DISCARDED

W9-DGZ-025

WOMEN IN TRANSITION

A Feminist Handbook on Separation and Divorce

Coordinator: Carolyn Kott Washburne

Editors and Researchers: Linda Backiel
Susan Daily
Carolyn Kott Washburne

Graphics Editor: Deborah Thomas

Poetry Editor: Susan Daily

Women in Transition, Inc., Joan B. Allen
Staff: Judith Bondy Brigham
Margaret Cox
Jennifer Fleming
Miriam Galper
Schree Hicks
Andi McKenna

Women in Transition, Inc., Jayma Abdoo
Legal Group: Leslie Austin
Martha Bush
Leslie L. Engle
Donna Lenhoff
Barbara Rosenberg
Cindy Rosenthal

Contributors: Don Bergeron
Peter Brigham
Janet Costner
Lyn Davis
Anita Dimondstein
Sarah Furnas
Stephen Gold
Nancy Hancock
Joan Hubbard
Kathy Jennings
Ann Marcelle Leventhal
Tom Linsley
Donna Shields
Thomas Shields
Steve Unger
Stephanie Weil Davis Weaver

WOMEN IN TRANSITION

A Feminist Handbook on Separation and Divorce

WOMEN IN TRANSITION, INC.

Charles Scribner's Sons, New York

WOMEN IN TRANSITION developed from THE
WOMEN'S SURVIVAL MANUAL, A Feminist Handbook
on Separation and Divorce, published by Women
in Transition, Inc. in 1972 for women in the
Philadelphia area. It received such an
enthusiastic response--and generated so many
questions from readers in other areas--that
this expanded, national edition, WOMEN IN
TRANSITION, was prepared.

Copyright © 1975 Women in Transition, Inc.

This book published simultaneously in the
United States of America and in Canada -
Copyright under the Berne Convention

All rights reserved. No part of this book
may be reproduced in any form without the
permission of Charles Scribner's Sons.

Library of Congress Cataloging in Publication Data

Women in Transition Inc.
    Women in transition.

    Bibliography: p. 511
    Includes index.
    1. Divorce--United States. 2. Divorcees.
3. Women--Employment. I. Title.
HQ834.W68 1975   301.42'8   75-15728
ISBN 0-684-14258-9
ISBN 0-684-14257-0 pbk.

301.428
W87w

1 3 5 7 9 11 13 15 17 19 C/M 20 18 16 14 12 10 8 6 4 2
1 3 5 7 9 11 13 15 17 19 P/M 20 18 16 14 12 10 8 6 4 2

Printed in the United States of America

CONTENTS

77-17060

We wrote this book because we have all been women in transition in one way or another. Some of us went through critical changes in our lives with the support of other women; some of us did it alone. All of us could have used a book like this. The material in this book is drawn from our lives and the lives of all the women who have been in touch with the Women in Transition Program. This is more than just a reference book, since there are many personal experiences in it, and we have also drawn some conclusions based on what we have learned. Not all the information will be relevant to your needs, and not all the personal statements will speak to your life experiences. But while every woman's situation is different, there are many commonalities. Many women have struggled with the problems you are facing and have survived, and we hope after reading this book you will feel that you are not alone.

We want to thank all the organizations that have helped support the Women in Transition Program over the past three years:

    American Baptist Churches, USA
    Church of the Brethren
    Dolfinger-McMahon Foundation
    Executive Council of the Episcopal Church
    Louis M. Rabinowitz Foundation
    Philadelphia Area United Fund-Community
       Development Fund
    Philadelphia Foundation
    Philadelphia War Tax Resistance Fund
    Sachem Fund
    Samuel S. Fels Fund
    Union Benevolent Association
    United Presbyterian Women
    West Philadelphia Community Mental
       Health Consortium
    William Penn Foundation

Grateful acknowledgment is made to the following for permission to reprint material copyrighted or controlled by them:

Boston Women's Health Book Collective. *Our Bodies, Ourselves*. Simon and Schuster, 1973. "What To Expect From Your Doctor," and "What To Expect From Your Hospital."

Citizens' Advisory Council on the Status of Women. *The Equal Rights Amendment And Alimony And Child Support Laws*. Department of Labor, 1972. Selected passages.

Frankfort, Ellen. *Vaginal Politics*. Bantam Books, 1973. Quote from page xxiv.

Goldman, Emma. *Anarchism And Other Essays*. Dover Press. Selected passages.

Grahn, Judy. *The Common Woman Poems*. The Women's Press Collective, Oakland, California, 1970. "Vera, From My Childhood."

THE BATTLE OF THE PRONOUNS

We had a difficult time deciding what pronouns to use throughout the book, and we have not been consistent. Many people automatically use "he" when describing someone who could be a man or a woman (such as a doctor or a child or a tenant), but we think it's important not to erase women from the English language quite so simply. When we use "he" it is usually to refer to a professional, such as a doctor, most of whom are men, and we usually include a note explaining why. Other times we use "she or he" or switch back and forth. We're sorry about the awkwardness, but it's the best we can do until a nonsexist language is developed and widely accepted.

►►► *FREDA*

"To she, who has suffered like me, you are not alone."

It's a proven fact that when you are lonely and depressed and in an impossible situation it helps to talk to a close friend. But when you are separated or divorced with little children, you might find yourself short of close friends. Of course there are agencies with faceless people who will talk to you all night on the phone. That is, if you can bring yourself to call a stranger and if you have a phone. So, being lonely and separated with four little kids, I'm writing this little note in the hopes that maybe one other woman in my situation will read this and feel a little bit better to know that she is not alone, and to stick it out, 'cause things do get better. I think it's a matter of mind, and though we think it's impossible today, and not really worth it, hang in there. Because the sun will shine tomorrow.

This is dedicated to every mother alone:

- whose welfare check has at one time or another got "screwed" and has had to steal peanut butter and bread from the supermarket so her kids wouldn't starve;

- who has a boyfriend that she supported who has promised her marriage and the rest of "the world" and who walks out because the responsibility of the kids is too much, even though the last one is his;

- who has been evicted because she won't sleep with the landlord;

- who has impulsively moved into a crummy shack with an ultra high rent because she had to put a roof over her kids' heads and has a landlord who smiles to her face but hates her guts because she's on welfare;

- who has a sick child and can't find a doctor who accepts "the card" and can't go to the hospital because she has no carfare or no one to watch the other kids and if she leaves them, a helpful neighbor will report her to her caseworker because "women on welfare just have it too easy."

To every woman alone, you are not alone. I have experienced every one of these things and many more. We each have our own private hells. I could write these examples all night. But what I'm trying to get across is that now I feel that finally I'm making it. It's not much, but I did it on my own and you can too.

When I finally got the guts to leave my husband, with the responsibility of four little kids on my hands, I found it wasn't easy. In fact, it was downright difficult because I listened to people who said, "Wow, how do you manage with four little kids! It's impossible." And I believed them and felt sorry for myself and ended up depressed and in the hands of a shrink. He also went the "you poor thing" route which depressed me more than ever. Then came love again and I stopped seeing the shrink. Then it was like an explosion with my life being rapidly blown to bits until I found I had nothing left (so I thought). Love went. I got evicted. Out of desperation I moved to a small town and in the process had a car accident and lost my savings.

Suddenly one cold night in January I awoke to find myself all alone. I had no friends or neighbors. No car, no phone, and thanks to a good old-fashioned welfare screw-up, no money or food for my kids. I lay down on my bed and cried like a baby and could feel what must be insanity coming on and decided I was better off dead.

Then something happened. It wasn't a ray of light like in the movies. It was pure anger. Anger at the way life treated me, anger at the welfare system, but most of all, anger at myself for lying there and letting it happen and not doing anything about it. Now you can say, well, what the hell could you do in that situation? And the answer is only one thing. Change your whole attitude and make something worthwhile living for. And believe me, no one knows better than I how difficult this is. It's a slow process, and there is no one to say, "Keep your chin up, baby." It's got to come from within. But as you slowly move up you'll feel a tremendous sense of satisfaction and self-worth 'cause you've done it on your own and you know you must be some kind of great to be making it with the odds stacked against you.

In my case it's a slow day-to-day climb getting my life in order and preparing to go to nursing school in the fall. My days are filled with the kids and the knowledge that by keeping this attitude I'm helping them and of course myself. For when I'm happy, they are, too. And an unhappy, depressed mother makes way for disastrous children. The nights are still very lonely, but I'm hanging in there. If this letter helps no one else, in a small way it has helped me, for it has filled the empty space of another lonely night. Thank you for reading this and letting me express my thoughts. You are not alone. We are all together.

ONE: WHO WE ARE
AND WHY WE EXIST

THE PURPOSE AND HISTORY OF WOMEN IN TRANSITION

Women in Transition is a resource program providing survival skills and emotional support to women experiencing separation, divorce, and/or single parenthood. The program began in the spring of 1971 when some of us working with the Philadelphia Women's Center realized that the Center was getting many calls from women thinking about or going through separation or divorce or raising children alone. The change in what is considered a woman's most important role in this society--that of wife and mother-- was generating a lot of needs in the women who called us. The requests we got were varied--calls for legal counseling and services, referrals to good therapists, job training, employment counseling, information on housing, day care, emotional support--but the same needs were voiced over and over again by different women.

A group of us came together to design a program to try to meet those needs. The Task Force on Women in Transition, as we call ourselves, consisted of eight women of different backgrounds, ages, skills, and resources. We shared the conviction that with the right kinds of supports, separation, divorce, and single parenthood didn't

1

have to be the debilitating trauma it often is and might
even become a creative learning and growing process. Most
of us were separated or divorced ourselves and felt that
the support of other women had been crucial to us, both
during the transitional period and afterward as we
settled into our new lives. We wanted to design a program where women could help each other in a structured way
through these difficult times. It was our goal to help
women realize their potential as strong, independent people regardless of whether they chose to remain in a marriage, follow through on a divorce, or remarry.

We were lucky enough to be funded by a few foundations,
some in Philadelphia and some national, and we formally
opened our doors in September 1971, with a full-time staff
of two and many volunteers. The program has undergone a
number of changes over the three years as we have learned
what is effective and what isn't. We now have a full-time
staff of seven, four of whom do legal work and three of
whom work on the emotional support part of the program.
In addition to the paid staff, we have a Planning Group
which takes responsibility for major policy decisions, a
legal group composed of lawyers and self-trained legal
workers which serves as back-up to the legal staff, and
a group of "sisters" who are facilitators for the small
groups we run. We come from a variety of experiences and
backgrounds--separated, divorced, single, married, with
children, without children, lesbian, heterosexual, black,
white, middle-class, working-class, with professional
credentials and without. The staff works collectively,
which means we all have an equal share in policy-making
and an equal share in the unglamorous aspects of running
the program (taking out the trash, answering the telephones, mimeographing, etc.).

At the present time the program is divided into two main
areas: emotional support and legal support. The emotional-
support part of the program has several facets.

Small Groups

We run four-week support/discussion groups where women
share feelings, ideas, and experiences about marriage,
separation, children, and future plans and goals. Although these are basically self-help groups, two women
who are trained by us serve as group sisters/facilitators.

Photo by: Diana Davies

Photo by: Emi Tonooka

Photo by: Emi Tonooka

Photo by: A. C. Warden

During the four weeks the sisters try as much as possible
to share what they know about group process so the women
in transition can form ongoing groups after the initial
four weeks if they wish.

Therapy

Not every woman in transition can benefit from and give to
a small group. We also provide therapy evaluation and
referrals for women who have emotional problems which are
too serious for the group process to alleviate. The
therapists we refer to have all been interviewed by us and
are sympathetic to the women's movement. This includes
both therapists in private practice and in mental health
centers and social agencies. With every referral we make
we hand out a *Therapy Information Packet for Women* (see
the bibliography for Chapter Eight for more about this)
which has information on how to choose a therapist, how
to evaluate a therapy experience, and other articles about
women and psychology.

Consultation To Agencies

Because we can help only a small number of women through
our program, we think it is important to reach workers in
more traditional social service agencies to explain what
we do and what we are learning about women. Our hope is
that as agencies become more sensitive to the needs of all
women, but especially those going through separation and
divorce, programs like Women in Transition will no longer
be necessary. In the meantime we hold workshops and
seminars at the request of agencies which recognize the
need for raising their awareness about women's problems.

The legal part of the program also has several facets.
When women call us with individual problems, we share with
them what we have learned about their options related to
separation, divorce, and single parenthood.

Pro Se Divorce Clinic

We are operating a *pro se* (for herself) divorce clinic
where we assist women who cannot afford private lawyers
to file divorce forms without a lawyer if the divorce is
uncontested. This enables women to obtain divorces for
about one-fifth the cost. This is being done in other
cities but is new to Philadelphia.

Outreach

We conduct workshops in low- and middle-income communities
on women's legal rights and options. Information in these
workshops covers separation, divorce, common-law marriage,
"illegitimate" children, welfare, support, child custody,
legal services, beatings, and rights of women. Some of
the workshops have developed into ongoing emotional support groups for their members.

WHY WE WROTE THIS BOOK

GAIL

*I went to the group looking for some answers. Well,
I didn't get very many answers, but they helped me
to know what I need. What I want. To know that in
order for me to be really happy, I have to change
myself. The only thing that I didn't get was how
to do this. I need some answers.*

*How do you change? Where do you find that someone
who really cares? How do I answer my daughter's
questions? How do I forget my husband, who I think
I still love? How do you begin again? Where do
you get the courage to try marriage a second time?
I could probably fill this page with my questions.
But I guess I know the answers have to come from
within me. Time will help, I'm sure. But there
is so little time.*

Soon after Women in Transition began we recognized the
need for a pamphlet for women in the Philadelphia area
which would give answers to some of the commonly asked
questions we were getting. As we started writing it,
however, it got longer and longer, and a year and a half
later we had produced a 271-page book called *Women's
Survival Manual: A Feminist Handbook on Separation and
Divorce*. It contained not only factual information, but
creative material and personal experiences of women who
had been connected with the program. The response to
the Philadelphia edition was overwhelming, both locally
and nationally. Women from many different cities wrote

to Women in Transition asking, "Is there a book like this for women from Milwaukee [Detroit, Durham, Boston. . . .]?" Some women wrote us that they were using our book and writing supplements for their local areas. Other women said that even though the specific referrals were of no use to them, they still got a great deal from the emotional-support section of the book. We have decided to write this national version in such a way that it can be used by an individual woman to find the resources and the strength she needs to survive and also by groups wishing to establish Women-in-Transition-type programs in their areas. Chapter Eight explains how to do this.

MARRIAGE AND THE NUCLEAR FAMILY: ALIVE AND WELL IN AMERICA?

We think it is important in this introduction to explain some of the basic things we have learned over the last three years. We will talk about all of this in more depth in later chapters, but we want to explain briefly the scope of the problems we are dealing with. The more we learn, the more myths about separation and divorce dissolve before our eyes, and we are always revising our opinions. But here are some of the truths which have emerged already.

Divorce and family disorganization are a fact of American life. Government statistics indicate that two marriages in four end in divorce, desertion, and/or separation. Marriage counselors estimate that only 25 percent of American marriages can be considered happy, yet the number of couples who have unhappy marriages far exceeds the number of couples who seek counseling. According to U.S. Civil Rights Commission, 1973, 34.6 percent of black families and 9.6 percent of white families in this country are headed by a woman, which means the daddy-mommy-two children families we see on television are not the kinds of families many of us live in. Even these figures seem low to us. A female-headed household is defined as one where there is no man present at all. We know of many situations where a man is still counted as the head of the household even though he isn't around much and contributes little or nothing to the family income.

The rapid increase within the last few years in the divorce rate in this country is misleading. Marital breakdown has been with us a long time; recent liberal divorce laws merely recognize an emotional split which has already occurred. The majority of couples obtaining divorces in the last few years have been separated for ten years or more but were unable to obtain divorces under more restrictive laws or were unable to afford them.

Legal roadblocks and public opinion about divorce often serve to increase the guilt and confusion felt by both women and men. No-fault divorce or divorce by mutual consent is available in a majority of states; for the rest, a guilty party must be named and made to pay--in terms of money and/or psychological burdens.

Domestic problems are seen as essentially private matters and legal settlement of such matters is considered a "luxury" by lawyers and the public alike. The accompanying adjustments in our personal, family, or emotional life, even when they are fundamental changes which alter our economic and social patterns, are not considered really important. This attitude, coupled with high court costs, is responsible for the fact that uncontested divorces obtained through private lawyers are almost beyond the means of most people. Contested divorces, where one party is actively opposing the divorce through legal means, are beyond the means of most people, since each party has an attorney and the proceedings can drag out for a long time.

Women who are on welfare or who have a low enough income to qualify for Legal Aid or the OEO-funded Community Legal Services can get a low-cost or free divorce but often need to wait for long periods of time (up to a year in Philadelphia). They often appear in Juvenile or Family Court--where matters of financial support and child custody are decided--with no legal representation at all. Thus, many women remain unaware of their legal rights and often make vital decisions without knowing about the consequences to themselves or to their children.

Two households are more expensive than one. Both men and women are subject to pressing economic burdens when they separate. More often than is commonly believed, however, it is the woman who has the heaviest burden--regardless of her social class. In the January 1972 report on "The Equal Rights Amendment and Alimony and Child Support Laws," the Citizen's Advisory Council on the Status of Women states:

*The rights to support of women and children are much
more limited than is generally known, and enforcement
is very inadequate. A married woman living with her
husband can in practice get only what he chooses to
give her. The legal obligation to support can generally only be enforced through an action for separation
and divorce, and the data that is available, although
scant, indicates that . . . alimony is granted in
only a very small percentage of cases; that fathers,
by and large, are contributing less than half the
support of the children in divided families; and that
alimony and child support awards are very difficult
to collect. (p. 1)*

WHO ARE WOMEN IN TRANSITION?

When our program first began, we were aware that there
were differences between the separation and divorce experiences of middle-class women and poor women, but we had
difficulty structuring the program to meet those different
needs. We hoped that our program, which put a lot of
emphasis on small groups for emotional support, would meet
the needs of women whatever their class and race. We
found, however, that in order to be helpful to low-income
women we needed to develop the part of the program which
provides them with survival skills. In the last three
years as we have worked with many older women and many
low-income women--black, white, and Puerto Rican--and as
women from those backgrounds have joined our staff, we
have found it increasingly difficult to generalize about
the "divorce experience" for women. The experiences of
middle-class and low-income women, we have found, are different in some significant ways.

Some middle-class women, especially those with professional
credentials, may be able to manage without undue financial
hardship, especially if their husbands are cooperative
about child-support payments. Their emotional and social
life may be in chaos, but financially things haven't become
significantly worse. Other women, however, who may have
been described as "middle class" by their husband's job
and status, often find themselves with little or no financial resources and few marketable skills with which to
support themselves and their children. Married women in
this situation are usually either not working outside the

home, or are simultaneously working at home while holding down an outside, often "women's work" job. We think of "women's work" as jobs including waitressing, clerical work, baby-sitting, housekeeping, sewing, and related jobs--all very low-paying, de anding, and sometimes boring. A young woman with children or an older woman may find she cannot get even these jobs. Accustomed to limited and prescribed financial responsibilities within the marriage, many women have little experience supporting a family and managing large amounts of money.

The emotional problems of middle-class women contemplating separation and divorce are often as frightening as the financial ones. Subtle and not-so-subtle accusations of selfishness, immaturity, and failure--from friends, relatives, therapists, lawyers--produce feelings of guilt which make the process of separation more painful than it needs to be. It becomes difficult for the separated woman to relate to many of the people who were part of her married life, just at the time when she needs the most support. The assumption that separation is a terrible trauma for the children involved often turns into a self-fulfilling prophecy. For an older woman who has spent many years caring for her husband and family, the prospect of reorganizing her life, perhaps working for the first time, can be terrifying.

And those women who seek professional counseling to alleviate some of this pain report that some counselors in traditional agencies encourage them either to keep a failing marriage together or imply that they will only be "normal" again when they have established another relationship with a man. Since this does not sufficiently acknowledge the emotional realities of a woman in transition--her anxiety, grieving, depression--it is less than immediately useful advice. For a woman who has several children, or who is older, this may not be a realistic option anyway, so her future can appear even more dismal.

Many of the experiences of low-income women are significantly different from those of middle-class women. The needs of minority and low-income women are much more immediate and concrete than those of women who have resources from their husbands, or of their own, to fall back on. Minority and low-income women are much more dependent on social service agencies than their middle-class sisters

for help with housing, child care, financial, legal, and
other problems. While many low-income women have worked
at one time, or perhaps continuously, they are unlikely to
get interesting, well-paying jobs with which to support
themselves and their families.

Low-income women are often forced to confront their husbands
in Family Court to obtain support orders and child-custody
decisions rather than negotiate these matters with private
attorneys. The Department of Public Welfare, which rarely
intervenes in the lives of women not on public assistance,
may bring suits in Juvenile Court to place children of low-
income mothers in foster care or state institutions. Low-
income women are bounced back and forth from Supreme Court
to welfare offices, where caseworkers tell them (erroneous-
ly) that they must sue their husbands for support. Their
problems are magnified if they are not married to the
father of their children; the children are labeled "illegitimate," are processed differently in Family Court, and
are discriminated against financially. Legal Aid and Community Legal Services are inadequately funded to meet the
legal needs of low-income people. Waiting periods are
long and many become discouraged by the delay.

This is not to suggest that low-income women do not experience guilt, fear, failure, and isolation as do middle-
class women. In fact, low-income women have the double
burden of being poor and female, and the hopelessness and
despair connected with this status can be overwhelming.
Often a low-income woman has a lot of her survival needs
to deal with first before she can focus exclusively on her
emotional needs. Although none of the existing options
may really work to provide her some relief from what she
is experiencing, a low-income woman may try to get help
through a local mental health center or family agency (private therapy would be too expensive).

SHARI

*The [Women in Transition] group became a mirror for
me--I no longer felt ugly and deformed by the stigma
of divorce. In the beauty of these other women, I
became more able to accept myself, and later even to
be a little proud of my condition.*

I suppose my discovery that I can love women was not new for this kind of group. Still, it is so profound for me, has affected my outlook on other people (men, too, a little!) so much, that it continues to be the point I most frequently mention when talking about Women in Transition.

I feel that four weeks was too short to undo a lifetime of taught jealousy and experienced disgust with the lot of women. I still rage inside over the willingness of other women to accept all manner of disappointment and humiliation simply to protect their dearest desire: to have a home for their children and a sense of worth. There is so much to be done and so much to be done inside me.

ON BECOMING A SEPARATE PERSON

It is our hope that this book will be useful to any woman, regardless of her economic or social situation. It has been our experience that women undergoing marital crises often feel lonely, dependent, and without resources to cope with the seemingly overwhelming problems that confront them. Most of us have been raised to view a successful marriage as our primary goal in this society, whereas men define themselves more directly in terms of a personal ambition or career. Thus the breaking up of a marriage is often more traumatic for women than for men, for both emotional and financial reasons.

It is our belief that the experience of separation provides a woman with the opportunity to reevaluate her lifestyle and goals. The honest admission that a marriage relationship is not working out can be the first step toward building a more satisfying life for everyone involved. It is our hope that this book will be useful to women in all stages of "transition"--those of you who are thinking of separating, those of you who have done so-- and those of you who have been separated or divorced for some time and are trying to create a new life for yourselves. Most women are in some transition most of their lives, and there are ways in which all of us can become stronger, more whole people. We don't want to overwhelm you with "shoulds" but we hope that this book will encourage you to take one step at a time toward your new goals.

We do not encourage women either to leave their marriages
or to stay in them. In fact, a number of women who go
through our program decide to stay in their marriages but
have a much clearer idea of what they want and how to get
it. We encourage a woman in transition to locate resources
within herself to free her from dependency on her husband
or her family. We also encourage a woman who is dependent
on institutions and agencies to begin to develop expertise
in using the services of institutions effectively, as overwhelming as this task might seem. In this way she can
begin to gain the power to escape the patterns of poverty,
racism, and neglect which often result in her seeing herself as a failure, as a worthless human being in general
and an inadequate woman in particular. As women, we do
have choices; our energy need not be totally invested in
marriage or remarriage. The time of transition can be a
difficult one, but it can also be a chance for growth. It
is our hope that this book will help all of us to make
these choices wisely.

the ladies in the knife-throwers ring

"God created woman, but it was
Rockefeller and his pack of thieves
who invented ladies." Mother Jones

so many women
walk about
with a look
of small shock
at the knives
that pin them
to their cardboard back-drop
of the supermarket and the fashion page
and they look
     as if they had been caught
          between motion
    (perhaps a flight of autumn birds)
          and inevitable death
and as if they do not know why
and do not ask how,
and are afraid to ask anything at all

I used to be pinned there
chloroformed like a prize butterfly
weakly wiggling in protest now and then.

I pulled out
            first one knife,
                        and then another.
I tell you, the pain is not so bad
it's the fear that holds you stiff.

                                Susan Daily

▶▶▶ *JOAN*

I was born in Chicago but grew up in Philadelphia
after age six. I have an older brother whom I
was very close to when I was growing up. My
mother died when I was a baby, and I was raised
by my stepmother, whom I've called mother. I
never considered myself a part of my family,
because no one ever really answered my questions
about my real mother, and we were farmed out a
lot to relatives. Although she tried, I never
felt close to my stepmother. My father wasn't
around much. He was either working or drinking.
I liked school, learning, and playing sports, and
it was these things that kept me going. In my
early teens, a group of us girls formed a club
and had parties and went on different outings.
Most of the girls either found steady boys or
moved away.

I started liking boys when I was 13 and only
went out with them because it was the thing to
do, even though I didn't like them that much.
You had to have a boyfriend in order to go anywhere or do anything, and besides there really
wasn't that much to do. I really liked the
boys with money and cars. We got out of the
city and just rode around the country. That
got tiring also because they were after only
one thing.

Seventeen is a pretty good age to be. I'd convinced myself, because I so much wanted it to be that way. At that age, I was the apple of Daddy's eye, a heartache to Mom, and my brother's baby sister, on my way to being an adult. To stay seventeen for twenty years and remaining a girl takes hard work. I closed my eyes to everything, and was successful at not growing up.

I began to feel trapped coming out of high school, working in an office. I felt that my life should have more to it, but didn't know what. The boys I was dating were mentioning marriage, which I didn't want. But not knowing what I did want and not having anyone to talk to about my vague dreams, I resolved the conflict by getting pregnant. I admired a cousin of mine who wasn't married, who traveled and seemed to have been enjoying life. To me she seemed free. My father didn't approve of her. He was constantly saying she should get married and settle down. She was the first black woman I'd ever seen who had lots of friends but no steady boyfriends and was leading a free life. I had mentioned to my mother that I had wanted to go live with her after I finished school. There was never an answer to this. Four months after I discovered I was pregnant, I was told my parents had planned on sending me there, everything had been arranged. I was very angry at the whole world after that.

When I told my family that I was pregnant, they acted as though I'd ruined their name. I told them I had no intention of getting married as the man was already married. When my son was born, I felt as though I was all those names my father called women who have "illegitimate" children. I got another job, found another man, and had another baby, a pattern I was to repeat over and over again through the years: men, babies, alcohol, pills, drugs.

In January 1973, I started growing up. I was then 37. All of us do not need psychotherapy. I did. Therapy helped me save my life. I learned I was not the sweet innocent baby that everyone was taking advantage of. I had something to do with letting things happen as they did, simply because I cared nothing about me.

My mother thought being a woman was a curse. She also favored male children. When I was pregnant with my third child, I finally broke down and got married, to save face and to have someone pay the hospital bill. The marriage was an enslaving job, washing, cleaning, cooking, and taking care of two babies (my husband and the new baby). Trying to feel like a queen when kingy came home, but really feeling like a washed-out old rag. I was pregnant with my fourth child when I left my husband. I returned home to Mama, where I have spent most of my life.

From 1957 to 1969, I floated from man to man, always hoping that the next man would be "Mr. Right." In 20 years you can run through a lot of "Mr. Rights." Fortunately I had enough sense not to get divorced from my husband, because I probably would have been stupid enough to get married again. To keep from going through all the anxiety of the marriage trap, I lived with men. But it never dawned on me that whether you're living with a man or married to one, when you separate the feelings are all the same-- desertion, loss, failure, fear, loneliness, and anger.

I was fortunately always able to get fairly decent jobs, although much of the time I seemed to be in a state of sleepwalking. My children were becoming teen-agers during my 20 years of being 17, and my many separations from my "lovers" caused some feelings to start surfacing--the guilt, the shame, the despair, and the terror of not being in control of my life. They were overwhelming at times, and I sometimes felt like someone had pushed me into a corner and was saying, "These are your children, this is your life, what are you doing?" I found myself stuck in many situations I felt powerless to change.

I eventually found ways of covering up the feelings. Alcohol was the first, but that made me physically ill. Pain pills, tranquilizers, and sleeping pills did a beautiful job of keeping the feelings covered up, making me feel I was still Daddy's baby and seventeen. Pills didn't make me feel sick the way alcohol did, so whenever I felt as though I was being smothered by guilt or chained to an impossible relationship, I took pills, pain pills for the never-ending headaches, tranquilizers for the anxiety, and sleeping pills to numb me at night. All of this took a few years, of course; nothing happens overnight.

One of my "lovelier" relationships was with a man who used to get his kicks from beating me up. After one time when he broke my nose and ruptured my eardrum, I feared for my life so I got a gun. The next time he came at me, I shot him in the legs. For this I got 2 months in jail and two years probation.

During my heavy pill period, I managed to buy a house, then lost it at a sheriff's sale. I was hospitalized for two weeks because I was having blackouts and seizures. I didn't tell the doctors how heavy I was on the pills. While in the hospital, I went through hell. I learned later when I was in therapy that what had happened here was barbiturate withdrawal, and the blackouts were caused by overdoses of barbiturates. But during my stay in the hospital I knew nothing except that I secretly wanted them to send me to the nuthouse or any place but home. Home was the kids I couldn't cope with and the bills I couldn't pay.

I thought I'd reached rock bottom. But I hadn't really gotten into heroin yet. By then I was so busy hating myself that I couldn't see anything good about me. I was going from doctor to doctor and preparing to move deeper into the ghetto. After moving there, I felt I was home at last. The gang fights every night, roaches, noise, dirt, overcrowded, and everywhere you look desperation. Here and there you find a few trying desperately to keep the place clean, make it look livable, and the greater majority working desperately to make it look even worse. You hear all the time about the ones that make it horrible to live here, but you never hear about the ones that are really trying to make it worthwhile. At that time I knew what side of the fence I was on.

It was here that I met the person that changed my life. She was my white female therapist. First let me say, I have always been led to believe that the whites hate and fear us blacks. The only reason they work in mental health centers is to get more satisfaction on how animalistic we are. The first few months of visiting her, I did my best to show her that this view of black people was correct. I really gave her the going-over. The way things turned out, we became friends. I gave her my facts, she came back at me with feelings. She told me about how she felt in similar situations. She was not analyzing me, she was talking to me, sharing her life with me, letting me see that I am not alone in my feelings. This middle-class white female therapist was becoming a part of me. She cut through the tough hard cold outer shell and got into my heart, because she shared her experiences with me. This above and over everything else got to me. This is when I really began to see me as I saw myself. I considered myself a pretty rotten person, the lowest.

At one point in my therapy she suggested I join a woman's group. I told her she was crazy. To sit among a bunch of women and actually talk about all the shit, to let them know I was nothing but a bitch, a whore, and a junkie, she was out of her mind. I had a fear that I would lose her and I really did not want any part of that. To lose my strength, my backbone, the only person I had ever believed in, no, no, no way.

She got transferred out of my district. This is when I hit the bottom. Judy was gone. This separation was the worst I had ever felt. After that there were deliberate overdoses, attempted suicides, a psychiatric hospitalization, and a slow awakening. None of these suicidal attempts were working, there had to be another way.

I took Judy's advice, I joined a drug program. Here I was able to talk to other people that were in my same situation. We all talked, we learned how to feel feelings, we learned how to deal with feelings, together. We learned to talk about our feelings, we learned how to handle them. The awakening, the beginning of a new life. The beginning of learning to appreciate me as a woman,

*as a black woman, as a human being, not having to be
a stereotype because. . .*

*In learning to like myself, I have learned to like
other people. I appreciate my parents, my children,
myself. I am better able to help my sons and my
daughters. In my vain hope of not becoming like my
mother I became just like her. I am better able to
help my children. I can tell them that I see them
going into the same pattern I went into, give them
examples of my own life to show them the similarity,
tell them I would not be able to see it so well in
them if I had not done the same things myself.*

*When I left therapy, I took a factory job. I worked
there for four months. My friend, who had been my
therapist, told me of a job opening making twice the
money I was making at factory work. I am working at
that job now. I am trying to help other women that
are going through transition.*

*My experiences as a black woman are very mild compared
to some of the black women that I know. There are some
that are getting help, but there are so many who feel
that they are "doomed" to their way of life. This is
a false belief. Women, black, white, poor, or middle-
class, are human beings before anything else. Me, I
am not trying to run the world, I am only trying to
run my little corner.*

*As for men, there is no difference in feelings, they
are "stereotyped" also. They have the same feelings
as women, fear, loneliness, desperation, anger. My
"Mr. Right" will never come because he was a dream,
but I know that there are men who feel as I do. Just
because I am a woman I do not have to smother my feelings and because he is a man he does not have to do
likewise; we get along better when we share our feelings.
Sharing is living.*

TWO: EMOTIONAL SUPPORTS

Separation and divorce are different for different women.
While the experiences of all women alone are somewhat
alike, women struggle with different problems and different solutions depending on whether they are middle-class,
poor, black, white, educated, or undereducated. This
Emotional Supports chapter deals with the problems, fears,
strengths, and weaknesses that women in transition have
shared with us. Some of the information will apply to
you and some won't. It is important for any woman
experiencing separation and divorce, however, to know that,
with some variations, millions of women are going through
it with you. You can learn from them, you can derive
strength and support from them, you can find new directions
and ways of thinking which will enable you to see that you
are not only ending an old way of life, you are starting
a new one.

A FEW WORDS ABOUT MARRIAGE

As females, from a very young age we are taught to define
ourselves in terms of being married or attached to a man.
Marriage is painted as the be-all and end-all of our
existence. We are told that marriage is a sacred institution, the basis of society, the one institution that is
designed to "protect" us. There are not many among us who
did not, as young girls, envision ourselves in a beautiful

white gown, being escorted down the aisle by the man of
our dreams, being romantically carried over the threshold
of our vine-covered cottage, experiencing the "wedded
bliss" that we had been told was waiting for us. This is
the one thing that we have been put on earth to do, and
we must do it right.

How do we measure up to the image of the blushing bride,
the happy housewife, the adoring mother? How well we
measure up often has a lot to do with our self-image. The
closer we come to what the women's magazines say we should
be, the better we tend to feel about ourselves. All of
this is tied up with the fact that as women, we have been
socialized to accept our "place." Some of us, usually
those who are white and middle-class, are taught to be
docile, weak, and passive. Others of us are forced to be
strong to survive, but all too often that strength is not
valued but is seen as an unfortunate necessity.

In fact, the independent, strong woman is labeled as the
castrating bitch, society's outcast. Historically, women
who choose not to be dependent on men have been viewed
with fear, hostility, and/or pity. Many of us learned to
make ourselves an acceptable product for men by costuming
our bodies and disregarding our minds. We viewed other
women merely as competition for men. So what *really* happens once we have made our catch?

If the women who come through Women in Transition are any
indication, marriage is not all it's cracked up to be.
Once married and raising a family, women may feel disillu-
sioned, isolated, bored, sometimes crazy, wondering why
they feel this way and guilty that they do. In her book
The Future of Marriage, a sociologist named Jessie Bernard
tells us (if we didn't already know from our own experiences!)
there is considerable evidence that marriage is actually
good for men, despite the bad press that it has. Married
men live longer, are healthier, more successful, and in
general happier than unmarried men. Marriage for women,
however, is another story. Married women show more symptoms of psychological stress--that is, depression, fear,
passivity--than married men *or* unmarried women. It appears
that many women are literally being driven mad by marriage.

Many women do manage to make a success out of an institution that is not designed to meet their needs, but marriages
are falling apart right and left. The emotional trauma that
accompanies such a break-up can leave us feeling that we are
failures as women. When our marriages fall apart, there are

Photo by: Joanne Kander

Artist: Bea Weidner

Photo by: Emi Tonooka

Photo by: Eva Shaderowfsky

Photo by: A. C. Warden

Photo by: A. C. Warden

no more illusions that we are living the life pictured in women's magazines. We tend to think that it's our fault-- we're scared, we're alone, and we need help. This is especially true if we have seen taking care of home, husband, and children as our primary occupation.

If you decide that it is time to think about *your* needs, *your* feelings, *your* future, it will be unforgivable to many who think that it is a woman's job to put others first. Often, those who succeed in a marriage do so by doing just that and denying their own needs. All too often the way the family is set up makes you feel as if you must be constantly sacrificing to keep things on an even keel. There have been a number of women who have gone through our program and have decided to stay in their marriages or to remarry. They report to us that it has been very difficult to retain a sense of self with the person they are relating to, but the struggle has been worth it. This is especially true if they have been married for a number of years to a man who always liked things the way they were and is very resistant to change. We believe that most of us need to be more self-reliant and self-aware in all areas of our lives, intimate relationships included. We know many strong and beautiful women who once saw their only worth in self-sacrifice. We don't think that enduring a bad marriage or being lonely are the only options a woman has. We have written this book to support those of you who have decided you want something different for yourselves.

Feminine Articles

What's marriage she said
but a change of clothes
Apron to nightgown
nightgown to apron
After five years I am
a lightning rod
waiting
Before a party I must eat
onions at dinner
on purpose
It protects me
from new men
like a ring
of marigolds
shields roses
from bugs

You're the type woman
who'd pay a rapist
the teased ones say
When I smile back
at them with the sweetness
of a flower my cunt
has teeth

> *My husband says*
> *I can do everything*
> *he does*
> *and more*
> *Cook his*
> *dinner Iron his*
> *shirts Pair*
> *his socks*
> *Soothe him*
> *when he hurts*
> *I could work*
> *twice as hard*
> *while dreaming*
> *of men I haven't met*
> *and he doesn't mind*
> *if I scrub the floor*
> *with vinegar*
> *and steel wool*

> *Alright*
> *if I had too much*
> *leftover energy*
> *I might expect things*
> *The right to my own*
> *ideas Maybe a male*
> *tennis partner*
> *one afternoon a week*
> *But I like to think*
> *of the Greek women*
> *cornered by Turks*
> *Rather than give in*
> *they joined hands*
> *began singing*
> *and danced their way*
> *off a cliff*

> *Maralyn Lois Polak*

The Experiences of Middle-Class Women

As we mentioned in the Introduction to this book, if you are
a middle-class woman, after a separation you are more likely

to maintain the standard of living that you are used to, especially if your ex-husband is cooperative about support payments to you and your children. If you have profession- al credentials or valuable job skills, you may be able to work at jobs which not only bring in some good money but will provide stimulation and a sense of being a competent, self-sufficient person on the job, even though you may feel like a pile of spaghetti when you think of your home situation. You may have family resources, both financial and emotional, to fall back on when things get tough.

You may be one of the many women who always thought of her- self as leading a comfortable, middle-class life, but in fact were dependent on your husband's job and status. You may not have worked since your marriage or since your chil- dren were born and now find yourself with few marketable skills with which to support yourself and your children. You may find yourself struggling along on a lot less money than before and stuck with a life-style that you can't sup- port. It is important not to panic. Losing the financial security that the marriage provided can be frightening, but you are not without resources, and you *can* cope.

When you think about the job possibilities open to you, they seem pretty dreary--clerical, waitressing, baby-sit- ting--and not likely to bring in a lot of income. If you have small children, employers may not want to hire you or you may not want to work until they are older, which leaves you even more financially dependent. If you are fortunate or maybe have worked out a good separation agree- ment, your ex-husband and/or your family can pay for job training or schooling for you so you can get some income- producing skills. If you have the chance to arrange some- thing like this, by all means try to do so. Planning for the future is an important way to get some control over your life. Also if you can afford it, pay a private law- yer to help you with a legal settlement. You may also want to see a therapist because you feel so disoriented (see the section on mental health in Chapter Seven). Count youself lucky if you have some choices about where to live or what kind of job to take so you can try to shape a new life for yourself.

If your financial situation is under control, or at least limping along in that direction, probably your biggest problems right now center around your social life and emotional well-being. Everyone in the world seems to be paired up, especially if you live in the suburbs, and you are the odd one out at parties, the PTA, etc. Don't feel embarrassed or abnormal--try to get together with other women in your situation. Often your children make you feel guilty by telling you how much they would like for Daddy to come back or by taking his side. On the other hand, your children can be a source of comfort and continuity when everything else is in flux. If you don't have children, you can feel relieved about not having to worry about how the separation would affect them, but you may also feel utterly alone as you realize your future plans for a cozy family life have evaporated. If your own family is far away, you may feel especially isolated.

Sometimes your friends don't help much by asking if you're dating yet. You may or may not be seeing men again. If you are, you discover it's a whole different ball game from before you were married--most men assume you want to sleep with them since divorcées are supposed to be sexually frustrated. If you aren't seeing men and want to, maybe you wonder if a man will ever again find you attractive. To the extent to which you have depended on your husband to make decisions, fix things around the house, etc., these things can now seem terrifying to you. If you live in a house, it may seem much too empty for you to be comfortable in and too big to afford. And if you have never worked or haven't worked for a number of years, you may feel you will never have the self-confidence necessary to get and hold down a job.

On the positive side, the more things you are able to accomplish for yourself, the more you will feel you can be independent and strong. If you have a job or are in school or a training program, you may find yourself making friends who didn't know you when you were Mrs. X and now know you simply as yourself. If your husband always put you down for being stupid or lazy or whatever, and you believed him, it may surprise you to discover that many people think you are clever and energetic and interesting. There is great relief at not having to face the day-in, day-out tensions with your ex-husband. You will still have to deal with him, of course, about the children, money, property, whatever, but hopefully you will be more and more able to assert what you want and not be pressured or bullied. And the thrill of belonging to yourself instead of to a man can be very heady, even if you only feel it once in a while.

The Experiences of Working-Class Women

If you are a woman from a working-class background, it may sometimes seem as if your world is being turned upside

down when you and your husband split up. It's not just the
fact that you can't stand it any more and it has to end,
but often he won't let it end. Friends seem to be few and
far between. If anything, family and friends often seem
to take his side, with attitudes that vary from "if she'd
been a better wife" to "well, if she doesn't like it she
should leave." The only thing is, it is very difficult to
leave, especially if you have children and not much money.
Whatever jobs are available are usually boring and disgust-
ing and pay very little. Planning for the future is difficult. Job training is hard to come by, even if you can
find baby-sitters that you can afford and feel good about.
If you have to go on welfare, the negative feelings that
you may have about yourself can be overwhelming at times.
If your husband has been working steadily, his paycheck is
hardly going to cover two homes even if he's willing to
pay, and all too often he isn't.

A lot of men get vicious at the time of separation and
insist on harassing their wives. Often they refuse to
leave, and it turns into a battle of nerves to see who is
going to be the one to give in first and finally leave the
house. Even after you are living alone, your husband might
decide to return periodically and give you a hard time,
which very often includes violence. One thing that we have
discovered at Women in Transition is that wife-beating is
a national pastime. Women need to be more open about this
because it is happening to many of us. Since the police
and courts seem to be powerless to do anything about it,
it's up to us to get together and put a stop to it. There
is more about this is Chapter Seven, "Taking Care of Ourselves."

Dealing with institutions is difficult. Support court is
not set up to benefit us as we are led to believe. Court
orders are notoriously low and hard to enforce. The welfare office treats us like objects, which only serves to
reinforce our already negative self-image. Going to
neighborhood mental health centers or to therapists can
sometimes be helpful, but often we are offered adjustment
to our sex role as the cure ("keep the marriage together"
or "find another man"). Sometimes we feel guilty and concerned about our children's emotional well-being, and
school counselors make us feel worse instead of better.
In general, things can look pretty bleak.

Survival is the issue. Strength is important. Contrary
to the popular belief that divorce is always hardest on
men, the legal and moral system that we live under is

weighted against you. You must not let it overwhelm you.
Planning and strategy are important in this. When you
decide on a course of action, try to move positively and
calmly in the direction that you have chosen, based not
on your feelings but on what in the long run will most
benefit you and your children. Get legal counseling if
at all possible. What has happened to your social life as
a result of your separation? If you have been doing much
of your socializing with your own or your husband's family,
you are going to be pretty lonely for a while, especially
if they disapprove of you and what you're doing. No woman
likes to be alone, but sometimes it gives you a chance to
clear your head out and do some serious thinking about your
future.

Try not to focus too much on things like revenge. Even
though you may be the one who has really been victimized,
you've got to spend your energy looking ahead. If you
really work at it, you may actually start to find things
that you enjoy about your situation, like not having to
worry about him any more, like being able to put yourself
first for a change, and like having peace and quiet at home.

Vera, From My Childhood

Solemnly swearing, to swear as an oath to you
who have somehow gotten to be a pale old woman;
swearing, as if an oath could be wrapped around
your shoulders
like a new coat:
For your 28 dollars a week and the bastard boss
you never let yourself hate;
and the work, all the work you did at home
where you never got paid;
For your mouth that got thinner and thinner
until it disappeared as if you had choked on it,
watching the hard liquor break your fine husband down
into a dead joke.
For the strange mole, like a third eye
right in the middle of your forehead;
for your religion that insisted that people
are beautiful golden birds and must be preserved;
for your persistent nerve
and plain white talk--
the common woman is as common
as good bread
as common as when you couldn't go on
but did.
For all the world we didn't know we held in common

all along
the common woman is as common as the best of bread
and will rise
and will become strong--I swear it to you
I swear it to you on my own head
I swear it to you on my common
woman's head

> *Judy Grahn*
> *The Common Woman Poems*

Some Experiences Common To All Women

There are some feelings and problems which are common to
all women who are alone, regardless of their class situation. Women from all backgrounds report to us their fears
about being lonely and about not being able to cope with
life, whether that means dealing with their hostile ex-
husbands, welfare workers, bosses, children, or neighbors.
Most of us have a big reservoir of guilt and insecurity
which comes bubbling up from time to time, and this is
certainly one of those times.

Most women tell us that they are resentful that their
husbands seem to have many more options for getting decent
jobs, meeting new women, and in general putting their lives
together. They also say that during a time of transition
their children are especially important to them. Even
though taking care of the children can be a real burden,
especially for women who have little money and/or have
sole responsibility for the children, for many women the
children provide a lot of continuity and stability and companionship.

Older women of all classes feel especially vulnerable.
Many of them have devoted their lives to "doing the right
thing" by taking care of their families and homes, and now
find themselves with very few options to get an interesting
job, meet people, and begin a new life. Besides, they are
tired of the constant grind, and had been looking forward
to getting older with the support and love of their families.

Finally, whether you have made the decision to leave your
husband or he has decided to leave you against your wishes
has a lot to do with how you may feel. It seems to be very
fashionable among middle-aged men to find themselves a
sweet young thing and decide to leave a wife of ten, twenty,
or thirty years. This can be terribly painful, especially
if you have contributed greatly to his growth and development over the years, only to have him leave. You may be

angered to realize that he has used you as his stepping-
stone to becoming the person that he is, and someone else
ends up reaping the benefits of your years of hard work.

Rejection is very difficult for women to handle, partly
because we don't have to face it as often as men do (at
work, when "dating," etc.), and partly because we are much
more dependent on other people's approval. Nonetheless,
if your husband has left you it is probably true that you
have gotten a dirty deal. It's true that he has been a
real villain, and the last thing that you should do is
look to yourself for the blame. On the other hand, you
cannot allow the situation to undo you, no matter how unfair it might be. It is understandable that you feel
rejected, unloved, and bitter, but you have to pick up
the pieces and keep going. Sometimes it may seem as if
it is very difficult to think about starting a new life
when the old one didn't always seem that bad, or at least
not bad enough to abandon it entirely. It might take you
somewhat longer to recover, although eventually, when you
look back on it, you may feel that the marriage was pretty
destructive and you may actually be glad it's over.

If you were the one who initiated the separation, things
are still difficult, but probably you felt as if you had
no choice if you wanted to survive. Women who leave their
marriages often feel stronger about being alone. It may
sometimes seem that you have made a bad choice. The terror of the unknown may make you long for the security of
the familiar, no matter how painful you know it is. Possibly your ex-husband and/or your children try to make you
feel guilty. For a woman to decide to live a life of her
own is to challenge a lot of myths and assumptions about
what a woman's role ought to be. As much as possible,
ignore your husband, your kids, your mother-in-law, your
neighbors, and seek out people who support what you are
doing. *You* know what is best for you, and it has become
necessary for you to end a destructive relationship. It
takes courage and strength, but we hope that you are determined to make a go of it. And try not to fall into the
trap of blaming your ex-husband for everything that went
wrong. Look honestly at yourself and your failings, so
you can avoid them in future relationships.

GETTING YOUR EMOTIONAL NEEDS MET

What we have said so far demonstrates the variety of problems and feelings that women in transition live through.
You may or may not feel really connected to what you have
read, but if you are a woman in transition, you have no
doubt known the feelings of doubt, guilt, isolation, fear,
and insecurity that we have touched upon. Pain seems to
be one of the primary feelings during the time of transition, and we would like to explore some ways in which that
pain can be dealt with.

*First, and most important, you're not always going to feel
this bad!* Honest. It *will* get better. You may find that
hard to believe in the beginning, but it becomes true for
the vast majority of us. It is important to remember this
when you are feeling overwhelmed, frustrated, and resentful.
As we have said, the degree of pain is influenced by a lot
of variables--how dependent you've been on your man to define yourself, whether you're working and must get up and
function each day, whether or not you have children, how
broke you are, how old you are, whether he left you or you
left him, etc.

There are a number of different stages in working through
feelings of separation. During the early days (weeks,
months, years), many women feel abandoned, panicky, depressed, sometimes suicidal, isolated, inadequate, and
lonely. They experience fear, guilt, failure, and anger.
You may find yourself unable to think of anything else
except the newly severed relationship. You may feel you
are boring your friends because you can talk about nothing
else. There's a reason for this repetition. Partly it's
a way to work through the grief and mourning process which
follows the death of a once-vital relationship. In a very
real sense you are mourning for a lost lover, a lost relationship, and a lost vision of a way of life. In order to
lay it to rest, it's sometimes necessary to examine it
over and over again until you understand it and have ended
its capacity to disrupt your emotional balance. It is
important to work on gaining control of your negative
feelings because they end up shaping your life in unproductive ways.

Here is how one woman worked in this direction:

*After my husband and I had been separated for about
a year, he began to play games with the amount of money*

that he was giving me. The arrangement was that he would give me a certain amount of money every week for the children. He would give me a check when he picked up the children on Friday night. Every few weeks, he would come in the door, assume a rather nasty manner, and inform me that he was taking out ten dollars or more that week. I would immediately get all upset and angry and would ask him, "Why?" His reply: "Because I feel like it" (usually spoken with the best of sneers).

At this point, I would be overcome with my feelings of anger and powerlessness, would get almost hysterical, would scream and sometimes throw things, and he would just get up and calmly walk out the door. After falling into this setup for a while, I started realizing that this was a device that he was using to continue to control me, and that in fact, his reason for doing it was to see the reaction, get the response, to see that he could still get a reaction from me, even if it was a negative reaction.

So, I decided to put a stop to it, and lo and behold, it worked. What I did was to stop reacting, no matter how hard it was, and believe me, it was hard. In the door he would come, make his grandiose announcement, and what did I do? Nothing! Not a murmur, not a peep. He would say, "I'm taking ten dollars out this week," and I would look up at him, smile sweetly, and say, "O.K."

Guess what? He stopped doing it. It no longer served his purpose, he did not get the rewards that he wanted so it was no longer in his interest to continue. What a victory that was for me. At first, I thought that it was a victory for me over him, but later I realized that much more importantly, it was a victory for me over me, over the part of me that was still allowing my anger to control me. It may seem like a small step, but actually it was the beginning of a whole new coming-out-from-under, a whole new understanding that I could decide what happened to me, that my life was finally becoming mine to control. It was a good feeling.

This woman's experiences along with those of many other women who came through our program have made us believe that we do have the ability to deal with our problems, and that the strength to do that comes from within ourselves

and from other women who have been through similar situations. Problems which seem insurmountable are in fact
solvable; situations which seem impossible can in fact be
changed for the better; lives which seem shattered can be
put back together, often with results that are far more
productive and healthy than you could have imagined.

It is important to keep reminding yourself that simply
surviving is an amazing thing in itself for a woman alone.
Sometimes it will seem that you are taking one step forward and two steps back, but you should know that it's the
same for everyone. Of course, you will feel discouraged,
weary, and even, at times, hopeless. We do think that you
should acknowledge that you will feel pretty low at times.
Don't try to avoid feeling bad at all costs, which might
mean you are burying some very real feelings. What we are
saying is that you should try to channel those feelings in
a positive direction, making them work for you rather than
against you.

Trust yourself! Do not allow guilt or self-pity to control
you. Don't listen to people who say things to upset you,
to make you feel that it's "a wife's duty to . . ." The
only responsibility that you have is to provide for the
welfare of yourself and your children the best way that
you know how. Staying in a destructive marriage may result
in far greater harm in the end to all involved, no matter
what others say.

Try to feel that this is not an end, but a beginning. It's
hard to face the fact that all of the years, all of the
hard work, all of the struggle seems to have been in vain;
but even though the marriage has failed, it doesn't mean
that *you* have failed, and hopefully, the growing and learning that you have done over the years will enable you to
strike out on your own in a productive and meaningful manner.

Do try new methods of problem-solving, new approaches to
your situation, but move carefully, with confidence, taking
small steps at a time. Many women have difficulty making
decisions anyway, and at this chaotic time in your life it
is important to sort out all the factors and options before
making any major decisions. We'll be willing to bet that
with some hard work and a little luck, you'll soon come to
feel that things are looking up and that maybe it's all
turning out even better than you would have thought possible.

Sometimes we can get so wrapped up in dealing with our survival needs that we tend to neglect our emotional needs,

feeling that first things come first. This is no doubt
true, but remember that as women we are conditioned to
always put others' needs ahead of our own. Getting food
on the table, the rent paid, our children off to school
are all things that we must do; but by the same token, if
our emotional needs are constantly being shoved aside, we
are not going to be in any shape to provide for ourselves
or our children. Also, some women don't want to talk about
their problems with friends or therapists because they feel
disloyal to their husbands or families or ashamed to admit
they have problems. We think it is important for you to
find an appropriate person or people whom you can share
your feelings with. Don't feel guilty about taking time
for yourself, spending some money on yourself, taking care
of *you*. You are entitled to it, you *have* earned it, you
are earning it.

GINNY

*Perhaps one of the most valid proofs of where I am
would be to tell you about my friend of 13 years.
She is a good person and for as many years had been
a terrific listener and "shoulder." I always envied
her and the large circle of close relatives and friends
surrounding her. Last month I was surprised to get a
midnight call from her. Her husband of 26 years left
her, and more shattering was the revelation that he
has had a 29-year-old "friend" for the past two years
(on the constant hunting and fishing trips that seemed
to multiply!). I was the first one she called for
help and I was able to steer her, be supportive, and
get her on her feet again--very shakily, I'll admit,
but she is functioning. She prefers me, I suppose,
to her family because I can understand and can help
her be more objective in her decision-making. I can't
say I was glad to have gone through my own divorce
experience, but at least the hell was helpful to someone else's avoiding the main portion of it.*

Friends

Does it seem as if you have suddenly found yourself basically friendless? This is one of the most common frustrations of the separating experience. Sometimes friends can
be a source of real support, and women have reported to us
that they "never would have made it" through the first
stages of the separation if it hadn't been for a warm,

supportive person, often another woman who has been through
something similar. More often, however, friends don't want
to take sides, they really turn out to be *his* friends (how
many of us never really made our own friends?), or they
feel threatened by the whole situation. Single women are
often seen as a liability in communities where everybody is
in couples.

It is probably most important to realize that friends can
probably never be a substitute for the intimacy you had
with your ex-husband, and that to expect them to replace
that will put impossible demands on them. Make some new
friends. Try to find other women who are going through
similar situations, and sit down and talk. Try not to
depend too much on friendships that may have been somewhat
shaky to begin with. But certainly take advantage of any
support you can get from sympathetic sources. And take a
good look at why an old friendship is fading fast. Are
you really a pain in the ass to have around, or is your
friend's marriage so shaky that it's frightening for her
to be around you?

Get out as much as you can, even if it's only to see a
movie or to get a pizza. By this, we don't mean rushing
from one activity to the next to fill time. After you get
used to being on your own, you should be able to relax and
enjoy being by yourself some of the time. Depending on
your background, life-style, and age, different things may
appeal to you. Bowling, going to bars, playing bridge,
bingo, visiting museums, working with church groups, sports,
going to the park with your children, reading, hobbies,
volunteer work--all of these things are possibilities.
Many cities now have women's centers and women's events
(film festivals, art shows, dances, lectures, etc.) where
you can meet other women who enjoy being with women. You
are probably finding yourself with new (or different)
energy, and you should make the most of it.

There are growing numbers of groups and places which cater
to "singles." Groups like Parents Without Partners and
Fifth Wheelers vary from place to place. Some chapters,
women have told us, are "meat markets" where men and women
(usually many more women) go to size each other up. Other
chapters provide a supportive place to meet other single
parents and to share fun activities with your children.
The singles' bar scene also varies from place to place.
Trust your judgment about whether any of these activities
is meeting your very real needs for companionship and fun
or whether you are putting up with a lot of degrading

things in the name of having a good time.

CHARLOTTE

Sometimes I would come home from work and if I didn't have any plans for the evening I would get really scared. I would think, how am I going to make it from now until it's time to go to work tomorrow morning? What if I get lonely? I could die here and nobody would know it. Sometimes I would make myself a big drink and drink it while I was reading the paper. This would make me so sleepy I would fall asleep until 9:30 or so and then I would get up and fix supper. I would stay up until 1:00 or 2:00, but the night didn't seem as long that way. Other times I would invite some friends over. But then I would get tired of having them there and wish they would go away. What was the matter with me?

Family and Children

Family can be a real source of support, especially if they live nearby and have been a part of your life before you separated. Many women have been taken in by their families until they could get themselves on their feet financially and emotionally. Families, on the other hand, can be a major pain. Often they think they should tell you how to run your life, they know what's best and all that. If you have no choice about it, you may have to rely on your family even if you don't want to. If you do have a choice, hopefully you won't become too dependent even if the relationship is basically positive.

Sometimes families disapprove of separation and/or divorce on religious or moral grounds: "It's a wife's duty," etc., etc. We suppose there's not much that can be done about that except to try to deal with whatever anger, resentment, or guilt you may be feeling. If you've been living with in-laws, breaking out can be especially traumatic. His family will more than likely take his side and possibly the neighbors will as well. We don't have to tell you that it's important to get out as soon as you can. Remember, you're outnumbered, so try to avoid getting involved in family feuds. Your energy is needed to deal with your situation.

You probably got custody of the children, which can often leave you feeling both good and bad. Children can be a real source of support, and they can also be an extra burden when you're the only one around to take care of them. Some women end up giving custody to the father for various reasons. We believe that fathers have as much responsibility to be parents as mothers and that an arrangement such as this should cease to be seen as the mother's failure to properly act out her role. Chapter Three, "Children In Transition," explores some ways in which you and your children can support each other positively at this time.

Men

At Women in Transition we neither encourage or discourage remarriage. We do feel that it is basically unproductive for a woman in transition to search desperately for another man to fill the gap created by the separation. Our goal is to promote the independence, both financial and emotional, of a woman in transition, so that *whatever* decisions she makes about her future are made from a position of strength, not weakness. During the early stages of your separation, you've probably isolated yourself from most people as you try to heal your wounds. Eventually the loneliness is going to get to you, and you will try to reestablish a social life.

Some women can't cope with being alone and put all their energies into another man. When this kind of rebound occurs, women can find themselves in a frying-pan-into-the-fire situation. Those women who want to relate to men often find themselves very timid and unsure of themselves and terrified of being hurt again. Many women are confused about how to handle the inevitable sexual pressures that arise. They obviously aren't teen-age virgins, but they also don't want to be seen as "loose divorcées."

Sometimes women settle for anyone, just to keep away those dark corners that loom out at all of us. The women in our program have generally found that getting support from other women at this time has made them stronger persons, and when they feel more secure and less needy, they have healthier relationships.

As women begin to feel better about themselves as people, they have less and less need for male approval, although they may enjoy spending time with men. Other women find their needs for companionship, affection, and love being met by other women and have little desire to be with men.

Many older women, especially those whose husbands have left them for younger women, feel sexually unattractive and as if their life is over, with absolutely no future. We admit this is a rough position to be in in this youth-oriented culture, but our experience again is that if you busy yourself with *you*, and stop trying to define yourself in terms of a man, you'll eventually find peace of mind. While you may find it hard to believe, you're eventually going to reach a day where you don't even think of your ex-man once! When this happens, you'll know that you're well on your way. You can draw strength and nourishment from friends and family, without the strings that come attached with many men.

Fantasy Chant

this fantasy
is a little bit like brandy
i taste it slowly
it makes me warm inside
and then tomorrow it will burn me

you're my southern comfort
calling me from texas
i wish my ears my ears would not remember you
talking to you almost hurts me
you're turning my thoughts askew just as you used to do

you try to give me your address
you want my poems in your record album cover
you dedicate a song to me
but still recall to ask about my lover

i won't promise anything but listening
so you say we ought to stop and see you
your wife is quiet and you don't believe she'd mind
she's out right now
buying wall paper for the house
is she going to pay your telephone bill
i wonder what would happen if i came to see you
would the four of us laugh and sing and get high
would i show you my in-de-pen-dence
my sep-ar-ation from your body

you know i'm a stronger woman now
strong enough to let you say you're feeling bad
strong enough to cry about your pain
strong enough to save you for a daydream
keeping you with my other fantasies
memories
you can stay there

Mary McGinnis

Consciousness-Raising Groups

Many of you have probably heard of consciousness-raising
groups, but aren't sure what they are. A consciousness-
raising group is a small group, usually between 6 and 10
women, which meets without a leader to discuss things
which are important to its members--their sexuality, feelings about their children, feelings about men, their self-
confidence, anger, etc. Consciousness-raising groups have
served as the basis of the women's liberation movement;
through the small group experience many women have developed a sense of their own self-worth. They learn that
they are not alone when the isolation, frustration, resentment, and guilt that are so much a part of women's daily
existence begin to feel overwhelming.

The Women in Transition program runs groups where women
can come together to talk specifically about the problems
of separation and divorce. Not all of the women in the
groups are separated or divorced. Some come because they
are thinking about separating and want help sorting out
their options. The dynamic of the group is one of encour-
aging interaction through an atmosphere of respect and
concern for one another. We talk about topics like "How
does it feel to be on your own?", "What are your needs
and goals?", "How do we feel about marriage?", and "How
is the separation affecting your children?"

MARJORIE

*I at first resisted the idea of a women's group
since I wanted to look for the return of my husband
or some other male who would leap in and fill the
breach. I felt that getting together with another
group of women to "share our miseries" was not going
to help me. In fact, I saw Women in Transition as
a group of desperate women taking second-best options
because firsts (males) were no longer around.*

*Although intellectually and experience-wise I knew
that there were women who opted to leave home or
their husbands, it was surprising to hear them and
their firm conviction in our group. I also could
find some comfort in the idea that there were women
who would voluntarily give up the idea of ever being
married. In fact, had made a considered decision
never to be. I found this a source of strength.*

It was also helpful to find people in the area who now feel free to call each other and share social times. I still find social evenings with women a little bit depressing, but it is better than nothing to do, and I foresee finding this as a more positive thing. Right now I am not yet geared to being alone.

For many of us who have often been hostile and suspicious of other women, this is a new and exciting experience. Women bring different strengths and weaknesses to a group, and these differences often complement each other. Practical advice is often shared. Women discover that their problems with husbands, children, friends, bosses, co-workers are not unique personal problems but are shared by many other women as well. The group is a place where women who feel the need to be somewhat dependent can do so, but in a way that is different from becoming dependent on a man or a therapist. The group is helpful to a woman as she passes out of an immediate crisis and begins to look at some more basic questions about how she will live her life.

We believe strongly that the small group is an important support for a woman thinking about or going through separation or divorce or who is a single parent. There is information in Chapter Eight on how to set up these groups. Unfortunately, these groups are available to only a limited number of women who happen to live in places where such groups have been organized. Even if you live in an area where Women-in-Transition-type programs exist, you may not feel comfortable in them because you are concerned about privacy or feel that you are sufficiently different from the other women in the group (because of your age, background, etc.) that you would have a difficult time sharing personal feelings about yourself or getting help from the other women.

Where these types of programs exist, they usually have been organized by women connected with the women's movement, but more and more community mental health centers and social agencies are creating groups for separating and divorcing women because the need is clearly there. Chapter Eight, "Reaching Out," talks about how to set up a Women in Transition program in your area. Chapter Seven, "Taking Care of Ourselves," explains how to find and evaluate mental health services where you live.

Therapy

Many women, especially those who travel in circles where
therapy is an accepted way of dealing with problems, feel
that therapy is the best way of coping with all the painful
feelings they experience after a separation. We have found
that many women who think they need therapy at this time
are able to get the support they need from a women's group.
The group is an especially good method for helping women
without fostering the traditional dependence that is frequently a part of the male-professional/female-patient
relationship.

We aren't suggesting, however, that consciousness-raising
is better than therapy or that group therapy is better than
individual. Different women have different needs at different times. Choosing what type of help you want depends
on which of your problems you want to work on and how. Some
women in transition choose to be both in therapy and in a
women's group. Others choose neither. Others try both and
find that nothing is really helpful in soothing the pain
of transition.

If you are not sure about whether you need therapy, we
would suggest talking with other women who have been in
therapy and/or a women's group and also seeing at least
two therapists if possible for an evaluation of your situation. Chapter Seven, "Taking Care of Ourselves," has a
section on how to decide if you need therapy and how to
choose and evaluate a therapist. If you do decide to go
into therapy, we think it is important to also be in a
women's group if possible so you can check out your
experience in therapy with other women.

Women In A Transition Group

This is the transcription of a tape made at one of our
Women in Transition group meetings in Philadelphia. We
have changed the names of the women. Miriam and Laura
are the group "facilitators."

Sue is 30 and has 3 children who are 11 and 10 (twins).
She has been separated for two years and is on welfare.
She is finishing high school and hopes to go to business
school.

Maryann is 32 and has a 5-year-old daughter. She has been
separated for a year and works part-time as a nursery
school teacher.

Ellen is 28 and has children who are 3 and 4½. She has been separated for 2 months and is a psychologist.

Shirley is 30 and has children who are 9, 6, and 15 months. She has been separated for 3 months and lives on support from her husband and partial welfare. She plans to get an office work job soon.

Miriam is 26 and has a 17-month-old son. She has been separated for a year and is not legally married to the father of her son. She is on welfare now but will soon be working as a counselor and organizer for a birth control clinic.

Laura is 30 and has a 10-year-old daughter. She has been separated for 18 months and works as a caseworker for the Department of Public Assistance.

Laura: What are some of the reasons we all got married?

Sue: Love, Sex. Loneliness . . . so I could be together all the time with my beloved. (laughter)

Maryann: Anybody else? What about a sense of humor?

Shirley: Yeah, a sense of humor. That was one of the things that really attracted me to my husband. . . .

Miriam: I wanted to have a child. . . .

Maryann: Yeah, but I didn't get one till four years later though. . . .

Ellen: To escape my family. . . .

Sue: Yeah, I'll vote for that one. If I didn't know that at the time, I sure know that now.

Laura: Because all my friends were getting married too.

Ellen: Yeah, that's a definite influence.

Sue: How about getting pregnant? (laughter) Is it a good reason? Today it's not a good reason, but then it was.

Laura: *Anything else?*

Miriam: *Security in general, the whole togetherness
          bit. It seemed like a stage, you know,
          like the next thing to do.*

Ellen: *Right, right. . . .*

Sue: *I just don't think anybody knows why they
          got married. Because I was 16 then, 2 days
          from my 17th birthday. I didn't have any
          reasons. . . . It has to do with society.
          I mean, I didn't know you should have
          reasons to get married, you know, you just
          did it. . . . (laughter) I'm sure no one
          thought they got married out of ignorance!*

Maryann: *I knew I was taking a risk but I loved it,
          so I didn't care.*

Miriam: *Uh, I thought I'd be happy.*

Ellen: *Happiness!* (sung not said)(laughter) *Shit,
          I wanted him and that was it as far as I was
          concerned, that was it. I think I married
          him so that everybody else would think that
          I was neat too. You know, young, married
          to a grad student, sweet, wonderful, perfect,
          adoring wife and nice husband. . . .*

Miriam: *Was that a good role?*

Ellen: *Yeah. Like I was, what's the word I want
          . . . an explorer, like an explorer.*

Maryann: *I thought I was really mature. I knew
          exactly what I wanted and I wanted him.
          And I had expected difficulties in our
          marriage because of his gambling, but I
          felt that he loved me so much that he
          would overcome this weakness in his life.
          . . . I was so immature. . . .*

Laura: *What about excitement?*

Sue: *I remember watching my girlfriend in the
          laundromat folding her guy's towels, and
          I remember thinking, oh, wow, this is it!*
          (laughter) *You know, it was exciting . . .*

folding your husband's towels in the laundro-mat. . . . (laughter) And I thought, yeah, that's what makes your life complete, folding towels in the laundromat.

Laura: *The thing is, if we'd had good marriages, and I'm sure there are a few around, we would never think like this. I think that this whole experience really forces us not to just get mad at our husbands and what is happening now, but to go back and look at why we got married in the first place and think about it and laugh.*

Sue: *I would get married now for all those reasons, because if I got those things out of marriage, I'd still be married.*

Maryann: *I never thought that marriages were made in heaven. You know, he went out one night a week with the guys and I thought, well, if this is the worst thing I have to put up with in my marriage, well, O.K. And he's just great and we're still really in love. I didn't know he was cheating on me at the same time.*

Miriam: *How do you feel about marriage now?*

Maryann: *Scared! (laughter)*

Sue: *Well, I think that I'll get married again but I think it will take me a long, long time. Like she said, I'd have to pick him over with a fine-tooth comb.*

Shirley: *I couldn't go through that again. My first response is uh uh, it would not work. . . .*

Ellen: *You want someone you know you can rely on, someone you can really count on.*

Maryann: *I'm so tired of carrying the ball, I'm so tired of being the one that mails out the bills, being the one that makes all the big decisions. Of being the one that really has to think out the future and how are we going to buy this house. I had to work for it, and I had to save my salary and I'm so*

*tired of handling things. I thought I
wanted someone to really handle everything.
But I found out something. I don't. I
want somebody to help me handle it, but I
want to "be in the know." There's nobody
that's going to lead me around by the tail.*

Shirley: *That's exactly how I feel.*

Miriam: *I just don't want to lean on him and say
. . . oh, you're so smart, you do it all,
I can't do anything, I'm not capable any
more. Bullshit. Oh, I know everything
now!* (laughter)

Shirley: *As far as Maryann was saying, carrying the
ball and everything, I do too. Everything.
I mean he didn't carry this much, and I
think that makes it easier for me to get
through this. But it never entered my
mind how many women's husbands put up storm
windows, go food shopping, take care of the
car, take the kids to the hospital. People
really have husbands like that* (laughter)
I never knew it existed.

Sue: *Yeah, yeah.*

Shirley: *And now that I found this out, I mean, I
couldn't cope with living with someone
like that now.*

Sue: *Yeah, I did it all myself too, everything.
. . .*

Shirley: *I took all the responsibility while he sat
on the couch. My God, when I think of all
that, I could kill myself. . . .* (laughter)
*But it really is less of a burden without
him. I really took care of him.*

Sue: *Yeah, I took care of his clothes; he was
like an invalid.*

Miriam: *Yeah, me too.*

Sue: *It's like there's only one parent in the
family and you are it.*

Miriam: For me what was worse--I mean he did a lot
            of things, but I felt like I was the one
            responsible for all the emotional stuff in
            the family. That anything that was going
            on, anything that was happening, I was the
            one responsible for analyzing it. . . .

Laura: Yes, yes.

Miriam: . . . for feeling it even.

Sue: He used to say, "I don't see why you say I
            have this problem with my mother." He
            couldn't see it.

Laura: Then you have to drag him to listen.

Sue: I was just thinking about that. You see, my
            husband's family is all nuts. I mean, they
            really are all emotionally unstable people.
            I used to have to keep all of them together
            and keep peace for ten years. It was so
            nerve-racking that I was the one in the end
            that thought that I was nuts. They used to
            say to me, you don't know how lucky you are
            that God gave you all this understanding and
            He gave you all of this sensitivity.

Miriam: You worked for it!

Sue: Right. That's what I said, fuck that God-
            gave-it-to-me. It's just how much you care.

Miriam: It's like when I was a kid, I was the person
            in the family who had to defrost and clean out
            the refrigerator. My mother always said to
            me, "Oh Miriam, you did such a nice job."
            "Well, Mother," I said, "I did such a great
            job because I'm the only one who does it, no
            one else had the experience of doing it, so
            of course I know how to do it so good."
            (laughter)

Ellen: I don't know how to get out of that. Even in
            relationships, not just in marriage. I mean,
            here I am 28, the people I see are in their
            late 20's and 30's. I already know how to
            cook better than most men and how to wash
            better than most men and how to do other

things. They already know more about cars
and more about this and more about that.
You know, when I'm in a relationship with
someone who basically agrees with the
sharing of skills, being more equal, the
very least you do is spend all this time
teaching each other and you come out with
almost never getting out of the teacher-
helper model.

Laura: Maybe you can take turns.

Ellen: Yeah, but like in maybe 10 years I'll know
as much about cars as most men. I feel like
it's too late, you know. If someone had
taught us when we were three, well. . . .

Miriam: It's a lot like a mother and child relationship. The mother knows everything really
well and it's so much easier, quicker, and
efficient if you do the cooking than if you
let the kids do it, but in the long run it's
much better for everybody if the kids go
through the messes, you know, make their mistakes. They learn what it is to do things
and to take care of something.

Ellen: I agree, but it's frustrating. I can't walk
into a situation and say O.K., we're equal.
I know how to fix cars and you know how to
cook. (laughter) Maybe if I hang around
professional men, they don't know how to do
anything either. (laughter)

Sue: Well, I was married to a man who didn't know
all these things that he was supposed to know,
and he was so egotistical that he would never
allow anyone to know it. Consequently nothing
ever got done because you weren't allowed to
have someone come in and do it for you--an
uncle, or a brother, or whatever. I used to
wind up doing it myself. I can panel, lay out
floors, all that shit. He was pissed off that
I did it but that was better than having
other men know that he couldn't do it.
Bullshit.

▶▶▶ *MIMI*

*I was very angry at all my friends who had children,
who never once mentioned the very bad times that a
baby brings. The constant demanding, the whole
topsy-turvy chaos that a newborn brings to a home,
the fact that your life isn't your own any more, that
any move you make in the future will have to be considered in light of how it affects the child. I always
considered myself to be a fairly well-educated person,
but nowhere, in any course I took, in any discussion
with a friend, a childbirth preparation class, a doctor, were the problems of motherhood discussed. I
felt angry and very cheated. Had someone told me all
this, I might have chosen to have a baby anyhow, but
I wouldn't have felt like I was going crazy because
the baby didn't bring me Happiness, like I always
believed it would. It brought me depression, isolation, and feelings of being very trapped.*

*I had worked for five years after I got married, and
my friends in the area where I lived were still working.
I was 30 years old when my son was born and I felt that
I had developed some feelings about who I was as a person. That may have been so, but I soon became a very
dependent person, and began to look to my husband to
fulfill my needs for knowledge of the outside world.
He would come home at night, and I was this lump of
Need--for a hug, for some sympathy, for some relief
from taking care of an infant who wanted to nurse every
two hours during the day and never took a daytime nap.
(His saving grace was that he slept all night from
his first week of life.) Back to my husband--the needs
I was asking him to fulfill were unreal. And my husband
had his own set of reactions to the birth of the baby
and the disruption in our relationship. Naturally, my
needs were not met, and there were lots of unhappy
times between me and my husband.*

*When my son Joshua was eight months old, I did two
things that saved my mental health, such as it was.
No, three things. I quit seeing the shrink. I began
to work again, first a day a week and then when he
was a year old, three days a week. (This strikes me as
funny now because the reason I said I wanted a child
was so I could stop working.) Anyhow, the third thing
I did was to call the Women's Liberation Center to
see if there were any consciousness-raising groups in*

my area. Yes, I was told that one was just forming.
That group lasted for two years and was my mainstay.
It was the first place that my feelings of disappointment in marriage and in motherhood were corroborated,
and I no longer felt that there was something wrong
with me. What a relief.

O.K., now it's years later. My husband and I have
separated. I should say that in between Joshie's
birth and the time we separated, Jeff and I had some
very fine times, the best we ever had together. But
they weren't fine enough for Jeff, and he wanted to
see what he could see without being married to me.
Josh was exactly four when we separated. In fact,
we stayed together one more week so Joshua could
have his birthday party with us all living together.

Try and explain to a four-year-old why Daddy is moving
out. We said the lines about we're not making each
other happy any more so we have to live apart, it's
not your fault, we both still love you very much.
Josh was in a total fog at first. He is a very active
child, but now for longer periods of time he would
just sit and stare. I guess you could say he was
depressed. It was so painful for me to watch him
like that and to know that something I was doing was
responsibile for his pain.

Then came his anger. He flailed about, throwing over
furniture, hitting and kicking--only just at me, not
Jeff. Jeff was feeling good about the separation,
and I think Josh might have gotten the message that
when he was with Jeff, he should feel good too. I
made no bones about showing my sadness and unhappiness,
and I guess Josh took cues from me too and showed me
his sadness in return. It was very difficult to know
when to hug and love him and when to say, "I've had
enough, and we can't be in the same room if you behave
like this." So I did a lot of both. It was also all
I could do to control or deal with my own feelings,
never mind having to handle his. I'd watch him
involved in fantasy play with miniature people, and
he'd have the father saying angrily to the mother,
"I don't like you any more. I'm leaving." He called
'em as he saw 'em, and he was right.

Josh began to have problems in all areas of his life.
His nursery school teacher reported that he was no
longer interested in participating in activities,

that he'd just go off to a corner and curl up. The
thought of that still breaks me up. Weeks and months
later, he'd still get hysterical when I brought him to
school. My impulse at times was to keep him with me,
since he was moaning about wanting to stay with me,
wailing, "Don't leave me." I never did take him back
with me, thinking of how school phobias start, and also
knowing that he got into the swing of things within a
few minutes, but sometimes I wonder if I wasn't being
too hard on him. Those indeed were hard times, with
me leaving for work every morning crying, still hearing
him crying as I got into my car. The baby-sitter Josh
went to after school, whom he has known for years,
reported that he became very difficult for her to handle
and that he kept yelling at her that he didn't want to
be there.

Jeff has always been a most involved father, and we
decided that neither one of us would have full custody
(a term I hate because it means possession of a child),
but that we would try to share being with Josh as much
as we could. The first few weeks after we separated,
neither one of us could bear the thought of being
without Josh for a few days in a row, so Josh spent
Monday, Thursday, and Saturday nights with Jeff, who
took an apartment nearby. I'll never forget the first
night I was home without Josh. Not only wasn't I a
wife any more, but I wasn't even a mother, or at least
I didn't have any responsibilities to my son. I just
walked around the house, moaning and crying a lot. It
wasn't exactly a pleasure to see Josh the next day
because he'd be so full of confusion and anger, but
at least it gave me a function in life and a reason for
being. Josh would ask me, "Where did I wake up this morning?" Within a few weeks we settled into a fairly stable
routine of me having Josh for four days during the week
and Jeff taking him for a long, three-day weekend. It's
not enough time for either me or Jeff to be with Josh.

It's been five months now since I separated, and some
things have gotten a bit back to normal as far as Joshie's
behavior is concerned. He seems to be having more fun,
but he is very apprehensive about being left at school,
or with a friend, and won't go off gaily with the
neighbors on outings like he used to. He needs to have
me close by, to be able to check in with me. When we
first separated, Josh complained a lot about physical
ailments. He'd say, "My body hurts" or "My brain hurts."
I've talked to some other separated parents about this,

and it seems to be fairly common, so I tried to tell myself that Josh didn't have a brain tumor, as I first suspected. I'd say things to him like, "Sometimes when people are sad or unhappy they say they don't feel good." One time I said, "Sometimes when people say they don't feel good, they really just want some attention." Then he said, "Can I have a hug, Mommy?" These complaints have lessened considerably, although just yesterday the conversation went like this:

Josh: I feel weak.

  Me: Are you unhappy about something?

Josh: Do I have to go to school today?

  Me: No, school is over for the summer. Do you still feel weak?

Josh: No, I feel O.K.

The first night after Jeff moved out, I'd had a long day, and came home to be with Josh. It was a shock to me to realize that I'd have to do the whole works myself--dinner, dishes, bath, bedtime stories, playing with him, etc. Now I realize that a lot of women do that all their lives, but I had always gotten some sense of relief when Jeff got home that I wasn't in it totally alone. And Jeff always did a lot of bedtime stuff and just about half of everything else that needed to be done. So I was in a panic about having to do it all myself. I realized that not only wasn't he coming home that night, he wasn't coming home any night. Those first few nights alone with Josh I didn't think I'd be able to cope--dealing with his craziness and mine, as well as all the practical work. But somehow we managed, and now I've gotten used to it and don't expect to be able to sit down to read the paper before 9:30 at night. The good effect of being alone with Josh is that I no longer rely on Jeff for interference in my relationship with Josh, so somehow it is more pure, if you know what I mean. Either we make it together, just the two of us, or we don't.

If I didn't have a child, I would pick myself up and move far away from here, in order to better, or more quickly separate myself emotionally from my husband, something I'm finding to be very difficult. But at this point I feel I don't have the right to pick up with Josh and go. I certainly wouldn't want Jeff to do that to me. At some time in the future I might consider going off by myself for six months or a year without Josh, but not right now. Anyhow, having a child makes contact with Jeff a necessity--over arrangements for pickup and delivery, we try to discuss Joshie's emotional needs and plan for them and deal with them as best we can--and that makes separating hard for me. The big Other Hand, though, is that Joshua is really a source of comfort to me. I don't think I use him in a sick way, but I do need a hug once in a while, and he is a huggy kind of kid, and I do get a good feeling from being with him. He is the most precious thing to me now, and I didn't always feel that way. I used to see him more as a drag on me, something that tied me down.

Also, it's good for me to have some schedule, somewhere I have to be at certain times. If I have to get some food on the table for Josh, chances are I'll eat a decent meal myself, instead of hitting the ice cream and cookies all night. There's something about a child giving me meaning for being, and while it might sound corny, that's where it's at for me now.

I look at Josh and think he's a really beautiful child, and then I think that I'll never have another child. I used to think that before I separated, too, but now it's because I'd never want to be responsible for making a child suffer so much, and I know that relationships are not permanent and there's every chance that it will happen again, in some form or another. Then I try to be optimistic and think that in the same way as for me, some growing and changing and maybe good things will come out of all this for Joshua, too. I don't really believe it, but I try to.

I've purposely left real names in my story. I want my son to be able to read this one day and know for sure that it is about him and me and what we went through together.

THREE: CHILDREN
IN TRANSITION

In this chapter we will discuss some of the problems (and
some of the joys) of living with children in transition.
Here we have very little definite advice to give. There
are too many differences between individual children to
even predict how the transition will affect your child.
But we do want to share with you some observations made by
mothers about how their children reacted to their parents'
separation and how mothers have tried to respond to the
problems that developed.

Many of the topics in this chapter are highly emotional
and deeply personal. No one can tell you how (or whether)
to live with your children. But you don't want to be told--
you want support and concrete help--day care centers,
freedom from financial worries, and the like. We can make
some suggestions about dealing with these day-to-day
problems in this chapter, and you will find other suggestions in the chapters on financial resources, housing, and
legal information. In this chapter we offer mainly the
support of many other women who have lived through transition with their children. Their experiences and what we
have learned from them give us a new perspective from which
we can say:

YOU ARE NOT ALONE.

YOU ARE NOT ALONE . . . in your wish to be alone, without the kids . . . for just one hour (day, week, month).

YOU ARE NOT ALONE . . . in your fear that no matter what you do, you will never make up for the loss of the child's father and a "normal" family life.

YOU ARE NOT ALONE . . . in your hope that your children will forgive you for disrupting their lives and grow up to be stronger, more independent people.

YOU ARE NOT ALONE . . . in your daily prayer that you will have enough money to buy school clothes, pay the rent, and have enough left over for groceries.

YOU ARE NOT ALONE . . . in your courage
in your strength
in your love for your children
in your struggle to be free.

FEELINGS

How Do You Feel?

There are a lot of practical problems related to being a mother in transition. At times these problems seem overwhelming. But often what makes them "overwhelming" instead of just extremely difficult is your feeling about the whole situation--the separation or divorce, your husband or ex-husband, your present financial status, the balance between your desire to be with the children and your need to be away from them.

Do you feel like a strong person now, eager to begin a new life? Or do you feel shaky, subject to attack, in need of protection and defenses? All these things will affect the way you feel about your children and the decisions you will make about where, how, and with whom they (and you) will live. Your feelings will affect the way you treat the children and the way they treat you. Once you appreciate the emotional side of the situation, the practical problems may seem much easier to tackle and solve.

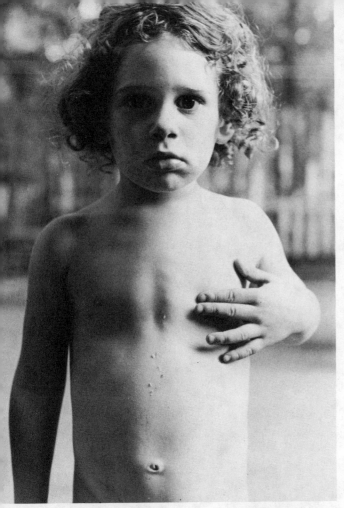

Photo by: Emi Tonooka

Photo by: Emi Tonooka

Photo by: A. C. Warden

Photo by: Emi Tonooka

Photo by: Joanne Kander

Photo by: Emi Tonooka

Photo by: Diane Deitchman Tong

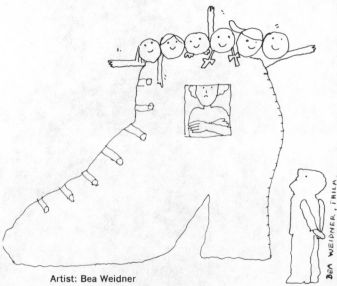

Artist: Bea Weidner

Feeling Trapped

One word used by many mothers in transition to describe
their feeling at this time is "trapped." Mothers of younger
children feel especially trapped because of their children's
greater physical dependence on them, but mothers of older
children report that more than ever they are seen by their
children as "the care-giver." Children of all ages have
greater needs for reassurance, contact, comfort, stability,
and love at this time. These needs often clash with your
need for time to be alone, to think about your own feelings,
time to plan, look for jobs, or go to work. Your emotional
resources are low; you just don't have enough energy to
give as much as your children seem to need. You begin to
feel they are growing more whiny and dependent every day.

"The more I feel trapped, the more desperate Mike becomes,"
said the recently separated mother of a four-year-old. "The
more he clings, the more desperate I am to escape." It's a
dangerous cycle, with anxiety and tension growing on both
sides. If you are beginning to feel trapped, stop and take
a look. Have you taken all the practical steps you could
to find help with your child? Is your child really asking
for more than you can give? Or have you misunderstood the
real need? Isolated motherhood *is* a burden and a trap. Do
you know other mothers in transition? Have you discussed
this feeling with them?

Are there ways to reassure your child other than being
physically close or at home all day? Have you considered
teen-age women or older women in your neighborhood or
building as possible baby-sitters? If your child is pre-
school age, have you looked into local day care centers?
(See the section on child care later in this chapter for
further information.) Have you considered a baby-sitting
or child-care cooperative where you would take turns caring
for each other's children? Or maybe a play group to allow
your child to fulfill some of her or his emotional needs
through peers? Or are you feeling backed into a corner
and playing a martyr role, feeling powerless--and enjoying
it?

Have you been honest with your child about the transition?
Maybe the clinginess comes from not knowing what is going
to happen. Does your child understand where she or he will
live in the future? Does your child know there are still
two parents who care for her or him (if this is the case)?
Have you done everything you can to reassure your child that

she or he did not cause the separation? Does your child
understand that you will not desert, even if the other
parent did?

You can relax a little in the knowledge that feeling
trapped is a natural and realistic response to raising
children alone. As long as this is not your *only* feeling
about being with your child at this time, you should not
feel worried or guilty about occasional moods. Look for
practical solutions after you deal with the underlying
emotions you both feel.

If your only reaction to life with your child is that you
are trapped, you should seriously reconsider your living
arrangements. It is immature to blame your child for your
situation and resent her or his existence. If you are
having such feelings, you should ask whether living with
your child is the best possible arrangement for both of
you. Is this a passing feeling? How do you think you
will feel in a year, or five years from now? If the
thought is unbearable, consider what alternatives there
are to your living alone (or at all) with your child.
How about living with another single mother? Would the
father be willing to share responsibility? Would he like
to live with the child all the time? Perhaps you should
be the "visiting parent."

If the father has deserted you or has no place in your
life, is there some other relative or adult who would
love and care for the child? Is the child young enough
to be adopted? If these questions sound like possible
solutions for you, you should get professional counseling.
Every state maintains a bureau of family services that can
provide or direct you to counseling in this area.

These are hard things to think about, no matter how boxed
in you feel. Women have been made to feel that choosing
not to live with their children is the worst crime they
could commit. This is far from the truth. Taking out
anger and frustration on your child, punishing him or her
for simply existing is certainly worse. The mothers of
"battered children" are not cruel, violent people; they
are, more often than not, mothers who felt so closed in by
and isolated with their children that their frustration
turned to anger and their anger to rage directed against
their children.

The truth is that these women are right to be angry--they
have just picked the wrong targets. We should all be angry

at the second-class treatment given women and children in
this society. Women and children are indeed trapped together between an economic system of discrimination against
women and a social system which leaves mothers with most, if
not all, the responsibility for child care. In many situations this includes financial responsibility.

But we as adults have a duty not to take out frustration on
our children. "Pecking orders" may be normal behavior for
chickens, but humans do have better ways of resolving problems. Be honest about your own feelings. Let yourself
really look at how you feel and then make the decision that
you think will be best for you and your child. You're only
kidding yourself if you think that staying with a mother who
desperately needs to escape from motherhood can be "best"
for any child. If you are considering not living with your
child, be sure to read the section "Living Without Your
Children" in this chapter.

On the other hand, maybe what you need most is some perspective on the situation. Your child is not going to be two
and a half forever. Teen-agers do become young adults.
When we are tired, lonely, or bored, time seems to stand
still, but it is important to realize that as your children
grow older their independence will increase. While you may
find that you and they have many more complex psychological
and social issues to deal with, at least you should have
more time for yourself.

It is especially important for women with very young children to realize this and to try to look ahead. Most
mothers find themselves at some time feeling they just cannot do another load of diapers or wash another bottle.
Usually this feeling passes. Do you know women with children just a year or two older than yours? You may be
amazed at how much more independent and self-sufficient
they seem. Yours will not be an infant or a toddler forever. It is important to have some patience now so that
when your child is able to express herself or himself you
two can enjoy warm and open communication.

This is not to suggest that your problems will be over
when your child reaches elementary school. Mothers of
older children indicate that people are less interested
in helping to care for older children because they are
less attractive--less pliable, more independent. "People
like little children because adults can have so much
influence over their lives," said the mother of three
older children.

MARY

When I was living with Joe and our son, Paul, I had a strong feeling that I had to get away from both of them. Paul had become a whiny, demanding kid, and I was seeing a lot of Joe in him. I went through a lot of trauma about this, mostly feeling guilty. And when I left I made arrangements for him to be with me one evening a week and every other weekend. Paul was 4½ at the time.

Six months later when I went to California, I felt pretty much the same. There were certain things I had to take care of in my life, like the fact that I had never lived alone, etc. And I didn't want to take Paul with me. I made plans for him to visit, though.

I returned to the East Coast after a year because things were not working out for me. Partly it was the constant nag of feeling guilty about Paul, but for the first time I was missing him. I didn't want to be so separated from him. I had to make peace with that issue.

All this time Paul had what could be called a stiff upper lip. Once he said, "Mommy, why don't you live with us any more?" I had no answer for him. I just said, "I can't--Daddy and I can't live together any more." But there was no big emotional scene for the three of us.

Paul finally did have a big blowup, though. He was visiting me once and he got angry about something. Then his anger turned into hysteria. It was like a volcano erupting--all the stuff that had been accu-mulating came out. That was true for me, too. I was crying and carrying on. Fortunately, Joe was right around the corner, so Paul and I went and got him and sat and talked. We tried to comfort Paul and be parents for him.

We try to do that all the time. We are both his parents and we try to check each other out on whether Paul has been to the dentist, what is happening at school, and how he is growing up. I am still his mother and Joe is his father. Joe and I have made what I think is a rather mature adjustment to being

*separated and working out our bitterness toward each
other. I am still exploring who I am as an individual
and what is important to me at this time. Since Joe
and I live 200 miles apart, I see Paul one weekend a
month. And I just spent four weeks with him. What's
important to me is what's in Paul's best interests,
including having a "together," happy mother.*

Feeling Guilty

Many mothers in transition experience strong feelings of
guilt. This is especially true for mothers of school-age
children, partly because these children have already spent
from five to seventeen years before this transition period
living with both parents in a "normal" family. Another
reason mothers of school-age children feel more guilty than
others is because their children are still quite dependent
on them, but old enough to talk about their own feelings.
"I'll never be happy again," one twelve-year-old proclaimed
upon hearing of her parents' separation. It took her mother
considerable soul-searching, waiting, and strength to say
later, "But I don't think that's true."

Although many women don't care to analyze their own feelings, it seems there are three basic things they feel
guilty about: divorcing the child from the "norm" of a
two-parent family, separating the child from the other
parent, and depriving the child of a "male model" or "father
figure." It might be helpful to look at these feelings one
at a time to see where they come from, what they mean, and
how to live with them.

While children should not suffer in any way for the mistakes of their parents, most divorced and separated mothers
have a lot less to feel guilty about than they believe.
Your own attitude toward your new one-parent rather than
two-parent home will make a big difference in how your
children experience their new living situation. If it
seems like a disaster to you, they are likely to feel the
same. If you feel that the "norm" of a two-parent family
with children was not working and that your present situation marks the beginning of an attempt to find a better
alternative for you, your children are more likely to have
positive feelings about the change. It is true that children often feel insecure if they feel they are "different"
from their friends and schoolmates, and in some communities
divorced parents are rare. But many "differences" are more
important to us as adults than they are to children. When

the three school-age children of a lesbian mother who
lives with her lover were asked how they felt about their
living situation, they replied that they thought it was
fine. They could see no outstanding differences between
their situation and everybody else's. They had chores,
homework, fights with their parents like everyone. True,
they only saw their father on occasional weekends, but they
lived with two adults who were responsible for them and
cared for them.

"The real difference," another mother commented, "is the
difference between what the kids' lives were like before
the separation and what they are like now. It takes time
to adjust. The two-parent family is all they've ever
known for a whole lifetime--six years or more. Living
with one parent, or living with one parent half the week
and another for the rest of the week, is a big change. It
may take another lifetime--six or more years--to get used
to this, and then this will be the norm."

Many mothers are very concerned about separating their
children from the other parent. There is no need for a
divorce between two parents to mean a divorce between the
children and their parents. If the father stops paying
attention to the children, he is the cause of this separation, not the mother, and your feeling guilty is not
going to help. It takes two mature people who are sincerely concerned about the welfare of their children to
insure that the children are not permanently separated
from the parent with whom they are not living. Children
of divorced parents can enjoy warm and stable relationships
with both parents.

"I think what's important is that the children have secure
independent relationships with each of us," said one separated mother. The next time you are feeling heavy with
guilt about separating your children from their father,
ask yourself: How much time did he spend with them before
the separation? Did the children have a strong independent
relationship with him before the separation? How much time
do children of two-parent families spend with their fathers?

Of course, you must do more than make yourself feel good
by making this kind of comparison. You must work to encourage your children's relationship with their father,
to show that you respect their need to be with him, at the
very least. One of the really cruel things parents can do
is to use their children as pawns in a contest to see which
parent has more power. Don't play emotional tug-of-war

with your children. Respect their independent relationships
with their father. Don't use them to find out about his
life, and don't let him use them to find out about yours.
If you find he is asking your children about your social
life, try to talk to him and explain that it is unfair to
ask the children to report on you. He should ask you
directly or (better still) not at all.

As the time you have been separated increases, you may
find that your children are being exposed to two different
life-styles and two different sets of values as they go
from your house to their father's. If you believe their
relationship with their father is important, you must not
fight for control of your children's minds any more than
you would fight for control of their bodies by not allowing him to visit with them. Exposure to different life-
styles and values can be one of the positive aspects of
your separation for your children. They will have more
than one perspective from which to understand things, and
will be better able to make intelligent choices about their
own values and life-styles. Your children may at least
understand that there is more than one kind of family,
more than one kind of parental relationship. They may
also have a more realistic understanding of marriage and
family life. They will, that is, if you are feeling good
about yourself and the separation and communicate this to
your children.

This is not to deny or minimize the real pain and trauma
that comes with a child's first separation from a parent
she or he has known and loved and lived with for a whole
lifetime. It is important to listen to and deal with the
real pain, and not to ignore it or hope that if you wait
long enough it will just dissolve like a lump of sugar.
It won't. You must deal with your child's pain and confusion *now* by answering as many of her or his questions as
honestly as possible. Just remember that guilt is *your*
problem, a problem that you have to solve for yourself,
and your allowing this problem to overwhelm you is certainly not going to help your children.

Of course the truth will hurt your child, make her or him
feel sad, maybe even cry every night until she or he falls
asleep. This kind of pain is hard for us to face. It
would be so much easier if we could avoid it--but we can't.
We can only stall and put it off until it develops into a
much bigger pain.

Don't avoid your child's questions or lie about the future.
Don't give her or him false hopes. If the question is "Why

can't we all live together like before?" or "Will we ever
live together?", don't say, "Maybe we will," or "Maybe
some day" if you have no intention of ever living with
your ex-husband again. It's better to say, "I know how
hard it is for you, but your father and I cannot be happy
living together, and we both feel that it is better for
us and for you if we live apart and each has a special
time to be with you."

One mother found she had to remind herself to ask her
three-year-old daughter periodically, "Do you wonder why
Daddy and I are not living together?" The explanation
would be understood and last a few months, and then the
child would be upset about the separation again and need
more explanation and new assurances. Don't think that
one explanation is going to settle things for all time.

Finally, some mothers are concerned about the absence of
a "male model" for their sons or a "father figure" for
their daughters. "I think a male model is important,"
said the mother of a four-year-old boy. "A man who's a
good person and cares about children . . . to counteract
all the terrible images of men they get elsewhere. How
else is my son going to learn to be gentle, or the kind
of person who takes responsibility for children?"

Another mother, who while pregnant left her husband and
now has a three-year-old son, had a different opinion.
"There are a lot of male models," she explained. "It's
harder for him to see good models for women. I want him
to be a strong independent person first, and a man later.
I try to reinforce him as a *person*, not as a boy or a
girl. What difference does it make?"

What difference it makes is a hotly debated question among
psychologists and mothers these days. Traditional psychology puts a great deal of emphasis on boys learning how
to be men from their fathers and girls learning how to
be women from their mothers. Parents of the opposite sex
also provide lessons in relationships with that sex, they
insist. Some psychologists insist that "proper sex role
identification" is essential to the mental health and well-
being of every individual.

Many people today are questioning and challenging this
notion. They feel that "proper sex role identification"
is just another way of saying that children must learn very
early to play their part in the systematic oppression of
women *and* children that is known as sexism.

The mother of two sons and a daughter said, "I'm much more
worried about my daughter feeling good about herself as a
woman. I think it's hard for girls, seeing what their
mother had to go through, to feel that it can be good for
them to be women." A single mother has a lot of work to
do to counteract the negative role this society has for
women. Weak, passive, dependent, illogical, and impractical. Hardly the picture of someone you'd want to be.

Maybe there's a source of guilt you have overlooked--your
own feeling that you have failed at the one thing you were
supposed to excel in, the one thing you have been trained
for all your life--marriage and motherhood. As a result of
your separation and possible divorce, you may be in the
process of reexamining the validity of these strict sex
role definitions for yourself. Your own economic and
emotional survival may demand more than marriage and
motherhood. Now is a good time to look at what those
roles will do to your children as well.

If you believe that it is important for your child to see
men taking responsibility for children and women living
strong independent lives, you will have to provide contact
with such people for your children. You may be able to
point to their father as a man who cares for children
and takes some responsibility for them. You might find
male relatives who want to spend time with your children,
or you can offer to trade child-care responsibilities with
men who have children. You will probably be the closest
model of how women can live for your own children, and
your children will also learn from your friends. If
Susan is an accountant and Jane a construction engineer,
let your children know this, encourage them to learn what
different women do for a living.

Some women with children live in a communal setting in
which male members take care of children. You may have
male friends who enjoy spending time with children. The
sad truth, however, is that as a result of years and years
of sex role training most men are not willing to take this
responsibility. And your problems may not dissolve with
the appearance of a male friend who enjoys being with your
children. You should be wary of seeking out father-substi-
tutes in your male companions. One mother observed, "I
guess it's made a difference having John around, and it
obviously means so much to the children. They all really
care about each other. But I sometimes wonder what it
means for me. Am I trapped again?"

Other women offer the following: "Don't forget--children can be tyrants!"

- *After the separation I had this image of me against the world, forging ahead with a child in either hand, until I looked down and noticed that they were gnawing off my legs below the knees.*

- *They're very perceptive--enormously sensitive to where you feel weak and uncertain. They can use your guilt as a way of controlling you. I have one friend whose eight-year-old son manipulated her into getting married. He was enormously disapproving of her dating, and was furious at her for depriving him of a father.*

- *My daughter used to yell and scream at me after visits with her father, "And I miss my Daddy"-- like it was my fault. I felt terrible. It's hard to separate out the real pain from the manipulation.*

When we're feeling guilty and/or trapped, we're often afraid to set limits for children, give a definite "yes" or "no" answer to their questions or their behavior. This is a real mistake. Often children are giving you some outrageous behavior to react to. "Please set limits, please give me something definite, some boundaries for my feelings and behavior," they may be saying.

Your children may be begging you to exercise some authority so that they don't have to make all the decisions themselves in a world full of emotional chaos. Especially if they were used to a good deal of structure and definite limits at home before the separation, some adult authority and some definite behavioral limits may be both reassuring and stabilizing for your children. If you feel in danger of giving in to your children's emotional manipulation, ask yourself, "Would I really want my children to tell me how to run my life?" As adults, we have a responsibility to manage our own lives, and to teach our children how to do the same.

How Do Your Children Feel?

A BROTHER AND SISTER DISCUSS THEIR REACTIONS TO

THEIR PARENTS' SEPARATION

B: *I felt sad when I found out my father was leaving. I don't know how I feel now. I think I'd say they're both happy. I would say to other kids to talk about it if your father leaves. It helped me.*

S: *The hardest thing to get used to is that Dad wasn't around any more.*

B: *Yeah, he wasn't here all the time any more. I missed seeing him and missed not having him to mess around with. There's a difference now because before I would play with Dad and he would help me with things but now he can't.*

S: *I don't feel strange when I'm around other kids at school when they talk about their fathers and mothers. We still have a father and a mother.*

B: *I'm happy that I can be with both my father and mother. Sometimes I felt like it was my fault. But not always. I just didn't know what it was. I think my mom has changed, but our relationship hasn't changed.*

S: *We get to see our father more than we did before. Before he was working and on weekends he was working on the house and at night playing in the band. Now he spends more time with us. We still see him on weekends and sometimes we stay for a week.*

B: *We don't see more of him but we have more fun when we see him. We do more things. Sometimes he still brushes us aside once in a while when he wants to do something by himself. I think the hardest thing to get used to besides Dad leaving was not having enough money. But now I'm not afraid about not having enough money. I know we'll make it. It took me about a month to feel OK.*

S: *I don't know if I feel OK yet. I'm not sure things*

*are all right.   I still feel sad.   I'd like to
be with my dad more.   Sometimes we can't be
with him.*

It's hard enough, sometimes, with all the emotional,
financial, and legal problems you have during transition
to keep your family going and figure out how *you* feel.
Knowing how your children feel is even harder. For one
thing, they don't often tell you.

Or it's hard to understand what they do tell you. "When
I grow up, I'm going to live in an apartment and visit
my children." Has this child made such a marvelous adjustment to the separation that he now sees this as the
"norm"? Or is he hurt and confused about how his father
feels about him and just waiting for a chance to use the
same kind of power on his own children?

It may be hard to face what your child is saying. "Mommy,
I don't want to go stay with Daddy now, I want to stay
with you." We may say that Daddy is expecting our children, but deep down inside we know the reality is that we
don't want to live with them all the time. "I don't want
to move to California, I want to stay here with Daddy,"
your child may insist, even though you know that her or
his desires are not going to change a decision that has
already been made.

Our first impulse may be to run from our children's feelings, to avoid dealing with their pain. It's hard not to
get caught up in guilt and self-pity. But this won't
help our children. They *are* feeling pain; they are feeling confused, deserted maybe, and maybe angry or guilty
themselves. It's not good enough to comfort your child
or help her or him to go to sleep, and special treats
won't take his mind off his questions and pain for long.
If your child is to benefit from your new life, or even
grow to adulthood without being scarred by this experience,
you must listen to the real questions your child has, and
deal with her or his real feelings and problems.

Children experience separation quite differently from
their parents. Parents, after all, are the ones who decide to separate. At least one parent has reason to believe her or his life will benefit from the separation,
despite the initial pain or economic hardship. Children
often have no reason to feel positive about being in
transition.

Exactly what feelings a child in transition is likely to
have depends on many different factors, including age,
whether there are brothers or sisters, and the relationship between the child and the two parents. Of course,
the way the two parents treat each other and what each
says to the child about the other will also have a considerable influence on what the child feels--not just about
the other parent, but about herself or himself and the
whole experience of being in transition.

Perhaps the most important thing you can do at this time
is to listen to what your children are saying. There's no
need to defend what you have done--just listen. Listen,
and acknowledge the feelings your children have. If they
are not talking about the separation at all, you might say
something like, "It must make you feel bad that Daddy and
I don't live together any more; I know it's scary," or "I
know there are a lot of children who feel the way you do
and wish their parents had stayed together." Doing this
won't take away the pain they're feeling, but they will be
reassured that someone they care for is listening and concerned about what they are feeling.

Feeling Insecure

*I think the divorce affected me by making me feel
really insecure. Whether I realized it or not, I
always thought I had a family that was there. All
of a sudden, I didn't. Even though I was grown,
that affected me a lot, that feeling that they weren't
there. It scared me to see my mother floundering.
She'd always been the strong one.*

Probably the only children in transition who escape feeling insecure are those whose parents separated before the
child was born. If the parent with whom the child is
living feels strong and positive about the separation, the
child is less likely to be haunted by feelings of insecurity. Most other children of separated parents are haunted
by these feelings at some time during the transition period.

It is only natural for children to feel insecure at this
time. The pattern of their lives--however long--has suddenly undergone a dramatic change. Perhaps it was an un-
anticipated change. Even if you tried to prepare them for
the transition, they may not have been able to understand--
or accept--what it would mean.

Children are much more disturbed by sudden unexplained

changes than by ones they can anticipate and understand--
just like adults. If your children were living under the
illusion that Mommy and Daddy loved each other and were
perfectly happy together, your separation may come as a
shock to them. It may also cause them to feel that they
cannot trust the world to be predictable, understandable.
If you have a chance to prepare your children for the
transition and communicate that you believe you are moving
to a better situation, they will feel more secure.

Although children may be asking a lot of questions about
"why" you and your husband are not living together any
more, they are less interested in the adult emotions involved than in how these will affect their lives. They
want to know if the entire family is threatening to dissolve, or if one of their parents is likely to stop loving
them.

"I try to make it more a logistics problem," said the
mother of two boys--4 and 6--who shares custody with their
father. "I flubbed a lot," she admits. "But I explained
to them that both of us loved and wanted to live with them,
and that we couldn't live together any more. I stressed
that we both wanted to live with them always. It's a hard
kind of reality, but we both love them in ways that make
us feel responsible for them. We're changing the only
reality the children have known in their entire lives; it
will take time until the separation becomes another reality."

No matter what you say to reassure your children, talking
can only go so far. Often their "whys" really mean "how?"
"How are we going to live without Papa?" "How are we going
to live in two houses?" "Are we going to leave all our
friends in the old neighborhood?" At some point explanations
are no longer comforting. The child's problem isn't intellectual; it's immediate, emotional, and practical. So your
response must be.

Stability, continuity, and predictability are far more
reassuring than lots of adult explanations about why the
change has occurred. Children need to feel secure in
their new lives, with new routines to replace the old ones.
They need to know that sudden drastic change has not become
the norm for their life, that transition is one meaningful,
if drastic, disruption which will soon be replaced by a new
pattern, a new life.

New adults in their lives, or adults your children have
known who are now taking more responsibility for them, can

be helpful to both you and your children. But be sure they
do not get to feel they are on a merry-go-round, with new
places to stay each week and a different person to care for
them each time you are not there. If your children feel
that you are the only constant in their lives, they will
probably become extremely dependent on you. On the other
hand, adults who care about your children and who are willing to commit themselves to a responsible relationship with
them can fill some of the empty, lonely spaces often left
after a separation.

Finally, the less you disrupt the patterns your children
were used to before the separation, the easier the transition will be for them. This may mean trying to stay in the
house they have always lived in and asking your husband to
leave, if you will have custody, or being willing to leave
the house if the children will stay with their father. It
may mean staying in some proximity to the children's father
if you wish to share custody or have frequent and informal
visitation arrangements. If your children go to school,
try not to change their school if you can avoid doing so.
If possible, keep in touch with their regular playmates
and arrange for them to play together after the separation,
as before.

Trivial things like regular mealtimes, new routines like
each child being responsible for certain chores (even if
it's only a three-year-old carrying her or his dinner
plate back to the kitchen, or helping to set the table),
regular quiet times for the children alone and with you
can be very important in making the transition period
less confusing and painful for all. If your children are
going to be removed from familiar surroundings and/or
their style of life will change considerably, it is particularly important to reinforce familiar routines. This
can go a long way toward helping children feel that they
have not entered an entirely new and strange world.

Feeling Angry

Insecurity may be the most common and the deepest reaction
your child may have to transition, but there will be other
intense emotions as well. Many children feel rejected by
the parent with whom they are not living, and hurt by and
angry at both parents.

Angry children may be the children of angry parents. If
you express your own anger toward your former husband to
your child or in the child's presence, you may be adding

fuel to her or his own anger. It is important to be honest with your children about the events that affect their lives, and it is dishonest (if not impossible) to hide some of your real feelings from children, no matter how young they are.

However, you should think twice before exposing your children to whatever hostility you may feel toward their father. You may be setting them up for a terrible conflict of loyalties, at the very least. There is little to be gained by causing children to lose respect for the other parent, and it is unfair to try to get them to take sides in this adult problem.

It is very confusing for children to hear someone who is important to them belittled, and it is frightening to feel pulled in opposite directions by two adults who are locked in conflict. It is your responsibility, as an adult and a parent, to cooperate with your children's father as much as possible on matters related to the welfare of your children. You should also try to encourage and improve the relationship between your children and their father if you feel the children would benefit from it. Of course, there's no reason to assume that just because half their genes belong to him they would benefit from the relationship. Think about what you know about your children and their father as people, and leave your own feelings about him out of the picture for a minute.

If at all possible, encourage your children to respect their father and explain that he did not leave the family out of anger, hatred, or dislike, but because you and he agreed that it was not good for all of you to live together any more. You should explain that his feelings about them have not changed, and that the conflicts and problems are strictly between you two adults, and that you are both still their parents.

If your former husband is being irresponsible to the children--for example, promising to see them and then not following through--you should not feel that you have to make excuses for him. You might want to warn the children not to expect too much, that he may mean well but not be able to carry out all his promises. If he did leave the family in anger or desert you, you might explain that he was not able to live with the family and care for all of you as he should, so that it is better for him to be elsewhere.

If your children's father is not around for reasons beyond

his--and your--control, you should make this clear. He may
be in prison, in a mental hospital, or he may have been
encouraged to leave by your desperate financial situation
and welfare laws which force men to leave their families so
that you and the children will be eligible for welfare.

This situation will probably be very hard for your children
to understand, and it may be difficult to prevent their feeling angry and losing respect for him. Don't cover up for
him if he isn't coming home; this may only destroy your
children's respect for you as well and make them feel even
more angry. Instead, be as honest as you can and let them
know how this situation makes you feel.

Finally, if you are the parent who left the family, you
are likely to bear the brunt of your children's anger.
Don't try to avoid this by blaming the other parent. It
may be good for your children to feel angry at someone
for disrupting their lives. From the child's point of
view, there may have been nothing wrong with the previous
arrangements, and your child's most fervent wish may be
to return to it. The child may be right--the separation
and new living arrangements may be quite arbitrary and not
at all as good as the life she or he was accustomed to.
Some of your child's anger is justified.

By expressing this anger, your child is asserting her or
his independence in what may be a particularly painful way
at a bad time for you. Nevertheless, you should respect
this statement of independence. This may be one of the
first of many times that your child will tell you in no
uncertain terms that her or his needs are quite distinct
from yours, and sometimes in outright conflict with yours.

You might want to tell your child that you understand the
anger and you feel it is justified, but that there is no
way for you to return to the old situation, and the best
thing for all concerned would be to make the best of the
new situation. The separation may be just one (although
a very large one) of the many disappointments your child
will have to face in life, and making this difficult adjustment can help her or him become a strong person with a
new flexibility and self-confidence. Emphasize the positive aspect of the transition.

Other Feelings Your Child Might Have

Insecurity and anger are two of the most important reactions
your child may have to transition. There are many other

feelings your child may experience, both good and bad.
Some children feel that they must have been the cause of
their parents' separation. This feeling is more common
among children where there was bitter argument or a
courtroom battle over custody. Children usually feel
guilty about their parents' separation because they have
not been given any information or any other explanation
for what happened. In most situations it should not be
difficult to prevent your children from feeling that they
are to blame for the separation. Once they develop this
feeling it may be harder to reassure them than it would
have been to give them some more realistic explanation
in the beginning for what has happened.

Don't ignore the good feelings your children may have as
a result of the separation. If there is less tension in
the home, your children will show it. "The kids are
freer now, more expressive since their father moved out,
and our discussions are much more intimate. They're more
honest knowing he isn't there to criticize. He's a very
rigid person, and they're more relaxed now," one mother
observed.

Now is also a time when your child is likely to do a lot
of growing up--becoming more socially and emotionally
mature. It's a time to share new responsibilities in the
house and make your children feel a real part of the day-
to-day upkeep and running of the house--including decision-
making. You may not have the time or energy to do all the
picking up and cleaning you used to. You might want to
have weekly meetings to talk about how things are going
and to divide jobs that have to be done around the house.

Being in transition may provide the impetus you need to
look at your relationship with the children and make some
much-needed adjustments. Are you still thinking of them
as "babies"? Are you still doing a lot of the little
chores and picking up after them that they could be doing?
Asking yourself questions like these may not only save
you time and energy, but also help make them more self-
sufficient, independent human beings.

HOW AND WHERE YOUR CHILDREN WILL LIVE

Making The Decision

In addition to dealing with all the feelings you and your
children and your husband have about the separation, you

are going to be making some very important practical decisions about how and where your children will live during
the next few years. You will find some suggestions about
how to make these decisions in "Keeping It In The Family,"
a discussion in the custody section of Chapter Four. We
strongly urge you to read that section along with this one.
You should also consider the information about various
living arrangements in the chapter on housing.

Once you have resolved the legal issues--who will officially have custody and what are the visitation arrangements--
you still have the hardest part of the job ahead of you:
figuring out how to live with the decision, how to live
with (or without) your children. In this section we will
discuss some of the practical arrangements you might make
and how they can affect you and your children.

Living With Your Children

Most women in transition end up living with their children.
The uniformity ends there. There are almost as many reasons why mothers are the ones with the day-to-day responsibility for their children as there are women and children
in transition.

One of the reasons, of course, is that the mothers and
children want to live together. But there are other reasons which are just as strong as the desires of the individuals involved, including the popular prejudice that
"mothering" is a job that only a woman can do. One woman
who has decided to share custody of her two children and
work part-time insists that "parenting" is the ability to
have responsible relationships with your children, and
this is something that men can learn to do, just as women
have learned.

Economic factors often play a decisive part in determining
with whom the child will live. Often it would mean that
considerably less money would be available for child support if the mother worked and the father gave up his job
to stay home to care for the children. On the other hand,
in many low-income communities there are no jobs at all
for men, and women must go out and work. If there is a
custody battle, some mothers feel they must give up custody
of their children because the father is better able to provide for them.

Ideally, you are living with your child because you want
to, and because you believe this is best for you both.

If you are happy with the decision and the child seems to be doing well, relax and enjoy it. Don't be overanxious, always looking for signs of trouble. Give the children time to express their own feelings. Sooner or later they will, although not always in response to direct questions.

Stick to familiar patterns and routines as much as possible. The fewer material changes, the easier it may be for your children to deal with the emotional changes. Some mothers feel it is a good idea to let teachers, child-care workers, or others who come into daily contact with your children know about the transition, where the child will be living, whether he or she is with you all the time or only part of the week, and other information which might affect the way the child works, plays, and gets along with others in school. Other mothers feel it may be dangerous to give this information to people at the child's school because they start to expect that the child will have trouble, or offer unwanted sympathy. You have to decide which you feel is more likely to be true in your situation.

You should let your children know that you are available to talk about the problems and feelings they are having. It is much better if they can tell you they are angry at you (or their father) for leaving them or disrupting their lives than if they have to keep all the anger inside. It helps if you can be somewhat honest with them also. "Sometimes I miss him too, but I think in the long run we will all be happier this way," will let your child know that the subject of their father is not taboo, and that you have confidence that this new living arrangement is for the best.

If you are living with your children but feel pressured into this decision and never had any real choice, you should watch and listen carefully to how your children are feeling about their living situation. How do you feel about it? Do you grit your teeth every morning and pray you'll last until they're in bed again? Are they suddenly doing poorly in school, acting much younger than their age, or otherwise behaving strangely?

No living arrangement or custody decision is permanent; these should always reflect the changing needs of the children and parents. If you felt pressured into a decision to live with your children, or had no opportunity to make a decision, and things are not going well among you, you should consider consulting a professional counselor--and possibly changing your present living situation.

Questions a professional counselor might ask include: Would the children rather live with their father? Is he available? Is their preference realistic? Would he want to have custody? Would he be able to take care of children? Could he make the necessary changes in his life?

You might consider other alternatives. Would living with another woman who is raising a child alone be helpful? Is the problem that you are alone with the child all the time? Would day care or baby-sitters make a difference? Are there any relatives you would feel good about asking for help?

Do you absolutely have to stay at home all the time with a young child? Some mothers have taken their children to work with them. Toddlers and infants can be found in many offices, schools, and other places which do not provide day care. These places may, in the future, provide day care in response to the presence of these children "where they don't belong."

The Visiting Parent

S: *I feel O.K. about Mike's visits with his father. Before the separation his dad would leave the house early in the morning and get back after he was in bed. He'd see him maybe three or four hours a week. I think he gets more quality time now.*

C: *I don't know about that "quality time." It becomes so artificial, they forget what each other is like as a person. It's a new lark every Saturday. Jenny got this white knight picture of her father. He'd come scoop her up and show her fairy castles and dump her back with this wicked mother.*

Many children tend to romanticize and glorify the absent or visiting parent--the less they see him the taller and kinder he grows. Don't be afraid to correct some of your child's wildest super-hero stories about an absent father, but don't needlessly put him down. Let your child know that his father is an ordinary person.

A variation of this problem is experienced by mothers whose children visit with their fathers for the weekend, come home with little presents, tales of amusement parks, and no naps. Living together every day is much harder--

and not nearly so much fun--as visiting on weekends. You
might remind your children that they would get sick if
they ate cotton candy all week. Explain that because
their father cannot live with them all the time, he is
quite anxious to please them and have a good time when
they are together. Most children can understand that
life is not one long vacation, and that love can be
expressed by one who disciplines as well as one who gives
presents.

Don't ignore the fact that your children are feeling some
confusion and conflict about the visitation too. They
may feel guilty about having a good time with their
father, and afraid to let you know they enjoy being with
him. Some children will be especially "bad" just before
it's time to go to their father so you'll be glad to get
rid of them. Others may insist that they don't want to
go to their father's for the weekend, or become whiny and
dependent just before it's time to go.

Try to make them understand that you must all try hard to
make this new arrangement work, and that although it does
not seem like it now, you believe this is the best arrangement. Explain how disappointed and hurt their father
would feel if they didn't come. How would they feel if
he couldn't visit with them at a time they expected him?
Finally, you may want to tell them you have made other
plans and couldn't possibly take care of them at this
time. Be firm about what the plans are and don't waiver
just because the routine is new. If it is ever going to
work, it must become firmly established from the beginning.

If your children's father is none too predictable about
visitation, talk to him about the effect this has on the
children. Try to get his cooperation in establishing a
pattern so the children know when they are going to see
him next and are not worried about the possibility of a
long separation or being deserted by him. If you know
that no amount of talking is going to make him more responsible this way, be honest with your children in telling
them not to expect too much from their father. Don't make
excuses for him, but let them judge for themselves.

Finally, as we mentioned above, do not allow visitation to
become the scene of an emotional tug-of-war between you
and your husband. If you take the children to his house
or he comes to yours to pick them up and return them, make
the goodbyes short and definite. Don't hang around to
comfort them if they are upset at your leaving or insist

they don't want to stay with their father. Unless, of
course, you have reason to believe that they shouldn't stay
with their father--in which case, don't even consider going
ahead with the visitation. Call him up and call it off.
Have a talk with your child and your husband, maybe all
three of you together (or with a counselor). Don't get
into playing games for your child's approval or use her or
him as a little spy on your husband's activities. Demand
the same from him.

Don't forget that neither one of you is likely to be pleased
with the new arrangement. You feel martyred because you
are with the children all week when the pressures of running
a household and/or working at a job are the greatest. You
get the kids up for school or day care, pack their lunches
and give them supper, fight over homework and bedtimes.
You are jealous of the easy relaxed weekend times he has
with the children.

On the other hand, he feels shut out of the childrens' real
lives and obligated to provide a continuous joyride all
weekend. If you are able to discuss this situation with
your ex-husband, it might relieve some of the tension that
you and the children are feeling. You might also make it
easier for him to relax with the children and have more
"normal" times just sitting and talking, watching TV,
going for walks, or reading books or doing other quiet
things together if you keep him informed of their weekly
activities and share some decision-making with him. Cooperating on fairly trivial things like birthdays and
holidays can be very reassuring to your child. Some
separated parents also share in more significant decision-
making about the child's education or other activities.
The advisability of such a plan for you depends entirely
on the relationship you have and the particular circumstances of your separation.

Some parents continue to do things together with their
children after the divorce. Again, the wisdom of this
arrangement depends entirely on the circumstances and the
relationships among all of you. Some mothers fall into the
trap of spending time with their ex-husbands (whom they
don't want to see) because they think it will make the
children feel better.

Sometimes a clean break is the best possible solution--
especially if you have any doubts or regrets about the
separation or are feeling especially bitter and/or hurt.
You should know that sometimes visitation is just a way to

win back Mommy. Sometimes it's an opportunity to make her
feel bad or even beat her up. If you feel this may be true
for you, avoid being alone when he comes for the children,
and don't go to his house alone. In extreme cases, you can
ask the local family court to order visitation only outside
either of the houses.

Living Without Your Children

---

*I didn't want to have a child. Later he told me he
made me have the child just to slow me down, to
punish me. But he wouldn't do anything for the baby,
from the very beginning. I'd sneak out to the
library to get books for the week and leave Jimmy
with his father. When I got back the baby was
laying there in dirty diapers. He'd been like that
for hours. "Why didn't you change him?" I'd ask.
"I didn't know," he'd answer. He couldn't even
feed Jimmy without eating all the food. It would
be two for me, one for you.*

*We separated when Jimmy was four. I had him all the
time then, day in and day out. Then one summer his
father took him so I could go back to school. I had
him only on the weekends. It was amazing; I found I
could function and still care for him. Jimmy seemed
to be much happier that summer. But at first it was
inconceivable--it just didn't seem right in my mind
for him to live with his father.*

*After that summer Jimmy came back to live with me.
He was having trouble in school; he could read anything but couldn't tell time or count money. Psychiatrists said I had overestimated him. But something
wasn't right. He began acting like a baby. I was
always so busy figuring--how I could send him to a
private school, how I could buy a house with a yard
so he'd be safe and secure, how to go back to school,
get a better job. I was going crazy living under all
the tension.*

*Finally when he was eight I said, "Do you want to
live with your father?" "Yes," he said, and I knew
that's what he'd wanted all along. Every time he
visited his father he came back more relaxed. I
don't know what it was.*

So I bought a ticket and sent him to his father. His father was furious with "the way it was handled," but I knew I couldn't give him a chance to think about it. He's that kind of person; he'd never say he wanted to live with his son all the time; he'd say he wasn't organized or responsible enough--he wasn't--until he had to be--just like me. Think I knew how to take care of him when Jimmy was first born? And another thing. I couldn't tell Jimmy his father didn't want him. He had to hear that from his father.

Just before it was time for him to go--the last two or three days, he acted really terrible--to make me glad to get rid of him, I think. It's amazing the change in the child since he's been living with his father and visiting me. He's much freer. And he almost failed second grade cause he couldn't count and last year he got all A's.

His father has learned to be organized. He's even getting to work on time for the first time in his life! He's moved down South to go back to college, so I send money for Jimmy's support. I don't think that's guilt money. I just want to make sure he has enough to eat.

I think I can stick out this job I'm in now for a few more months. I'm applying to law school. I'm not going to get weighed down again. I've learned my lesson. I think I have a right not to want to live with my son.

"How could you do that? Abandon your own child? What kind of mother are you?" These are typical reactions to a mother who has decided to let the child's father raise the child. Many people consider such a decision "unnatural"--which just goes to show the strictly biological pigeonhole women are put into. If you give birth to a child you are supposed to feed, clothe, and care for it until it's old enough to be on its own. No matter that you never asked to have the child. The fact that there is also another adult responsible for bringing this child to life doesn't matter either. If the child came out of your body, it's yours, for better or for worse, until it's grown.

Of course these attitudes have nothing to do with what is best for children; they are concerned with enforcing a rigid role stereotype of women in general and mothers in particular. Mothers are supposed to (and often do) perform miracles. There is an almost religious belief in the values and virtues of "motherhood"; it may be America's last sacred institution.

Women who have made the decision not to live with their children come up against the full force of these beliefs. They are made to feel tremendously guilty--cold, cruel, heartless. Their own mothers are often most outraged. The force of these reactions makes one wonder. Men are understandably threatened--they might end up being mothers! Women might enter the job market in increasing numbers. But what makes women--our own mothers--so upset? Is it the possibility that their own sacrifices will seem futile if they see that they could have chosen not to give up their jobs, educations, their own lives? There are no clear answers to questions like these, but women who consider not living with their children (and all women should *consider* it rather than live with their children simply *because* they are mothers) will have to find some way of standing up to enormous amounts of social pressure, often from people they are quite close to.

Feeling guilty and giving in to this pressure can be bad for both you and your child. Many women who do not want custody of their children feel ashamed to ask for visitation privileges, for example. There is no reason why mothers shouldn't be the visiting parents just because fathers usually are. If you have decided not to take custody of your child--because your husband wants more than you do, because you believe that your child would be happier with him, because you need time to go to school or pursue a career, or because you just don't feel capable of raising a child right now--you should consider what visitation arrangements will be best for you and your child.

It is important to your child to know that you are not rejecting her or him. She or he may hear people (grandparents, your ex-husband's friends, people at school) say that you are a terrible mother and have deserted your child. It is important to reassure her or him that she or he is very important to you, and that you believe your visits are the best way for you to be together. You might explain that when parents separate the child usually lives with just one and visits the other. The only thing that is different about your situation is that most often the fathers visit and the mothers live with the child.

Of course, if the child has indicated a strong desire to

live with the father, she or he is less likely to feel abandoned by you. If your child does indicate a preference for living with the father and this arrangement makes sense to you, be careful not to show any resentment over your child's choice. Don't let your anxiety about what people will say decide how your child will live.

If you are living without your child because you have lost a custody battle or lost because of a bad negotiating position (this happens, for example, to many lesbians who are "persuaded" to agree not to sue for custody or even visit their children), you have a different set of problems. If you are unhappy about the loss of visitation privileges, you should try to talk to your ex-husband and/or contact a lawyer immediately.

LESBIAN MOTHERS

Many people still think of "lesbian mother" as a contradictory term. "How can a woman be a lesbian and a mother?" they ask. Many lesbian mothers often have the same question, but for very different reasons. Questions such as this are common because people in this society are stereotyped according to their sex and their sexuality. "Man hater" is what comes to mind when many people hear the word lesbian. The man on the street will probably tell you that "lesbians are women who don't have sex with men." A negative definition of a woman if there ever was one!

Fortunately, real life is much more rich and complex than such simple formulas would indicate. Many lesbians *are* mothers; many are or have been married. Not all lesbians hate men; not all lesbians have lovers. Lesbians come in as many sizes and shapes, classes, colors, and flavors as any other category of people. What sets the lesbian apart is that she loves women. One lesbian has said,

> *Lesbianism is not simply sleeping with other women. Lesbianism is the time, energy, and love of women flowing into each other, a reaffirmation of ourselves and each other as women, an awakening to the harmony and peace possible from within. Learning to love another woman is learning to love yourself.*

The following section was written with the help of many lesbian mothers in the hope that it will touch on some of the many questions and problems you may be facing, and help you know you are not alone with these problems. Everything

that has been said about being a mother and having children
is true for lesbian mothers--only more so. This section of
the chapter is about the "more so"--the additional questions
lesbian mothers must answer, the additional problems, conflicts, and pressures they feel. As in all the other sections of this chapter, we can offer no magic formulas and
few concrete solutions; we can share experiences and offer
support.

What's So Difficult About Being A Lesbian Mother?

Plenty. Like the fact that in the eyes of most people
you're either sick, crazy, confused, perverted, immoral,
illegal, promiscuous--or all of these. Like the fact that
"most people" probably includes your mother, your children's
teacher, your husband if you are married, or your boss if
you work. Your children are being taught to think you're
all these terrible things by subtle and not-so-subtle
messages in school, in the media, and on the street. Unlike most mothers, you stand a strong chance of losing
custody of your children if your sexual orientation becomes
public knowledge. On the other hand, if many of your
friends and associates are lesbians who are not mothers,
you may find little support for the particular problems
you face as a mother.

"Lesbian mothers spend a lot of time running between a
culture that rejects them and a culture that rejects their
children," one lesbian mother observed. The "straight"
heterosexual culture rejects women who are lesbians;
lesbian culture may tend to reject lesbians who are
mothers. Perhaps the most common reaction to this dilemma
is for a woman to reinforce the "straight" side of her
life--wife and mother--at the expense of her lesbian self.
There is so little support for lesbianism and so much
(purely verbal) support for marriage and motherhood that it
is hard *not* to make this choice. It is not easy to learn
to love yourself in this culture--especially if you are a
woman.

Many lesbians who are not mothers have rejected a "motherhood mania" which they believe enslaves so many women.
They decide not to have children and, as a result, have
little contact with children. Because they are not often
around children, or children and their mothers, they may
feel that it is *children* rather than isolated motherhood
which oppresses women. As a result, lesbian mothers often
are left feeling apologetic for ever having had children.
There is currently a great deal of discussion and

consciousness-raising among lesbian mothers and other lesbians about children, child care, motherhood, and the ways
in which non-mothers can share in the joys and pains of
raising children.

Building The Lesbian Nation

"We have to reject both cultures and know that we are
building something entirely new," a member of one lesbian
mothers' group insists. A culture which respects both
women and children and leaves them free to live their own
lives without oppressing each other. A culture in which
women have children if and when (and only if and only when)
they want to. A culture in which children are cared for by
people who love them--not just their biological parents.

What will this new culture look like? What does it have to
do with the way lesbian mothers live now? For some lesbian
mothers it is the way to live now, so that many more can
live this way later. It means not choosing to be *either* a
mother *or* a lesbian, but insisting on being both. Sometimes it means fighting custody battles in court, more
often it means being honest with yourself and your children.

A woman who lives with her lover and her children aged 8,
10, and 11 explains that the emotional, financial, and
moral support she finds in this living situation is infin-
itely preferable to marriage. "Do your children know that
you are a lesbian?" she was asked. "Oh, yes," she answered.
"At first I told them that Susan was very dear to me and
had helped us out a lot, but now that they are older they
understand that we are lesbians." "And what does that mean
to them?" one woman asked. "It means two women who commit
themselves to each other, have sex together, love each
other," she answered.

In the last few years more and more lesbian mothers have
been seeking out other lesbian mothers to share ideas,
problems, and support. Lesbian mothers' groups have been
formed in many major cities, and are accessible through
lesbian hotlines, women's centers, and gay switchboards
and counseling centers as well as national publications
such as *Momma* (a quarterly publication for single mothers,
listed in the bibliography for this section), and through
the national headquarters of the Daughters of Bilitis:
DOB Center, 1910 Vermont Street, Los Angeles, Calif. 90007.

Lesbian or gay coffeehouses and newspapers and women's

bookstores are sometimes places for lesbian mothers to meet
and contact others who are interested in forming support
groups, sharing ideas, energy, and resources. These groups
can provide the lesbian mother with an opportunity to share
some of the most difficult problems she may be facing.
Questions like whether, what, when, and how to tell your
children can be treated realistically and sympathetically
by women who have made their own decisions about these and
other strategic questions unique to lesbian mothers. The
groups can also be a place where lesbian mothers figure out
ways to raise the consciousness of non-mothers about children and motherhood. They may provide advice, strategy
moral, and financial support if child custody becomes a
legal fight. Mothers in the group may share baby-sitting
or make other child-care arrangements and provide each
other with contact with other segments of the lesbian and
women's movements.

Of course, no paper and ink can substitute for the inter-
change with real live people, but in the next few pages we
shall consider some of the topics that might be discussed
in a lesbian mothers' group and share the experiences of a
few members of one group.

What Should I Say To My Children?

What do they want to know? What is meaningful to them?
How will this relationship affect *their* lives? Most children will not be impressed with the political significance
of your sexual orientation. They want to know what the
woman you care about is like and will she care about them?
Will she live with you? Will they see her often? Does
she have children? They may also be afraid that your love
for another person is going to take away from the love you
have for them. It is important to reassure them that this
is not the case. Jealousy can be very destructive in this
situation. Make sure they understand that no one is going
to replace them in your affections, that you will not
desert them for her.

Do not try to tell your children more than they could
possibly understand or care about. Even six-year-olds are
probably not going to have heard or understand the term
"lesbian." If you want them to understand this as a positive word you might want to use it to describe yourself or
women who love women or live with other women. But remember
that your concern about your identity and your sexuality is
pretty far from their concerns.

Older children may hear the word "lesbian" used in a derogatory way--sometimes they may hear it so used to describe their mother. If you want to prepare them for this possibility you might want to tell them that this is one of the many prejudices popular in America. You might want to compare the use of the word "lesbian," "dyke," or "queer" to the word "nigger" and explain that these words are used by people who have been prejudiced to hurt others. City children are more likely to hear "faggot" and "queer" than any other term to describe lesbians, and they may use these terms in a derogatory manner without having any understanding of their meaning.

Some women feel that it is important for them to tell their children they are lesbians. Not to do so would be to live a lie and set an example of dishonesty which might close off communication from their children. Some mothers feel it would be hypocritical not to share this information with their children. "I think they are seeing a much more positive image of women, living together, doing not so typically feminine things and caring for each other; I think they have a much healthier picture of women," said the member of one lesbian collective with two children.

Many lesbians feel the heterosexual norm is dangerous and must be attacked head-on by offering a positive alternative to the kind of sex role stereotyping and nuclear family models they are exposed to in school and elsewhere. This belief almost always provokes the classic heterosexual question: "Aren't you afraid they'll turn out to be homosexual?" The classic response, of course, is that homosexuals all came out of heterosexual unions, and a culture which promotes a strongly heterosexual norm. Why shouldn't children know that there is more than one way to live and choose for themselves?

> *I can see no better way to move toward developing your potential than for a woman to be gay, and although I don't feel that I should impose my values on my children, I would hate to see my daughter fall into the traps of female passivity and early motherhood. . . . I don't want to see her go through what I went through.*

Some mothers feel that their children's knowing they are lesbians is too great a burden. It forces children to face the social rejection that their mother may have chosen, but which they did not. Conformity is very important to most children, they will point out. It's terrible for them to feel "different," and they can be cruelly rejected by peers whose parents may not tolerate any variation from the norm.

Many of the mothers who do not tell their children about their being gay cannot tell their husbands for fear of losing custody. They feel that it would be dishonest for them to encourage their children to be "open and honest" and then warn them not to tell their fathers that their mothers are gay. Other women believe they cannot trust their children to keep this secret. They may be right. Some lesbians have told their children and asked them to keep this information from their fathers, and are confident this was a wise decision:

> *They knew they couldn't tell their father and it was clear from the beginning that their survival as well as mine depended on their attitude. I guess they were about seven and nine at the time. I felt they were more than capable of realizing that there are just some things that you can't talk about and now it's four years later and they have no problem keeping the fact that I'm a lesbian to themselves.*

There are no answers to the question of whether and how to tell your children you're a lesbian. It depends a great deal on the age and maturity of your children, their peers and the community you live in, and whether their father knows. Chances are that most of the children of lesbian mothers who do not have custody know why.

When you are thinking over this question, be sure to consider just what would be important and understandable to your child. And look for other lesbian mothers and other sources of support. The more support you have and the more lesbianism is a real part of your life, the easier it is (and the more important) for you to share this with your children.

What Should I Say To My Husband?

Again, the answer to this question depends on many factors. Are you still living together? Are you considering continuing to live with him? Why? Has he had any positive contact with lesbianism or homosexuality? Is he completely ignorant? Prejudiced? What is his attitude toward child custody? Would he be likely to try to take your child away from you? Do you want custody? Is he likely to carry out his threats? Are you in a position where his revealing your lesbianism would mean disaster? Who else knows? Do you plan to make your lesbianism public? Tell your parents?

In other words, before you decide whether or not to tell your husband, try to figure out what he will do with this information. Is it important to you to tell him? Why? One woman who has been very active in feminist and lesbian politics said:

> When I decided to come out I did not tell my husband. I felt that I would be left in a very vulnerable position if I did, and that if I did tell him, it was only because I wanted to have something to hit him over the head with and to hurt him. It would serve no purpose except to get me involved in a custody suit which I do not want. Although I think that he suspects I am a lesbian, I have never admitted it to him, and he finds it more convenient to pretend that it isn't true.

Another woman whose husband immediately threatened a custody suit upon learning that his wife is a lesbian is presently living with her lover and her children. "Get out of our lives" was his first reaction, but after thinking it over for a week he realized he wanted to have no part of full-time child-care responsibilities, and suggested they sign an agreement giving her custody "for a year." "Unless I initiate it," she says, "he will let it stand that way forever. I have asked my children if they would rather live with him, but they say that they are more comfortable with me."

Some lesbians who continue to live with their husbands and children tell their husbands, hoping to find a little freedom to pursue the relationship with another woman. Many husbands may be quite irate; this is a tremendous blow to the masculine ego. Some husbands will tolerate the lesbian relationship, not wanting to risk the comfort and security of their marriage, or fearing public knowledge would harm their careers. Often they hope the lesbian relationship is a passing fancy and will go away. This puts the lesbian mother in a position of being forced to give the lesbian relationship second place in her life if she wants to live with her children.

Before you tell your husband, try to understand why you want to do this. Do you want to shock or hurt him? Are you looking for revenge? Do you really want his approval? Or do you think he could respect your choice and leave you alone to live as you wish? What do you think the consequences of your telling him will be for your children? Will he try to keep you from living with them? Do you want to live with them? Can he carry out his threats?

If you are separated and/or planning to be divorced and you think he may have a strong negative reaction to knowing that you are a lesbian, be discreet. You can avoid a lot of trouble if you do not wave your relationships in front of him like a red cape. If you have decided to tell him, or if he is likely to try to find out even if you don't tell him and you think he may be reasonable, don't deliberately antagonize him. Stay on speaking terms so that you can settle the custody question by agreement without going to court. Read carefully the "Lesbian Custody" section of Chapter Four before you go any further. Lesbians almost *never* win in court. You don't want to be a test case unless you have to. Send your support and contributions to a lesbian mother who is already fighting the battle in court. (See the bibliography.) And whatever you do, if you want to live with or visit your children, don't sign an agreement to the effect that you waive all custody or visitation rights. He may try to use the knowledge that you are gay to force such an agreement on you. *Don't sign it.* If you have already signed such an agreement, read the "Lesbian Custody" section of Chapter Four and contact a lawyer immediately.

Moving Forward

If we look only at the present, today, and yesterday, it's easy to get discouraged. There is still a great deal of prejudice and very little understanding of what lesbians, mothers or children are about. The strong (sexist) arm of the law often comes between lesbians and their children. If lesbian mothers do live with their children, they are forced to choose between living a lie and risking loss of custody. Their children are expected to conform to straightjacket stereotypes. Everywhere we look, the two-parent nuclear family seems to be flourishing. Society is built to accommodate and encourage it, and to discourage women loving women and women living alone with children.

Lesbian mothers have to keep in mind that we are building something, but we're not quite sure what it will look like when we're done. We know it's an alternative to the present family structure and the present male/female role models. It's nothing less than an alternative to sexism (and heterosexism).

We know it's a society where people are free to love whom
they choose, openly and honestly, without having to lie or
apologize. It's a society where women are respected and
children are nobody's burden, everybody's responsibility.
A society in which "family" means people, children and
adults, who have made a commitment to one another, who will
support each other emotionally, financially, and spiritu-
ally.   A society in which children are encouraged to
develop all their interests and explore all the possibilities for living rather than be channeled into a narrow mold
depending on sex, class, or race.

If those who have more comfortable, traditional lives tell
us that this is utopia, we must admit that it is. "But,"
we must tell them, "we have no place else to live." The
world we inherited does not have room for us; it has
smothered and crazed many already, and our children cannot
grow here without being twisted and distorted. So we must
build, with all those who are willing to help, a new home
for ourselves, our friends, and our children. We cannot
rest here, content with the present. We must, like children, live at the egd of tomorrow.

ALTERNATIVES

Shared or Joint Custody

"Oh, Mommy, I have too many rooms to water plants in," said
a four-year-old who lives with his father four days a week
and with his mother three. But both parents believe this
is the best alternative for the child and for both of
them. Both parents want to live with the child--all the
time. But they care enough about their child to know
that any more complete separation than already exists would
be very painful for all concerned--and unnecessary. Many
psychologists and psychiatrists believe this arrangement is
dangerous. Children need one stable home, they say. You
should consider this warning before you decide to share
custody.

If you and your ex-husband live fairly close to one another
and both have strong desires to live with your children, it
may not be necessary to fight it out in court or draw straws
for custody. Sharing custody gives you a chance to be
yourself and relieves a lot of the tension that comes from
children being isolated with "Mommy" all the time. "When
you live alone with a child, you can't even get angry at
each other--you've got no one else," said the mother of one

child who lived alone with her son for several years.

Some parents feel that commuting from one house to another --often from one life-style or value system to another--is too difficult for their children. For others, the situation results in too many conflicts (and contacts) between the parents. Many children may be confused or disoriented by arrangements like this. If your children have been accustomed to a fairly stable, secure home with little need to develop flexibility and adapt to different situations, they may not benefit from a shared custody agreement. But do not underestimate them. Weigh the risks of extended separations (weeks or months) from one parent against the risk of confusion in commuting between the two of you. Any custody arrangement should be for the benefit of the children, not just the convenience of the parents.

Changing houses every three or four days may be too often for children, if not for adults. Some parents have divided custody between the school year and summer vacations; some alternate years during which they have children during the year with years during which they are with the children during the summer. Whatever period seems good to you, don't forget to look at it from the child's perspective too. For very young children, the anxiety involved in long separations from either parent may be greater than the confusion about living in two places. Older children may need longer periods so that they can have stable social lives and not need to reorient themselves in the middle of the school week or term.

Should Children Have A Choice About Where They Live?

Q: *What if your daughter decided to live with her father?*

A: *After the last visit with her father, Beth said she wanted to live with her father for a whole summer. The thought terrifies me--a whole summer, not taking her swimming, not watching her legs grow longer. I don't know, I panic when I'm not with them. My identity melts away. There's nobody's junk to pick up. What is my function? Of course, if she chose to live with him, I don't know what I'd do. She knows her word counts. If she doesn't like school or her teacher or something like that, I take her seriously*

> *I look into it. So she knows I take her choices*
> *seriously. I guess if she really wanted it, we'd*
> *have to try it. I can't weigh the risks. If*
> *that's what she really wants. . . .*
>
> *Q: Do you think all children should have the right to*
> *choose?*
>
> *A: I think it depends. If a child is used to having*
> *to make choices, having a lot of responsibility*
> *for her own life, I think her preference should be*
> *respected. We can't always know what's best. But*
> *if a child is not used to having this kind of*
> *responsibility--I think it would be shattering.*

If your children are school-age or older, you might consider
discussing the possible living arrangements with them.
Would they prefer living in one place all the time, or would
they rather have a chance to live with both parents? How
would they feel about seeing one or the other of their
parents for "visits"? Which parent should this be?

Some people feel that it is not wise to ask your children
these questions, that it places too heavy a burden on them,
and that the adults should resolve these questions and present their answers as final. Others feel that children
should have a say in how and where they will live, and
that any decision in which the children have a say is
better than one made by adults "in the best interests" of
the children. You should think about these issues in relation to your own children and decide what is most appropriate for them, depending on their age, maturity, the degree
of responsibility they are used to, and other factors.

Single Parenthood

"Single parenthood" has many different meanings. Once it
was nothing but a euphemism for the phrase "unwed mother"--
a woman who was forced to pay for her "sin" in poverty and
humiliation. There never has been a word to describe the
fathers of these children. The Puritan morality is still
with us, as any mother on welfare can tell you. It was
only recently that the Supreme Court of the United States
decided that midnight raids to see if there was a man in
the house were illegal invasions of a welfare mother's
privacy. And many caseworkers still insist on having the
name of the father of the children of welfare recipients
as a condition for granting welfare. What all this has to do

with whether or not you're poor enough to qualify for welfare is not clear, but these practices and attitudes make
a lot of sense if you assume that one of the purposes of
welfare is to punish people for being poor.

Today more and more mothers are choosing single parenthood,
or ignoring the stigma traditionally attached to it. Although birth control and abortion are still not available
to many poor women, fewer and fewer children are born today
without a decision on the part of the mother that she
wants to raise the child. Often she knows, or decides from
the beginning, that she will be raising a child alone.

Much of what we have said elsewhere in this chapter about
living alone with children is applicable to single mothers.
The "survival techniques" discussed are particularly important since you are probably the only parent responsible
for your children.   It is important to express your feelings and allow your children to express their feelings as
honestly as possible--even when they want the impossible
("Mommy, why can't you stay with us during the day?").
Too often mothers have believed their feelings about living
alone with children, their feelings about work or other
problems, had to go unexpressed. "It would be a burden on
the children," they say, or "It might make them feel bad to
know how hard I work."

It may not be easy or pleasant for children to share in
some of the hard realities of their mothers' lives--but
the alternative is a slow smouldering resentment of your
children. You must work all day and come how to work at
night, sacrifice your social life and free time for them--
and they don't even know or care what you're feeling! Of
course, they can't care if they don't know. You don't
have to tell them to hurt them or in a way that makes them
feel responsible for your problems. Sometimes it can help
to say, "I sure had a lousy day at work, and I have a terrible headache. I'd like to rest quietly before dinner,
O.K.?" You might explain what happened later, and ask
your children what happened during their day. They might
even fix dinner for you!

Sometimes you will feel like screaming at the children.
They are being inconsiderate, not cooperating at all,
ignoring assigned jobs, or not picking up after themselves.
Sometimes it's good to scream when you're angry--let them
know how it makes you feel to have to clean up after them
all the time or keep after them till they've done their

jobs. If you've been hesitant to express your feelings and frustrations to your children, they may have learned to think of you as a person without feelings, a superwoman who never gets ruffled. It's important not to feed that illusion if you want to have any kind of open communication with them.

And don't forget that your children have strong feelings and problems which need to be expressed--especially their feelings about their lives at home and problems they have growing up and being themselves. The pressures of being a member of a single-parent household can aggravate these problems, but the pressures of the situation can also force us to learn new ways to find support and help.

Many single mothers are learning to work with others to help one another have better times with their children and more free time alone. Cooperative nurseries or day care, shared baby-sitting, or car pools help mothers get some free time alone, and give women a chance to work together and talk about common problems, needs, and goals. Day care and free lunches are available to the children of poor families at local Get Set centers in the neighborhood at no cost. Many churches, community organizations, and other groups sponsor child-care centers for children aged 2 or 3-5. Women in some neighborhoods have organized co-operative play groups for young children where each mother takes turns watching the children in her home or in a larger space which may be rented or donated by a local church or other organization. Others have formed "baby-sitting co-ops" in which mothers earn baby-sitting credits for taking care of one another's children. Each hour worked is an hour earned. This way no one pays for baby-sitting in money, and children often get to play together while one mother cares for the others' children. For more information on day care and other child-care arrangements, see the "Child Care" listing in the bibliography.

Another way to make the responsibilities of single parenthood more bearable is to share the housework with your children. Everybody eats, everybody wears clothes and needs more or less order in the house; it's only fair that everybody shares in the work of preparing meals, getting clean clothes, and keeping the house in order.

Three-year-olds can learn to carry their plates away from the table, put their dirty clothes in one place, and clean up their own rooms. Four- and five-year-olds can help by setting the table, carrying food to the table, picking up after themselves, and helping with some of the simple

cleaning tasks. Older children can do many household
chores including sweeping, mopping, dusting, doing the
dishes, and cleaning bathrooms. Many single-parent
families divide all the household tasks among all the
family members. These tasks may be assigned on a weekly
or monthly basis, rotating duties at the end of each
period.

---

*Brenda and Pat are seventeen-year-old single mothers
who are best friends. They live in a housing project
with Joan, Pat's mother.*

Joan: *I'm trying to be my own Joan, because I
hate the role of motherhood. I hate it.*

Brenda: *I was fourteen when I got pregnant. At
first I was ashamed about having a kid so
young, but then I began to hold my head
up. By now I'm used to raising him alone.*

Pat: *Well, I wasn't ashamed, I was happy,
because I thought I was grown then.*

Joan: *How did you feel about me telling you to
get an abortion?*

Pat: *I didn't like that, because I felt it was
my decision. That's one of the reasons
I got mad.*

Brenda: *If I didn't have a baby I'd still be
running around. You have a baby and
then you're grown. Calvin really helped
me by coming along. He helped me make up
my mind. I probably would have dropped
out of school. I'd probably still be
running around the street all day. I
was always following behind someone. I
never could make up my own mind. I'd
let someone else do that for me, but
now I do what I'm going to do.*

Pat: *I'm still in school, and I work summers
and winter too and take care of Jimmy.*

Brenda: *You know, I know a lot of girls who don't
even have babies, and I say, "Damn, I'm
doing better than them."*

Joan: *Yeah, you really are.*

Brenda: *I'm lucky I'm doing good. They drop out of school like nothing's holding them back. Can't get a job. It's hard. I'll probably have a hard time getting a baby-sitter and stuff, but I'm proud. I'm doing good. I'm really proud of myself. Calvin really made a difference. He really straightened me out. He helped me see what I was doing.*

Raising a child alone is not easy, as any mother who's been alone just one day with her child knows. "It gets so that by five o'clock you'd be glad for *anyone* to walk through that door, just anyone to share the responsibility with, to take up some of the intensity of just you and them all day."

Mothers who work rather than stay at home with their young children have other problems--coming home to a house full of work and children who seem to need an extra measure of support and reassurance because you've been gone all day. Only you've scarcely got the energy to fix dinner and put them to bed, and start on the housework.

It is easy for single parents and their children to work themselves into a situation where there's a lot of tension in the house from everyone feeling her needs are not being met. When this happens to you, try to remember that both you and your children have needs and rights. A little peace and quiet, some time alone, is as important to the well-being of your family as time for you all to be togeth-er. Single mothers and their children must expect more from each other than families with more than one adult. There must be a lot of give and take on both sides, with parents and children helping each other.

All single mothers don't do so badly! Helen Morgan, the 21-year-old 1975 Miss United Kingdom, told the news media in Britain that she is the mother of a 15-month-old little boy. "I'm not married, but I'm not ashamed," she said.

New Families

Some mothers are looking for alternatives to the one- (or

two-) parent "nuclear family" model with a mommy and a
daddy and their children. In some communities this family
model has never been allowed to work. Economic conditions
and centuries of slavery have often forced black men to
leave their families; the single mother and her children
adapted as best they could by sharing whatever resources
there were--including time, love, and energy. In many
poor communities and ethnic communities some kind of "extended family" is common, with cousins, aunts, and grandparents sharing responsibility for the children of single
mothers.

More and more young, white, or middle-class single parents
are imitating the "extended family" style of child raising
--often not with relatives, but with peers and friends
they trust and who have made some commitment to helping to
raise children who are not "their own."

"Mommy is not my name," Alice tells her three-year-old son.
"I have a name just like everyone else. I don't call you,
'Hey kid,' do I?" Alice lives in a collective with four
other adults. For a while her son was calling both men in
the house "Daddy." "What do you think he meant by 'Daddy'?"
she was asked. "Well, I don't think he knows it means,
you know, the man who helped make you. I think he thinks
it means a man you live with who cares for you. He has
always been around adults who cared for him. It's not
just me and him. I think that's important, that he knows
there are other adults he can count on."

Eileen and Penny are both parents to Penny's children, who
are now 7 and 5. "The relationship that I have with the
kids has grown over the last three years," Eileen says.
"In the beginning I saw it more as baby-sitting, not the
kind of parenting I do now. Financially in the beginning
the kids were Penny's responsibility, but now we split up
the financial needs equally among all the adults who live
in the house. There isn't any vocabulary to define what
we're doing, but I think it's become more and more clear
to the kids that we are a family. They know I'm part of
the family but they don't have a tag for it."

The section of the "life space" chapter entitled "Group
Living" explores in more detail the pros and cons of living
in an intentional "extended family."

ANDI

I got separated from my husband when I was 3½ months pregnant. I went to Wisconsin to live in a collective with a group of my old friends from before I was married. I hadn't really wanted to have Sean and it gave me time to reconcile how I felt about having a child. It gave me time to know Sean as a person without a lot of extra burden and strain on me. I wasn't too stable at the time.

There were 9 people living in the house. From the time I was pregnant, we talked about everyone taking responsibility for my child when he was born. Everyone took a day that they were responsible, so I only had to take care of him one day a week. Since that happened from the time that he was born, he was really familiar with those people, and he related to them as much as he related to me. I think the only thing that separated me from them was that I breast-fed him for the first 3 months.

When he was 9 months old he got measles and he was really sick. They thought they were going to have to hospitalize him. For 3 days and 3 nights he was running a temperature of 106° and up. He went equally to everyone in the house. It wasn't necessary that I had to be with him all the time when he was sick. Although I was around most of the time because I was pretty worried, I could leave and go sleep and he could be around the other people and feel comfortable and safe.

I was working in a day care center. Since I was raising him alone, it gave him other people that he could trust and relate to and be with without constantly depending on me. Especially since that was a time in my life when I was pretty untogether and having a lot of trouble adjusting to being a mother, especially a single mother.

The drawbacks in that kind of situation are that you have to work out 9 different ideas of how children should be raised, 9 different ways of discipline, etc., and it was pretty hard to decide who would have final say about what would happen with Sean and who had ultimate responsibility. As he got older, it got harder for me to let everyone have equal responsibility, to relinquish my control of Sean. But the benefits of

*having more than one person for him to relate to
definitely outweighed the struggles that we as a
group had to go through in making decisions about
Sean. He was really well loved by all those people,
which was better than just being loved by one person
who was hassled and burdened by taking care of a
child. It freed all of us up to do what we wanted
to do and still take care of a child without feeling
that it was holding us back from where we wanted to
go.*

MENTAL HEALTH SERVICES FOR CHILDREN

The stress of a separation or having to live on a survival
level can profoundly upset a child. Some of this is "normal" reaction to stressful situations and can only be resolved over time. Sometimes, however, a child's behavior
seems essentially destructive and out of proportion to what
she or he is going through, and it seems to be getting
worse rather than better. It is very hard to draw the
line between what is "normal" and what isn't. In addition,
you are most likely confused about the powerfulness of your
own emotions. It is hard enough for you to figure out if
you need professional help for yourself, much less for your
children.

We suggest you read our section on finding and evaluating
mental health services in the chapter "Taking Care of Ourselves." Many of the criteria you would use to select a
therapist for yourself can be used to select one for your
child. Word-of-mouth referrals are especially helpful
here; try to find a children's therapist who is recommended
by a friend or by a therapist you trust. We feel it is
important that the therapist be trained in working with
children, because there are specialized skills in that
area.

Some therapists tell parents they are pushy or overbearing
if they want to know what is going on between the therapist
and the child. While we don't think a therapist should be
expected to explain or justify everything she is doing, we
would be suspicious if a therapist refused to talk with
you about what she thinks is happening with your child,
what progress is being made.

In many ways we think family therapy, where the whole
family is seen as a unit by the therapist, is a sensible

approach. A child's problems aren't just hers or his,
they are symptomatic of problems the whole family is
having. A skilled family therapist can help children and
parents talk in a more open way about the tensions within
the family. The biggest drawback of family therapists is
that they are trained and do their work in the same kinds
of institutions as other therapists--those steeped in
traditional notions about the way the world is. These
notions are about what the family is and what women's
role in it should be, how poor people behave, why black
people are the way they are, etc. It is important to
look for a family therapist who is trying to free herself
or himself from these oppressive ideas.

A word about school guidance counselors: Most of us get
pretty intimidated when a school counselor says that our
child is having problems and tells us what we should do
about them. Sometimes their observations are insightful;
school counselors do pick up on things that we might
overlook at home. But sometimes, especially if a school
is very traditional, a child may be labeled a "problem
child" just because she or he is different--by being
aggressive or daydreaming or not mixing well with the
other children. School counselors, especially those who
aren't well trained, sometimes get carried away with themselves and the power they have. They are likely to mis-
diagnose problems or find problems when they aren't there.
This is especially true for children of single-parent
households; counselors are often so sure that a "broken
home" is traumatic for children that they interpret
everything in that light. Our best advice if a school
counselor says your child is disturbed and you are uncomfortable with that is to get a second opinion from
someone you trust. You can also talk with friends whose
children have had similar problems.

CHILD CARE

You have probably already had the experience of trying to
find adequate child care for your children. The problem
becomes even more acute if you are the only adult responsible for the children most of the time. As you establish
your new life, your problems finding good child care may
persist after most of your legal, housing, and financial
problems have been resolved.

In the past few years there has been much interest on the
part of federal and state governments in developing day

care facilities for women on welfare. The rationale behind
this interest involves "breaking the poverty cycle" from
generation to generation by training welfare recipients
into "desirable" occupations (usually traditional, low-
paying "women's" jobs like clerks, hairdressers, household
workers). These programs, however, serve the state better
than they serve the women and children who use them. They
are often designed primarily to get women off welfare, and
are not intended to help either the children or their
mothers.

There has been less interest in establishing day care for
middle-class mothers, who are still encouraged to believe
that mothers and young children belong at home together.
There is a small but growing force exerted by the women's
movement which is demanding low-cost child care available
for all who need it. Finally, a number of corporations are
also investigating the profit-making possibilities of day
care, and may soon sponsor some on a profit-making basis.

The result is a hodgepodge of options, most of which are
inadequate, overcrowded, or expensive. Women who can
afford the price of private child care (baby-sitters,
housekeepers, nursery schools, women in the neighborhood
who take in children) often, although not always, can work
out something satisfactory. Women with the time and energy
can participate in parent cooperatives where they can have
some say over the kind of experience their children are
having. Sometimes it is possible to find a warm, loving
person who enjoys being with children, or a child-care
center which provides a meaningful social and educational
experience.

Women who can't afford private child care often have to
leave their children with people they don't trust because
they simply don't have other options. You may not like how
your grandmother gets along with your son, but since she's
free and close, you feel you can't complain.

It is important that we have a say in what happens at the
child-care centers our children attend. But with the
pressures of work and taking care of our houses and children, this is out of the question for most of us. You may
find yourself in conflict with the atmosphere and teaching
methods at the center where your child goes, but feel too
tired and too powerless to do anything about it. Perhaps
as things settle down and your life becomes more regular,
you will be able to make arrangements elsewhere, or work
with other parents who feel the way you do to change things.

There is still some federal money available to start day
care centers for the children of low-income families. One
quarter of this money must be raised through state, county,
or local sources, including contributions from government,
businesses, industries, large institutions like universities and hospitals, and private foundations or individuals.
If there is no "Get Set" or other free day care program in
your neighborhood, you might find other mothers who would
be interested in meeting with local agencies and organizations to get funds for a day care center in your area.
Organizations like the Urban League, the N.A.A.C.P., child
welfare agencies, or local day care councils may provide
help in writing proposals and finding local sources of
money.

Women in several housing projects have started their own
day care programs in the meeting rooms and playgrounds of
the projects. Social service workers, community action
programs, or the local Office of Economic Opportunity might
be able to help you organize your own day care center or
get funds for a full-scale developmental program with professional teachers.

Finally, don't overlook colleges and universities that may
be in your neighborhood as excellent locations for day care
centers. Often women's groups on campus are pushing to get
day care for students and community people provided by the
university. This is an especially good idea if the university has departments of education, early childhood development, or psychology. Locate the women's group on campus
and find out if they are working on university-supported
day care.

You may have already considered many of the following child-
care options, but we want to list them here to cover any
you may have overlooked.

1. Relatives: paid or in exchange for housing or food; not
    paid, in your home or theirs.

2. Unrelated baby-sitters: paid or in exchange for housing
    or food; not paid, in your home or theirs.

3. Employee day care at work.

4. Nursery schools or play groups.

5. Exchange baby-sitting or co-ops.

6. After school: neighbors, friends, activities at school
    or elsewhere.

7. Federally funded programs such as Get Set.

You can find out about most of these through word of mouth
(friends, neighbors, doctors, hairdressers, etc.) or adver-
tisements (newspaper, bulletin boards at church, food
co-ops, local stores).

Other options you might want to think of include:

1. Working at home (tutoring, typing, telephone sales,
    baby-sitting, dressmaking).

2. Taking your child to work with you.

3. Sharing your home with another family, woman in transi-
    tion, student, or older person in exchange for baby-
    sitting.

4. A live-in housekeeper if you can afford one.

▶▶▶ *SARAH*

*I have four sons, all now teen-agers. If my perspec-
tive seems biased, I hope you'll understand. I began
this motherhood trip eighteen years ago, when I was
17. At that point I was very much a girl of the
Fifties; marriage was my only real goal. My pregnancy quickly answered the question of whom I would
marry and when. Four children and five years later
the age of The Pill arrived. It was the first
contraceptive I'd tried that really worked. Freed
of constant preoccupation with pregnancy, I could
finally step back and take stock of my life. It
seemed unreal. I felt as if I were in somebody
else's movie.*

*After a couple of years of indecisiveness, I finally
got up the guts to strike out on my own with my four
sons, and promptly fell flat on my face. Having been
"taken care of" by first my father and mother and
then by my husband, I had never developed any real
independent strength, and I ran frightened into the
arms of the first man to come along who promised to
take care of me. When this disastrous relationship
ended after a few months, I was totally wiped out.*

*I felt as though there was no hope for me, that I was
a complete failure as a woman.*

*My kids saw me through a divorce where I had no market-
able skills and had to work as a dental assistant for
$42 a week. I realized I had to get an education and
took courses whenever I could schedule them. I used
to get up at 6:30 to watch "Sunrise Semester" for a
literature course, for which I got three credits. I
went to Community College taking one course at night.
And then through hustling scholarship money I was able
to go to school full-time. During this three-year
period we all lived on maybe $100 a week, which in
those days (1967) seemed like enough money, but it
wasn't.*

*My sons were growing up through all this time and
trauma. In the beginning I'd socialized them the way
I'd been socialized; boys don't cry, don't hit girls,
etc., etc. While I was struggling, so were they, but
while they were generally helpful and cooperative
(they needed to be in order for us to survive), I don't
think they really understood what I was going through.
For that matter, I didn't have much energy to help
them with their struggles. I assumed they were sensitive to my problems as a woman. They saw me, for
example, being turned down for jobs because I was a
woman, and this affected them directly. As I became
involved with women's liberation seven or eight years
ago, I thought they'd be strong supporters. This
doesn't seem to have happened, certainly not to the
degree I thought it would. It's hard to do a complete
turnabout in attitude and bring kids right with you.*

*Let me tell you about them. Jim, the oldest, is
eighteen and has been through the heavy drug scene.
He feels very pressured by society to take responsibility as a "man." He enjoys cooking, but he often
seems to treat his girlfriend in a very chauvinistic
way. I wonder where he learned this. He and I have
a reasonably comfortable kind of peace for now. But
in what seems some sort of a throwback to the years
when I was much less emotionally available, he feels
that I should be at home, "available," even though
he's now out most of the time. I feel his need,
and this is the constant conflict I feel as a mother:
my life or theirs?*

Bruce, my second son, is seventeen, studying horti-

*culture without much enthusiasm, and engaging in a
continuing series of hassles with me. I seem to be
the target for his frustrations with his girlfriends.
One day a friend of mine came to visit while I was
out. She and Bruce talked for hours, and she found
him a delightful young man. I walked in the door,
and he went through a complete personality change,
becoming a petulant child. She couldn't believe
it. Neither can I, sometimes.*

*David is just fourteen and our real "adolescent in
residence." He's artistic and excels at basketball.
He told me recently that he felt embarrassed because
he was the only one in his group of friends who had
to cook and do the dishes (once a week). Rational
argument went nowhere; all that was important was
the opinion of his friends.*

*Michael, the youngest, is just thirteen. So far he
seems to comprehend me and my life in a way his
brothers don't. He's excited by learning, open to
the many adventures life offers, and is very sensitive and loving. I guess I dread most the day he
turns away from me. I'm hoping that by the fourth
time it won't be as painful. Still, I felt hurt
when I offered to play ball with him one night
after supper, and he said it would embarrass him
because none of the other mothers play ball!*

*I yearn to share my struggles with another mother
of teen-age sons, but most of my friends have younger
kids. And I find only a parent of a teen-ager can
empathize with that particular experience. I wish
that I had a daughter at times. It gets kind of
funny living in a house with five men. When we had
a woman student staying with us I really got a lot
out of it. She was someone else who shared my perspective on the world. I think women are just easier
to talk to. I am the minority person in my household,
yet I'm also the one most responsible for management
of things because men don't see the importance of
getting the dirt out of the corners or vacuuming
under the beds once in a while--things that I've
been socialized into and just can't let go of.*

*I've remarried and fortunately in my current rela-
tionship I'm able to have a great deal of freedom.
I can take a trip if I need to or be with other
friends--I can be a separate person from my husband.*

It's funny though that even though my kids know the relationship is good, that my husband and I really care about each other and love each other and respect each other, they still get nervous when I do these things. I'm still not acting like a mother should act. It's as though they feel somewhat abandoned by my not carrying out that traditional role. I guess I hope in the long run of their lives that the example of me as a woman will carry more weight than their present peer relationships.

Being a mother has dominated my life since I was seventeen. It's not a role you can quit or take a vacation from; once caught, you're into it for a long haul. I resent often the constant demands and responsibilities of motherhood. Within the limitations of this role, I try to find as much freedom as possible, but it's awfully hard. I think at times about what my life would be like if I didn't have kids. I get through the difficult parts of my life by putting time limits on it--there, there, dear, just hang in there for a few more years and this will be over. I did that with school. I'm looking forward to the time when they move out, but I wonder, too, how long I'll be contented with a quiet, tidy house and a full refrigerator. I'm hoping that the empty nest syndrome is a myth, too.

One week later: We're vacationing on an island, and my perspective has changed. I realized that with all the outside pressures on all of us, we spend very little real time together. Here we can focus more on our relationships, and I feel more in touch with my kids. There's a surprising amount of affection and caring and voluntary cooperation in daily chores. They are treating me and each other more as people, and we're all having fun. They tease me about "women's lib" when I have trouble swinging an ax, but it's done with affection. I guess I've been overreacting a lot to what they say, and have missed some of the subtle things that suggest that they do understand. If we could only live on an island forever!

Three weeks later: We're back home and back to hassling about who's going to put the dishes in the dishwasher. Is it possible to really live in any sane way in this city? We've got to keep trying to find a way to live as if we were still on the island, but how?

FOUR: WHAT THE LAW SAYS

INTRODUCTION

"Before all else, you are a wife and a mother."

*"That I no longer believe. I know the majority
thinks you're right, but I can't go on believing
what the majority says. I have to think these
things over myself and try to understand them."*

--Henrik Ibsen
A Doll's House

And with this fiery speech, Ibsen's heroine Nora exits
from the stage--and from real life. While many of us
reach this same realization at some time in our marriages,
we are given no graceful exits. In fact, the real world
often seems to begin here--the world of looking for apartments, getting credit, and trying to survive as a woman
alone (or a woman alone with children). No one applauds
as we march from job interview to loan office or from
family court to welfare office. We find ourselves without
well-rehearsed lines covering what to say to social workers, employers, creditors, in-laws, our children--ourselves.
And sooner or later we begin to feel like we have fallen
down some rabbit hole and are seeing the world through a
strange looking glass called "The Law."

Suddenly the law seems to have something to say about almost every aspect of our lives--our children, our houses, our bank accounts, whether we are employable or good credit risks or good tenants, whether we can get the doctor bills and the grocery bills paid--even what names we should use.

Like most women in transition, those of us who have worked on this chapter were both awestruck and ignorant of the law when Women in Transition first opened. It did not take long to learn that helping women to understand the legal system and to use its services effectively had to be one of our first and primary tasks. We began, with no expertise or training, to gather whatever information we could about the legal aspects of separation and divorce, in order to advise women who were anxious to know about their legal rights as wives, mothers, welfare clients, and consumers of legal services.

Over the last three years we have read and studied and talked with many lawyers. Some of us have gone to law school, some have graduated and are working as lawyers; some of us have jobs as legal workers doing technical and non-technical work in law offices. But we have learned the most from the women who came to us for information and support.

We have learned about the high cost of separation and divorce, about the delays in the judicial process and the sexism behind the laws regarding marriage, separation, divorce, and custody. This learning reflects our experience with women who came to us with a wide variety of problems and many different backgrounds. Women who wanted to avoid paying high taxes on the property settlements or alimony payments and women who wanted to know whether they could have their husbands evicted from their public housing accommodations; women whose children had been kidnapped by their husbands and women whose children had been placed in foster homes by a public agency; women who had been beaten by their husbands and women who were afraid to demand decent amounts of support from their well-to-do husbands. All these women have taught us something we could never learn in law books or classes or law offices and courtrooms. They have taught us a lot about what the law *does* as well as what it says. We hope we can pass along their experience to you.

Please note that this information is gathered from our experience in Women in Transition and the legal training

Artist: Gale Russo

Feminist Resources

Artist: Alice Neel

Liberation News Service

some of us have acquired as a result of that experience.
Although most of us in the group that helped write this
chapter are not lawyers, we have collectively learned at
least as much about uncontested divorces, child custody,
property settlements, separation agreements, support court,
and welfare as most attorneys who do not specialize in all
these areas. The information contained in this chapter
has been carefully read by several lawyers who are trained
and experienced in the area of the rights of women in
transition.

We believe that this information can help you make some of
the decisions you face as a woman in transition; however,
we do not intend this chapter as a substitute for qualified
legal counsel (or personal moral support). Particular laws
differ widely from state to state, and their application
from urban to rural areas, and from the rich to the poor.
It would be impossible for us to give specific information
in all the major areas that would apply to every state in
the nation. For the most part, you will have to discover
the details of the law in your own locality as well as how
the practices differ from the letter of the law.

This chapter is designed to help you figure out what legal
questions you will have to ask in order to get on the road
toward a more independent, self-sufficient life. In many
cases you will need the advice and support of qualified
legal counsel as well. We emphasize "qualified" and "counsel" because we do not assume that every lawyer is "qualified" to help you, nor that the most qualified people in
this area are always lawyers. In order to help you decide
what kind of legal counsel you need and evaluate particular
counselors, we have included the following sections.

Using Legal Services

Legal services have traditionally been available in this
country only to those with rather high incomes. The cost
of divorce contributes significantly to the number of de-
sertions, illegal marriages, and "illegitimate" children
in this country. In the last decade some progress has been
made toward providing legal services to all who need them,
although this goal is still far from being reached. Many
people still are not aware of their legal rights because
they have not been informed of their right to free legal
services.

The term "legal services" covers a wide range of activities,
from professional counseling and court appearances by a

lawyer to a telephone or in-person question-and-answer session with a non-lawyer who has been trained in domestic relations or other fields of law. What kind of service you will get depends on your needs (and, to some extent, your means).

If you want professional advice or services from an attorney, you will probably have to pay at the rate of somewhere between $25 and $60 an hour. However, if your income is near the level of the maximum welfare grant in your area, you may qualify for free legal services through a legal aid program (called "Legal Services," "Community Legal Services," or "Legal Aid" and listed in the white pages of your nearest city telephone directory). The major drawback to these free services is that there are not nearly enough centers and lawyers for all the eligible people who have legal problems. There may be considerable waiting time involved, especially if you want a divorce. However, if your problem is an emergency by their standards--for example, you have been summoned to appear in court on a specific date--you should explain this to the person answering the telephone at the center where you call for an appointment, and you should get one promptly.

How To Use This List Of Sources Of Legal Services

Potential sources of legal services for each state are listed in the following order:

1.   State or municipal commissions on the status of women. These are usually government-funded and have very different budgets from state to state. Each state has particular projects--e.g., employment, education, or other "women's rights." If you have problems in these areas, or other problems related to sex discrimination (e.g., name change, credit), this is a good place to start. Also, if there is no legal service agency in your area, the state commission might be able to direct you to a sympathetic lawyer in your area.

2.   The local or state chapters of NOW. This is one women's organization which has at least one chapter in every state. If you have trouble finding legal assistance, the local NOW chapter may be able to give you information about helpful lawyers or other alternatives.

3.   Local Legal Aid offices (free services in some areas,

"modest fees" in others) and Lawyers' Reference Services
(referrals to private attorneys who may or may not charge
less than the standard fees).

Note that all these addresses are subject to change, but were
accurate as of publication of the Women's Rights Almanac
(1974).

Legal Service Agencies And Other Sources Of Legal Help

For Women In Transition

> Women's Legal Defense Fund Legal Project
> Domestic Relations Counseling
> 1736 R. Street, N.W.
> Washington, D.C. 20009
>   (202) 232-5293

> Neighborhood Legal Services Programs,
> Office of Legal Services,
> Office of Economic Opportunity
> 1200 19th Street, N.W. L509
> Washington, D.C. 20506
>   (202) 254-5218

You may write or call this agency if you cannot locate the
legal services office nearest you. This office publishes
a directory of all the legal service programs in the country, which you may obtain by writing "Legal Services Projects and Legal Services Project Directors," OEO Pamphlet
6140-2, May 1972, at the above address.

> Southern Action Legal Movement
> Post Office Box 54472
> Atlanta, Georgia 30308
>   (404) 876-5257

Alabama: National Organization for Women (NOW)
                  Post Office Box 2204
                  Main Station
                  Huntsville 35804

      or

                  454 S. Goldthwaite Street
                  Montgomery 36104

Alabama Women's Commission
Samford University
Birmingham 35202

Legal Aid Society of Birmingham
318 Jefferson County Courthouse

or   Legal Aid Society of Lauderdale County

or   Committee on Legal Aid
Mobile Bar Association
New Courthouse Building

or   Lawyers' Referral Service
121 Royal Street, Mobile

or   Montgomery Legal Aid Office
4th Floor, Courthouse

or   Lawyers' Referral Service
Montgomery County Bar Association
19 Adams Avenue, Montgomery

Alaska: Alaska Commission on the Status of Women
Post Office Box 492
Petersburg 99833

Fairbanks NOW
306 10th Street, Fairbanks 99701

Arizona: Arizona Governor's Commission
on the Status of Women
First National Bank
Post Office Box 20551
Phoenix 85036

National Organization for Women
6802 Opatas
Tucson 85715

Maricopa County Legal Aid Society
706 Security Building
Phoenix

or   North Central Lawyers' Reference Service
Maricopa County Bar Association
Title and Trust Building
Phoenix

The Legal Aid Society of Pima
  County Bar Association
Pima County Courthouse Annex
112 West Pennington, Phoenix

or   Lawyers' Reference Service
Pime County Bar Association
82 South Stone Avenue, Phoenix

Navajo Legal Aid Service
The Navajo Tribe
Window Rock

Arkansas: Arkansas Governor's Commission on
  the Status of Women
State Capitol
Little Rock 72201

National Organization for Women
8205 Louwanda Drive
Little Rock 72205

Sebastian County Legal Aid Society
Welfare Building
Fort Smith

Pulaski County Legal Aid Bureau
901 Pyramid Building
Little Rock

or   Lawyers' Referral Service
Pulaski County Bar Association
733 Pyramid Life Building
Little Rock

California: State of California Commission
  on the Status of Women
4028 Huntington Road
Sacramento 94814

*(There are municipal commissions on the
status of women in many large California
cities.)*

NOW
Eve Norman, State Coordinator
1157 S. Spaulding
Los Angeles 90019

          or   NOW
                  Helen Damouth, Assistant State Coordinator
                  935 Peninsula Way
                  Menlo Park 94025

                  Legal Aid and Lawyers' Reference Service
                  County Bar Association or Courthouse
                  (In almost every county)

Colorado: NOW
                  Diana Berghausen, State Coordinator
                  1501 Village Lane
                  Fort Collins 80251

                  State Commission on the Status of Women
                  Mrs. Arthur T. Cowperthwaite
                  1218 Denver Club Building
                  Denver 80202

                  Boulder Legal Aid Clinic
                  University of Colorado Law School
                  Boulder

          or   Lawyers' Referral Service
                  County Bar Association
                  National State Bank Building
                  Boulder

                  Legal Aid Society of Colorado Springs
                  461 Independence Building
                  Colorado Springs

          or   Lawyers' Referral Service
                  El Paso County Bar Association
                  Independence Building
                  Colorado Springs

                  Metropolitan Legal Aid Society of Denver
                  314 14th Street (and branch offices)
                  Denver

          or   Lawyers' Referral Service
                  Denver Bar Association
                  525 Mile High Center
                  Denver

                    Legal Aid Society of Pueblo
                    Thatcher Building
                    Pueblo

        or   Lawyers' Referral Service
                    Pueblo County Bar Association
                    303 Bon Durant Building
                    Pueblo

Connecticut: State Commission on the Status of Women
                    Office of the Governor
                    State Capitol
                    Hartford 06115

                    NOW
                    Judy Picerking, State Coordinator
                    28 Lincoln Avenue
                    Norwich 06360

                    Legal Aid and Lawyers' Referral Service
                    County Bar Association or courthouse
                    Bridgeport, Hartford, New Haven,
                    New London, Norwich, and Waterbury

Delaware: Helen R. Thomas
                    Council for Women
                    Scott Plaza
                    1228 Scott Street
                    Wilmington 19806

                    NOW
                    Muriel Durhan, Convenor,
                    151 Thorne Lane, Apt. 7
                    Newark 19711

                    Legal Aid Society of Delaware
                    412 North American Building
                    10th and Market Streets
                    Wilmington

        or   Lawyers' Reference Service
                    Delaware State Bar Association
                    Room 153 Public Building
                    10th and King Streets
                    Wilmington

Florida: Marie Willard Anderson
                    Florida Commission on the Status of
                       Women
                    2840 S.W. 28 Terrace
                    Miami 33133

                    NOW
                    Karen Coolman, State Coordinator
                    1911 Bayview Drive
                    Fort Lauderdale 33305

                    *Legal Aid Societies and Lawyers'
                    Referral Services, housed in county
                    courthouses or Bar Association offices
                    in Clearwater, Gainesville, Jackson-
                    ville, Miami, Orlando, Pensacola,
                    St. Petersburg, Tampa, and West Palm
                    Beach.*

Georgia: State Commission on the Status of Women
                    Dorothy W. Gibson
                    1646 Mt. Paran Road
                    Atlanta 30327

                    NOW
                    Martha W. Gaines, State Coordinator
                    2444 E. Adina Drive
                    Atlanta 30324

                    *Legal Aid and Lawyers' Referral Services
                    in Athens, Atlanta, Augusta, Columbus,
                    Macon, Marietta, and Savannah. Housed
                    in county courthouses or Bar Association
                    offices.*

Hawaii: State Commission on the Status of Women
                    Margaret Ushijima
                    Post Office Box 150
                    Honolulu 96810

           or   NOW
                    Mildred E. Kersh, Western Regional Director
                    2301 Fairview East
                    Apartment 214
                    Seattle 98102

or   NOW
      Dr. Vivian Walker, President
      1948 Puowaina Drive
      Honolulu 96813

or   NOW
      Jo Ann TeSelle, Convenor
      184 Puueo Street
      Hilo 96720

      Legal Aid Society of Hawaii
      813 Alakea Street
      Honolulu

or   Lawyers' Referral Service
      Bar Association of Hawaii
      813 Alakea Street
      Honolulu

Idaho: Honorable Marjorie Ruth Moon
          Idaho Commission on Women's Programs
          Room 102, Statehouse
          Boise 83707

          NOW
          Anne Burdick, President
          2161 Aegean Avenue
          Idaho Falls 83201

          Lawyers' Referral Service
          Third District Bar Association
          First National Bank Building
          Boise

          Lawyers' Referral Service
          Ninth Judicial District
          Bar Association
          c/o Probate Judge
          Idaho Falls

          Lawyers' Referral Service
          The Book Arcade
          Bannock Hotel
          Pocatello

Illinois: Senator Esther Saperstein
                   Commission on the Status of Women
                   Chicago Board of Health
                   Chicago

                   NOW
                   Irene Bennet, State Coordinator
                   7620 78th Street
                   Rock Island 61201

                   *Legal Aid and Lawyers' Referral Services
                   in Aurora, Champaign, Chicago, Glen
                   Ellen, Lansing, Pekin, Peoria, Rockford,
                   and Sterling.*

Indiana: Margaret Ginzler Robb
                   State Commission on the Status of Women
                   Purdue University
                   Administrative Building
                   Lafayette 47902

         or   Dr. Lee Ellen Ford, Executive Director
                   Office of the Governor
                   Indianapolis 46805

         or   *Municipal Commissions on the Status of
                   Women in Columbus, Fort Wayne, Gary,
                   Indianapolis, and West Lafayette.*

                   NOW
                   Pat Gillespie, State Coordinator
                   2612 Eastgate Lane
                   Apartment 16A
                   Bloomington 47401

                   *Legal Aid and Lawyers' Referral in Fort
                   Wayne, Indianapolis, and South Bend.
                   Legal Aid only in Evansville. Courthouse
                   or county Bar Association offices.*

Iowa: Christine Wilson, Chairperson
                   State Commission on the Status of Women
                   1141 Garden
                   Des Moines 50315

NOW
Irene Talbott, State Coordinator
2002 Motley
Des Moines 50315

*Legal Aid Societies in Des Moines and
Waterloo; Lawyers' Referral Services in
Davenport, Des Moines, Douds, Ottumwa, Storm
Lake, and Waterloo.*

Kansas:
Cora Hobble, Chairperson
Kansas Governor's Commission on
    the Status of Women
1101 Polk
Topeka 66612

NOW
Kathy Rand, Regional Director
10 W. Elm
Apartment 701
Chicago 60610

or   *Local chapters in Lawrence, Manhattan,
Ottawa, Topeka, and Wichita; Legal Aid
in Kansas City, Topeka, and Wichita.
Lawyers' Referral Service in Emporia
and Kansas City.*

Kentucky:
Mrs. Ronald Abrams, Chairperson
State Commission on the Status of Women
306 Castleview Drive
Louisville 40207

NOW
Carolyn Weeks, State Coordinator
2380 Vakley Vista
Louisville 40205

Legal Aid Society of Louisville
205 S. 4th Street
3rd Floor
Louisville

                    Lawyers' Referral Service
                    Kenton County Bar Association
                    Covington Courthouse
                    Covington

                    Lawyers' Reference Service
                    Louisville Bar Association
                    400 Courthouse
                    Louisville

Louisiana: Myrtle Pickering, Chairperson
                    Bureau on Status of Women
                    2609 Leaf Lane
                    Shreveport 71109

     or   Gwen Redding, Acting Director
                    Louisiana Bureau on the Status of Women
                    Suite 402, State Office Building
                    Baton Rouge 70801

                    NOW
                    Margaret P. Stanley, State Coordinator
                    9508 Wild Valley Road
                    Baton Rouge 70810

                    *Legal Aid and Lawyers' Referral Service
                    in Baton Rouge, New Orleans, and
                    Shreveport. County courthouses or
                    Bar Association offices.*

Maine: Ruth Zrioka, Chairperson
                    Advisory Council on the Status of Women
                    42 Longfellow Drive
                    Cape Elizabeth 04107

                    NOW
                    Lois Reckitt, State Coordinator
                    38 Myrtle Street
                    South Portland 04106

                    Lawyers' Referral Service
                    Cumberland Bar Association
                    97-A Exchange Street
                    Portland 04111

or	Legal Aid Office Courthouse Portland 04111

Maryland: Anne Carey Boucher, Chairperson
            Maryland Commission on the
               Status of Women
            Western Run Road
            Cockeysville 21030

or   Elaine L. Newman, Executive Director
            1100 N. Eutaw, 6th Floor
            Baltimore 21201

or   *Numerous county commissions.*

            NOW
            Casey Hughes, State Coordinator
            1400 Bayside Drive
            Edgewater 21037

            Legal Aid Bureau, Inc.
            People's Court Building
            Fayette and Gay Streets
            Baltimore 21202

or   Lawyers' Referral Service
            Bar Association of Baltimore City
            617 Mercantile Trust Building
            Baltimore 21202

Massachusetts: Ann R. Blackham
                 Governor's Commission on the
                    Status of Women
                 33 Canterbury Road
                 Winchester 01890

or   Municipal Commission
            Boston

            NOW
            Patricia T. Desmond, State Coordinator
            18 Kilby Street
            Quincy 02169

Legal Aid Societies in Boston, Cambridge (Harvard Law School), New Bedford, Springfield, and Worcester.

or   Lawyers' Reference Service
Boston Bar Association
35 Court Street
Boston 02108

Michigan: N. Lorraine Beebe, Chairperson
Michigan Women's Commission
24424 Fairmont
Dearborn 48124

NOW
Lee Lavalli, State Coordinator
1750 Culver
Dearborn 48114

Legal Aid in Battle Creek, Detroit, Flint, Grand Rapids, Jackson, Kalamazoo, Lansing, and Pontiac; Lawyers' Reference Service in Detroit, Flint, Grand Rapids, Hamtrack, Kalamazoo, Mount Clements, Muskegon, Pontiac, Port Huron, and Saginaw.

Minnesota: Phoebe Kent, Chairperson
Women's Advisory Commission
1202 Washburn Avenue, N.
Minneapolis 55411

or   Betty Howard, Director
Division of Women's Affairs
Minnesota Department of Human Rights
Room 60, State Office Building
St. Paul 55101

NOW
Roberta I. Petit, State Coordinator
1767 Blair Avenue
St. Paul 55104

Legal Aid Department
Family Service of St. Paul
104 Wilder Building
St. Paul

Lawyers' Referral Services in Duluth,
Minneapolis, and St. Paul; Legal Aid
in Duluth and Minneapolis.

Mississippi: Judge Mildred W. Norris, Chairperson
                Commission on the Status of Women
                Post Office Box 1633
                Hattiesburg 39401

                NOW
                Ted. R. Williams, State Coordinator
                199 Treehaven Drive
                Jackson 39212

                Legal Aid of Jackson
                Public Welfare Building
                355 S. Congress Street
                Jackson 39201

Missouri: Alberta J. Meyer, Chairperson
                Missouri Commission on the
                   Status of Women
                507 East Capitol
                Jefferson City 65101

                NOW
                Mary Ann Seday, State Coordinator
                3716 Fairview
                St. Louis 63116

                Lawyers' Referral and Legal Aid in Kansas
                City, St. Louis, Springfield; Lawyers'
                Referral only in Clayton and Farmington.
                County Bar Associations and courthouses.

Montana: Natalie Conner, Co-Chairperson
                Status of Women Advisory Council
                2130 Highland
                Helena 59601

or   Evelyn Hottenstein, Co-Chairperson
        618 N. Davis
        Helena 59601

        NOW
        Billie Bohanan, Convenor
        1840 S. Higgins
        Missoula 59801

or   NOW
        Valerie Anne Littlefield, President
        36 Birch Street
        Great Falls 59405

or   NOW
        Geraldine Cooney, Acting President
        1447 Dewey
        Butte 59701

        *There are apparently no Legal Aid or
        Lawyers' Reference Services in Montana.
        Check local telephone directories for
        large cities with local NOW chapters or
        write to national sources listed at
        the beginning of this section.*

Nebraska: Virginia L. Portsche, Chairperson
            State Commission on the Status of Women
            1700 Crestline Drive
            Lincoln 68506

            NOW
            Ellie Shore, State Coordinator
            3225 Holdrege
            Lincoln 68503

            Lincoln Legal Aid Bureau
            College of Law Building
            Lincoln

            Omaha Legal Aid Clinic
            Creighton University Law School
            26th and California Streets
            Omaha 68131

Nevada: Majorie Da Costa, Chairperson
                   Governor's Commission on the
                     Status of Women
                   Post Office Box 1550
                   Reno 89505

          or   Mary Frazzini, Chairperson
                   Reno Commission on the Status of Women
                   1630 Van Ness
                   Reno 89503

                   NOW
                   Ethel Barinia
                   3861 Royal Crest Street
                   Apartment 6
                   Las Vegas 89109

                   Clark County Legal Aid Society
                   1622 S. Commerce Street
                   Las Vegas 89102

New Hampshire: Carol Pierce, Chairperson
                   State Commission on the Status of Women
                   State House Annex
                   Concord 03301

                   NOW
                   Eleanor Marshall, Convenor
                   16 Hilton Drive
                   Merrimack 03054

          or   NOW
                   Kate Tuckerman, Convenor
                   5 Conant Road
                   Hanover 03755

                   *Again, there may be no Legal Aid or
                   Lawyers' Reference Service as such,
                   but check local telephone directories,
                   local NOW, and national sources.*

New Jersey: Dorothy B. Mery, Director
                   Office on Women
                   New Jersey Department of
                     Community Affairs
                   363 W. State Street
                   Post Office Box 2768
                   Trenton 08625

or   Sylvia Sammartino, Chairperson
             New Jersey Commission on Women
             160 Ridge Road
             Rutherford 07070

             NOW
             Debbie Hart, State Coordinator
             15 Roosevelt Place
             Montclair 07042

             *Legal Aid and Lawyers' Referral Services
             in most large cities.*

New Mexico: Dr. Dorothy I. Cline, Chairperson
             Governor's Commission on the
               Rights of Women
             1721 Ridgecrest Drive, S.E.
             Albuquerque 87108

             NOW
             Pat Booneau, Contact
             1220 Orange
             Deming 88030

or   NOW
             Marcy Levine, President
             Post Office Box 26262
             Albuquerque 87126

or   NOW
             Ruth Theobald, President
             1063 48th Street
             Los Alamos 87544

or   NOW
             Carol Mast and Susan Edwards, Co-Presidents
             605 S. Dallas
             Portales 88130

or   NOW
             Clara Kawkes, President
             1550 6th Street
             Apartment 53
             Santa Fe 87501

Lawyers' Reference Service
Albuquerque Bar Association
First National Bank Building
Albuquerque 87101

or   Legal Aid Society of Albuquerque
          46 County Courthouse
          Albuquerque 87101

New York: Evelyn Cunningham, Director
                 Women's Unit of New York State
                 Office of the Governor
                 22 West 55th Street
                 New York 10019

                 Nola Clair,
                 State Coordinator
                 1804 Jefferson Tower Building
                 Presidential Plaza
                 Syracuse 13202

                 *Lawyers' Reference Service and Legal
                 Aid in most large cities.*

North Carolina: Dr. Margaret A. Hunt, Chairperson
                 North Carolina Commission on Education
                     and Employment of Women
                 1011 Benjamin Parkway
                 Greensboro 27408

or   *Municipal Commissions on the Status of
          Women in Salisbury, Greensboro, Green-
          ville, Rockingham, and Winston-Salem.*

          NOW
          Rebecca Patterson
          State Coordinator
          1155 C. Salem Drive
          Charlotte 28209

          Lawyers' Referral Service
          Twenty-Sixth Judicial District
              Bar Association
          Law Building
          Charlotte 28202

or   Legal Aid Office
Legal Aid Committee of the
   26th Judicial District
     Bar Association
Charlotte Courthouse
Charlotte 28202

Lawyers' Referral Service
Lumberton Courthouse
Lumberton 28358

Legal Aid Society of Forsyth County
O'Hanlon Building
Winston-Salem 27101

North Dakota: Nita Fox, President
North Dakota Commission on the
   Status of Women
1806 Dres Drive
Grand Forks 58201

NOW
Anita Wasik, State Coordinator
570 Carleton Court
Grand Forks 58201

Lawyers' Referral Service
Cass County Bar Association
Cass County Courthouse
Fargo 58102

Ohio: Emily Leedy, Chairperson
Advisory Committee on the Status of Women
Director of Women's Service Section
Ohio Bureau of Employment Services
145 S. Front Street
Columbus 43215

or   *Both Cincinnati and Cleveland have non-*
governmental citizen's committees on
the status of women.

NOW
Jan Burnside, State Coordinator
67 E. Kossuth
Apartment D
Columbus 43206

Lawyers' Referral Service and Legal Aid in most large cities.

Oklahoma:

Maxine Looper, Chairperson
Oklahoma Governor's Commission on
  the Status of Women
Heavener 74937

NOW
Astrid Clark
State Coordinator
318 N.W. 20th Street
Oklahoma City 73103

Stephens County Legal Aid Society
Duncan Courthouse
Duncan 73533

or   The Legal Aid Society of Oklahoma
    County, Inc.
622 County Courthouse
Oklahoma City 73102

or   Lawyers' Referral Service
Payne County Bar Association
County Attorney's Office
Stillwater Courthouse
Stillwater 74074

or   Tulsa County Legal Aid Society
603 County Courthouse
Tulsa 74103

Oregon:

Sharon Langeberg, Chairperson
Governor's Committee on the Status
  of Women in Oregon
Post Office Box 38
Beaverton 97005

NOW
Cindy Barret and Sally F. Fronsman-Walker,
Co-Convenors
219 S. 11th Street, No. 306
Klamath Falls 97601

or   NOW
Post Office Box 843
Portland 97407

or   NOW
Carolyn Hutton, President
920 Tamarack, N.E.
Salem 97303

Legal Aid Committee
Lane County Bar Association
Lane County Courthouse
Eugene

or   Lawyers' Referral Service
Lane County Bar Association
858 Pearl Street
Post Office Box 1147
Eugene 97401

Legal Aid Committee
Oregon State Bar Association
826 County Courthouse
Portland

Salem Legal Aid Clinic
College of Law
Willamette University
Salem

Pennsylvania: Alma Fox, Co-Chairperson
Governor's Commission on the
  Status of Women
7124 Apple Avenue
Pittsburgh 15206

or   Lynn Scheffey, Co-Chairperson
Governor's Commission on the
  Status of Women
628 Main Capitol Building
Harrisburg 17120

NOW
Eleanor Smeal, State Coordinator
132 Sunridge Drive
Pittsburgh 15324

Legal Aid and Lawyers' Referral Services in most large cities. Often located in county courthouse or with county Bar Association offices.

Rhode Island: Freda Goldman, Chairperson
                    Rhode Island Permanent Advisory
                      Commission on Women
                    Roger Williams Building
                    Hayes Street
                    Providence 02906

        or   Anna M. Tucker
                    Executive Director
                    Chief, Division of Labor Standards
                    Rhode Island Department of Labor
                    235 Promenade Street
                    Providence 02908

                    NOW
                    Miriam Kapsinow
                    State Coordinator
                    18 Whitin Avenue
                    Warwick 02888

                    Legal Aid Society of Rhode Island
                    100 North Main Street
                    Providence 02903

        or   Lawyers' Referral Service
                    The Rhode Island Bar Association
                    1114 Industrial Bank Building
                    Providence

South Carolina: Donna Culberton, Chairperson
                    c/o South Carolina Democratic Party
                    2825 Millwood Avenue
                    Columbia 29205

                    NOW
                    Pat Callair
                    State Coordinator
                    6-15 Prince Hall Apartments
                    Spartanburg 29301

                    Charleston Legal Aid Office
                    33 Broad Street
                    Charleston 29401

South Dakota: Ann Thompson, Chairperson
                     Governor's Commission on the Status
                       of Women
                     Box 1072
                     Pierre 57501

                     NOW
                     Mary Lynn Myers, State Coordinator
                     1312 E. Church
                     Pierre 57501

                     *Check local telephone directories to see
                     if there are any Legal Aid or Lawyers'
                     Reference Services available.*

Tennessee: Osta Underwood, Chairperson
                     Tennessee Governor's Commission
                       on the Status of Women
                     921 Andrew Jackson Building
                     Nashville 37129

                     NOW
                     Pat Welch, State Coordinator
                     502 Linwood Lane
                     Nashville 37204

                     *Legal Aid offices in Chattanooga, Knox-
                     ville (University of Tennessee College
                     of Law), Memphis, and Nashville.
                     Lawyers' Referral Service, Chattanooga,
                     and Nashville.*

Texas: "Inactive Commission" on the Status
                       of Women--write:
                     Office of the Governor
                     State Capitol
                     Austin 78711

         or   *Austin, Fort Worth, Huntsville, San
                     Angelo, and San Antonio all have
                     municipal or "mayor's" commissions on
                     the status of women.*

                     *NOW: Chapters in Arlington, Austin,
                     Dallas County, Fort Worth, Houston, San
                     Antonio, Waco, Bay Area, Denton, Hidalfo
                     County, Huntsville, Texarkana, and
                     Val Verde County. For addresses, write:*

NOW
Jackie Frost, Southern
  Regional Director
5017 Malibu Drive
Charlotte, North Carolina 28215

Legal Aid and/or Lawyers' Referral Service in Abilene, Amarillo, Austin, Beaumont, Bryan, Corpus Christi, Dallas, El Paso, Fort Worth, Houston, Midland, San Antonio, Tyler, Waco, and Wichita Falls. Located in courthouses, Bar Association offices, and law schools.

Utah: Beth Gurrister, Chairperson
Governor's Advisory Committee on
  Women's Programs
820 Eliason Drive
Brigham City 84302

NOW
Carole Toomey, State Coordinator
473 First Avenue, No. 3
Salt Lake City 84103

Legal Aid Society
509 Atlas Building
Salt Lake City

Vermont   Lenore W. McNeer, Chairperson
Governor's Commission on the
  Status of Women
Vermont College
Montpelier 05602

NOW
Susan Paris, State Coordinator
Box 187
Shelburne 05482

Bennington Legal Aid Service
100 South Street
Bennington 05201

or   Legal Aid Committee
Chittenden Co. Bar Association
62 West Allen Street
Winooski (Burlington) 05404

Virginia:
                  Mrs. Julian A. Kean, Chairperson
Commission on the Status of Women
3901 Kensington Avenue
Richmond 23229

      or   Alexandria Committee on the
                  Status of Women (municipal)
405 Cameron Street
Alexandria 22314

      or   *County Commissions on the Status of
Women in Arlington and Fairfax counties.*

NOW
Barbara Keershov, State Coordinator
39 Nash Street
Herndon 22070

Legal Aid Bureau
Courthouse Square
Arlington 22216

      or   Lawyers' Referral Service
Norfolk and Portsmouth Bar Association
Bank of Commerce Building
Norfolk

      or   Legal Aid Bureau
Family Service Society of Richmond
221 Governor Street
Richmond 23219

      or   Legal Aid Receptionist
Roanoke Family Service Association, Inc.
442 King George Avenue, S.W.
Roanoke 24016

Washington:
                  Dr. Inga K. Kelly, Chairperson
Washington State Women's Council
N.W. 400 Orion Drive
Pullman 99163

      or   Giesela E. Taber, Executive Director
Washington State Women's Council
305 Insurance Building
Olympia 98504

or   Mildred Henry
        Director of Women's Division
        Office of Human Resources
        (Seattle Municipal Commission on
          the Status of Women)
        88 S. Main Street
        Seattle 98104

        NOW
        Jan Swanson, State Coordinator
        20015 43rd S.E.
        Boothell 98011

        *Legal Aid office in Whatcom Co. Courthouse
        (Bellingham), 325 Lyon Building (Seattle),
        Courthouse Annex (Spokane), and 625
        Perkins Building (Tacoma).*

West Virginia: Alma Ferguson, Chairperson
        Governor's Commission on the Status
          of Women
        Harrisville 26362

        NOW
        Karen Kuhns, Convenor
        Charleston NOW
        1591 E. Washington Street
        Charleston 25305

or   NOW
        Letty Stewart, President
        Route 4, Box 266
        Morgantown 26505

        Legal Reference Bureau
        Kanawah County Bar Association
        Transit Building
        Charleston

or   Legal Aid Society of Charleston
        203 Berman Building
        612 Virginia Street E.
        Charleston 25301

Wisconsin: Dr. Kathryn Clarenbach
        Governor's Commission on the Status
          of Women
        Room 247, Lowell Hall
        610 Langdon Street
        Madison 53706

NOW
Margo V. House, State Coordinator
432 West Grand Avenue
Eau Claire 54701

*Legal Aid offices in Beloit, Janesville,
Madison, Milwaukee, Oshkosh, and Racine.
Lawyers' Reference Service in Galesville
and Milwaukee.*

Wyoming: Edna Wright, Chairperson
Wyoming Commission on the Status
  of Women
114 E. Walnut Street
Rawlins 83201

*NOW chapters in Casper, Cheyenne,
Laramie, and University of Wyoming.
For addresses write:*

NOW
Mildred E. Kersh, Western Regional Dir.
2301 Fairview E.
Apartment 214
Seattle 98102

*Check local telephone directories for
Legal Aid or Lawyers' Reference Service
and consult national listings.*

District of   Mary Dublin Keyserling, Chairperson
Columbia: Commission on the Status of Women
Room 204, District Building
14th and Pennsylvania Avenue, N.W.
Washington, D.C. 20004

A major failing of the present legal services system is
that people whose income is between welfare level and
middle-income level have almost no legal services available at a price they can afford. Many lawyers will
arrange time payments for their services, but some demand
the entire fee before filing any papers for you. Even
with time payments you end up paying an average of about
$750 for an uncontested divorce. In some "no fault"
states the fee may be less--$300 to $400. A separation
agreement may cost anywhere from $100--if all the lawyer
has to do is write it up and witness the signing--to many
thousands, depending on the amount of time a lawyer must

spend working on it and, often, the amount of property involved in the settlement.

Paying For Legal Services

If you qualify for free legal help, congratulations! The
process may seem terribly slow, but you are reasonably
certain of getting competent legal help at no cost. If
you do not qualify for these services, welcome to the crowd
of women who wonder how they will ever *afford* a divorce--
the money is all either your husband's or sitting in a
jointly held account. You can get legal services, but it
takes some looking and some planning.

You might begin by looking for women lawyers. Often they
are more understanding of your financial situation, more
sympathetic to the problems of women obtaining a divorce,
and more likely to treat your case as an important one.
Women's centers (there is a list at the end of this book),
women-in-transition projects, the local office of the
National Organization for Women, and other similar groups
may be able to direct you to some feminist lawyers in your
area. Often these women cannot afford to charge lower fees
for divorces, however, as their own economic situation may
be none too secure yet. Many large cities operate a "lawyers' reference service" which will refer you to a lawyer
and give you one consultation session with a lawyer for a
minimal fee (under $25).

Once you have found a lawyer you think you can work with,
the next step is to figure out how to pay her or him. Your
lawyer might suggest suing your husband for "alimony *pendente
lite,* counsel fees and costs." If your lawyer does not suggest this, you might. Alimony *pendente lite* is the amount
of support your husband is legally obligated to provide you
(not just your children) during a separation until a divorce
is final. He is also obligated in most, if not all states,
to pay your attorney's fees and the court costs of a divorce--
assuming he has the money and you don't.

The catch is that many lawyers are not willing to work on
this basis. With good reason--in order for you to collect
your temporary alimony (that's what alimony *pendente lite*
is called in plain English) and your lawyer to collect his
fees he must do a certain amount of paper work and appear
in court with you. At the end of all this a judge may order
your husband to pay your lawyer $100. Many lawyers figure
it's not worth the trouble. If your husband could easily
afford the lawyer's fees and you have found a sympathetic

lawyer, you should be able to get enough money from your husband to make it worth the lawyer's trouble.

If your husband has a fair amount of property, or the two of you have accumulated property during the marriage worth more than a few hundred dollars, many lawyers will be interested in taking your case on a "contingent fee" basis. This often sounds like a wonderful idea to the woman in transition. It means the lawyer will take a percentage of whatever you receive as a result of a property settlement. If you receive very little, so does the lawyer. It means you don't have to have any cash in your hands when you come to the lawyer's office, and it means you won't be charged more than you have. Many people feel this is a dangerous arrangement, however, because it encourages your lawyer to hold out for the highest possible amount of money for you, while other items, like child custody--or just reaching some kind of agreement and finalizing the separation--may be more important to you. Your lawyer is not supposed to be an interested party in the negotiations. She or he is sup- posed to be a disinterested party whose objectivity can make communication and compromise between you and your husband easier. Obviously, this is not the case when the lawyer is negotiating for her or his fee.

Whatever payment arrangements you make, be sure you under- stand how you will be charged and what you will be charged for. Many women do not realize that the friendly telephone conversations with their attorneys are costing them a dol- lar a minute or more! Discuss with your attorney how she or he plans to charge you. We think that a "flat fee" sys- tem is by far the best. This means that your lawyer will tell you at the first interview that the fee for the divorce--barring unusual complications--will be a set amount. This amount should include court costs, the lawyer's fee for all the time she or he spends on your case, including phone calls, research, court appearances, and other inci- dentals (like expenses--Xeroxing and postage).

Again, some lawyers are not willing to work on this basis. There's no such thing as a simple divorce, they insist. You can never tell whether complications will arise or how serious they could be. It's simply unrealistic and unfair to try to work for a flat fee. While there is some merit to this argument, some lawyers *do* work that way, and it is certainly the best way for women in transition. Otherwise you may find yourself with a divorce--and a bill for a thousand dollars or more.

What To Look For In A Lawyer

> *if you have questions about*
> *separation, divorce, child custody,*
> *or name changes*

1. What is the lawyer's *reputation*? Were you referred to her or him by someone you trust, by someone who has had experience with this lawyer's legal work?

2. Has the lawyer had *experience* with the judges and courts of your city or county? What kind of legal problems does your lawyer handle?

3. What kind of *attitudes* does your lawyer have? Does she or he make stated or unstated assumptions which would prevent her or him from working in your best interest? Does she or he assume that mothers should always have the responsibility for their children; that a woman who put her husband through school or a job-training program may be entitled to money from her husband to put her through school or a job-training program after there's a divorce (or even if there isn't a divorce); that women in general (or you in particular) are simpleminded and inferior? Does the lawyer respect you as a person? Can the lawyer imagine herself or himself in your situation?

4. What is the lawyer's *fee*? The prices private lawyers charge for their work vary from person to person and firm to firm. A standard charge for an uncontested divorce in most of the no-fault states is approximately $750 (including court costs). Anything less is a bargain (in the eyes of lawyers) and anything more is outrageous. Standard fee for a separation agreement is about $350, although you may be able to get one for less as part of a "package deal"--agreement and divorce. The charge for a support hearing is usually about $250 for the plaintiff (the person who brings the suit) and $150 for the defendant (the person who answers the charge--your husband in a support action). However, some lawyers will perform all of these services for less. If you are getting a divorce and you want to retake your prior name, be sure to state that at the outset. Other than a nominal filing fee, there should be no additional charge in many states.

Over the telephone or at your first appointment with the lawyer, get a financial estimate for the work. Do you expect your divorce to be contested by your husband? It is important to know this from the outset. Contested divorces are much more expensive than uncontested ones. If you want a separation agreement, do you expect much resistance from your husband on the terms of the agreement (on support money, child custody, property division)? Is there much or any property to divide? Do you want the lawyer to represent you at the family court in obtaining a support order, or in determing child custody and visitation rights? Lawyers will have different fees for each of these tasks, depending on how much work is involved, how much money you or your husband have, and how much the lawyer is used to being paid.

We suggest that you and your lawyer draw up and sign a written agreement of what services the lawyer will perform, how much time the work should take, and what the lawyer's approximate or maximum fee will be. You and your lawyer can negotiate a new agreement if the conditions under which the first agreement was made change significantly: for example, if your own financial situation changes or if more work is involved in the divorce because your husband decides to contest the divorce, or your husband disappears and must be located. The important thing is that you will know what is happening and for what and how much you are being charged.

5. Does your lawyer have good *communication* with you? Does she or he let you know what's happening with your case? Does your lawyer talk in language that you can understand? Many professionals (including lawyers) use all the technical terms they can so their clients think they are doing terribly complicated and expensive work. Others talk that way because it's a habit. If there is ever anything you don't understand, ask for an explanation. Your lawyer must have a good reason for doing something, and she or he may not. *Ask. And keep asking until you get a satisfactory answer.*

In most situations, you will probably have several options. Your lawyer should let you know what the choices are and discuss possible consequences. However, you should determine what your own goals and priorities are. Your lawyer is there to advise you, but it is your choice and you have to live with the consequences of the decision. It may be helpful to bring a friend when you see your lawyer. Remember that most decisions don't have to be made there in the lawyer's office. If you need time to think something over, take it.

Few lawyers have all the above qualities--good reputation, valuable experience, empathetic attitudes, reasonable fees, willingness to communicate. Depending on your situation and your goals, some qualities will be more important to you than others. We hope that as we become better consumers of legal services, the law will seem less mysterious, lawyers will become people just like the rest of us, and fees will drop.

SEPARATION

Thinking About Separation

When we are trying to decide whether or not a separation is appropriate, we are often overwhelmed by conflicting feelings. Many of the traumas associated with separation can be avoided by a little calm thinking at the time crucial decisions are being made.

For many women, separation means a loss of income and a lower standard of living. Our financial resources may be lowest at that time when they are most needed. Finding a new home, a job, new child-care facilities, etc., demands more of our time and money than we had anticipated, and we find ourselves plagued by fears and doubts that lead us to question our capabilities and the wisdom of our decision to separate. Some of these practical and emotional problems can be avoided by careful planning before you make the big move. Some other chapters in this book can help you with specific decisions.

* The chapter on housing outlines what you need to consider when deciding whether to stay where you are or move to another place.

* The chapter on children in transition gives suggestions for making the transition as untraumatic and as meaningful for them as possible.

* The custody section of this chapter will help you make negotiations with your husband about custody and visitation more fruitful.

We have found that no matter what the cause of the breakdown of the marriage, it is very important for you to continue on the best possible terms with your husband, especially if you have children. It is advisable that you reach some kind of agreement, in principle if not on paper, before

one of you moves. If this is not possible, you should try
to reach an agreement as soon as possible after the move,
with the help of lawyers if necessary.

It is never too early to seek legal advice, and you don't
need to have decided on a divorce before you talk with a
legal counselor. Ideally, a separation agreement should
be ready for signing before either of you moves. Of course,
sometimes situations get to the point where it is important
to act and talk about it later. But remember that you and
your children have nothing to gain by antagonizing your
husband. If you are eventually able to reach an agreement
as to support and custody, you will be a lot more comfortable than if you let a court make those decisions for you.

Marriage: The Unwritten Contract

> *"Love and marriage have nothing in common."*
> *Emma Goldman,* Anarchism and Other Essays

Over half a century ago Emma Goldman tried to strip marriage of some of the fairy-tale myths and make women more
aware of the legally binding but unwritten contract they
were entering into when they became wives. A Russian
immigrant who came to this country in the late nineteenth
century, Emma had grown up in a society where women were
told whom to marry and when. Once married, these wives
had little more freedom than serfs and slaves--just what
the master gave and no more.

American women could have much more freedom than their
Russian sisters, she concluded, if they were better informed about the terms of the marriage contract and exercised their freedom to marry wisely or not at all. The
marriage contract, she decided, was not so different from
an insurance contract. The wife gets security in exchange
for services she must perform for her husband.

> *It [the marriage contract] differs from the ordinary*
> *life insurance agreement only in that it is more*
> *binding, more exacting. Its returns are insignifi-*
> *cantly small compared with the investments. In taking*
> *out a life insurance policy, one pays for it in dollars*
> *and cents, always at liberty to discontinue payments.*
> *If, however, a woman's premium is her husband, she*
> *pays for it with her privacy, her self-respect, her*
> *very life, "until death doth part."*
>
> *Emma Goldman,* Anarchism and Other Essays

"But marriage isn't anything at all like a life insurance policy," many of her contemporaries argued. "It's a sacred institution based on human love." And love, she would reply, is not part of the contract. Few women (or men) are aware that there is any kind of contract involved in a marriage. It's a well-guarded state secret. The state sets the terms of the contract but never writes them down, and never shows the contract to the parties to see if they understand it. The only clues about the terms of the contract may be found in the state's divorce laws.

"But marriage isn't like that today. . . . There's open marriage, communal living, and women's lib," answer many of *our* contemporaries. Quite true--and yet, the terms of the marriage contract have not changed since before Emma Goldman's days! Ever wondered about the "to have and to hold" part of the ceremony? Originally this indicated that two people wished to transfer possession of a piece of land. This is why the father "gives away" his daughter. First her father, then her husband give a woman her name--her identity--and have some right to control her. If this doesn't sound like anything you ever thought about during your marriage ceremony, it's because there's not much of a hint as to what you're agreeing to anywhere in the ceremony. Who would know that a wife has a legal duty to live in any "suitable home" provided by the husband, and that if she refuses to, he (and not she) may have grounds for divorce! And most grooms are probably not thinking about the fact that twelve years from now they may be sued to pay for the support of the children of this marriage--even if the now-blushing bride has since remarried. In reality this burden on the father-to-be is relieved by inefficient family courts and sympathetic (male) judges. The bride has a lot more reason to worry. While he agrees to provide her with food, clothing, and shelter, she is contracting to do free housework and child care as long as the marriage lasts.

Would you sign this contract? (You did.): I, Jane Doe, do hereby solemnly agree that upon pronouncing the words "I do" shall become legally obligated by the terms of the contract which follows:

1. Wife hereby agrees to engage in sexual intercourse with the husband and none other for the duration of the marriage.

2. Wife shall follow husband to any suitable living place of his choice and live with him there so long as he wishes to remain.

3. Wife shall provide the following domestic services for husband:

    A. Housekeeping--including but not limited to light and heavy cleaning, cooking and laundry.

    B. Child care and education, transportation, and nursing services.

    C. Food purchase, budgeting, and preparation.

    D. All other essential and incidental tasks related to the comfort, safety, and well-being of all household members.

4. Wife hereby waives all right to payment for the above-mentioned services performed at home.

5. Wife hereby waives all right to file any criminal or civil complaints against husband for acts which, if performed by any other, would constitute the crime of rape.

Each state defines the marriage contract in effect in that state. The terms of this contract represent many of the basic terms found in most states.

6. In exchange for all the promises made by wife, husband agrees that he shall:

    A. Engage in sexual intercourse with wife and none other for the duration of the marriage.

    B. Provide wife with suitable shelter, food, clothing, and other necessaries of life according to his ability.

    C. Provide children with suitable shelter, food, clothing, and other necessaries according to his ability.

7. Husband and wife hereby admit that the terms of this contract cannot be changed by mutual consent or the desire of either party.

8. Husband and wife agree to abide by the terms of this contract, regardless of their personal beliefs or desires, until the state shall decide this contract has been breached and is no longer binding.

IN TANDEM

*It's actually
built in
to the bike
this need
for loyalty
and trust
My handlebars
fused to your
seat
You front
me rear
If I try
to steer
we'll spill
I pace
My pedaling
to yours but
even on side-
walks our strides
never match
It's easy
to miss seeing
a rock until
we crash
or slip backward
on a hill
Your voice
dies in the wind
though I
am a practiced talker
at backs
This dependency*

Maralyn Lois Polak

*"A married woman living with her husband can
in practice get only what he chooses to give
her."*
            *Citizen's Advisory Council on the Status
            of Women, "The ERA and Alimony and
            Child Support Laws."*

Perhaps the unwritten term of the marriage contract which
handicaps and humiliates the largest number of women is
the absolute economic power most husbands have over their
wives. Unless the wife is independently wealthy and

manages her own money, she is reduced to depending on her
husband's generosity. So long as the marriage is congenial
and the husband generous, many women don't mind. But as
soon as the marriage goes sour, or if the husband turns
out to be unusually frugal, the wife becomes a beggar.

In 1953 when Mrs. McGuire petitioned the Nebraska court
to force her husband, a well-to-do farmer, to provide her
with a $50-a-month allowance, she was living in a house
with no toilet, no hot water, and no kitchen sink. The
court refused her petition, reasoning that since the marriage was thirty-three years old and Mrs. McGuire had never
come to court to complain before, there was really no problem.

> *The living standards of a family are a matter of
> concern to the household, and not for the courts
> to determine, even though the husband's attitude
> towards his wife, according to his wealth and cir-
> cumstances, leaves little to be said on his behalf.
> As long as the home is maintained it may be said
> that the husband is legally supporting his wife and
> the purpose of the marriage relation is being car-
> ried out.*

> *(McGuire v. McGuire, 157 Neb. 226,*
> *59 N.W. 2d 336, 1953)*

Mr. McGuire was apparently not so severely affected by the
lack of a kitchen sink, and he found the living conditions
quite adequate. Mrs. McGuire had to take what he gave her,
no matter how little.

In no state in the nation is a woman entitled to be paid
for the work she does at home. She had, instead, a right
to be fed, sheltered, and clothed. These are precisely
the same "rights" granted to slaves under the southern
"Slave Codes." Should a husband choose to ignore his
duty, most courts will do nothing so long as the parties
are living together. This is not, they reason, really a
question of a breach of contract or one person denying
another her rights; it is a mere "budgetary problem" in
which the courts are reluctant to become involved.

Some legal writers insist that marriage is a purely civil
contract--like a sales contract or an employment contract.
If this were true, however, the parties of a marriage
would be free to write their own contracts, including
whatever terms they saw fit. But the traditional view is

that the terms of the marriage contract cannot be varied to suit the parties and may not be canceled by mutual consent. Even in "no-fault" states, the state must give its permission before the parties can effectively end their marriage.

Many people are becoming so dissatisfied with the terms of the uniform marriage contract that they have decided to write their own. You *can* write your own. Whether this contract is enforceable and whether its terms can take precedence over those of the standard contract is another question. Most opinions indicate that a marriage contract which includes terms which contradict the traditional contract are neither enforceable nor capable of superceding the traditional terms.

What this means is that if two people who plan to marry write a contract specifying that the wife shall retain her original name and that the husband will be under no obligation to support either her or the children, neither party could go into court to enforce those provisions because they conflict with the terms of the official contract. But if people want to make agreements like this, they are perfectly free to. And if they can manage to abide by these terms rather than those of the state, so much the better. They just can't depend on the state to enforce their terms.

Some counselors and lawyers are suggesting that these marriage contracts may not be such a bad idea. They give people a chance to think over areas of potential conflict in a marriage and figure out how they would like to deal with these before a real problem arises. This may not be a bad idea--so long as the parties are also aware that they will be bound by the terms of the traditional contract, no matter what their private agreement says.

> *"Marriage is not only a contract, but a status and a kind of fealty to the state as well."*
>
> *(Bove v. Pinciotti, 45 Pa. D. & C. 1942)*

Marriage, in other words, is too valuable an institution to leave in the hands of the people who are involved in it. Marriages are not made in heaven, but in the legislatures, explained the United States Supreme Court:

> *Marriage, as creating the most important relation in life, as having more to do with morals and civilization . . . than any other institution, has always*

been subject to the control of the legislature.

(Maynard v. *Hill, 125 U.S. 190, 205, 1888)*

One may still wonder, all the same, why the state is so concerned with the marriage relation. It does not appear at first glance to be an item that would concern senators, congresspeople, and judges. The roots of the state's great concern with marital and family relationships go deep into history (and economics).

Centuries ago in Europe, a woman deserted by her husband was considered a terrible burden on the community--all the more so if she had children--because it was considered a community obligation to support her from public money. Fatherless children presented a similar problem. In order to plug up this rather serious drain on the community "welfare" sources, laws were passed giving the local government rights to sue the rogue so that the community could be reimbursed for supporting his wife and children.

In many states today "desertion and nonsupport" by a husband or a father is still a crime. It was from this practice of the *state* suing the husband for the support of his wife that the theory that a husband had a legal duty to support her was first developed. But note that the duty was owed to the *state* so that the wife could not become a drain on the public treasury. The state's obsession with children it labeled "illegitimate" springs from similar roots. Thus, the state has a vested (economic) interest in keeping married couples and families together.

Such human problems and legal policies hardly went out of style in the Middle Ages. They are still very much with us. One of the popular arguments used during this decade against "no-fault," "do-it-yourself," and other forms of divorce which would allow the parties to decide for themselves when a marriage is over is the argument: If such reforms were incorporated into our divorce laws, the federal and state governments would end up supporting even more families with dependent children than it presently does. Of course, unemployment and poverty are much more closely related to the health of the national economy than they are to the marriage and divorce rate.

> *"Because they are esteemed as one person*
> *in law, they are presumed to have but one*
> *will."*
>
> *(Hawkins Pleas of the Crown, 4th ed. Bk. i,*
> *1792)*

It was not until 1960 that the United States Supreme Court laid to rest--and then for the purpose of accusing a woman of conspiring with her husband--the legal doctrine that makes a wife a mere extension of her husband's will and identity. The legal doctrine known as "coverture" was spelled out by William Blackstone, among others. He announced: "By marriage, the husband and wife are one person in law; that is, the being or legal existence of the woman is suspended during the marriage, or at least is incorporated into that of the husband, under whose wing, protection, and cover she performs everything." This doctrine, which has been invoked to keep women from buying or selling land without their husbands' signatures, entering into employment contracts, and testifying against their husbands in civil and criminal actions, has been condensed into the maxim that a married woman is "civilly dead."

"Married women may purchase sewing machines."

(Act of February 29, 1872, Pennsylvania)

The inequality built into the marriage contract has long been questioned; some of the explanations come from the "natural superiority of man" philosophy. The more practical interpretation is that it is necessary to decide once and for all which of two people in a lifelong relationship is going to have the upper hand. Many people believe that "it is only natural for the man to wear the pants in the family," and many legislatures turn this into law.

The progress toward legal equality between husband and wife has been slow. But important. Beginning in 1839 when Mississippi became the first state to pass the "Married Women's Property Acts," wives have been slowly resurrected from their civil deaths by similar acts passed in every American state. The wording of these acts varies widely from state to state, but in almost every state, they have restored to married women the rights to enter into contracts, make loans, sign leases, buy and sell land, and conduct businesses in their own behalf.

Passage of the Equal Rights Amendment to the United States Constitution would make even more changes. Perhaps, after the passage of this amendment and several years of its application to marriage and divorce situations, many of the still-existing legal handicaps of married women will be done away with.   For the present it is impossible to understand the legal position of wives--married, separated, or divorced--without knowing something of the obsolete laws that continue to "rule us from the grave."

Common-Law Marriage

Many people who go through the trouble and expense of
getting a divorce have been led to wonder why it is so
easy to get married and so hard to get divorced. It has
been suggested that states should make it harder to get
married. People who want to get married should understand the terms of the marriage "contract" and be aware of
the emotional and financial cost of divorce. But while we
see marriage and divorce in terms of human institutions
and problems, legislators mumble about limited welfare
budgets and the sanctity of the family. Marriage continues to be encouraged and divorce discouraged for
economic reasons.

"Common-law" is the easiest of all marriages to get into.
However, it is just as hard as any other kind of marriage
to get out of. Many people think that "common-law marriage" is just a polite name for no marriage at all.
Others believe that "if you live together for seven years,
you're common-law married." Neither of these very popular
myths is true. But common-law marriage does exist in 17
states.

In order to have a common-law marriage, you must agree to
live together as wife and husband until death (or divorce)
separates you. Promises to get married in the future don't
count. "Sure, honey, I want to get married," is not a
good substitute for an exchange of vows. Neither is "Don't
I treat you just like you were my wife?" On the other hand,
acting as if you are married, when it is not done to mis-
lead, is good legal evidence that you consider yourself
married. The essence of common-law marriage is that both
parties consider themselves married to each other, and so
do their neighbors, friends, and families. Of course, a
requirement for common-law marriage is also that both parties are legally free and capable of getting married. That
means that marriages entered into by minors or people who
are already married to someone else do not count--in fact,
they are illegal.

States which have decided not to recognize such marriages
base their decisions on the fact that common-law marriages
are usually claimed when one of the parties has died and
the other wishes to collect certain benefits which would
normally go to a legitimate spouse--social security, workers compensation, death benefits, life insurance, or other
inheritance. Since one of the parties to the alleged
marriage is dead, it is difficult to prove. The surviving

spouse must bring enough evidence to convince a judge and/
or jury that the parties had indeed intended to be married
and not just "living together." Exactly what you must do
to prove a common-law marriage differs from state to state.

States which have decided to recognize common-law marriages
base their decisions on the importance of families and of
keeping children off welfare rolls. Another consideration
frequently raised is the state's reluctance to "bastardize"
children. There is strong feeling that the stigma of "illegitimacy" is a terrible burden to place on a child. It
certainly is--but the state's concern has led very few
states to take the logical step of abolishing the status of
"illegitimate" altogether. (See "Questions and Answers on
Illegitimacy.")

The following states currently recognize common-law marriages as having the same legal effect as licensed marriages.

ALABAMA	IOWA	RHODE ISLAND
ALASKA	KANSAS	SOUTH CAROLINA
COLORADO	MONTANA	SOUTH DAKOTA
FLORIDA	OHIO	TEXAS
GEORGIA	OKLAHOMA	DISTRICT OF
IDAHO	PENNSYLVANIA	COLUMBIA

The following states have recently repealed their laws
recognizing common-law marriage and will not recognize any
new common-law marriages. They do recognize common-law
marriages entered into before the dates specified below:

INDIANA, January 1, 1958

MICHIGAN, January 1, 1957

MINNESOTA, April 26, 1941

MISSOURI, April 4, 1953

NEBRASKA, March 3, 1921

NEVADA, 1923

NEW JERSEY, March 29, 1943

NEW YORK, December 1, 1939

MISSISSIPPI, April 29, 1933

Common-law marriage is forbidden in all other states. Some states which do not recognize common-law marriages entered into within the state do recognize those which were entered into in another state which does recognize them.

People involved in a valid common-law marriage are just as legally and permanently married as those who have a license. The same duties and rights arise from common-law and official marriages, and the children of common-law marriages are as officially "legitimate" as those of formal marriages. Common-law wives are entitled to support from their husbands and may sue for support if they are separated.

The problem with common-law marriage is not that it is a less official or less valid form of marriage, but that you have a hard time proving that you are married without a certificate or other concrete proof of marriage. Before a court will enforce any of your marital rights, you must prove that you were in fact living as husband and wife with a mutual understanding that you were married and not just "living together."

In order to prove this marriage, you will have to show evidence of the following things:

1. Intention and promise or agreement that the relationship is a permanent husband/wife relationship.

2. Actual cohabitation--that the two of you did live together at the same address for some length of time. The longer the time, the more convincing, but in most states the number of years will not prove anything without other evidence.

3. Your reputation in the community as married people. A lease in both your names, your using his last name, bills, accounts in both your names, joint tax returns, testimony of neighbors and other disinterested people in the community and children born of the common-law marriage are all considered pieces of evidence tending to show you had a valid marriage.

Warning: Many courts and legislators are hostile to common-law marriages. In Pennsylvania, where they are still recognized, they have been called "a fruitful source of perjury and fraud . . . to be tolerated, not encouraged." (*Baker* v. *Mitchell, 143 Pa. Super. 50*).

The parties claiming to have a common-law marriage have to bring a significant amount of convincing evidence into court with them. And the judge will be skeptical.

A final warning about common-law marriage: It is just as
hard to get out of as an official marriage. You can't end
a common-law marriage by walking out the door either. If
you want to be free to get legally married again, you must
get a divorce. In order to get a divorce, you must prove
that you are married, which is not easy for people in a
common-law marriage. If this reminds you of a dog chasing
its own tail, you've got the picture.

Instances in which you might want to prove a common-law
marriage include the following:

1. If you are going to have a baby and don't want the
    hospital records or birth certificate to indicate that
    the child is "illegitimate," insist that you are mar-
    ried. You don't have to call yourself Mrs. John Jones
    if your name is Sarah Smith, but it would probably
    make things a lot easier.

2. If he has left you without any support and has a decent
    income, you might get him to sign a separation agreement,
    or you can sue him for support. But note: Fathers of
    "illegitimate" children are also legally obligated to
    support their offspring, so you can get support for the
    children regardless of any kind of marriage.

3. If he should die and there are widow's and/or other
    survivors' benefits for you and/or your children, you
    will want to prove that you are his wife. Sometimes
    these benefits go only to "legitimate" children (which
    is probably unconstitutional), so it's important even
    if you only want to collect for them. These benefits
    might include social security, workmen's compensation,
    life insurance, employee benefits, death benefits, and
    inheritable property.

4. If he should later try to get "officially" married to
    someone else and you are concerned that he will end up
    supporting the second family at the expense of yours, or
    if you are afraid he will try to use his official mar-
    riage to get custody of your children, you might warn
    him that: (a) he will continue to be legally obligated
    to support your children, and you can get a support
    court to order him to do so, and that (b) unless there
    is a divorce between the two of you, his second marriage
    is bigamous and the children born of it will be "ille-
    gitimate."

There are some advantages to a common-law marriage. Among them:

1. It is better than no marriage at all in situations such as those listed above.

2. It is no better than an official marriage, ever. The qualifications are the same (not already married to someone else, of the right age, and not too closely related), and the contract is the same. A common-law marriage is just as hard to get out of (officially) as a regular marriage.

3. If you are pretty sure he'd never go through with an official marriage, but you want some legal protection as his wife, you might have a little home ceremony, or take other steps to make it easier to prove your common-law marriage.

4. There are disadvantages. A marriage certificate is pretty good proof of marriage. People claiming common-law marriages often have a very hard time proving the marriage exists because courts (and other officials-- like hospital records-keepers) are skeptical of this form of marriage.

Separation Agreements

What Is A Separation Agreement?

The "separation agreement" or "marriage settlement" is a formal document describing the legal consequences of your separation. Perhaps the most important thing for you to know about such agreements is that they are quite different from a divorce. In many states, a couple may get divorced without ever entering into any agreement or otherwise dividing property or settling questions of child support, custody, and visitation. In others, a written agreement is the first step in the divorce process.

A separation agreement is a legally binding private contract between a husband and a wife which spells out how the two of you will divide the assets and responsibilities accumulated during the marriage. It is also an agreement that the two of you will live "separate and apart, free from any control, restraint, or interference by the other, in all respects as if each were unmarried." This means that your husband agrees, for example, not to break into your apartment in the middle of the night (or any other

time). It is "as if" he were no longer your husband in
this respect--although he is still your husband until a
divorce is granted to either party.

Theoretically you could live apart forever, abide by the
terms of the settlement agreement for the rest of your
lives--and still be married. Usually people start thinking
about separation agreements when they start thinking about
divorce. A separation agreement is not a declaration by a
court; it is an agreement between two private people. Once
a court speaks and says, for example, that you are now divorced (or that you now have legal custody of your child),
you are divorced now and forever--no two ways about it.
Agreements between private people are a lot trickier, as
you probably know. A separation agreement says a lot more
than that you agree to separate. It also says who will
have custody of the children and who will visit when, it
says how much support will be paid by whom and when, who
will live in the family house and who will move, and how
the financial assets of the family will be divided. Promises, promises--they may be kept or broken.

Broken promises are hard to enforce in court. If your husband fails to pay the support, move out of the house, or
return the children after visiting with them, you must hire
a lawyer and go into court, convince the judge that you
have a legally binding contract, that he violated it, and
that he should be ordered to comply with the agreement.
This can take more time, energy, and money than you can
afford. So basically, the private-contract kind of separation agreements are "word of honor" agreements. They are
valuable because they help two people deal with practical
problems in a very emotional situation and make the trauma
of transition less. They work usually because both parties
feel they represent a fair resolution of the problems and
represent a fair distribution of the resources and responsibilities accumulated during the marriage.

In many states a separation agreement can be made more
easily enforceable and more official. In some states--
most of the "no-fault" states or states in which voluntary
separation is a ground for divorce--you must live apart
for a specified length of time and abide by the terms of
an agreement. In other states the judge granting the
divorce decree also divides the marital property and decides the child custody and support questions.

If the parties are able to reach an agreement beforehand,
this agreement forms the basis of the judge's official

order. If they are not able to come to an agreement, the
judge dictates the terms. In still other states, a separation agreement may be "incorporated" into the divorce
decree upon request of either party. All these are ways
of making a separation agreement more enforceable, or of
forcing people to settle the practical problems of dividing
up family resources.

The advantage of making these more formal arrangements is
that once the terms of an agreement become part of a court
order they are much more easily enforced. Instead of starting a suit for breach of contract, you contact the judge
who made the order or issued the divorce decree and inform
him or her that the terms have been violated. You ask for
a hearing on whether your husband should be held "in contempt of court" for violating an order of the court. You
do not have to prove that you had a legally binding con-
tract--it is presumed that a judge's order is legally bind-
ing--and you do not have to prove what the terms of the
contract were because they are spelled out on an official
document which is part of the court record. And finally,
you have more than the threat of a civil suit against your
husband should he not abide by the terms of your agreement--
you may seek to have him held in contempt of court, which
may carry a fine or imprisonment as well as an order to
abide by the agreement. Breaking promises is one thing,
but disobeying a court order is quite another!

In the following states, however, a separation agreement
is the *only* way to ensure a fair distribution of marital
property after a divorce. In these states judges have
little or no authority to order property distribution:
Alabama, Florida, Georgia, Maryland, Massachusetts, Mississippi, Montana, New York, North Carolina, Ohio, Pennsylvania, Rhode Island, South Carolina, and Virginia.

Who Needs A Separation Agreement?

Despite the fact that most divorce laws do not require
separation agreements, it is strongly recommended that
you have one if you have children and/or property about
which there is or may be some question. If your husband
has deserted you, or if you have no children and no property to speak of, a separation agreement is useless.

If you do have children and your husband is able to contribute to their support or would want custody or visitation rights now or at some future date (e.g., if he should
remarry), or if you have any property of value (including

bank accounts, car, house, etc.), a separation agreement is
the best way to ensure a fair resolution of your more concrete problems. Occasionally it is helpful in resolving
some not-so-concrete problems. For some wives, getting the
husband to sign the agreement to live separate and apart is
more than half the battle. Look at your own situation and
decide for yourself whether an agreement is likely to be
helpful and possible for you.

When Should I Start To Think About A Separation Agreement?

An agreement is best entered into as soon as you are sure
that you are involved in a permanent separation. If you
are only experimenting with living apart, with a view toward
a possible reconciliation, an agreement is not necessary.
But if you are reasonably certain that the separation will
be prolonged and may well end in divorce (though a divorce
need not be in your mind before you enter an agreement),
you will want to have an agreement drawn up as soon as
possible.

It is essential to your own and your children's future
security and peace of mind that you make every effort to
continue on speaking terms with your husband. Once communication has broken down, you will have to speak through
lawyers who often as not are representing their own interest as well as, if not better than, yours.

If you and your husband are not able to figure out how
best to settle your differences, some of your financial
resources are going to be eaten up by lawyers. If you and
your husband are on speaking terms, you may be able to
draw up your own agreement and avoid the legal fees; if
communication is poor and your husband is being represented
by an attorney, however, you should also have a legal ad-
viser in whom you have confidence.

How Do I Get A Separation Agreement?

Before you even think about what a final agreement will
look like, sit down and make notes of how much money you
will need to live on (check the itemized expense list from
Chapter Five) and what items you want to have in the agreement. Next consider what your husband's reaction to each
of your requests is likely to be. Is the amount you need
to live on an amount he could afford to provide? Could he
provide half that amount? What can you expect to earn?
If he is going to object to custody or visitation arrangements which are essential to you, what items could you live

without? Leave these items in your original proposal so
you will have some room to negotiate. Your first draft of
an agreement should be like a contractors' estimate--
realistic, but padded.

Depending on your circumstances, you will either talk over
with your husband the items you want in the agreement and
learn what he wants in the agreement or you will take your
items to your lawyer and have her or him draft an agreement
for your husband to look at. The more of this work you do
(like talking to your husband and incorporating what he
wants into the agreement you suggest to the lawyer), the
less you will have to pay for the agreement. If your lawyer has to do all the talking with your husband and his
attorney, you will pay for all those conversations. If
your lawyer has to write three separate drafts of the agreement either because you were not sure what you wanted or
didn't have any idea what your husband would accept, your
costs will go skyrocketing. The best possible plan is for
you and your husband to reach an agreement, inform the
lawyer of the terms, and have her or him write it up.

If your husband is the one whose lawyer drafts the agreement, you should look it over carefully before signing.
Compare it with the sample included in this chapter and
the checklist. If you have any doubts or questions, consult an attorney. The fee for one consultation should be
minimal, and could save you a great deal.

If you reach an impasse in arriving at mutually agreeable
terms, you might consider submitting your dispute to an
arbitration team. This may consist of a group of people
chosen by you and your husband, or a more formal group
composed of members of the American Arbitration Association.
The function of arbiters is to announce what they believe
is a fair resolution of the conflict. They are impartial
third parties whose decision binds those who request their
services. Some separation agreements also provide that
should any dispute arise in the future with regard to the
terms of the agreement, or any violations of the agreement
be charged by either party, the matter will be submitted to arbitration rather than a formal court.

Sample Separation Agreement

The following agreement is set out here to give you an idea
of what a completed agreement might look like, and to familiarize you with some of the standard terms and language of
separation agreements. It is not intended to be a model

which you should copy to solve your own problems. Agreements are as unique as the individuals who enter into them.
There is no formula for a "good separation agreement."

In some instances, a very low support figure might be accepted for an important custody provision. In other agreements there may be generous medical insurance coverage but
a lower support figure. Some agreements may reflect the
cancellation of an old debt between husband and wife. All
agreements will reflect the relative bargaining power of
the parties involved. The party who wants the divorce
usually has somewhat less bargaining power in writing the
agreement. The threat to contest a divorce (depending on
the party's ability to carry out the threat) can be a serious bargaining weapon.

For an idea of what kinds of questions would be covered in
a more complex agreement, see the checklist which follows
this sample agreement.

Agreement

This Agreement made on the first day of April, 1975,
between George J. George, residing at 201 Maple Street,
Oldtown, in the state of Grief, herein called Husband,
and Mary Freewoman George, residing at 1523 Parrish
Avenue, Newtown, in the state of Anticipation, herein
called Wife,

Witnesseth:

The parties were married on or about the 30th day of
June, 1967, in the city of Euphoria, state of Forever-
more.

Two children have been born of this marriage, who are
now minors, one Doris Mary George, born January 1, 1970,
and the other, Dennis James George, born June 13, 1972.

As a result of irreconcilable differences, the parties
are now living apart. It is their intention to live
apart for the rest of their lives, and both wish to
settle for all time their respective property rights
and agree on terms for the support of wife and the support and education of the children.

Wife has presented to husband and to Richard R. Right,
his attorney, copies of this agreement, and Husband,
having been fully advised of his rights, desires and

agrees to the terms hereinafter set forth.

NOW THEREFORE in consideration of the promises and the mutual undertakings herein contained, the parties hereby agree and intend to be legally bound as follows:

1. Husband and Wife shall at all times hereafter each have the right to live separate and apart from each other and to reside from time to time at such places and to engage in any employment for his or her separate benefit as he or she shall deem fit, free from any control, restraint, or interference direct or indirect, by the other, in all respects as if each were unmarried.

2. Neither party shall molest the other or compel or attempt any legal or other proceedings to compel the other to cohabit or dwell with him or her. This provision shall not be taken, however, to be an admission on the part of either the Husband or the Wife of the lawfulness or unlawfulness of the causes which led to, or resulted in the continuation of, their living apart.

    a. Husband shall pay to Wife for the support, maintenance, and education of each Child of the parties, the sum of $4,680 per year, in equal weekly installments of $90 each, consisting of $45 for each Child until the death or attainment of majority of each such Child;

    b. The foresaid payments shall be made in advance on the first day of each month commencing on December 1, 1975.

        Provided, however, that in the event either or both such children should attend a college, university, or other form of higher education or training, Husband agrees to pay the incurred tuition costs and expenses and to support such Child or Children at a rate and sum agreed upon by the parties at that time.

        Provided, however, that in the event that any such Child at any time after attaining sixteen years of age should elect to reside with Husband in his household, the payments herein required of Husband for such Child shall thereupon terminate.

c. In the event that the Husband's income increases
    or decreases by any amount in excess of $1,000
    per year, Husband shall increase or decrease the
    sum specified in this section 3(a) for the sup-
    port and education of each Child by two-thirds
    of the percentage rate of the income increase
    or decrease.

d. Wife shall pay for any expenses incurred by each
    Child of the parties that are in addition to the
    basic maintenance and education expenses covered
    by the $4,680 figure contained in Section 3(a)
    of this agreement. These expenses will include
    all extracurricular activities and further educa-
    tion, gifts, entertainment, vacations, and hobbies.
    Wife agrees to pay these expenses which are in-
    curred by each Child during the periods of time
    that the Children are in her custody.

4. Husband represents that he is presently carrying for
    the benefit of the Wife and Children (i) hospital
    service insurance (Blue Cross); and (ii) major medi-
    cal expense insurance under a group insurance plan
    in effect at A.B.C. Enterprises, Inc., where the
    Husband is presently employed, and underwritten by
    the Mutual Insurance Company of North America. The
    Husband is entitled to the benefits of the aforesaid
    major medical expense insurance only so long as he
    is employed by A.B.C. Enterprises, Inc.

    a. The Husband shall maintain the present Blue
        Cross policy or its equivalent during his life-
        time (1) for the Wife so long as she does not
        remarry, and (2) for each of the Children until
        they respectively reach the age of twenty-one,
        obtain an undergraduate degree from a college
        or university, or complete other formal train-
        ing, or die, whichever first occurs.

    b. So long as he continues in the employ of A.B.C.
        Enterprises, Inc., and the group insurance plan
        is in effect there, the Husband shall maintain
        the major medical expense insurance for each of
        the Children until they respectively reach the
        age of twenty-one, obtain an undergraduate
        degree, or complete other formal training, or
        die, whichever first occurs.

        If the Husband for any reason ceases to be

employed by A.B.C. Enterprises, Inc., and if there is a similar insurance plan in effect at any other employer with whom he may be subsequently associated, he shall make the benefits of that plan available to the Children for the periods and on the conditions stated above. However, nothing herein contained shall obligate the Husband to secure or maintain any major expense medical insurance on any basis other than as above set forth.

5. Wife shall be liable for all medical expenses incurred for the Children not covered by Blue Cross or other major medical insurance in effect at the time. Husband shall not be liable for Wife's medical, dental, surgical, nursing, or hospital expenses, whether ordinary or extraordinary. However, if any expenses are incurred for any of the Children as a result of any extraordinary illness, and such expenses exceed the coverage of the medical insurance, Husband shall contribute one-half the amount of such excess, provided (a) he is consulted in advance on the expenditures and approves of same, and (b) his contribution does not reduce his net spendable income below $_____ a year. "Extraordinary illness" means any accident or illness that confines a Child for more than two weeks, or any accident or illness that requires surgery.

6. Husband represents that he is presently carrying for the benefit of the Wife and Children a life insurance policy in the amount of $_____ with the _____ Insurance Company, bearing number _____. Husband represents and warrants to the Wife that the Policy is presently free and unencumbered and that he has not heretofore borrowed against the same. Husband agrees to maintain this policy or its equivalent in a free and unencumbered state during his lifetime.

a. Husband shall not change the beneficiaries on the Policy, except that in the event of an absolute divorce being granted to either party, he shall remove Wife as primary beneficiary and be obligated to name the Children irrevocable beneficiaries, in equal shares.

b. The Husband shall not borrow against this Policy;
he shall not pledge or otherwise encumber it;
and shall pay all dues, premiums, and assessments
on it.

7. The parties heretofore filed certain joint income tax
returns.

a. The Husband represents and warrants to the Wife
that he has heretofore duly paid all income taxes
on such returns; that he does not owe any interest
or penalties with respect thereto; that no tax
deficiency proceeding is pending or threatened
against him; and that no audit is pending with
respect to any such return.

b. If there is a deficiency assessment on any of the
aforesaid returns, the Husband shall give the
Wife immediate notice thereof in writing. He
shall pay the amount determined to be due, together with interest and penalties, if any, as
well as all expenses that may be incurred if he
decides to contest the assessment.

c. Husband shall hold his Wife harmless from any
claim, damage, or expense arising out of any
such deficiency assessment.

d. If there is any refund on any of the aforesaid
returns, it shall belong to the Husband.

e. For every year that he abides by each and every
term of this Agreement, Husband shall have the
right to claim the Children as dependents for
federal income tax purposes.

8. Wife shall have the custody, care, and charge of
both Children at all times during their respective
minorities except as otherwise specified in this
section (8).

a. Husband shall have the custody, care, an charge
of both said Children three days per week com-
mencing Friday morning and ending Sunday evening, the times of pickup and discharge of said
Children to be mutually convenient to the parties and the Children.

b. Wife shall not change the residence of the

Children without the written consent of Husband, which consent cannot be unreasonably withheld.

c. Custody of the Children during Christmas and Easter holidays and during two to four weeks of their summer vacation may be decided by further negotiation between the parties each year as these periods approach.

d. This provision (8) may be changed from time to time by mutual agreement of the parties, and is independent of all other sections.

e. Each Child shall have the right to decide with whom such Child desires to reside after attaining the age of sixteen years, and on such decision the parent whom the Child selects shall have the right to the custody and charge of such Child.

9. By quitclaim deed executed simultaneously with this Agreement, Husband does remise, release, and quitclaim to the Wife all his right, title, and interest in the real property located at 1523 Parrish Avenue. Husband agrees to continue to make the required payments on the mortgage, insurance, and taxes for such property until such time as the mortgage (together with interest) has been paid in full.

10. The death of the Husband shall terminate the requirements of this agreement for any and all payments by Husband, and neither his personal representatives nor his estate shall be liable hereunder except for installments due and unpaid at the time of his death.

11. The Wife acknowledges that the provisions herein made for her support and the support, maintenance, and education of the Children are fair, adequate, and reasonable, and satisfactory to her. Accordingly, she accepts the same in lieu of and in full and final settlement and satisfaction of any and all claims and rights that she may now or hereafter have against the Husband for her support and maintenance and for the support, maintenance, and education of the Children.

12. So long as Husband commits no breach or default of this Agreement, the Wife shall not contract or

incur any debt or liability for which Husband or
his property or estate might be responsible, and
shall indemnify Husband from any obligations incurred by her. In the event Husband shall at any
time hereafter be obliged to pay any debt incurred
by Wife, Husband may deduct and retain the sums he
may be obliged to pay out of any future payments
required to be made by him under this agreement.

13. If the husband fails in the due performance of his
    obligations hereunder, the Wife shall have the
    right, at her election, to sue for damages for a
    breach of this agreement, or to rescind the same
    and seek such legal remedies as may be available
    to her. Nothing herein contained shall be construed
    to restrict or impair the Wife's right to exercise
    this election.

14. The following disposition shall be made of the
    furniture, household goods, appliances, equipment,
    tablewear, and books owned by the parties:

    a. The parties have agreed on a division of cer-
        tain of these items. The division is set forth
        in Schedule A, attached hereto. The items
        listed in this Schedule as belonging to each
        party shall constitute his or her exclusive
        property, free and clear of any claim or
        right of the other party.

    b. The parties shall confer on the division of the
        remaining items. If they cannot agree within
        sixty days after the execution hereof, the
        matter shall be arbitrated under the provisions
        of clause 19 of this agreement.

    c. Except as above provided, and except as may be
        directed by arbitration, each party shall here-
        after own, have, and enjoy, independently of any
        claim or right of the other party, all items of
        real and personal property (tangible or intan-
        gible) now or hereafter belonging to him or her
        and now or hereafter in his or her possession,
        with full power to dispose of the same as effec-
        tively as though he or she were unmarried.

15. The counsel fees of the Wife amounting to $_____
    have been paid simultaneously herewith by the Hus-
    band to the Wife's attorneys, who have accepted the

same in full payment of their services in connection with the preparation and execution of this agreement and all negotiations prior thereto.

16. Except as otherwise herein expressly provided, the parties shall and do hereby mutually remise, release, and forever discharge each other from any and all actions, suits, debts, claims, demands, and obligations whatsoever, in both law and in equity, which either of them ever had, now has, or may hereafter have against the other upon or by reason of any matter, cause, or thing up to the date of the execution of this agreement.

17. Each party hereby releases and relinquishes any and all rights that he or she may now have or may hereafter have as spouse under the present or future laws of any jurisdiction (a) to share in the estate of the other party upon the latter's death; and (b) to act as executor or administrator of the other's estate. This provision is intended to constitute a mutual waiver by the parties to take against each other's last wills under the present or future laws of any jurisdiction whatsoever.

18. No modification or waiver of any of the terms hereof shall be valid unless in writing and signed by both parties. No waive of any breach hereof or default hereunder shall be deemed a waiver of any subsequent breach or default of the same or similar nature.

19. Any claim or dispute arising out of or in connection with this agreement or any breach thereof shall be arbitrated by the parties under the rules then obtaining of the American Arbitration Association. The cost of arbitration shall be borne as the award may direct. The arbitration shall be held in _____ (city). The award shall be binding and conclusive on the parties, and shall be rendered in such form that judgment may be entered thereon in the highest court of the forum having jurisdiction thereof.

20. Nothing herein contained shall be construed to bar either party from suing for absolute divorce in any competent jurisdiction because of any past or future fault on the other's part. This agreement shall be offered in evidence in such action, and if acceptable to the court shall be incorporated by reference

in the decree that may be granted therein. Notwith-
standing such incorporation, the agreement shall not
be merged in the decree, but shall survive and same
shall be binding and conclusive on the parties for
all time.

21. This agreement shall be construed according to the
     laws of _____ (state).

22. Each party shall, at any time and from time to time
     hereafter, take any and all steps and execute, ac-
     knowledge, and deliver to the other party any and
     all future instruments and assurances that the other
     party may reasonably require for the purpose of giv-
     ing full force and effect to the provisions of this
     agreement.

23. This agreement constitutes the entire understanding
     between the parties and there are no covenants, con-
     ditions, representations, or agreements, oral or
     written, of any nature whatsoever, other than those
     herein contained.

In Witness whereof, the parties hereto have executed this
Agreement, this _____ day of _____ (month), 1975.

                                    _____
                                    George J. George

                                    _____
                                    Mary Freewoman George

Witnessed by:

_____
As to George J. George

_____
As to Mary Freewoman George

It is impossible to write a "typical" agreement; everything depends on the details of your marriage--what your
financial condition was, whether you were working, what
kind of education or income potential you have, how old
your children are, etc. This agreement is written with
the following considerations in mind:

1. The wife in this agreement asked for no support for
    herself, as she plans to be working soon at a regular
    job with a satisfactory salary. The husband has, how-
    ever, agreed to continue to pay the mortgage and
    insurance and taxes on the house, which will belong
    to the wife when it is entirely paid.

2. The parties are on reasonably good terms with each
    other so that they can agree to confer on some matters
    relating to the children and have slightly flexible
    visitation provisions.

3. The personal property owned by the parties is not of
    great value and they can agree between themselves
    how to divide it.

4. The wife trusts the husband on the terms of this agree-
    ment. Otherwise a "Security" clause would have been
    included, in which the husband puts certain amounts
    of money or stock in escrow to be used by the wife in
    case of default.

5. The support figure for the children is fairly low, but
    the children will be living with the husband three days
    a week, and the husband has agreed to maintain medical
    and life insurance for the benefit of the children.

Writing Your Own Agreement

If yours is a relatively simple situation with little or
no property and no controversy about support, visitation,
or custody, you might want to write your own separation
agreement. You can use this agreement as a basic model
and/or go to the library and browse through the books on
domestic relations until you find a book of sample separation agreements. (See the bibliography for specific titles.)

Whatever models you use, remember that these are all standard forms, samples. You may need fewer or more clauses,
and the precise terms of your agreement will vary from the
model.

If you and your husband are on exceptionally good terms
you might agree on what should go into an agreement and
then draft one together. If you are on less good terms,
but still feel you can arrive at an agreement without a
lawyer, you should not be afraid to try to write your own.
Or you might both want to draw up an agreement and see how
the two differ. The party who drafts the agreement has a
tactical advantage. If you are the author of the agreement,
your husband will have to reply point by point to your terms.
Even if he does not completely agree with any of them, you
have the advantage of having defined the issues.

What To Do With An Agreement Presented By Your Husband

If you are not the one to draw up an agreement, and are
presented with one to "sign," take your time. Read the
agreement over carefully, and consult a legal counselor if
at all possible. If the agreement seems basically fair
and you would like only a few changes, you may take his
version of the agreement and insert your additional terms
or cross out those which are objectionable in ink. You
can then return the agreement to him and he will probably
return it to his lawyer for revision.

If the whole agreement seems unfair to you, or you feel
that many changes must be made, you should get a counter
proposal drafted. Eventually, you must both agree to one
statement of all the terms of your agreement. Never
accept two separate agreements. And never sign an agreement containing any terms you do not understand or any
terms you do not think you could live with. NEVER ACCEPT
AN ORAL PROMISE NOT TO ENFORCE THE TERMS OF THE CONTRACT
OR TO DO ANYTHING NOT WRITTEN INTO THE CONTRACT.

The checklist that follows suggests some of the more important provisions which should be included in more complex agreements involving custody and/or property. It is
not intended to be an exhaustive list of all the possible
clauses, but rather attempts to indicate some of the more
typical ones which you should look for or write into a
sophisticated agreement.

If you are presented with an agreement drawn up by your
attorney or by your husband's attorney, you might want to
check it against this list, and if relevant provisions on
the list do not appear in your agreement, consider whether
they would be useful. If you feel they would, write similar terms with details appropriate to your situation into
the "ready-made" agreement. If you are presenting a list

of items you would like in your agreement to your lawyer, consider whether any of those below would be good for you.

REMEMBER: You want to "pad" your demands a little. Put in a few items that are not outrageous, but ones which you are willing to throw away in order to obtain more important clauses. But be careful not to so overload your agreement with "giveaways" that it is unrealistic. But always ask for a little more than you are willing to settle for. And remember that an agreement will never reflect your ideal. It is a compromise between what you want and what your husband wants.

Checklist For Separation Agreements

1. Will support be in the form of a lump sum or in periodic payments? (Tax Note: "lump sum payments" are not considered income to the wife--even if the payments on the lump sum are stretched out over a period of up to ten years. Any payments which last ten years or longer, or are for an uncertain length of time--so long as wife lives, until wife remarries, or the like-- are considered "periodic" payments and thus are income on which the wife pays tax and a deduction for the husband. The husband does get to deduct lump sum payments.)

2. If there will be either permanent or temporary alimony or support for the wife, the agreement should contain a specific date for the commencement and termination of the payments--until a certain date, until death or remarriage, until wife earns degree, or the like.

3. The amount payable in the lump or in each payment should be specified.

4. A payment schedule should be spelled out. Often it is a good idea to have the checks payable to the local family court. The wife receives checks directly from the court and the husband thinks twice about "forgetting" to pay.

5. Sometimes the husband must post a certain amount of money or property as security in case of his default on payments. This is great insurance for wives--if you can get it.

6. It is wise to have an escalator clause tied to the husband's income. This way, if his income decreases, so does the amount of support he pays you--but only by a

fraction of the decrease. Likewise, if his income increases, you get a fraction of the increase. This is
much better than a "cost of living" escalator clause
for him because he gets to keep most of the increase
in his income. Remember, the cost of living is going
to rise just as fast for him as it is for you. You
may want to fix a minimum floor below which his support
payments should not fall, regardless of his income.

7. If you don't like the idea of alimony, or he balks at
    "supporting you," you might suggest he pay your tuition,
    fees, and living expenses for a certain period while
    you complete your education or receive additional train-
    ing. This is especially appropriate if you interrupted
    your education to enable him to complete his.

8. You may want your husband to continue carrying you on
    his health insurance plan. Sometimes the cost is so
    minimal that this is no problem. It might also decrease
    the amount of money you would need to live on, because
    you would not have to save for medical emergencies.
    This is especially appropriate if you are not in a
    position to get good, inexpensive health insurance.
    Note: Many policies will cover separated wives, but
    not ex-spouses.

9. Your agreement should include a clause stating that
    your husband agrees to pay your attorney's fees and
    court costs unless you have enough money to do this
    yourself.

10. If either of you has made a significant loan to the
    other, a schedule for repayment should be worked out
    or incorporated into the support or property settle-
    ment figures.

11. The idea is still controversial, but some wives are
    asking for a lump sum to compensate for their loss of
    earning power while they were out of the job market
    performing domestic work at home for free. Others
    see the lump sum as unpaid wages for work done at home.
    Another possibility is to get your husband to agree to
    support your education in consideration of your work
    at home.

Regarding custody, the agreement should:

1. Specify with whom the children are to live at what
    times. You should read carefully the custody section of

this chapter and the "Children in Transition" chapter of this book before making any final decision or signing any agreement about which you have the slightest question.

2. Spell out visitation times, places, and conditions as much as you think is necessary in your situation. This clause should, at the very least, include the days and times of visitation, how the children will get from one parent to the other, and whether the visitation will occur in the visiting parent's home or elsewhere.

3. Specify where the children will spend school and summer vacations, especially if it varies the regular custody/ visitation schedule.

4. State that neither parent could move outside the area within easy commuting distance of each other (or the jurisdiction of the court in which the agreement is filed or order entered) without the written consent of the other parent.

If the wife has custody, the husband usually pays a specified amount per week or month. If possible, checks should be made out to the family court. Both amount and payment schedule should be spelled out in the agreement. (Tax Note: Child support is not income to the wife and not deductible by the husband. As you would suspect, there is a lot of pressure from husbands to call everything they pay "alimony" and from wives to call it "child support.")

The party who contributes more than 50 percent of the child's financial support for the year may claim that child as a dependent on his or her personal income tax for that year. I.R.S. tends to respect parents' written agreements as to which parent this will be. They are mainly concerned that there are not two parents claiming the same child, so specify.

Provision should be made for a father with good medical insurance to continue the coverage for his children, especially where the cost to him is minimal and the wife would have to spend a great deal or is not in a position to obtain such coverage. The agreement should specify which party will pay all expenses not covered by insurance.

It is a good idea to get your husband to agree to maintain any present life insurance policies, naming the children as "irrevocable beneficiaries."

If there is any chance he will cover and can afford inci-
dental expenses like extracurricular activities, extra lessons, camp, and the like, by all means include this in the
agreement. Usually this burden falls on the parent with
custody. But remember that if that parent has a lot less
money, the child will be penalized for the parents' divorce
unless she or he is given all the advantages (or most of
them) she or he would have enjoyed had there been no divorce.

If there are any decisions about the child's future education, health care, or any other matter which you believe
should be made by both parties, this should be spelled out
in the agreement. Otherwise the party who has custody
will have this right.

You should specify at what age support, medical insurance,
and other payments for the benefit of the children shall
be terminated.

Some parents wish to specify an age at which they will
abide by the child's decision as to which parent the child .
will live with. For a discussion of the wisdom of this
policy, you may want to read parts of both the "Children
in Transition" chapter and the custody section of this
chapter.

Regarding property settlement, including real estate, bank
accounts, stocks, bonds, business, the agreement should:

1. Identify all jointly owned property and/or income
    therefrom, along with the appraised value of each
    item.

2. Specify what proportion of the total assets or which
    individual assets shall be distributed to each party.
    Means and effective date of distribution should be
    specified if possible.

3. Provide for the distribution of income from any prop-
    erties which will continue in joint ownership as well
    as describe the liability of each party for expenses
    or debts incurred in the maintenance of this property.

4. Specify which party is to remain in the marital home
    and which party will pay the costs and expenses related
    thereto including mortgage, insurance, and taxes.

5. Contain a list of all debts for which the parties are
    jointly liable. If at all possible, these debts should

be paid out of jointly held assets prior to division
and distribution of these assets between the parties.

In dealing with personal property, most agreements simply
state that the parties agree to an "amicable settlement" of
all property acquired by both parties at the time of or during the marriage. This is much easier than spelling out who
gets which lamp. However, if you cannot trust an "amicable"
division of this property, it should all be enumerated in
the agreement. Also, any exceptions to the amicable division should be noted--for example, a particular piece of
furniture that you want to be sure will be yours.

The agreement should state that each party will take all
property owned by that party alone prior to or acquired by
gift to that party during the marriage.

In some cases you might want the agreement to provide for
the party who is leaving the marital home to take such
furnishings, etc., as will minimize the expense of establishing two houses. Obviously, this provision only makes
sense in a situation where the marital home has more than
enough to support the party staying in the home. This
provision is particularly appropriate when the party leaving the home will be living elsewhere with the children.

Be sure that all property settlement provisions indicate
the effective date and means of transfer of all property
described in the agreement as property to be transferred
from one party to another. In some cases this will mean
one party agrees to buy the other's interest in a particular property. In others the property division will be
made by the judge making the divorce decree. If no agreement can be reached, the parties might agree to submit the
property settlement to arbitration. Finally, if no agreement can be reached, one party may have the right to compel a sale of the property to recover her or his share.

The tax consequences of every transfer of property should
be figured before the entire agreement is signed (or even
drafted). Having a tax advantage can mean you are willing
to take a much lower support figure or are willing to give
him some property he considers important. Or, he may be
willing to pay a higher amount of alimony rather than increase the child support because alimony is deductible for
him (and taxable for you) while child support is neither
deductible for him nor taxable to you.

For federal income tax purposes, you may agree to file

joint returns during the separation period until a final
decree is granted. If his income is much higher than yours,
it may be worth a good deal of money to him to have the advantage of this low tax status. This means you can bargain
with him over whether or not you will file joint returns.
Filing a joint return gives you an easy way to keep track
of something like his true income. On the other hand, you
can be held liable for any fraud or other violation or crime
he commits on the joint returns. If he underpays, you can
be held liable for the entire deficiency.

Your agreement should also indicate whether or not you intend it to continue in full force and effect should a
divorce be granted to either party. In most states, you
cannot agree to make any provision in the agreement contingent on either party's obtaining a divorce. In these
states you also may not agree that one of the parties will
institute divorce proceedings.

It should specify what effect, if any, the death of either
party will have on the terms of the agreement. For example,
will a husband's estate continue to be liable for the
wife's support payments? Will the wife be able to inherit
from the husband if he dies before a divorce is granted?

Remember that no term of the agreement which is illegal
or "contrary to public policy" is enforceable. This includes your agreement not to receive child support. It is
a good idea to have a clause stating that all the clauses
of the agreement are independent and that all the rest remain in effect in the event that one of the clauses should
be found invalid, illegal, or otherwise unenforceable. A
clause providing for the independence of the various provisions will also insure that you need not rewrite the
entire agreement should you wish to modify support figures
or visitation arrangements.

And Remember . . .

1. Two households are more expensive than one. Most
    families will simply not be able to continue at the
    same economic level after a divorce. Thus, in planning
    your agreement, you should recognize that many small
    luxuries--necessities even--will disappear. Your hus-
    band will, in almost every case, not have the money to
    run two houses in the same style as the one you shared.

2. Remember that you have to live with the results of this
    agreement. The support and property provisions should

represent a reasonable compromise between what you and
your children need and what your husband can afford.
It is precisely at this often intensely emotional time
that your future security is being determined. Calm
deliberation and careful planning will result in a
better agreement and one which is more likely to be
carried out by both parties.

3. Try, as much as possible, to leave emotional considera-
    tions out of your calculations. A separation agreement
    is not an instrument of revenge and may never get nego-
    tiated (leaving you with nothing) if it is considered
    that way by either party. On the other hand, don't
    sell yourself short. If you put your husband through
    professional school and paid for two-thirds of the
    property acquired during the marriage, you should ask
    for that proportion of the property when splitting up.
    If your husband was your sole source of support and
    "income" during the marriage, however, you are entitled
    to half the jointly owned property, regardless of the
    fact that he had all the capital. Your free labor
    enabled him to earn that money!

4. Remember the two basic aims of a separation agreement:
    security for your children and financial independence
    for you. The agreement should be arranged to accom-
    plish the first goal for as long as possible (until
    the children are able to be self-supporting) and the
    second as quickly as possible. You might look at the
    agreement as a sort of down-to-earth declaration of
    independence, and measure its effectiveness by the
    extent to which it enables you to be a separate person
    as soon as you are economically able.

5. Respect the rights of your children and insist that
    your husband do likewise. They have a right not to be
    punished for their parents' incompatability. Sometimes
    a divorce is the only way to avoid their further suf-
    fering, but all too often parents see their children's
    rights to support and custody as negotiable items, and
    the children become pawns in the parents' struggle.

    If, during the marriage, your husband had planned to
    maintain a fund so that your children could attend the
    college of their choice, he should continue to do so
    regardless of a divorce. On the other hand, the in-
    creased expense of having two households may make
    things like private school for the children impossible.
    Be realistic, but cautious. Try to avoid bargaining

away your children's rights and make sure your husband understands that support and other payments for the children are for the children and not for you.

Suppose We Can't Agree?

It has been suggested that the law serves a kind of first-aid function in society; it will deal with those emergency situations that cannot be resolved by ordinary social means-- discussion, negotiation, bargaining, and the like. It is important to remember this as you look to the law to help you solve some of your problems as a woman in transition.

The law cannot make you and your husband agree on a fair amount of support, or who gets to keep the car. It can't assure you of a decent standard of living or dull the pain of separation. It can serve a much more limited function-- helping you to enforce some of your basic rights to support for your children (and yourself in some states), a fair hearing of your case, and enforcement of its orders.

Many separating husbands and wives simply cannot work out agreements. Usually this is not because they disagree about specific items--these can be negotiated. The real cause of failure to agree is often an inability on the part of one or both of the parties to deal with the *emotional* realities of the situation. This is why many people use lawyers and have them draw up the agreement and do the negotiating. Fine if it works--if you have the money.

For many women, however, court-ordered child support and alimony, property division, or custody decrees are important alternatives to a separation agreement. For still others, welfare is the only alternative. This is most often the case when the husband's income simply can't stretch any further, or when the husband has disappeared.

If you believe a support suit in family court (sometimes called "domestic relations" or by some other name) is the best solution to your immediate economic or custody problems, read the support section of this chapter. If you are convinced your husband would not comply with a court order for support and that the court-ordered figure would not be much higher than the local welfare levels, read the welfare section of the "Financial Resources" chapter before you decide whether to go to support court.

If you are going to be separated or divorced and plan to go to court for support for yourself and/or your children,

you should familiarize yourself with the functions and
authority of the local courts in your county (located in
the county seat) or city. The areas usually handled by
family or domestic relations courts include: granting
separation and divorce decrees, determining the ownership
and distribution of property, awarding temporary or permanent support for wives and/or children, awarding child
custody and visitation rights, granting protective orders
or injunctions, and determining who should own and occupy
the marital home. Although you are often at a distinct
advantage in these and other courtrooms with a lawyer,
you have a right to file your own petitions in most family
courts. Filing fees are usually modest (except for divorce)--$10 or less. In some cases the fee may not be
required at all if you are a welfare recipient and show an
identification card proving you are on welfare.

Support Court

> *The legal obligation to support can generally be
> enforced only through an action for separation or
> divorce, and the data available, although scant,
> indicated that . . . alimony is granted in only a
> very small percentgae of cases; that fathers, by
> and large, are contributing less than half the
> support of children in divided families; and that
> alimony and child support awards are very difficult
> to collect. (Citizens Advisory Council On The
> Status Of Women, "The Equal Rights Amendment and
> Alimony and Child Support Laws," Women's Bureau,
> U.S. Department of Labor, Washington, D.C.)*

Where Do I Go?

Let's assume that you and your husband cannot reach an
agreement on the amount of support he should pay. You
have given up all hope of ever negotiating a separation
agreement, and want to proceed with the divorce. Your
problem now is how to provide for yourself during the time
of transition until you are economically self-supporting
and how to enforce your husband's legal duty to support
his children.

First: Learn your rights in your state. Every state requires that a father support his minor children. Some
states also require that a husband support his wife after
divorce (alimony) or during the period while the divorce
is pending (known as alimony *pendente lite* or temporary
alimony).

Your first question will be, "Am I entitled to sue for support for myself as well as for my children?" If, under the law in your state, you are entitled to some form of alimony, you should consider whether this will encourage your independence from the marriage or only further increase your dependence. You may need alimony for a limited time or for a specific goal. You may decide you don't need it at all. Remember: The less you depend on him the happier you'll be. But if alimony would enable you to return to school or get some kind of training you've always wanted, by all means take advantage of this opportunity.

Once you have determined what kind of support you need and for what purposes, try to prepare a realistic estimate of your expenses, along with an estimate of your projected income for the next year. You might want to use the itemized list of expenses from the "Financial Resources" chapter for this. Then estimate your needs, and subtract the amount of your estimated expenses from your projected income. How does this figure compare with your spouse's income? With the figure you get when you subtract his expenses from his income? Is what you are asking realistic from your point of view--could you live on your earnings plus his contribution? Is it realistic from his point of view--can he meet his expenses and still pay what you are asking?

If you have reason to believe his income could provide support for you, you should head for the local family court (or its equivalent in your area). If you think your husband is likely to be represented by an attorney, you should arrange to get a lawyer. This is especially important if you think your husband would be able to conceal much of his income. This is possible if he is self-employed or if a substantial part of his income comes from sources other than regular paychecks.

If your spouse's income is fairly regular and you signed joint tax forms which you believe accurately reported his income, you may learn exactly what this amount was by obtaining a copy of the joint return from the I.R.S. Commissioner in Washington, D.C. Sometimes the local I.R.S. office can help you.

Representing Yourself In Family Court

If you are sure your husband will not try to conceal his income and will not be represented by a lawyer, you may want to represent yourself in support court. But be cautious in deciding that he will not conceal his income or be represented. The courtroom is a familiar battleground to lawyers and judges. It can be an unfriendly territory for an untrained person, particularly one who is emotionally involved in the issues. If you do decide to represent yourself, take time and study the situation carefully, then remember: Confidence and sincerity are your best weapons.

Before the hearing, you may be asked to attend a "conference" with your husband and a social worker. The court would like you to enter a voluntary agreement so they would not have to supervise your husband's payments or go through a time-consuming trial. Many husbands will agree to pay support in front of a social worker at a conference without the slightest intention of keeping this promise.

If you think your husband will not voluntarily agree to pay you, or would agree to do so only to avoid a hearing and never carry out his promise, you may waive the conference and go straight to the hearing. At the hearing you present the judge with your list of itemized expenses, receipts which tend to document these expenses (rent receipts, paid bills, medical expenses, etc.). You show what your income is (pay stubs) and what your husband's is (tax returns), then ask the court to order support.

In order to begin the support action against your husband you must file a "petition" with the court. There is usually a small filing charge. In many places you can fill out this form yourself with the help of a clerk or "intake officer" at the family court offices. Once this petition is filed your husband will be notified or receive a subpoena ordering him to appear in court on a certain date.

After the hearing, the judge will usually announce his decision and put it down in a written "Order" of which you should get a certified copy. Once a support order is made, your husband should begin regular payments. Many courts have set up a special office to receive this payment from the husbands. The husband writes the check to the court and the court issues a check to you. This plan makes it a little less likely that your husband will fail to pay the ordered amount on time.

You might want to get a certified copy of the support order, especially if your husband will not be paying through the court, but directly to you. The copy will help if you ever have to go back in court should he fail to pay according to the order.

What Can I Expect?

When you go to Family Court for a support order, you are asking for two things: First, you are asking a court to determine how much support you should get from your husband. Second, you are asking the court to stand behind its order with enforcement when your husband fails to pay.

Amounts of support awarded vary considerably, from region to region, city to country, and from judge to judge. A 1965 study of Michigan courts indicated that a father whose weekly income was $120 a week would be ordered to pay $24 per week to support one child, and $84 to support six or more children. Although wives are theoretically entitled to up to one-half their husbands' income (after taxes, social security, and all other mandatory deductions have been taken out) for the support of themselves and their children, awards are usually much lower--one-third or less. This is especially true if the husband remarries, regardless of the fact that the amount required to support his former wife and children does not decrease.

Factors which influence the amount of support awarded include the living standard of the couple, the respective incomes of the parties, the physical and mental health of both, the length of the marriage, number and ages of children, and the relative earning power of each party. Also considered are the amount of money or property each contributed to the marriage and how the family income was obtained. The social position of each party before the marriage is sometimes a factor. Where there are additional dependents--such as parents--this will also be considered. If one of the parties (usually the wife) sacrificed a career for the marriage, she should get a little extra compensation. Sometimes who was at fault influences the support figure, especially in cases where it is obvious there was or still may be much bitterness or suffering.

If you consider your own situation in light of these criteria, you may get a fair idea of what amount you can expect a judge to order for support. A factor that's very hard to predict but very important is the judge's personality and personal feelings about marriage, divorce, and support. Finally, your lawyer and/or the preparation you have done ahead of time can be a most important factor. The better your documentation of his income and your expenses the more likely you are to get a realistic amount of support.

Enforcement

Once you have managed to get a support order, you have
every reason to believe your economic situation is at least
fairly stable. Unfortunately, your financial problems may
not end here, or even take a brief rest here. What do you
think will happen if your husband thinks the support order
is unfair? What if he's vindictive, or thinks he doesn't
owe you a penny? How about if he's forgetful, or a spend-
thrift? Your support check is only as reliable as he is.

Of course, you have a legally enforceable right to receive
the decreed amount each month. But enforcing that right
is often harder than getting the order. A 1955 Wisconsin
study shows that one year after the divorce and support
order, only 38 percent of the fathers studied were still
sending the proper amount regularly. Twenty percent had
"partially complied"--some of these having made exactly
one payment. After ten years, 79 percent of the fathers
with outstanding orders were no longer paying anything at
all.

There are, of course, penalties for noncompliance. In
some states he may be fined, held "in contempt of court,"
and even imprisoned. In some states his wages may be
attached so that you receive your check before he gets to
spend his pay. One of the problems in the enforcement
system is that you can't run down to the court the first
time his check is three days overdue, even if the oil company won't deliver on credit and it's the middle of winter.
A week overdue? Maybe just a delay in the mails. In many
large cities complaints about missed and overdue payments
will not be heard until he is at least one month behind.

Assuming you can live for a month without payments (you
must budget for such emergencies), you file a request for
a hearing on his nonpayment and wait for the hearing date.
Lo and behold, a check arrives in the mail. Maybe not for
the full amount, but just enough to keep the court from
holding him in contempt.

Or maybe you can show the court he is $1,000 or more in
arrears. If he doesn't have this money in his pocket, you
may never see all those back payments. Sometimes the court
will increase the weekly payments for a certain length of
time to make up for the missed payments. But no matter
what the court does, you're never going to get the money
if he doesn't have it. And if he does have it, enforcement
still depends most of all on how willing he is to give it
to you.

Sad to say, unless your husband's income is regular and
fairly substantial, you may be better off on welfare. At
least there you get a regular (if exceedingly small) amount
every two weeks. If welfare is a possibility for you, read
the welfare section in Chapter Five before going to court.
Try to decide which plan would give you more money and more
security. Don't forget that if your husband misses two
payments a month, you're going to be living on *half* the
amount a judge would order--and these amounts are not very
high to begin with. Compare what you think you might receive from your husband under an order and what you would
receive from welfare before you decide.

Emergencies, Temporary Orders, And Other Measures

In many states you may file for an emergency support order.
Contact the intake office of the nearest family or domestic
relations court in order to file your petition for support.
You should have rent receipts, utility bills, and other
evidence of your expenses ready to take with you. You
should also have your itemized list of expenses.

In some states your husband's employer and his bank may be
notified that you have filed for support; in some cases he
will be prevented from withdrawing money from his bank account until the support has been paid.

Courts, even when dealing with "emergencies," move slowly.
In the time between the day he leaves you with no money,
no bank account--nothing but bills and hungry children--
and the time a court orders him to make payments, you could
starve. If you find yourself in an extreme financial emergency you have two options: Apply for emergency welfare
money (see Chapter Five) or, if you are known in the area
and your husband's credit is good, you might take advantage
of your legal "oneness" with your husband. Under the law,
you are entitled to buy "necessaries"--including food and
clothing--at any store where your husband's credit is good,
and charge it to his account. Hopefully, he hasn't been
thorough enough to close his accounts and put a public
notice in the paper that he'll only be responsible for his
own debts.

*What Is The Effect Of "No-Fault" Divorce On Property
Settlements And Support Orders?*

While no-fault divorce laws are making it easier for people to get divorced, they are also making it harder for
economically dependent spouses (almost always wives) to

bargain for decent support and property settlements. Where there are only fault grounds for divorce, a husband may be willing to agree to a higher support figure or better property settlement in order to avoid a contest from the wife, or in order to avoid the publicity involved in either a contested divorce or a courtroom settlement.

The Uniform Marriage and Divorce Act (see the divorce section of this chapter for a discussion of this Act) was drawn up with sections relating to property division, child support, economic maintenance for a "dependent spouse," child custody, and enforcement. But most of the states which have adopted the Act or added no-fault grounds to traditional divorce grounds have failed to enact the portions of the Uniform Act relating to support, custody, and enforcement. Five states have adopted many of these provisions--Colorado, Kentucky, Missouri, Washington, and Arizona.

None of the states whose "no-fault" ground is separation, desertion, or incompatibility have adopted the economic sections of the Uniform Act. This means that in all but the five states listed above, while divorce will be easier to get, a fair economic settlement will probably be harder than ever to arrange because husbands can safely refuse to negotiate an agreement with adequate provisions for the wife and/or children, and rest secure knowing that judge-ordered support levels are notoriously low, and collection and enforcement of these orders highly ineffective.

The Act also suggests that the family house should be awarded to the party with custody of the children. There are two proposed ways to divide the remaining property under the Act; it is up to the state to decide which alternative to use. One proposal is that all property acquired during the marriage be fairly divided, and recommends that "fairness" requires a consideration of what each party contributed to the property, *including contribution of a spouse as homemaker*. The alternative to this proposal suggests that a fair division of *all* the property owned by the parties be made, including the husband's separately owned properties--stocks and bank accounts as well as real estate.

Child-support payments under the Act would be based on the standard of living the child would have enjoyed had the marriage not been dissolved. This provision seeks to keep children from being economically punished for living with the less affluent parent (also usually the wife).

Section 312 of the Act authorizes a court to order a spouse paying child support or maintenance to "assign" a part of his income to the persons receiving payments. Under this procedure, a father would never have a chance to skip or skimp on child-support payments because once he's "assigned" those funds, they are out of his control--they may be deducted from his paychecks just like federal income taxes.

Unfortunately, these rather realistic ways of dividing property and providing for support are presently only available in five states. In Michigan, Nebraska, Oregon, Alabama, Connecticut, Georgia, Hawaii, Indiana, Maine, Maryland, Montana, and New Hampshire, parties who take advantage of the "irretrievable breakdown" standard for no-fault divorce have neither bargaining power with respect to separation agreements nor sensible guidelines and decent enforcement.

The economic provisions of the Uniform Marriage and Divorce Act, while far from perfect, do offer several important safeguards to economically dependent spouses and to parents who have custody of minor children. These include a provision for the "maintenance" of either spouse if that spouse doesn't have enough property to provide for her or his needs, and is unable to support her or himself through "appropriate" employment, or has custody of a pre-school or school-age child. Factors to be considered in fixing the amount of "maintenance" payments include the standard of living during the marriage, the length of the marriage, the age, physical, and emotional condition of the party seeking "maintenance."

▶▶▶ *ROSE*

I don't know where to turn, I just don't know where to turn. I've been married for 45 years, and now my husband says he wants to leave me. I don't know what to do. My children are all grown and they don't seem to really care. I don't know what's come over him all of a sudden, after all these years. It's never been really right, though. I knew for years that he's been running around, but I figured that as long as I provided a good home and meals on the table--I've always put meals on the table. Every night when he came home there was always a meal on the table. I've raised 5 children. I was a good mother. But now this girl--I think he wants to marry this girl. She's really putting the pressure on him to marry her. You know, she's half his age.

He must be going through his second childhood or something.

I got married and I did everything that you're supposed to do. I never worked, except for one time my husband was on strike. I got married when I was very young and I had the children right away. My husband took care of us. He gave me most of his money every week. I really knew how to spend it. I never spent money on myself, I always spent it on the children. Once in a while I would go to the hairdresser, but other than that I never spent it on myself. He would complain all the time. I tried to tell him how hard it is to make ends meet when you have 5 kids, but he would always complain.

Then he started running around. It's been going on for 15 years now, and there must have been a good half dozen. But I said to myself, look, as long as he comes home, as long as he gives me the money, takes care of the family, I've got a roof over my head, I'll put up with it. He even admitted it more than one time. He said so what, what are you going to do about it? I asked him many times if he wanted a divorce, but he said no, he wasn't leaving his house, he wasn't leaving his children.

So I said well, it could be worse, it could be worse. I've still got my children, I've still got my health. But now it's too much, now he says he wants a divorce. I don't even have my health any more. I've just been so sick. I've been to the doctor so many times, and I don't know what's wrong. I know a lot of it's my nerves. Anyhow, it's getting harder and harder for me to get around. I'm 63.

I have no money, I have no family to turn to. My children don't want to be bothered. They're all grown now, with families of their own. I haven't been to a lawyer. I wouldn't even know what to say to a lawyer. My husband has sort of left the house. He comes home a couple nights a week now. He doesn't give me any money any more, just enough to buy a little food. He doesn't pay the bills on the house any more. I'm afraid we're going to lose the house, even though it's almost paid off. I don't know if he has been to a lawyer. He said he's going to go see a lawyer because he wants a divorce. He spends all his money on this girl. Just yesterday he came *in and I said, please, you've got to give me some money, you've got to pay the the phone bill, the electric bill. You know what that son of a bitch gave me? A $10 bill, that's what he gave me.*

If I had it to do over again, I don't know how much of it I would change. I know that I never should have been so dependent all those years. These young girls today, they've got the right idea. They've got their own bank accounts, their own jobs. I wanted to work after my children grew up, but what could I do? I went through the tenth grade. Back then it was much more common for people to quit school. In my day girls didn't even graduate from high school, let alone go to college.

One time when my husband was on strike I had a job. I worked in a factory making model railroad trains. I didn't like working, it was worse than staying home. I was treated like a piece of machinery. I wasn't even allowed to talk on the assembly line. Back then we didn't have the unions that they have today. It exhausted me. It was just too much working all day and then going home and cooking and cleaning and doing the wash. My husband never did any of that, no time, ever. Like I said, these young girls today, they've got their husbands helping them. In my day that was women's work.

My children have been a real source of strength for me in the past. Sometimes we would go on vacations, and then it would be O.K. with my husband. But now, like I said, my children can't be bothered. At least my children, they're settled. My oldest girl is married. She's got children of her own, and my oldest boy went to college, and he's got a good job. But I'm going to tell my oldest daughter, she'd better make sure she can do something so she can't be left in the cold like this. That goes for the rest of my girls, too. One of them, she's just ungrateful. She's no good. The others, though, they're busy. They are trying to raise their families. Two of my youngest girls, they both work. I just don't feel right telling them all this. They've got problems of their own.

I've been to the minister, but he's been no help. He tries to understand, but he tells me just to have faith in God. I've had faith in God all these years. Like I said, I've been a good woman. I go to church every Sunday. I think I need something more than faith now.

*I get together with some of my friends from church
and we talk about old times and our children. And
then I can forget my problems for a while. But when
I come home, they're still there.*

*So I just don't know what to do now. I need some
help. What's an old woman going to do? Can he
just do this and go out and get a divorce and leave
me after all these years of being a good wife and
mother? Doesn't the law say something? Don't I
have any protection? I thought when I got older
it would be my time to rest. I've done my job and
been a good wife and mother, and now I get to the
age when I could sit back and rest and maybe try
to enjoy life a bit. I thought maybe we'd sell
the house and maybe stay down at the shore after
he retired. We've got a place down at the shore,
you know. I don't know what's happening to that.
He takes her down there. To our house, our house
that I helped to fix and paint and clean. I don't
go down there any more. I hardly get out of the
house any more. I suppose maybe it will be all
right in the end. I mean, maybe I'll find a way
to get through it.*

DIVORCE

Who's Who In A Divorce?

1. If you want the divorce.

    A. You file. You are the *plaintiff* ("innocent and injured" party in fault situations).

    B. He files. You are the *defendant* ("guilty" party in fault situations). You receive the Complaint but do not contest or countersue.

2. If you don't want the divorce.

    He files. You are the *defendant*. You contest. (You may decide to countersue instead. In that case, you are the plaintiff in another action.)

3. If you don't care about the divorce, but want support or custody problems to be resolved. He files. You are the *defendant*. You:

    A. Present a separation agreement.

    B. Threaten to contest if it's not signed.

    C. Contest if the agreement is not signed or being negotiated in what you think is a reasonable manner (assuming you have legitimate grounds on which to contest).

Remember that the party who goes to a lawyer and files for a divorce is called the *plaintiff*. In states which have not adopted any no-fault ground for divorce, the plaintiff plays the role of *innocent and injured spouse*.

The *defendant* is the one being sued; the defendant plays the role of the *guilty spouse*. If the defendant doesn't want the divorce to go through, she *contests* or *countersues*.

In states which have adopted no-fault grounds there is no innocent party and no guilty party.

When You Might Not Want A Divorce To Go Through (although you really don't care all that much whether you're married or not):

1. If you have been married nineteen years, don't let him divorce you until your twentieth anniversary. After twenty

years of faithful service, you get to collect on his social security. If your divorce is final one day before your twentieth anniversary, no social security.

2. If he's filed for a divorce in another state in order to escape support responsibilities in your home state, you might want to countersue for divorce in your state and prevent the foreign divorce from being granted. (See foreign divorce section of this chapter.)

3. If you are the defendant in a state where "fault" is considered a factor in awarding custody or support, you could still get a divorce from him by instituting your own suit as plaintiff.

4. If you are already separated and you feel certain he will stop supporting you once a divorce is granted (assuming you need the support).

Getting Ready To File

"I hope you can help me, I want a divorce," says a tired voice on the other end of the telephone. She must be in her late forties. Sounds like she's lived in this city all her life.

"Well, tell me a little about your situation," I say. I wonder what problems she wants a divorce to solve. Is she bored, tired, angry, or lonely? Have her children all left home? Does her husband beat her up? Is she looking for a new life, or just trying to survive in this one?

She's feeling a little of all of the above. Mostly frustrated and worried. Very worried. What's she to do with herself? She suggested going back to work-- it would help the financial situation--but he's dead set against it. "My wife doesn't have to work! What will people think--I'm not earning enough to make you happy?" That was a long time ago. It's getting harder and harder to talk about it. He's drinking more, sometimes he roughs her up . . . "a little. Nothing serious."

She went to a counselor. Feels she's tried everything. Divorce seems to be the only way out. "I feel so boxed in." I tell her about legal services and ask her to call back if she cannot find a lawyer or has any trouble with one. Is she interested in discussion groups? "No, I'm a pretty private person," but I can hear her smiling.

She's one of hundreds of anonymous women. Some mornings I think every woman in the city over twenty must be thinking about divorce. Sometimes I worry. Do they think of divorce as a new lease on life? A magic solution? Are they prepared for the indignities? Telling the most intimate details of their lives to stony-faced judges, fresh young (almost always male) attorneys, and curious constables? Are they ready for the brusque lawyer who's carefully noting every six minutes of conversation? Can they afford a divorce? Are they going to be even more lonely and isolated afterwards?

Because divorce is just the final, formal step in a long march toward emotional and economic dependence, we emphasize the importance of getting ready for a divorce. Not just emotionally ready--although that's important. Here are some of the things we think you should do before you ever talk to a lawyer about a divorce.

Decide what you want from a divorce. There's a lot more in it than just freedom from your husband. What are your positive goals for your own life? What do you want to be doing a year from now? Five years from now? Fantasize for a moment. Do you want more education, a better job, a different life-style? How can you accomplish these goals? What stands in your way? What will help you? You should look at the chapter on financial resources and housing before you decide to give up some of your more realistic fantasies. Now is a time to explore, see what is possible.

Set your goals before you see a lawyer. Remember: A divorce by itself will not work any miracles. After the immediate relief (and/or loneliness) wears off, what will you have? You might find yourself bitterly disappointed if you haven't planned in advance for what comes after the divorce.

You might want to talk to psychologists, therapists, close friends, or women's groups if you feel you need help in evaluating your goals and figuring out how to achieve them. It is often difficult to decide for yourself which of your ideas is unrealistic, which too modest.

Do not expect any help from your lawyer with these questions. A lawyer can help you navigate through the seas of
legal papers and bring you to one of your goals--that of
no longer being legally married. The emotional part of
the divorce and the development of a new life for yourself
is in your hands.

Separate your legal from your non-legal questions. Many
women look to divorce to solve all their problems and go
to a lawyer as a first step toward preparing for their new
life. The lawyer should be the last person you see. Lawyers are the most expensive source of advice you can get
for anything but strictly legal problems. Most of your
initial questions will have nothing to do with the law.
They will have to do with putting your life in order and
planning for the future. Save the decision-making process
for those who are qualified to help you make decisions--
friends, therapists, and others you trust. Use the law to
inform yourself about your rights and to give a concrete
shape to the decisions you have already made.

Make divorce the final step. Settle property, support,
and custody first. Once you decide to begin the legal
process of getting separated and becoming independent,
take care of long-range questions first. Support, property division, custody, and visitation should all be settled
by the time a divorce is granted; the divorce is the *final*
step--a seal on your declaration of independence. The
divorce itself won't solve any problems; it can only announce the solutions you have already made. Remember: The
creative part of being a woman in transition comes from
the decisions you make. Independence is not something
that a court or a lawyer can win for you.

> *The legal structure in the United States is based
> on a generally held societal assumption that a
> woman should secure an adequate standard of living
> through pleasing her husband and through womanly
> wiles. If the marriage fails, fault may be
> ascribed to her lack of femininity or skills in
> being a good wife and mother. ("Recognition of
> Economic Contribution of Homemakers and Protection
> of Children in Divorce Law and Practice," Citizen's
> Advisory Council on the Status of Women)*

From No Divorce To No-Fault: A Brief History

Not too far back in the history of the Anglo-American
legal system, there was no such thing as divorce, at least

not as we know it today. In the days when there were two
legal systems--one run by the state and one run by the
church (of England)--divorce was a matter which could be
handled only in the church ("ecclesiastical") system.

The church, of course, had very strong ideas about the institution of marriage. It was begun with a sacrament and
was considered an almost sacred institution. You might
well suspect that everybody but Henry the Eighth had an
awful time trying to get a divorce. The church just didn't
believe in it, and at that time, the state had nothing to
say about it.

Two rather limited forms of divorce were created to accommodate the likes of Henry the Eighth and other influential
people who had made unsatisfactory marriages. The first
was "annulment," which is not really a form of divorce at
all. An annulment declares that the marriage was *never
valid.*

Like divorce, there were (and are) very specific grounds
for annulment, such as the fact that one or both parties
were under age, mentally incompetent, drunk at the time
of the marriage, or already married to another party, but
these were often elaborated and interpreted to fit some
most unlikely situations.

The other form of divorce in the ecclesiastical system was
the divorce "from bed and board." It permitted the husband
and wife to eat at separate tables (boards) and sleep in
different beds. It did not change the fact that they were
married to each other, and neither party to this form of
divorce was allowed to remarry. This form of "divorce"
also survives in some states today as "separate maintenance" or by the old name--divorce AMET (*a menso et thoro*--
bed and board).

This form of divorce was usually considered fair because
it allowed the wife to live apart from the often offending
husband, but continued his obligation to support her as a
form of punishment (and incidentally saving public chari-
ties for those unfortunate women without men to support
them).

Eventually the state won most of the battles for control
of the courts in England. Divorce became a "civil" matter,
and slowly (very slowly) the rules and grounds for divorce
became slightly more realistic. We must emphasize very
slightly. It was not until 1966 that New York residents

could get a divorce on any grounds other than adultery!
During the early 1970s several states lept forward into
the twentieth century. California, Iowa, Florida, Oregon,
Michigan, and Colorado had adopted a "no-fault" divorce
law and several other states, including New York and New
Jersey, had adopted a modified "no-fault" divorce by mutual
consent and separation for a specified period.

"No-Fault" Divorce

Ever since New Mexico made "incompatibility" a ground for
divorce in 1933, states have been inching toward "no-fault"
divorce. By 1963, 21 states allowed divorce after a specified period of separation (in most of these states some
kind of intent to desert--usually a malicious intent--was
also required).

In 1970 the National Conference of Commissioners on Uniform
State Laws proposed a "Uniform Marriage and Divorce Act"
which was ready for adoption in any state whose legislature
would approve it. Unlike most of the recommendations of
the prestigious Commissioners, this one was not popular
with the American Bar Association or the legislators. Most
observers take this as a rejection of no-fault divorce on
the part of lawyers who feel that "no fault" will mean
less money for divorce lawyers.

Under the Uniform Marriage and Divorce Act (UMDA), a divorce
may be granted if a court finds the marriage is "irretriev-
ably broken," even if one of the parties believes the breakdown is *not* permanent.

If the parties do not agree that a divorce is appropriate,
the court can order a conciliation conference. In some
states the "conference" is mandatory--at least in form.
"Irretrievable breakdown" is currently the only ground for
divorce in Arizona, Colorado, Florida, Iowa, Kentucky, Missouri, Michigan, Nebraska, Oregon, and Washington.

"Irretrievable breakdown" is defined by the UMDA as a
situation in which: (1) the parties have lived separate
and apart for a period of more than 180 days . . . or
(2) there is serious marital discord adversely affecting
the attitude of one or both the parties toward the marriage."

The difference between this ground and the "modified no-
fault" grounds in New York and New Jersey, for example, is
that in the "modified no-fault" states, both parties must

agree that the marriage is irretrievable, and in many of
these states the parties must have already been living
apart and abiding by the terms of a separation agreement
for a specified period--usually 12-18 months.

"Irretrievable breakdown" of a marriage has been added to
the traditional grounds for divorce in Alabama, Connecticut,
Georgia, Hawaii, Indiana, Maine, Maryland, Montana, and New
Hampshire. In these states the parties have a choice between fault and no-fault. In the strict "no-fault" states
listed above as having adopted the UMDA, there are no-fault
grounds.

Most other states also have "separation" for specified
periods of time as a ground for divorce. Illinois, Massachusetts, Mississippi, Pennsylvania, Ohio, and South Dakota
are conservative strongholds where you will find nothing
even faintly resembling a no-fault ground for divorce.

Thus, in all but about a dozen states divorce is the expensive prize you must win by playing a legalistic game
which pits power and skill against chance. In private and
among colleagues most lawyers and legislators will frankly
admit that no-fault is not, in reality, such a departure
from the traditional scheme. Anyone can get a divorce
today, even in the strictest of states--if she is only
willing to lie a little.

Many women are disturbed when their lawyer urges them to
lie under oath--and rightly so. The perversion of justice
involved in sticking to obsolete divorce laws is disturbing. Unfortunately, most legislators and lawyers, it seems,
would rather counsel people to lie and continue to collect
their large fees than work for realistic divorce laws.

A Word About Divorce Information

Now let's assume that you have thought about the decisions
you must make to shape your future and you have a separation agreement, or have agreed to accept a judicial decree
on support, custody and visitation, and property division.
It's time to start working on a divorce.

Unless you are going to do your own divorce, your lawyer
will know all the details about local law and procedure.
What you want to know is what a divorce means and how the
divorce laws work. The answers to these questions vary
widely from state to state in particular details, although
certain general principles remain true in every state.

There are, for example, approximately ten basic grounds for divorce, although not all of these are used in every state, and the same ground might have different names in neighboring states. In the section that follows we will describe the basic features of the divorce laws in most states, but it is important that you keep in mind that none of this information can be relied upon to tell you precisely what the law or procedure is in your own state. To learn this, you must ask a local attorney with a domestic relations practice, read local texts, form books, and rules of court, and find other people with current experience in divorce law.

Grounds for divorce are decided upon by your state legislators. They are enacted into law and written into the statute books for your state. These have titles such as "Illinois Revised Statutes," or "North Dakota Century Code," and may be found in any law library or larger public library. The statutes or laws themselves are remarkably brief and cryptic. For example, to charge your husband with "Indignities" in the state of Pennsylvania, you simply write on the Complaint in Divorce that the defendant "did from [write the date when the offensive treatment began] until [write the date of separation or the current date] offer such indignities to the person of the innocent and injured spouse, as to render her condition intolerable and life burdensome."

As you can see, it is almost impossible to know what these laws mean from reading the statutes. They only make sense once they have been interpreted by various courts. If you want to know exactly what kind of behavior and how much constitutes "Indignities" in Pennsylvania, you have to read what various courts have said about what this language means.

The easiest way to see what the grounds mean is to look for an "Annotated" version of your state statutes. These contain notes summarizing the most important interpretations given the laws. Some states publish a state *Law Encyclopedia* which explains the interpretations of all the state statutes. To find an explanation for divorce grounds, check the index under "Divorce." Another way to find out what these grounds mean is to talk to lawyers and legal workers and other people (like people who have recently been involved in a divorce) about what situations constitute which grounds.

Grounds For Divorce And Some Standard Interpretations

The grounds for divorce have traditionally been based on violations of the unwritten marriage contract. Originally adultery was the only ground for which a divorce could be obtained in most American states. In some states (Massachusetts, for example) adultery was so defined that it could be committed only by a married woman! Thus men could get divorces from their "unfaithful" wives, but a woman who was married to the town's Don Juan had no legal release from "the chains of marriage." Gradually more grounds were added until there are now over 40 different "fault" grounds recognized in various states. Some of these may have different names in different states, but mean approximately the same thing--e.g., "mental cruelty" and "indignities." Listed below are some of the most common grounds and their standard interpretations.

"Abandonment" or *"Desertion"* are grounds for divorce in every state that has not adopted the strict "no-fault" approach to divorce. Each state defines "desertion" or "abandonment" a little differently, however.

Usually you will be required to prove several things to get a divorce on this ground:

1. That your spouse intended to desert you--that he hasn't just been accidentally or absentmindedly absent and that his absence is not beyond his control. Of course, it's hard to prove what anybody else's intention was. Usually things like his saying, "I'm leaving," "I don't want to live with you any more," or "You'll never see me again" are good proof of intention. You might want neighbors, friends, or relatives to testify as to what they heard him say about his intention to leave you. In some states you will not need witnesses at all, but have to indicate what he said in a sworn written statement.

2. You will also have to show that you did not consent to his leaving, that the separation was *not* mutually agreed upon. This is true in all the strict fault states.

3. You must show that the desertion occurred more than a specified number of months ago. Usually this period is between one and two years. Warning: If you have had sexual intercourse with your husband at any time since the date of the alleged desertion, you must consider that the desertion occurred on a date after you

last slept with him. Sleeping with your husband
just once breaks the "desertion" period and you must
start to count the months all over again from the
date you last slept with him.

4. You should show that he had no good reason to leave
    you. Remember: His getting a job in Sacramento and
    moving there is not desertion if you stay in Milwau-
    kee--*you* are the one who deserted here! You must not
    have given him any good reason to leave you. Some
    courts will consider that living with your mother
    is good reason for him to leave.

5. In some states attempts at reconciliation are con-
    sidered significant. It certainly looks better if
    you tried to get him to come back and he refused. It
    may look a little funny if he "deserted" you but moved
    just a few blocks away and you made no attempt to talk
    to him since that time.

"Nonsupport" or *"Neglect Of Duty,"* a husband's failure to
support his wife, is by itself grounds for divorce in every
state *except* the following:

ALABAMA	NEW YORK
DISTRICT OF COLUMBIA	NORTH CAROLINA
GEORGIA	PENNSYLVANIA
HAWAII	SOUTH CAROLINA
ILLINOIS	TENNESSEE
LOUISIANA	TEXAS
MARYLAND	VIRGIN ISLANDS
MINNESOTA	VIRGINIA
MISSISSIPPI	WEST VIRGINIA
NEW JERSEY	

In the above-listed states, your husband's failure to support you may be added to other kinds of offensive behavior
to constitute some other ground (e.g., "mental cruelty"),
but may not be used alone as a ground for divorce.

In all other states, you may get a divorce based on the
sole fact that your husband failed to support you. What
does "failed to support you" mean? It is obvious that your
husband need not support you in luxurious fashion. On the
other hand, he is required to see that you don't starve,

go naked or homeless.

Thus, in half the states you have a right to divorce your husband if you can show that he deliberately failed to fulfill his duty as a provider. This is qualified by several factors. He is only obligated to support you according to his ability. You can't sue him for divorce just because you'd like a higher standard of living, but you may be able to get a divorce in these states if he refuses to work or look for work. Courts today will also consider your earning ability when you claim "nonsupport" as a ground for divorce.

"Adultery" is a ground for divorce in every state in the union (except those with strict "no-fault" grounds only). Adultery is defined as sexual intercourse with anyone other than the complaining spouse. Wife or husband swapping does not count--you consented to that adultery (even though you may now wish you hadn't). Nor can a party who has been guilty of adultery complain of her spouse's extramarital activities. The reasons for these two rules may be found in the section on defenses to divorce.

Contrary to detective shows and popular myth, adultery is not a popular ground for divorce. It is difficult to prove and can, in many cases, be easily "defended" (see section on defenses to divorce). A party suing for divorce on the ground of adultery is often trying to get revenge. In some states there is an additional "penalty" attached to this ground. If the complaining party so chooses, he or she may name the party with whom the alleged adultery took place and prevent those two parties from marrying during the lifetime of the complaining spouse.

Most spouses, no matter how embittered, do not carry out their threats to sue on the ground of adultery. It just is not practical. To prove adultery the plaintiff must convince a judge that the defendant and a specific third person did, at some specific time and place, have the desire and the opportunity to have intercourse. The time, place, opportunity, and inclination or desire must all be proved by the plaintiff. Merely knowing that your spouse is seeing another person is not enough to prove adultery, although it might form the basis of a charge of mental cruelty, indignities, or incompatibility. If you have considered using adultery as a ground for divorce, read over some of the other grounds and see if they don't just as accurately describe the harm that has been done to you. Other grounds are a lot easier to prove and much more

dignified. You will probably save no small amount in lawyer's fees by choosing the less complicated ground.

Of *"Alcoholism," "Drug Addiction,"* and *"Insanity,"* alcoholism is a ground for divorce in all but fourteen states.
Drug addiction is recognized as a ground for divorce in
only eleven, while insanity is a ground for divorce in all
but twenty states. In states where these are not specific
grounds, they may form the basis of other grounds, such as
"mental cruelty" or "incompatibility."

Alcoholism and drug addiction must be prolonged and continuing conditions in order to constitute grounds for divorce. There is usually a specific length of time over
which these conditions must exist, and they must continue
into the present time. You may not divorce your husband
because he has been an alcoholic in the past if he is no
longer an alcoholic (or a drug addict).

Basically, the plaintiff using either of these grounds must
show that her spouse has a long-standing and apparently uncontrollable (or at least long-uncontrolled) habit of using
intoxicants to such an extent that it disrupts the marital
and/or family relationship.

Some states allow divorce on the ground of insanity, while
a few others make insanity a "defense" to a divorce--in
other words, your spouse's insanity makes it *impossible* for
you to divorce him. In states where insanity is a ground
for divorce, the plaintiff must show by psychiatric evidence that the defendant was or should have been (depending on the state) committed to a mental institution. If
your husband is presently seeing a psychiatrist every day
of the week and has been diagnosed as psychotic, you
probably do not have grounds for divorce. Not unless you
can also find a psychiatrist who will testify that he
should be committed to a mental institution.

Divorces on the ground of insanity are expensive for the
plaintiff--she must pay the psychiatrists for their expert
opinions and she must pay all court costs. Often a divorce
will be granted on this ground only on the condition that
the divorcing spouse shall pay all institutional and medical costs for the insane spouse so long as they both live.
In some states, divorcing an insane spouse is virtually
impossible because the state does not want to take on the
financial responsibility for his care and treatment.

"Mental Cruelty," or *"Indignities," "Cruel and Inhuman*

Treatment," along with "desertion" and "incompatibility"
are the most popular grounds in most states requiring
fault. The name varies from state to state, but in each
of these states you will find one ground for divorce
based on one spouse's utter disregard for the happiness
or well-being of the other. Incidents which qualify as
examples of this kind of treatment may range from mere
insults to physical abuse of all but the most severe
kind.

Usually these grounds require a course of conduct over a
fairly long period of time (specified in some states, un-
specified in others). A single insult or a single slap in
the face does not constitute grounds for divorce, but a
persistent pattern of behavior showing your husband's
total lack of respect or care for you as a person does.

Obviously, legislatures and courts are not going to allow
divorces for the normal stresses involved in a marriage.
Whatever the name of the ground and whatever actually happened to you, you must be able to demonstrate (or at least
swear) that your husband's conduct is making your life
miserable ("burdensome" according to some states).

You will include in your proof of these grounds such
things as insults to you in public, physical assaults
short of those which give you reason to fear for your
life (see "Cruel and Barbarous Treatment"), a pattern of
inattention to you and/or your children, gross insensi-
tivity, and the like. It is important to show how you
were injured by his conduct. If you ignored his insults
and injuries and haven't suffered, you don't deserve a
divorce. If you got migraines, ulcers, or had sleepless
nights, or got bruises, rashes, or any other physical or
mental disturbance as a result of his treatment, you are
a good candidate for a divorce on one of these grounds.
If you consulted a doctor, psychologist, family counsel-
or or therapist, or missed work or school, you have still
more evidence of the seriousness of the harm done to you
and the importance of a divorce to your general well-
being.

There is one enormous drawback to using grounds like
these. They are terribly undignified and often painful
ways of getting a divorce. Of course, there is not usually any more dignified or less painful way possible. If
you use these grounds in a state which requires testimony
before a judge, you will be required to reveal some of the
most intimate and painful details of your life to a middle-

aged man (who probably has heard them all before and finds his job a terrible bore) who is the judge, a few lawyers, and other people who are waiting to tell their sad and embarrassing stories. You must simply familiarize yourself with the stylized "story" made up of the incidents that tend to prove your ground for divorce exists, then steel yourself to recite it before a bunch of unconcerned strangers.

Another problem for many women is that their husbands never really did beat them, insult them in public, or stay away from home three nights in a row without calling to say they were all right. "Do you have to lie to get a divorce?" they want to know. Most lawyers, if they are honest, will answer "Yes." If you want a divorce, if you have no other ground and your state does not recognize voluntary separation, incompatibility, or some "no-fault" ground, you must lie if you are determined to get a divorce. That's the way the divorce law is written, and most judges and lawyers ignore the enormous amount of perjury created by these laws.

"Physical Cruelty" is a ground for divorce in almost every state which has any fault ground for divorce at all. Acts which constitute physical cruelty must be much more serious than those which constitute "mental cruelty" or "indignities." In some states you must have been given reason to fear for your life as a result of physical injuries (not just threats) received from your husband.

If you are considering using this ground, you should have medical evidence of the injuries received, their extent, frequency, and seriousness. Mere hitting and slapping, even if it resulted in a broken nose, will not qualify for physical cruelty (although it could be part of a charge of "indignities" or "mental cruelty," and would certainly be good evidence of "incompatibility"). Nor can you use merely accidental injuries as evidence of physical cruelty.

You must show that the physical acts indicated either an uncontrollable and dangerous tendency to violence on the part of your spouse, or that his feeling toward you was manifested in the physical cruelty. In some states, the insistence of a party infected with venereal disease on having intercourse will constitute physical cruelty if the other spouse becomes infected. In most states a spouse's unreasonable sexual demands are more appropriately included in "mental cruelty" or "indignities."

"Voluntary Separation" is a ground for divorce in the following states:

ALABAMA	NEW JERSEY
ARIZONA	NEW MEXICO
ARKANSAS	NEW YORK
DELAWARE	PUERTO RICO
DISTRICT OF COLUMBIA	RHODE ISLAND
HAWAII	SOUTH CAROLINA
IDAHO	TENNESSEE
KENTUCKY	TEXAS
LOUISIANA	UTAH
MARYLAND	VERMONT
MINNESOTA	WASHINGTON
NEBRASKA	WEST VIRGINIA
NEVADA	WISCONSIN

There are three basic kinds of "voluntary separation" grounds.

1. New York, New Jersey, and several other states have recently adopted "voluntary separation" as a modified "no-fault" ground for divorce. In these states both parties must have agreed to live separately and have done so for a prescribed length of time (12 to 18 months usually). Some states require efforts at "conciliation" or have voluntary conciliation conferences for those who wish them. In some states a divorce on "voluntary separation" grounds will only be granted to parties who have abided by the terms of a written separation agreement for the prescribed time.

2. Many states have recognized "voluntary separation" as a no-fault sort of ground for many decades. Length of time for the separation runs from one year to seven years. So long as the defendant does not contest the divorce, fault is irrelevant for this ground. Connecticut, North Carolina, New Hampshire, and Vermont all recognize this type of "voluntary separation."

3. A more ancient form of "voluntary separation" is recognized in many other states. The "seven years gone--presumed dead" rule makes it possible for spouses to obtain a divorce after their errant partner has disappeared, so long as *no one* has heard from the "absent" one.

Other important grounds for divorce include:

Incompatibility (Alabama, Alaska, Delaware, Kansas, Nevada, North Dakota, Oklahoma, and Vermont).

Fraud, if the fraud is related to an essential basis of the marriage--e.g., mistaken identity. In eleven states this is a ground for divorce, in most others it is ground for annulment.

Under Age Of Consent is a ground for divorce in only four states. In some states it is a ground for annulment.

Incest (5 states).

Attempted Murder (2 states).

Religion Forbidding Intercourse (Kansas and New Hampshire).

Imprisonment or *Conviction of a Felony* is a ground for divorce in several states.

Beware of "Collusion"

A divorce may be denied in "fault" states if the judge
finds there is too little contest. If it is clear that
you both really wanted the divorce and you agreed to help
each other get the divorce, you may lose your chance to
get unmarried! You are guilty of collusion! An agreement
to get a divorce is called "collusion," and states that
require fault as part of the ground for divorce require
the plaintiff to swear that there is no collusion involved.
This does not mean that the defendant must contest the
divorce, but it does mean you and your husband are not
supposed to sit down together and figure out who will file,
what the charges will be, and who will pay the attorney's
fees. Technically this is collusion. In reality, it may
seem like a civilized way to get a divorce.

Very few uncontested divorces are denied. Occasionally
this happens. A judge may deny a divorce where there is
evidence of collusion, or where he or she finds that there
are grounds for divorce on both sides. If it is clear
from your testimony that both parties contributed to and
are responsible for the marital breakdown, a judge may
find that there is no "innocent and injured party." You
deserve each other and not a divorce. For further explanation of the thought behind denying divorces for these
reasons, read "On Contested Divorces and Defenses"--but
remember, a judge may find that these defenses exist in
your case even though your husband does not contest; on
the contrary--he may have been too eager to help you get
divorced!

On Contested Divorces And Defenses

Contested divorces are long, drawn-out, expensive, and
usually bitter affairs. The vast majority of divorces
are never contested, for just this reason. Even when the
defendant would rather not be divorced, it's seldom worth
the $1,000 or more it may cost to keep a divorce from
going through.

There are, however, often good reasons for threatening to
contest a divorce. This may be one of your best bargaining weapons in a difficult separation agreement negotiation.
If you are the defendant in a divorce action and you do not
want it to go through, you may want to contest. If you are
the plaintiff, you hope the defendant won't contest, or you
give in on some difficult issue in a separation agreement
in order to avoid a contest. In either case you should

have a lawyer.

A contested divorce gives you an opportunity to see the "adversary system of justice" at what may be its most adverse moment. Witnesses in contested divorces must be prepared to undergo sometimes hostile cross-examination. The lawyer for your spouse will object to the introduction of much of your evidence and testimony on any of many technical grounds. Since you know the plaintiff in a contested divorce is almost certain to be represented by a lawyer, it is foolish to contest without a lawyer.

There are several ways in which to contest a divorce. The most obvious is to deny that you did the things charged in the divorce complaint. In many states, this involves filing a "Motion for a Bill of Particulars," in which the plaintiff is requested to spell out precisely which incidents in your marriage he has in mind as the basis for the ground he has chosen. You then deny that the events transpired as he says in a formal "Answer." Later you will both have a chance to tell your side of the story in court and be cross-examined by the other party's lawyer.

If you carry the contest to trial, your lawyer must convince a judge that the statements your husband is making about your behavior are either not true or, if true, not strong enough to meet the legal standard of proof for that ground in your state.

Another tactic is to claim one of the recognized defenses to a divorce. The three most important defenses have appropriately gothic names: "condonation," "recrimination," and "connivance." They all have in common the fact that they do not deny that what the plaintiff says in the complaint is true. Rather, they say, "Yes, but . . . ." For example, if you charge your husband with adultery, he may reply with, "Yes, I did commit adultery, but so did my wife."

It then becomes a question of who is telling the truth and what is the whole story? Does either party have grounds for divorce? Both of you? Or just one? If the judge finds that you both have committed acts which constitute grounds for divorce--no divorce: you deserve each other! This is the principle of "recrimination." When you were little it was called "getting even," or "he hit me first." At any rate, it won't work in a divorce situation, and you'd better be sure when you ask for a divorce that your husband will not be able to show (or would not be willing to show) that he also has grounds for divorce.

Next, there's "condonation." "Condonation" is a particularly quaint term. It means you forgave him for all the
hideous offenses--usually by sleeping with him. In order
to support a charge of adultery (or desertion in some
states) you must show, should he contest and assert the
defense of condonation, that you did not voluntarily sleep
with him (thereby forgiving him) after the offenses
occurred.

Finally, there's "connivance." You've heard of "conniving
women"? Well, connivance is tricking your husband (or
being tricked by him) into giving him (or you) grounds for
divorce. Basically it means that you can't actively encourage (or even consent to) what would be grounds for
divorce, then complain about it as an "innocent and injured" spouse. If you agreed to mate-swap and then decide
you got a bad deal, you can't sue him for adultery. You
consented. You can't support your husband's drug habit,
and then turn him in and get a divorce on the ground that
he has been sentenced to a term of imprisonment.

One of the few good things that can be said for these
defenses is that they are on their way out. They are
recognized in a limited number of situations (usually
adultery, sometimes desertion). Recrimination has been
abolished as a defense in several states, as even the
lawmakers can see that nobody benefits from a policy which
forces people to stay married once the marriage has broken
down by standards the state itself has established.

There is one other, seldom-used defense to divorce, called
"laches" or the "statute of limitations." This means that
if your husband is guilty of behavior which amounts to a
ground for divorce (like physical cruelty), you can't wait
until ten years later to due for a divorce based on that
incident.

Twenty-five years after the "adultery" may be too late to
complain--and the likelihood of "condonation" by this time
is pretty strong. This does not mean, however, that you
cannot get a divorce at the end of twenty-five years of
continuous mental or physical cruelty. You can always
say, "I've tried and tried, and now I know it just won't
work." (Or--"I just don't think I'll last much longer.")
What you *cannot* do is wait an unreasonably long time after
the last incident on which you base your complaint.

Migratory Divorce

State boundaries may have as little meaning to modern
Americans as they do to wild Canadian geese. Many of us
commute to work in another state every day. Ours is a
migratory society; people don't live in the same town they
grew up in; chances are you've moved since your marriage,
and it is quite possible that if you are separated now,
you and your husband are no longer living in the same
state.

State borders have little reality in the social and economic lives of Americans today. Unfortunately, our present
degree of mobility was not foreseen by the men who wrote
the Constitution. They regarded state borders as very significant and reserved for each state the right to make its
own laws affecting its own citizens.

The contrast between our mobile life-style and our state-
based laws creates much chaos and confusion in the area of
separation and divorce, support and custody. Authors of
law journal articles and Supreme Court justices mull over
the meaning of the "full faith and credit" doctrine* in the
Constitution while women in New Jersey try to enforce support orders against husbands in North Dakota. Divorce-
desperate spouses pack up and move to Nevada for six weeks,
or go to the Dominican Republic for a divorce weekend.

Often, the desperate spouses (and the deserted ones) are
understandably confused about the effect of a legal action--
such as a support order--entered in another state. They
are in good company. Many of these questions have yet to
be definitively answered by the United States Supreme Court,
so there are no clear answers, only reasonably safe predic-
tions and generalizations.

Adoption of a uniform marriage and divorce act would remedy
much of the present confusion but, as we noted earlier,
this does not seem likely in the near future. At least ten
states--Nebraska, New Hampshire, California, North Dakota,
Rhode Island, South Carolina, Washington, and Wisconsin
(Louisiana adopted and repealed)--have adopted something
called a "Uniform Divorce Recognition Act" which is neither

---

* Basically, the "full faith and credit" doctrine means
  that any judicial decision which is valid in one state
  should be enforceable in any other state. Unfortunately,
  after a few hundred years of interpretation by judges and
  lawyers, it is no longer so simple.

"uniform" nor an act recognizing foreign divorces. In
fact, the Act has been adopted in only the above ten states,
and rather than provide for the recognition of divorces
granted in other states it does quite the reverse! It
specifies conditions under which migratory divorces will
be "of no force or effect" outside the state in which they
were granted.

In short, the topic of "migratory" or "foreign" divorce is
very complicated, highly theoretical, and hard to under-
stand--mainly because none of the lawmakers can come to
terms with the conflict between our present-day mobility
and the supremacy granted individual states in the United
States Constitution.

Of course, you are not interested in many of the theoretical aspects of migratory divorce. You just want to know
whether you are liable to become "undivorced" by walking,
driving, or flying across state lines. The following is
an attempt to help you decide how to answer that question
according to the facts in your life.

To begin with, let's consider what is meant by a "migratory"
or "foreign" divorce. The word "foreign" in this context
is revealing--usually something is "foreign" if it comes
from another nation. Foreign divorces, on the other hand,
are those which are granted in a state (or nation) other
than the state in which both parties have their permanent
residence.

If you and your husband have a permanent residence in Arizona but go to school in California for the summer and stay
there long enough to meet the residency requirements for
divorce in California, get divorced, and then return to
Arizona, you have a foreign divorce. Likewise if either
of you goes to California--temporarily or permanently--
and gets a divorce there while the other stays in Arizona,
you have a foreign divorce.

"O.K.," you say, "so it's exotic--who cares if it's a foreign divorce or a home-grown one? What difference does it
make where I got my divorce?" The answer is that it can
mean the difference between being divorced and being married, or between being divorced and bigamous. It can mean
the difference between having legitimate and illegitimate
children, or support and no support.

A very important basic principle to remember about foreign
divorce is: *No state is obliged to recognize a divorce*

granted in another state. Practically, of course, the
state does not care a whole lot whether you're married or
divorced. But some foreign divorces can be successfully
attacked and rendered void under certain conditions.
Whether the out-of-state decree can be successfully attacked can be roughly gauged by a few rules of thumb.

1. A divorce which is valid in the state where both
    parties had their permanent residence at the time
    of the divorce is valid in every other state. This
    is not a foreign divorce, no matter where you or
    your husband live after the divorce.

2. A divorce which is *not valid* in the decree-granting
    state cannot be valid anywhere. You may think this
    is too obvious to state. Before we are done with
    the Alice-in-Wonderland of foreign divorces, you
    will be thankful for these small certainties.

3. A divorce that is valid in the decree-granting state
    (e.g., Vermont) and which neither of the parties
    wishes to challenge at a later date is presumed to
    be valid and continues in effect in every other state.
    This could be called the "sleeping dogs lie" princi-
    ple. In order for a foreign divorce to be challenged
    and invalidated, one of the parties to the divorce
    must complain. Thus, divorces which are not contested
    and in which both parties participated (or acquiesced)
    rarely, if ever, present any problems. The prob-
    lem is usually with the "ex parte" (one-sided) divorce.

If the defendant did not participate in the divorce, but
was merely notified of the proceeding, she or he may have
grounds to challenge the validity of that divorce in
another state. The challenge is usually to the effect
that the defendant was not sufficiently notified of the
proceeding so that the divorce violated basic principles of
"due process" (procedural fairness) which is required for
any judgment to be valid. Requirements for what constitutes "fair notice" range all the way from publication in
a local newspaper to receipt of a registered letter marked
"Deliver to Addressee Only."

If you wish to challenge the validity of a foreign divorce,
you need a lawyer. If you have obtained a foreign divorce
which your husband threatens to challenge, you will also
need a lawyer--preferably one from the state where your
husband is bringing the challenge.

So what should you do if your husband goes to another state
and you are notified that he has instituted divorce proceedings against you? If you are just as happy to let him get
the divorce, do nothing with regard to the divorce itself--
support and custody are coming up in the next section.

Suppose you are not happy with his getting the divorce--
what can you do then? You should talk to a lawyer as soon
as possible. The lawyer may advise one of two things: Contest the foreign divorce. (This means having this lawyer
go to the state where the divorce is being brought or hiring
a lawyer in that state to represent you, and possibly having
to go there yourself.) Or refuse to participate in the divorce so that you can challenge it in your own state.

There is one other way to challenge a foreign divorce. If
you act immediately and your husband has not been out of
the state very long, you can try to get an injunction
against the divorce proceeding in the other state. In
order to do this, you would have to prove that your husband
is not actually a permanent resident of that state.

You should know that there is a danger in letting the foreign divorce be decided against you. Courts don't really
like to set aside divorces, especially if either party
has remarried. If you wait awhile before challenging the
foreign decree, the court in your own state may find that
you acquiesced in the decree, that you consented to the
decree, or that your failure to challenge the decree prior
to this time has led others (your husband and maybe his new
wife and family) to rely on the fact that you would not
challenge it. This is known as the doctrine of "estoppel."
It works in your favor when you are the one obtaining a
foreign divorce and when it is not challenged immediately.

Divisible Divorce

So far we have only been talking about the divorce itself--
the decree that announces a change in your marital status.
Most marriages involve a lot more than marital status--
there are usually children, property, and support obligations. In order to deal with the problems created by these
matters in families who live in different states, the law
has created the concept of "divisible divorce."

What this term means is that while a court might have
the power to grant a final divorce, it may not have the
power to decide where the children will live, how much
support the father will have to pay, and whether or not

the wife is entitled to alimony.

Questions of custody, visitation, property, and support are seen as "divisible" or separate from the question of the marital status of the parties. In order for a court to make a binding decision about these more complicated matters, both parties must be brought within the "personal jurisdiction" of the court to have their side of the story represented.

Thus, if your husband runs away and sues for a divorce, which is granted, and you have not participated in the foreign divorce proceedings--although you were properly notified--you have not lost your right to support for yourself or your children. He may get a perfectly valid divorce and still be liable for child support or even alimony if the state in which *you* live finds that you are entitled to it.

If you are the one to sue for divorce, you should always try to settle custody, support, and property division at the same time, either by agreement or in the same court that grants the divorce. If you are the defendant and your husband is suing you in another state, you may go to his state and sue him there. Any order for support, custody, or property division issued in his state will be legally binding and enforceable in your home state. This is the most certain way of enforcing your rights once he has left the state. You can, of course, hire a lawyer in the other state, but you will probably have to appear in that state eventually for the hearing.

Another possibility is to stay in your own state and sue him there. Many states have "long arm" statutes which will allow you to sue him in your home state after he has left if you were married in that state or if he committed the grounds for divorce in the state where you now live. If your state has no such "long arm" statute, or if you are now living in a state your husband has had little or no connection with, your only option is to sue for support in the state where he now resides.

If you have a support order which was entered in another state--the state in which your husband is currently residing--you may have it enforced in that state, and it is fairly safe to handle the whole matter through an attorney in that state without ever going there yourself. Enforcement hearings are fairly routine, and once you have the support order, your presence in the courtroom is not so

essential. You may not even need a lawyer in the other
state, however, thanks to the Uniform Reciprocal Support
Act, which makes support orders decreed in one state
effective in all the others. Once he falls behind or
stops paying as ordered, you may start enforcement procedures in your own state.

The question of custody in a foreign divorce is treated
somewhat differently from the question of support. In the
custody situation, the state in which your *children* are
living is usually the best place to bring a custody suit.
This may or may not be the state in which your husband is
living. It is obvious that if you are filing for custody
in another state, you will want to be there in person to
oversee the case and to testify, if need be, or negotiate
with whomever has custody.

Finally, property division can be made in the state where
the property is as well as the state in which the property
holder (your husband) is. So if you owned a house in Kentucky and he's moved to Georgia, you can sue for a divorce
and get the property settlement in a Kentucky court. If
he has taken all the proceeds from the sale of the house
with him to Georgia, you can sue him in the state where
he committed the wrong (Kentucky) if that state has the
proper long arm statute. Otherwise you must go where he
and the property are located.

After The Divorce: A Woman's Right To Her Own Name

"My name is the symbol of my identity which must not be
lost," declared Lucy Stone, who, in 1855, became the first
American woman to keep her own name after getting married.
In 1921 the Lucy Stone League, a group whose goal was to
establish the legal right of a married woman to use her own
name, was established. The League was important in winning
many early victories for women who wanted to use their
birth names. However, the right of a woman to use this
name after marriage remains a complex issue today. Married women who wish to use their birth names are still
faced with many bureaucratic and social obstacles.

Most states now recognize the right of a woman to retake
her birth name after a divorce. Some states put conditions
on this right--women with children may not retake their
birth names in Arkansas, Michigan, South Dakota, West
Virginia, and Wisconsin. In Kentucky, New Hampshire, and
Oklahoma, name changes are granted only to women who are
not at fault in the divorce.

Recently some of the obstacles which face a woman who wants
to retain or regain her birth name have been removed or
reduced by court decisions and state attorney generals'
opinions. Most of these are based on the common-law right
of any person to use any name she or he chooses so long as
she or he is not doing so to defraud creditors or others.
Hawaii is the *only* state in the United States requiring a
woman to take her husband's name. In all other states a
woman need not *ever* use her husband's name. In all other
states, a woman is able--in theory--to change back to her
birth name after using that of her husband without going
to court. In reality it is much harder to retake your
birth name than it is to keep it.

If a married woman has taken her husband's name and wishes
to regain her birth name or take another name, she has two
options in most states. Procedures vary from state to
state. The first option is to change her name through the
common-law process, which consists of simply adopting and
using her new name. In many states this procedure will be
complicated by opposition from state officials--voting
registrars, heads of departments of motor vehicles, and
the like. A woman who decides to change her name by this
method should (try to) collect as much identification
(social security card, driver's license, credit cards)
in her new name, in order to "prove" to stubborn officials
that she is now identified by this name.

A second option is the formal name-change procedure in
effect in your state. Although a formal court proceeding
may eliminate many problems in dealing with officials,
the procedure often has its own difficulties. In a few
places it may be easy, does not require a lawyer, and is
inexpensive; in other states a lawyer is customary and
court costs may be several hundred dollars. In addition,
a judge may require an explanation of why you want your
name changed. If he is not satisfied, he may deny your
request. Name changes which have been denied can be
appealed.

For further information, we suggest you contact the Center
for a Woman's Own Name--261 Kimberly, Barrington, Illinois
60010. The Center publishes a booklet dealing with applicable law and personal experiences of women who have changed
their names. Price: $2.00.

By custom, the surname of a "legitimate" child is that of
its father. However, most states do not have laws which
require this, and in the absence of such a law, common law

allows any name to be written on the birth certificate of a
newborn child. Thus, a child could be given the surname
of its mother, or a hyphenated name including the surnames
of both parents, or even a completely different name. However, even where such laws do not exist, the prevailing
practice of using the father's surname on the birth certificate is so entrenched that use of any other name is apt
to be strongly resisted (by the hospital administrators,
or whoever fills out such forms), and some kind of legal
action may be necessary to enforce your common-law right
to give the child a surname other than that of your husband.
If you wish to give your child any other name, you should
know precisely what the law does or doesn't say in your
state. Before you go to the hospital to have a baby, you
should be in touch with a lawyer who will speak to hospital
administrators if necessary.

In states where the common-law rule prevails, minors can
change their surnames without going through legal proceedings; however, the practice in most schools, for example,
is to require the use of the name on the child's birth
certificate, and nothing short of a court order will convince a school to accept a different surname.

Where legal proceedings are either required by law or made
necessary by practice as described above, it will usually
be necessary to have the father's consent to the use of
any surname other than his, especially where the parents
are together, or if the father is contributing to the support of the child and the parents are separated. This will
be easy, of course, in the case where both parents are
changing their names to a common one (as in a hyphenated
name), but if the mother has kept her name after marriage,
she will probably not be able to give her name to the children of the marriage without her husband's consent.

After divorce, the situation is much the same. A father
who is contributing to the support of his children who
are now living with their mother will probably be able to
block any name change of those children, even where the
mother has legally retaken her pre-marriage name or legally
changed her surname entirely. It is sometimes possible for
a woman to change her children's names under a name-change
law in spite of the father's objection, but this has usually been done where the wife merely wants to change the
children's name from that of her first husband to that of
her second.

For more information on children's names, write to the Center
for a Woman's Own Name, 261 Kimberley, Barrington, Illinois
60010.

►►► *BETTY*

*In April of 1971 I left my now ex-husband believing
that I was a total nothing as a person, inadequate
as a woman, a poor mother, valueless, unemotional,
and ready and wanting to die. My excuse not to make
an attempt to commit suicide was that I had two small
children whom I felt would be worse off with their
father than with me, although I wasn't that sure that
I could do much for them myself.*

*At the time of my separation he was taking drugs, not
working, forgot to come home, and used me as his
punching bag. His rage and violence caused black
eyes, bruised ribs, back injuries, etc. But most of
all it gave me the feeling of nothingness and a constant emotional state of depression. Being slapped,
punched, kicked, and dragged over furniture was/is
not my idea of showing love and affection. After
four years of living this way I realized that no
matter how I cared for him emotionally, I was beginning to hate him, and could not help someone who
was unwilling to admit that he had a problem. With
this in mind, I left.*

*In order to leave the house with my children it was
necessary to have the police there, as he was
attempting to prevent their going with me. Not
having pre-planned this, I didn't have much of a
choice as to where to go, and so went to the home
of my parents. Two days later he and his brother
entered my parents' home and forceably took my
children while I was working.*

*This began another round of battles. Magistrates,
court hearings, lawyers--this is where I spent much
time, energy, and all the money I could get my hands
on for the next two years. Because of the children
being used as pawns, it was necessary to obtain
legal custody. Since you must have a lawyer to do
anything in the county where I live, this cost
$250.00. It took about ten minutes in front of a
judge, a month of my visiting them while they lived
with their father, and an emotional upheaval that is
unexplainable. (When I went to visit the children,
I always took someone else with me as I was afraid
of being beaten.)*

The children were returned to me, and in June of that year we moved into an apartment in another section of the county. After several beatings and more court hassles, I discovered that I was a domestic problem. In my opinion this is worse than death beacuse no matter what action was taken legally, all my husband had to do was say he wouldn't do it again. I moved again, this time into the city.

Prior to this move and after seeing several lawyers, I began divorce proceedings. This was in May of 1972. The fee for divorce was $600.00, which included nine months of aggravation, no help from the lawyer when it was desperately needed, and no settlement agreement or any of the things that are normally included when you are paying someone for services.

Although I knew it was a usual practice to have a settlement agreement included in the divorce, I abided by the lawyer's advice that I should wait until the divorce was over. I have since learned that his reason for doing this was that he intended to charge $35.00 per hour to do anything outside the divorce. Because of my dealings with lawyers and the judicial system, I have become untrusting of our "system" and am no longer as legally naive as I was.

As I previously mentioned, we moved into the city, but I'm sorry to say this did not hinder my husband from breaking down my door and also the beatings continued. Still being told that I was a domestic problem and that there wasn't much that could be done, I was ready to give up completely. This was when I made my first contact with Women in Transition. It was with their support and their making me aware of the legalities that govern people in my situation that I became determined that something was going to be done and that I wasn't going to spend the rest of my life in fear. Let me add here that my fear was not a fantasy but a realization, for I had been told by doctors, a psychologist, a psychiatrist, and a social worker that my husband was/is capable of killing me.

After swearing out three private complaints and visiting the commissioner's office six times, it was sent before a judge. Because of my husband's feelings regarding the law and the fact that nothing was ever done before, he didn't appear at the hearing. Since he did not appear, he was considered to be in contempt of court. For this reason only was I able to have him arrested. However, after the arrest he was given a court hearing for the assault and battery charges and was put on two years' probation. He is now in the process of appealing this.

I am very much aware that he could do what he has done in the past again, but this was the first time he had been legally reprimanded. Perhaps to some this may not seem like much, but after two years of working in the system to accomplish something, I feel that a major step has been taken.

In July of this year he was also taken before a judge for non-support. The outcome of this was that his arrearages were lowered from $3,000 to $1,500 and he was ordered to pay the ongoing support order. To date I have not received one cent of this money, and he has visitation rights which I have not withdrawn because I refuse to use my children as pawns in any way.

My court battles aren't over yet, but I'm ready and able to fight back. In fact, I have another one in the very near future. Right now, with the laws and attitudes of the lawmakers being what they are regarding domestic relations problems, I know that I cannot teach my children in good conscience to respect our judicial system. It's an appalling situation when you see that in our society life doesn't mean much and money is the almighty God.

Although I have had my own hell and perhaps still more to come, I have been able to get myself together, know some of the things I want for myself, and, more importantly, I am determined to make it. I'm finding some happiness, enjoying my children, take each day as it comes, and know that I am a Somebody--mentally and emotionally. I'm a realist, and yet I am still a dreamer. But no matter, I know that I'll make it just as I know that you can. People care, and although you may think that you're alone, you're not.

CHILD CUSTODY

The purpose of this section is to help you understand what
the law has to say about child custody. We will also
offer some suggestions to help you decide what living and
visitation arrangements will be best for you. Most of
the information in this section is practical and legal; it
is aimed at helping you to arrive at a decision. We
strongly urge you also to read the "Children in Transition"
chapter as you consider where and how your children will
live. This chapter discusses some of the feelings you and
your children may have about being in transition, and
talks about how to live with the decisions you have made.

We have also included a discussion of how to defend yourself against the charge of a social worker or agency that
you have abandoned or neglected your child, or that you
are an unfit mother. Poor women, often raising their
children alone with no support from the children's father,
are often subject to these charges merely because they are
poor. This is a very difficult situation because you are
being asked to come up to the standards of the welfare
workers and the judges without having their advantages.
Good legal help is essential in this situation. You might
also want to look at the section on living without your
children in the "Children in Transition" chapter.

Although our main concern in this chapter is settling the
legal issue of child custody, our discussion is not limited to situations where this question will be settled in
court. In fact, one of the purposes of this chapter is
to help you *keep that decision out of court*. You and your
husband and your children are the best people to decide
how you will all live after a divorce. No matter how fair
and impartial a judge tries to be, the experience of having
to fight about custody in court will leave you all the
worse for wear. And it is doubtful that any third person
can make up for the fact that he or she knows nothing at
all about your family. A short hearing, with both sides
putting forward arguments and trying to make the other
side look bad, will not give anyone enough information to
make a wise choice. *If at all possible keep talking* so
that the people who know and care the most about the situation will be the ones to make the decision.

   *"We talked to a number of judges around the country
   and there seems to be a fairly uniform attitude
   among them. . . . In the main, judges are middle-aged
   or older, and they've learned their habits and they've*

learned their prejudices, their biases, over the
past thirty to fifty years. They were raised by
parents who were born at the turn of the century
and their attitudes today will reflect what they
were taught." (Bill Noble, author of The Custody
Cage, *interview.*

There is much discussion in legal books about the right of
parents to the "care, custody, and control" of their children. Not too long ago they also had a right to all their
children earned and a right to "chastise" them in any way
they saw fit. Fathers exercised these rights over their
children and husbands exercised the same rights over their
wives. We have made a little progress since those days--
but it's still far from "a long way."

The word "custody" in the legal books most often refers to
the right of one parent to live with the child. It borders
on a right to "possession," and is all too often considered
a right to possession. We use the word "custody" as a
shorthand for all the responsibilities which fall upon the
parent with whom a child lives.

Using the word "custody" to mean "possession" accounts for
one of the major sources of conflict and heartache in many
divorces--the belief that either parent has a right to a
child. *Children are not property. They are people, with*
rights and duties of their own. You may have a right to
own and use a certain piece of land or a certain automo-
bile. *No one can have a right to a child.*

Thinking of custody as a right like the right to a certain
piece of property is not a new idea. Courts and governments
have certainly seen it that way for centuries, and many
still do. Until the end of the end of the nineteenth century, the laws of New York and California, among others,
stated that "The father of a legitimate unmarried minor is
entitled to its custody." "Illegitimate" children were,
of course, their mother's problems, and married women officially belonged to their husbands. The mother of "a legitimate unmarried minor" had custody of her child only if the
"father is dead, or is unable, or refuses" to take custody,
"or has abandoned the family." (Field Code, Draft. N.Y.
Civ. Code Sec. 90; Cal. Civ. Code, Sec. 197)

So it seemed a step in the right direction when the states
began to change their laws in favor of the mother. She,
after all, was the one who had, in most cases, cared for
the child all along. Until quite recently, most states

gave the benefit of the doubt to the mother. This was done
by the "tender years" doctrine, which said that children
"of tender years" were better off with their mothers than
with their fathers. There was no firm rule about what ages
were included in the "tender years," but the term has been
used to describe thirteen-year-olds. Under this doctrine,
a father who wanted custody of a child would have to prove
either that the mother was "unfit" to care for her children
or had neglected or abandoned them. He could *never* be
awarded custody by a judge merely by showing that he preferred to live with his children and they with him. It began to look like the lawmakers had overcompensated for
their earlier mistake of giving fathers an absolute right
to custody.

It seems that some important changes are being made today,
but it may still be too early to tell just how real these
changes are. The present trend seems to be away from assuming that either party has a *right* to custody and toward
looking at the total family situation and figuring out what
would be best for the children. Some courts are trying to
develop some guidelines for how this decision is made while
in others it depends entirely on the feelings and prejudices
of a single judge.

You may wonder what any of this has to do with staying *out*
of court. Think back over the discussions you may have had
or your own feelings about custody. Chances are both you
and your husband have thought, "That's not fair! I have a
right to that child." You claim your right from the fact
that you gave birth to the child, fed and cared for her
or him. He claims his right from the fact that he's provided the financial support for the child (and maybe you).

Feelings like these are almost automatic. They show just
how much the law reflects and strengthens what most people
in our society already believe. The temptation to think of
children as a special form of property in which you have a
right of ownership is very strong. It is also very destructive. This attitude reduces children to the status of
slaves, and creates so much emotional conflict that it can
become impossible to make any decisions based on what will
be best for all concerned.

Making The Decision

We list below the most common situations of people with
child-custody problems. Locate yourself in one of these
situations and consider carefully all the choices you

might have before making any final decision. The three
basic situations are:

The ready-made decision: Either your husband left you *and*
the children or he left with the children. (We are assuming that if the children are with you now under any other
circumstances, custody is not a problem for you.)

You and your husband have failed to reach an agreement,
and the decision will be made in court.

You and your husband will agree on custody in a separation
agreement.

The Ready-Made Decision

1. He left you with the children.

Just because he left and never said anything about having
the children with him, don't think you will never have a
custody problem. He may call up six months or four years
later and say, "I want to see my child." Or, "I want my
child." Many men don't think about children when they are
running away from an unhappy marriage. It's not until they
are free from some of the immediate problems that they
realize how much they depended on their children for affection, esteem, love, and entertainment.

What should you do in the meanwhile? If you are in touch
with him, you should try to convince him to make some kind
of agreement so that the child's future will be somewhat
predictable and secure. Arrange for visitation, if he is
not too far away, on a schedule that is convenient to you,
your husband, and your children. If he is farther away,
consider summer vacations or long school holidays. If you
feel the children are too young to travel where he is, you
might agree that they should spend summers or other vacations with him once they reach a certain age. Any visitation agreement will reduce your risk of having to fight a
custody battle in court. Before you make any visitation
agreement, read the section on the visiting parent in the
"Children in Transition" chapter of this book.

An agreement is not just essential to your peace of mind;
it will also establish some security for your child. It
is important to make an agreement about custody as soon as
possible because the longer you are separated the less
likely you are to agree, and the more distant you are, the
more desperate he may be. Child-kidnapping between parents

who rarely see each other and cannot make decisions together
is not unusual. Parents are often anxious to see their children after a long absence, and they are just as anxious to
avoid painful feelings which would be stirred up by talking
about which parent the child should live with.

Usually judges aren't too happy about this process either.
One writer who interviewed many judges reports:

> *We've seldom talked to a judge who enjoyed custody
> cases. . . . They are torn because it's not a clear-
> cut legal issue; it involves too many human emotions.
> One judge said he likes to put off all his custody
> cases until later afternoon, because he dislikes them
> so much. (June Noble,* author of The Custody Cage,
> *interview)*

If your husband has taken your child away and you don't
know where they are, you have an even bigger problem.
First you must find them. The law will not help you here
because the legal definition of "kidnapping" makes it impossible for a parent to "kidnap" his or her own child.
Once you find your husband and child, try to talk things
over and stay out of court. You should consult an attorney immediately, but you should probably not make your
first contact through the lawyer.

If your husband has left the state you live in, it may be
best for you to go where he is to talk. If you have to
take the case to court, you will have to do so in the
state where the children are, not the state where you live.

Finally: If you are involved in a child-snatching situation
and he will not discuss or negotiate custody with you and/
or third parties, *you need a lawyer*. This is not a time to
try to represent yourself in court. Custody decisions may
be won or lost on technical questions like whether a psychiatrist was properly qualified to testify as an expert,
or whether the social worker's notes were admissible as
official business records. To repeat: if you are involved
in any courtroom custody contest, YOU NEED A LAWYER. Before
choosing one, read the section on legal services and what
to look for in a lawyer in this chapter.

Finally, as a practical matter, there is no end to the
kidnapping story. You *can* go and take the child back. He
can come and take the child even after custody has been
granted to you by a court order. He will be in contempt
of court for this, but he may not be thinking about the

consequences at the time he acts.

Of course, there is nothing to stop you from taking the
child away from him and making it impossible for your husband to get in touch with you. This is a last-ditch
measure that should not be resorted to without really desperate circumstances. For example, you have reason to
fear for the safety of your child or you feel certain your
husband cannot properly care for her or him. Otherwise,
you should try to reason with him first. Go to court only
as a last resort. Then, if all else fails, and you feel
your child may be in danger, you might consider taking the
child away from its father. Remember, the person who suffers in these conflicts is not your spouse, but your child.

Once your child has been carried off, there is not much
you can do to reassure her or him directly. The best
thing you can do is try to find your child and his or her
father, and persuade him to discuss the matter with you
and/or some outside person. You might suggest a counselor,
therapist, child psychologist, or lawyer. You may want to
consult a lawyer immediately, but we do not recommend having
your first conversation with your husband in the presence of a
lawyer. A lawyer may make your husband feel the decision
should be made according to legal rules (or tricks) rather
than by a serious consideration of what would be best for
your children.

The legal remedies for child-snatching are both inefficient
and traumatic. They are also time-consuming and can be
expensive. The parent who does not have custody must file
a "habeas corpus" petition, which says that the person who
now has the child in custody does not have a legal right
to custody. If your husband can be found and brought into
court, it is up to you to prove that he has no right to
custody and that you do. You are the one who must do the
work of convincing the court; he can just sit back and see
if you can persuade the court to order a change. Courts
are very reluctant to order a change in custody, no matter
how it was obtained.

Often filing a habeas corpus petition will mean bringing
the children into court and either having them testify or
having a judge talk to them in his office. This is bound
to be upsetting for both you and them.

Perhaps the most important thing you can do if your husband
leaves you and the children is to help them deal with the
confusion they must feel. Be as honest as you can in terms

that they will understand. You may want to tell them, for
example, that their parents were not able to get along very
well, and that although their father will not be able to
live with them, he continues to love them. Of course, if
the situation was quite explosive before he left, the children may feel more relieved than anything else. In this
case, you may not have to explain much about why he left,
but it will still be important to reassure them that *they
are not the cause* of their father's absence.

It is important to reassure your children about this no
matter how he leaves. Children see the world as a universe
controlled by their own experiences and desires. You should
do everything possible to help them understand that their
father left because of a problem between you two adults.
Of course, the more you and he fight over who will have custody, the less believable this reassurance is.

2. He left, taking the children with him.

"Child-snatching" is what we call kidnapping when it's done
by a child's parent. Child-snatching is the ultimate in
disrespect for a child. It is nothing but a larger, more
powerful person taking a smaller, less powerful one and
removing it from familiar surroundings. It is a belief in
the right to possession of children carried to the extreme.

There are a few extreme situations in which you might want
to consider running away with your child. These might include situations in which you have lost a custody case in
court, and have exhausted all your appeals or have run out
of money for an appeal. You must recognize, however, that
all the warnings and the consequences spelled out in the
preceding pages apply to you as well. Should this be your
only alternative, you should take extra care to see that
whatever bitterness you may have toward your husband does
not get deliberately communicated to your child. You must
also guard against the possibility that your child will
believe she or he is the cause of the bitterness and disagreement between you. This is, after all, a most logical
conclusion to draw after a series of in-and-out-of-court
arguments about who the child is to live with.

Letting The Judge Decide

We will assume now that, for whatever reason, you have found
it impossible to reach an agreement about custody, and that
both you and your husband are content to let a judge decide
the custody question. Usually a court action begins with

the parent who does not have custody filing a "habeas corpus" petition. In some places the parent who already has
custody can file a petition "for recognition of custody"
in order to prevent a parent running away with a child.
This petition asks that the court formally recognize that
the present custody arrangement is best. You do not have
to have a lawyer to file either of these petitions, but
you should get one as soon as possible.

After you file your petition with the proper court, it is
served on the person who has custody, ordering him to
appear in court with the child at a specified time and
place. Remember, you cannot bring your husband into court
unless the court where you file your writ has jurisdiction
over him personally. In custody cases this depends on
where he lives with the children. In cases where the children are with grandparents or someone other than the
father, you must file the writ in the state and county
where the children are now living.

The family court in the jurisdiction where you file your
petition may have some mandatory or optional interview with
a social worker or other counselor who will urge that you
and your husband try to settle your differences out of
court. In many states there is a free counseling service
attached to the court. It may be worth trying. Remember:
You're almost always better off if you stay out of court.
Churches and family service agencies also provide counseling, which you might consider if you think there is a
chance of reaching any real agreement, even at this late
date.

Once you decide that an agreement is absolutely out of
the question and you file your petition, you will receive
a special "answer" from your husband's lawyer. It will
tell you something about what the issues in the court case
are going to be. His answer may state that:

1. You abandoned the family. It may suggest that he and
    the children have been living comfortably together ever
    since you left, and that it would be unfair to remove
    the children from the familiar environment at this time.
    The longer you have been gone, the harder it is for the
    court to see why an apparently stable living situation
    should be disrupted.

    The truth might be that you moved out temporarily, in-
    tending to return. Now he won't let you come back.
    Or you may have moved out to look for a place for you

and the children to live, but have not been able to
find one. You may have moved out because he was threatening you, or simply because the situation was unbearable. He may have assured you that you could have
the children when you were ready for them.

2. His answer might also state that you are not a good
    parent for the child--you are "unfit," or that you
    have abandoned or neglected your children. It might
    indicate that the children are better off with him
    because he can provide a better home, spend more money
    on education or baby-sitters, or the like. He may use
    the fact that he got a divorce from you on the ground
    of adultery, the fact that you work all day, or the
    fact that you have been institutionalized or treated
    for mental or emotional problems. If you have a
    prison record or are a lesbian he is almost certain
    to mention these facts, and they will go a long way
    toward persuading many judges that you are indeed not
    fit to be a mother. In other words, he would mention
    all the same things if he were suing you for custody.

In making custody decisions, judges are supposed to follow
local law. Local law usually tells them to use one of
three basic principles for making the decision. In some
states, custody may be related to who was "at fault" in the
divorce. In other states who was "at fault" is not supposed to matter, and there is a strong feeling that mothers
should have custody of their children almost no matter
what. In still other states "the best interest of the
child" is supposed to govern. Let's look at each one of
these principles.

One is the matter of "fault." In some states the judge
granting the divorce decree decides the custody issue at
the same time. Sometimes his decision is affected by who
is officially "at fault" and what the grounds are. Sometimes the details of the divorce don't make a whole lot
of difference, but it is safer to be the "innocent and injured" party who files for the divorce rather than the
villainous defendant just in case. Of course, who sues
for the divorce usually has absolutely nothing to do with
the best custody arrangement.

Another is the "tender years" doctrine. In some states
the "tender years" doctrine means that the judge starts
with the principle that mothers are "naturally" better
able to care for children than fathers. In these states
a mother may have to do something pretty outrageous before

the judge will award custody to the father. Just remember
"outrageous" means what the middle-aged, middle-class judge
thinks is outrageous. While the assumption that mothers
should always have custody of young children is the only
slender thread of hope for lesbians and other mothers with
unconventional lives, it is not an assumption that benefits
women in general.

One of the hardest things about making up our own minds
about custody--even under ideal conditions--is the social
pressure mothers are under to play the role of mother.
You may feel forced to fight for custody because the idea
that women who choose not to live with their children are
terrible is so popular. If you are considering allowing
your children to live with their father, you should read
"Living Without Your Children" in the chapter on children
in transition.

A third is the "best interest of the child" doctrine.
Some states are less concerned with who was at fault in
the divorce or the natural ability of mothers to care for
their children than with what is called "the best interest
of the child." This principle is probably better than the
other two because it requires some consideration of the
child. Unfortunately, judges often apply their own
prejudices in deciding what's best for children. Often
the decision will be based on the same factors we mentioned earlier: who was at fault in the divorce, which
parent provided for the child economically, and which parent lives the more conventional life.

Some guidelines for the "best interest of the child" have
been developed, although they are often ignored and violated.
Some of the guidelines are spelled out below.

The "best interest of the child" should not be determined
by the economic and social status of the two parents. A
father should not be awarded custody just because he has
a larger income or lives in a bigger house or a better
neighborhood. Or at least these factors should not be the
only ones that determine custody. But you can bet that
the parent with the larger house, the better job, and nicer
neighborhood has a head start in convincing a judge that
living with him is in "the best interest of the child."

What the court is supposed to look at is the kind of living
situation the child would have in each home. Would there
be someone to care for the child at all times? If you are
working, you would want to show the court what kind of

child care you expected to have. What kind of physical
surroundings would the child have in each home, and how
would these affect the child's growth and development?
Again, if you live in a housing project or low-income
neighborhood you would have to work hard to convince a
judge that living with you would be better for the child
than living in a neighborhood with trees and yards. But
don't forget the judge is comparing what the child's
life would be like with you with what the child's life
would be like with the other parent. If neither one of
you has trees and yards, the physical surroundings may
not make any difference at all. A judge will compare the
opportunities for play, education, and physical exercise
in the two houses and neighborhoods.

Another thing a judge will look at--most carefully if
the judge is sincerely trying to do a good job--is the
relationship between each parent and the child. Things
like which parent has spent the most time with the child
and which parent the child feels closer to will be important. Occasionally a judge will say that children
should go with parents of the same sex. This is particularly true of older children and adolescents. Often
the "reasons" a judge gives for a decision are made up
after he decides.

If there is more than one child, there may be the additional question of whether to keep all the children together or divide them between two parents. The answer
depends on the circumstances of your family. If there is
a wide age range, it may be good for the children to live
with different parents. On the other hand, if there are
two or three fairly young children who have been close
throughout their lives, it does not make much sense to
divide them up just to be fair to the two parents.

The weight to be given a child's preference in custody
cases is controversial. Some judges think that children
are very bad judges of what is good for them. Others believe that they can learn a great deal about what is in
the child's best interest by observing the child, talking
about living situations, and asking the child her or his
preference. Sometimes a judge will hold a private conference with the child in his office. Both parents of the
child are excluded from this conversation, so the child
will be able to talk with the judge without being afraid
of hurting the feelings of either one. In some cases the
child may be represented by a court-appointed attorney who
is not working for either parent. Some parents have used

expert psychiatric testimony to help the judge determine what is in the child's best interest, but this practice is expensive and can backfire. On the other hand, if you have an unconventional life-style, or a history of emotional or psychiatric problems, psychiatric testimony may be ordered by the court and/or crucial to your case.

Custody In The Courtroom: Questions And Answers

Q: Will a court look at how I live my life in order to decide a custody question?

A: You bet!

Q: What things will they be interested in?

A: Just about everything--from how you dress to how mature and emotionally stable you seem. Do you have a job or a means of supporting yourself? Where do you live? What is your home like? Is it a good place for a child? Do you have any definite plans for where the child will live, how she or he will spend the daytime?

   The judge will also be interested in your work record, your social life, and whether you have any religious ties or belong to any community organization. In short, the more you conform to the judge's stereotype of what white, middle-class American women should be, the easier it will be for you.

Q: Suppose I don't conform? Suppose I can't?

A: If you don't *want* to conform, you have to make a tactical decision. Deliberate noncomformity (even going to the hearing in blue jeans) will probably offend the judge. You have to decide whether getting custody is worth a show of respectability. *Theoretically*, the judge is supposed to be more concerned with your relationship with your child than with the way you dress or the way you live. In reality, the judge has a lot of leeway in deciding what he or she thinks is in the best interest of the child.

Q: Are you suggesting that I'd better not live with my boyfriend during a custody suit?

A: Absolutely! To do so would be to invite the court to find you morally unfit and not capable of maintaining a "suitable" home for your child. And this is *not* the

time to try to enlighten a judge, or argue about changing values.

Q: If I know or suspect there will be a custody suit, what
      are some *good* things to do?

A: It depends on whether you are now living with the child
      or not. If you are living with the child, make sure
      that your home is presentable, that you have a regular
      form of child care for when you are not at home, and
      that your living situation is one which would raise no
      objections in the mind of the local P.T.A. president.

      If you are not living with your child, make sure that
      you are living in a place that would be considered suit-
      able for a child. If you are now living with your boy-
      friend, in a commune, or in the cheapest place you could
      find, you may want to consider moving in with your par-
      ents, with another separated woman with or without chil-
      dren, or to a larger apartment in a neighborhood with
      other children and adults who look after them. If you
      are not working now, you should consider actively look-
      ing for work, applying for school, and generally trying
      to develop a plan for how you will live with your child,
      should you be awarded custody. A realistic plan for
      living with the child can make an enormous difference
      in your case.

      As soon as you know there will be a custody suit, find
      a lawyer you trust and plan strategy with her or him.
      See "What To Look For In A Lawyer" and "A Word About
      Legal Services" in this chapter. If you are a defendant
      in a custody suit, the local legal services agency may
      help you find a lawyer even though your income is too
      high to qualify for their free services.

Q: This advice is all so depressing. You're telling me to
      rearrange my whole life and touch things up so it will
      look like I am somebody straight out of *Good Housekeep-
      ing*. Can't I live just like I always do and try to
      convince the court that this is what is best for my
      child?

A: You can, and maybe you should--only you'll probably
      lose. Very few family court judges have enough imagi-
      nation to believe that any living situation other than
      the one in which their grandchildren are presently
      living can be very good.

In some cases, however, honesty may be the best policy. Say your husband knows that you have been living
in a commune for the last four years. Your other
activities just don't add up to anybody's image of a
housewife and mother. If you have little hope of
presenting a consistent picture as one of the acceptable stereotypes--housewife, career girl, or the like--
your best bet might be to educate the court as tact-
fully as possible about the way you live your life.
But be careful not to be arrogant. This is a very
tricky situation, and your best strategy is to win
the respect of the judge.

Q: I am suing my husband for custody. Should I consider
      hiring detectives or anything like that?

A: Talk this over with your lawyer. How are you trying
      to win your case? If you want to convince the court
      the child should not stay with him because he's never
      home, has no regular plan for the child, leaves the
      child unattended, and spends all his money on enter-
      tainment, you may want to have some detective work
      done. But this is an ugly and expensive business,
      and even though you and your husband are now on oppo-
      site sides of the courtroom, you are going to have to
      continue to meet over your child. It does not benefit
      your child to antagonize her or his father.

Q: My husband is suing for custody. Should I be thinking
      about getting experts and other witnesses? How about
      psychiatrists?

A: In some situations the court will order a period of
      psychiatric evaluation. Otherwise it's up to you to
      decide whether or not you want this kind of testimony.
      Again, it's important what the issues in your case
      are. If the child's father is saying you are too
      emotionally unstable to care for your child, favorable
      psychiatric testimony would be very important.

      One of the drawbacks to this kind of expert opinion is
      that this kind of expert opinion is very expensive.
      The other drawback is that psychiatrists think like
      judges. They may even believe you are crazy for not
      wanting to be married any more.

      If you are considering using this kind of expert wit-
      ness, you might want to look for feminist therapists
      through referral services operating out of women's

centers or other similar places. Remember, it can be dangerous to have too much faith in experts, although there are times you really need one. This goes for yourlawyer too. Don't let a lawyer tell you what to do or how to think about what you want. Ask questions; make your lawyer explain what he's doing and just what the steps are. If you feel uneasy with the way your case is being treated, check the information against another source--another lawyer or a legal counseling service for women.

Q: What about witnesses? Who should they be? Does it matter how they dress or talk?

A: Judges (and juries) are going to be impressed by people with degrees and well-educated speech. Professionals in social service fields, psychologists, teachers, clergy, and the like are always good. However, judge and jury are also going to want to know how long and how well the witness has known you and your children. Does the witness visit your home often? Know your children well? Can she or he tell the court about the relationship between you and the child? In short, when you decide whom to present as a witness, try to get a balance between ordinary people who know you well and respected professionals.

Court Orders: What Do They Mean?

A court order will usually state who is to have custody of which children and what kind of visitation rights the other parent will have. It may specify conditions for visiting, or include the amount of support to be paid by the parent who does not have custody.

It is important to understand the effect of an official custody decision. It does more than a divorce decree, which often simply announces that your marital status has changed. Once the judge enters an official "order" for custody, any person who does not obey the order may be held in contempt of court and fined or jailed for disobeying the court's order. This might happen if the parent with custody denied the other parent visitation rights spelled out in the order, or if the parent without custody refused to return the child after a visit.

If your husband has custody and will not let you see your child, you should threaten to inform the judge. If necessary, you may ask the judge to hold him in contempt of

court. If you are the parent with custody and you believe
you have good reasons to refuse to let their father visit
your children, you should go to the judge who made the
custody decision and set up the visitation and inform her
or him of the change in circumstances which makes visitation unwise. If you can do this ahead of time, you will
avoid putting yourself in contempt of court and avoid the
risk of a hearing and fine or imprisonment.

Second Stage: Appeal

Once the trial judge hears all the testimony and sees
whatever evidence there is, he or she will either announce
the decision at the close of the case or "reserve decision"--
think on it a few days--and write an opinion. In either
case, you have a right to appeal any unfavorable decision.

Appeals are expensive, however, partly because of the
lawyer's fees, and partly because of the cost of "transcripts"--the official record of who said what during the
trial. These may cost as much as $1.00 per page. You
might, of course, find a sympathetic attorney (if you
think there are civil rights involved, try the local
American Civil Liberties Union) who will take the case for
a moderate fee and try to convince the court that you cannot afford to pay for the transcripts. If she or he is
successful in this argument, you may get free transcripts.

If you lose the case and don't have the money to appeal
or feel you have no hope of winning (often an appeal is
futile because higher courts won't reverse any decision
that falls within the "discretion" of the trial judge),
don't give up all hope. Custody decisions are *never* final.
They are always subject to review in light of "changed
circumstances." You should be aware, however, that the
change in circumstances must be pretty drastic, as courts
are reluctant to order any change in custody

Keeping It In The Family

By now you may be persuaded that it's best for all concerned to stay out of court. You believe you and your
husband could reach some kind of custody agreement. What
should you consider? What are the stumbling blocks? How
should you go about making the decision? These questions
depend a great deal on your circumstances, the personali-
ties of the people involved, the age and number of the
children, and how you've settled disputes before.

We offer some suggestions based on our experience helping
women settle custody questions with their husbands. Our
list of suggestions is by no means exhaustive, and is
bound to include suggestions you may not find helpful.
Decide which ones make most sense to you. We believe this
decision is one of the most important ones you will be
making for a long time, and that it is important to take
time to think about it, to live with your hunches and un-
certainties until you have a sure feeling about what seems
right.

If you are able to communicate in a calm, thoughtful manner
with your husband, so much the better. If you are absolutely unable to do so, make sure you have a lawyer or legal
counselor whom you really trust and stay in close contact
with her or him throughout the negotiations.

The First Step: What Do You Want?

What kind of custody arrangement do you want? Why? Be
careful of the motherhood mystique--the feeling that you
will lose your identity if you are not a mother all the
time. The most dangerous thing about the motherhood mys-
tique is that it makes you feel guilty for not wanting to
be a mother all the time. Probably everyone you know (or
almost everyone) has been infected by the motherhood mys-
tique. These people (and a little voice inside your own
head) may make you feel guilty for even thinking that it
might not be a bad idea for the children to live with
their father.

Figuring out what you want to do about living with your
children is part of defining your goals for your new life.
Do you want it to be as much like your old life as possible? Are you trying to make time for new things--a new
job, more training or education, or a new life-style? Do
you feel they have become too dependent on you? Or are
you starved for more time to be with them? Can you afford
to live with your children? Do you have a job? If you
will not be at home during the day, are there reasonable
child-care facilities available? Is their father in a
better position to care for them, or are you both living
on as little as possible?

The Second Step: What Does Your Husband Want?

Does he really want to live with the children, or is he
just threatening to get custody for revenge, or in order
to make you give in to something he wants in the separation
agreement?

If you feel his demand for custody is based on reasons
like these, you should talk with him and try to get him
to separate these other reasons from the custody questions.
If you cannot talk to him directly, tell your lawyer what
his motives are and ask his lawyer to reason with your
husband or his lawyer. Child custody is not something to
bargain with.

Often husbands are suspicious and confused about child-
support payments. They consider these "income" (tax free)
for mothers, a sort of bonus that goes to the wife if she
gets custody. It is important that he understands that
child-support payments could not possibly be any "bonus" to
mothers. Let him see an itemized list of your expenses,
indicating what portion of these are for child support.
(See the itemized list of expenses contained in Chapter
Five.)

If you believe he is asking for custody of the children
just to make you give in on some other part of the agreement, or as a form of punishment or revenge, be sure he
understands how unfair it is to punish children for their
parents' incompatibility. If you fail, his lawyer (or
yours) should be able to convince him that it is better
for all concerned if he is reasonable and cooperative on
this issue. It is important that you do not respond to
these tactics with bitterness and anger. Save these feelings for issues that concern just the two of you. Of
course, this is much more easily said than done, and it
is quite understandable that the more emotional the issue,
the less rational our behavior. Child custody is one of
those instances worthy of superhuman efforts to curb such
"natural" impulses.

If your husband wants custody of your children and you see
no real reason why this would not be good for them, don't
be too suspicious. His reasons for wanting to live with
the children may be as good as yours. Maybe it's time for
a change--you work or go to school while he looks after
the children.

Consider his reasons for wanting custody, and then look at
what this arrangement would mean to the children. What
would be the effect of their living with their father most
of the time? Would it be a good change for them? Is he
in a position to take care of them? Would they see enough
of him not to feel deserted?

Don't assume that just because he has not been a model

father while you were together, he'd be a totally inadequate
parent without you. Many fathers are lazy. They watch
mothers do the work and think how "natural" it is for women
to care for children. Left to their own devices, many
fathers learn there's more hard work than "nature" involved.
They also turn out to be excellent parents.

Finally, think about the relationship between your children
and their father. How do they feel about him? Would they
be comfortable living with him? Would he be comfortable
living with them?

The Third Step: Who Do Your Children Want To Live With?

Does any child have a strong preference for either parent?
Is this preference realistic in light of the willingness
and ability of that parent to care for the child? If so,
should the child's preference be given a great deal of
weight? How mature is the child? Are you sure you know
what the child wants, or are you speculating? Have you
ever talked with your child about this preference and the
reasons for it? What do you think this preference is based
on? The desire for a change? Does living with Daddy seem
more glamorous? Or is the child saying she would rather
live with you just to please you or avoid hurting your
feelings?

Consider the other ways in which your child's life would
be affected by living with each parent. Is your child
already rooted in a familiar place with many friends and
companions? Is one parent closer to grandparents or other
adults the child is used to seeing? What about school?
Would living with either parent force the child to start
all over again with new friends, new teachers, new schools?
What effect do you think this might have?

Sometimes your child might need a change as much as you do.
If your child has felt a lot of conflict at home, has been
upset and confused as a result, and has not been doing well
in school, or doesn't know anyone with separated parents,
it might be a good time for a change.

Finally, you should try to weigh the child's opportunities
for growth, security, and happiness with each of you. You
should consider the different values considered important
by each parent and how living with either parent would
affect the values your child has already learned.

Alternatives

If you are working out an agreement about custody and
visitation, you are free to make any arrangements you
think would be best for your child. You might want to
consider some alternatives to the traditional division
between the parent who lives with the child and has formal "custody" and the parent with whom the child "visits."

Many psychologists, child psychiatrists, and books on the
subject warn that any departure from this arrangement may
be dangerous for your child. You should carefully consider your own child's personality and the pattern of her
or his life to date before making any such decision. If
your child is used to a particular house or is the kind
of child who needs a home base for stability and security,
some of the "alternative" custody plans are probably not
for you.

Some families have a "shared custody" arrangement, with
equal responsibility and equal time for children with
both parents. The children might stay with their mother
from Thursday morning to Saturday night, for example, and
with their father from Saturday night to Thursday morning.
This way both parents spend both weekdays and weekends
with their children. An arrangement like this will only
work, however, if the parents live quite near each other
and are able to meet regularly without trauma. Otherwise
children will be shifted from one school or neighborhood
to the other in midweek.

Other parents share custody by dividing their time with
the children between the school year and the summer, with
one parent living with the children during the school year,
the other during the vacation (or summer and two long
school holidays). Where circumstances permit, the parents
sometimes reverse this schedule the following year. Some
parents have tried six-month schedules for children who
are not in school, and some have alternated on a week-by-
week or half-month basis.

In making arrangements like these, it is important that
you consider the effect they will have on the child above
the convenience and fairness to the parents. The shorter
periods seem to have more potential for disrupting a child's
routine and making her or him feel pulled and pushed between
two adults. The advantage of the shorter priods is that
the children are never separated from either parent for a
long time, and the transition from living with both

parents to living with just one may be easier. The disad-
vantage of the longer periods is that, although three
months may not seem long to you, it may be a very long time
for a child. Shorter periods may produce less anxiety
about being separated from the other parent. Again, what
is appropriate for you depends on your own circumstances--
the age and flexibility of your children and their feelings
about the separation, the proximity of their father, the
flexibility of your schedule and his, and your ability to
cooperate with each other.

Some parents are quite reluctant to agree on any definite
custody or visitation schedule, preferring to "play it by
ear," or "work it out as we go along." Our experience suggests this is not wise. Your children's lives should not
be made to depend on spur-of-the-moment decisions made by
you and/or your husband. Think about the issues now, and
decide what will be best for all. Don't avoid the problems,
they will only grow. Make a definite arrangement. You
can always change it if it doesn't work--but give it a real
chance. There are bound to be some problems and some hard
adjustments the first few months.

No custody agreement is final. Children grow, and the law
recognizes this. So be aware when you are making the agreement that this part, at least, is subject to change. You
should keep in mind that as the children grow, their needs
will change and you will have to adjust certain provisions
of the agreement as they do. You might want to state in
the agreement--just to remind yourselves--that the custody,
support (for children), and visitation provisions are subject to change by mutual (written) agreement of all the
parties. But be careful not to leave things too open-ended.
You are trying to define your new life, not tie it in to
the old.

Another change in the agreement you might want to provide
for is the increasing independence of the children. You
might want to agree to be bound by the child's decision
about which parent to live with as soon as the child has
reached a certain age. Parents have different ideas about
the age at which their children will be making responsible
decisions--some say as young as 12 or 13, others say not
until 16. It's up to you, but your agreement might provide
for an age at which the child has the right to decide.

Again, there are many warnings against such a flexible
provision. Some professional counselors argue that this

places a terrible burden on a child. It creates constant
pressure to choose one parent without hurting the feelings
of the other, they say. You have to decide whether you
think this kind of choice would amount to an unfair burden
or a vital part of the process of growing up for your
child.

Before making any final custody agreement, read the chapter, "Children in Transition," and remember: Having children means that you may not ever be as separated as couples
who never had any children. It is important to recognize
this now. Your agreement should contain a statement of
what major decisions involving the children will be made
by which parent, and which decisions, if any, will be made
jointly.

Lesbian Custody

On September 3, 1974, a Superior Court judge in Seattle,
Washington, made a small piece of history for lesbian
mothers who want to live with their children. He ruled
that two women, both of whom had been awarded custody of
their children on the condition that they not live together,
had the right both to live together and raise their children. So ruling, he overturned the earlier order which
made living apart the only way these lesbians could live
with their children. This condition was intolerable to
the women, so they fought and lost, and fought some more
until they won the first significant legal victory for
lesbian mothers in America.

This does not mean that judges are henceforth going to
smile at lesbians and approve their choices for living
partners and child-raising plans. It is still dangerous
to be a lesbian in a society with strong heterosexual prejudices and difficult to be a mother in an anti-child
society. Until quite recently, there was absolutely
nothing to write about how the law treated the lesbian
custody issue. For the most part, it didn't. Either
there was no contest--the wife signed away her right to
live with her children under threat of exposure--or one
party simply scooped up the children and moved away.

For many years, judges who did decide lesbian custody cases
failed to mention the real basis of their decisions, and
merely found either that the mother was not a fit person to
care for her child, or that it was in the best interest of
the child to stay with its father. It appears that the

lesbian and women's movements are educating the public
(which includes fathers, judges, and lawyers) to some of
the realities of lesbianism. As a result, a few rational
decisions are being made. But rationality is not the rule;
it is still the exception.

It is therefore even more important for you than for other
mothers to heed the warning to *stay out of court*. Regardless of your personal feelings, try to come to some suitable agreement with your husband. You may want to enlist
the aid of a lawyer or other legal counselor, a psychologist
(referrals are available through many gay switchboards),
social worker, or other third party. Before you start to
negotiate with him, be clear in your own mind what custody
arrangement you think would be fair and best for all concerned. Read the lesbian mothers section of Chapter Three
for additional information.

If you have custody of the children, or you are still on
speaking terms with your husband and he has custody, you
should do everything in your power to reach an agreement.
Study all the suggestions made in this chapter and Chapter
Three to reach an agreement. Remember to give him time to
cool off before you start talking about custody. "You'll
never see the children" is a typical father's reaction upon
learning his wife is a lesbian. Many of these men have not
yet thought about the time and trouble involved in carrying
out this threat.

If your husband knows or suspects you are gay and is
seriously threatening to take custody of the children, try
to talk to him in a calm and thoughtful manner. He must
understand that your children are not going to stop loving--
and needing--you because he is angry that you are a lesbian.
It may not make very much difference to them at all. He
must also understand that you are ready and able to work
for what you sincerely believe is the best interest of your
child. You must both respect your child's relationship with
the other parent rather than work to sabotage it.

If he is determined to take the issue to court, he should
be warned that he may be overconfident about his chances in
court. But even more important, you all stand to lose,
especially the children, by being unable to resolve your
own problems. The children will, of course, be affected by
the immediate trauma and the ultimate decision. But fathers
are not immune from the quirks of justice. Once either of
you submits the custody question to a court, you both lose

all control over the outcome. A court may find that both
parents are unfit. The father need not be an alcoholic to
lose custody; he may just not be prepared or able to care
for the children. If this is obvious to the judge, even
the most conservative might find that neither of you should
have custody, and refer the matter to juvenile courts.
Your children risk becoming wards of the court and shunted
from foster home to foster home.

This is not said to scare you needlessly, but rather to
emphasize the danger of taking your custody questions to
court. Both parents stand to lose, and the children are
inevitably losers whenever their parents can't agree on
their responsibilities. One last time, because it is the
best advice we can give: *If you can possibly avoid it,
stay out of court!*

Of course, you do not want to stay out of court if you are
unhappy about not having custody or visitation privileges.
If you are the one to initiate custody proceedings, your
first concern will be to find competent and sympathetic
legal counsel. This is by no means easy to find. One
woman of very modest means was offered the services of an
attorney who did a great deal of custody work--for $10,000.
Lawyers often consider custody "dirty work"--it involves
real feelings--and do not want to get involved in it without a large fee.

If there is a women's center, lesbian center, or project
for women in transition in your area, you should see if
there is any information about attorneys who would be good
in this kind of case. Often women will be more sympathetic,
but there are so few women lawyers that you shouldn't set
your heart on one. A lawyer with some experience with
custody cases can be very valuable. You should also try
the local legal aid or legal services program; sometimes
you can get a referral and sometimes good advice from
these agencies even if you do not fall within their income
guidelines. Local civil liberties unions (look in the white
pages of your telephone directory under "American Civil
Liberties Union" or under the name of your state for the
state civil liberties group) are beginning to take an interest and work on lesbian custody cases. A more complete
list of resources can be found under "lesbian mothers" in
the bibliography.

Lawyers will suggest different strategies, but it seems
likely that if your husband has any suspicion you are a

lesbian, he will use this in court. It's almost a sure
winner--for him. Therefore--if he doesn't already know and
you suspect he will not be able to agree about custody,
don't tell him. If you have told him or he suspects you
are gay, you should be prepared to deal with this in court.
Often you will have to educate both your lawyer and the
judge. One possibly helpful thing is the recent resolution
by the American Psychiatric Association declaring that homosexuality is no longer a "disease." Copies of this press
release and rationale may be obtained by writing: American
Psychiatric Association--Division of Public Affairs, 1700
W. 18th Street, N.W., Washington, D.C. 20009. Other suggestions may be found in the bibliography. You may also want
to call a psychiatrist or other counselor who understands
lesbianism and is sympathetic.

Finally, some familiarity with the historic Seattle case may
be helpful. In this case a judge ordered a court social
worker to visit the home where the two lesbians lived with
their children. She reported to the court that the home was
"most happy, well-organized" and "creative." She went on
to say that she and the psychiatrist and psychologist who
visited the home were all impressed by the fact that both
mothers were able to set limits for their children without
stifling their creativity, their inquisitiveness, or their
affection.

In this case the social worker admitted she was quite ignorant about homosexuality and its possible effects on
children. She did some reading, and found that the greatest danger was that the children would be hurt by society's
attitude toward lesbianism. *They* might feel rejected.
Here this danger was weighed against the immediate trauma
of being separated from their mothers, and it was decided
that the greater danger was the immediate trauma. It was
therefore in the best interest of the children to leave
them with their mothers.

All of this suggests that it is good to have professionals
on your side, and that the more calm-talking and educating
you can be, the better off you will be. It does not change
the fact that your chances of winning in court are pretty
slim.

When An Agency Is Suing For Custody Of Your Child

Poor women are sometimes faced with a different kind of
custody problem. Social workers, welfare caseworkers

counselors at community mental health centers, doctors, or others in public health clinics, and public school teachers may all believe it is their duty to supervise poor women in many aspects of their lives, from housekeeping to child-raising.

Often, the values and standards of these professionals are not met by welfare mothers or those who work outside the house all day for eighty or a hundred dollars a week. Sometimes the mother gets a lecture about what kind of clothes or breakfast her children should have. Sometimes she may get some useful information about additional services available to her. Occasionally her ability or fitness to care for and have custody of her children is challenged by a custody suit.

If you are ever summoned to appear in court with your children or otherwise notified that your custody of your children is being legally challenged by some agency or official, *get a lawyer immediately*. If you have been notified of a court date, call the nearest legal services agency and explain that you must appear in court on a certain date to defend your right to live with your children.

Do not hesitate to get in touch with a legal services agency, even when you are not certain that you could qualify for free legal services. You should also not play around with the idea of defending yourself. This is a very serious situation in which you need all the expertise of a professional attorney.

No matter when you are notified or what the date of the hearing, *do not go to court without a lawyer*, and *never take your children with you* to such a hearing unless you have a lawyer who has advised you to do so. Sometimes you may be ordered to appear in court with your children by means of a postcard or letter. You do not have to go unless you have been properly served--in person--with a subpoena. Many women who do not know this appear in court with their children, without legal representation. Some of these women lose custody of their children then and there. You should *never* take this risk.

What kinds of situations are likely to bring you into conflict with agencies or other public officials? The following are several of the most common situations which can lead to a custody suit against you. You should avoid these if at all possible.

1. Never leave your children alone or in the care of some-
    one less than 16-18 years old for any extended period
    of time. The longer your children are left unattended,
    the greater the danger. If at all possible, leave your
    children with adult relatives or responsible neighbors,
    or take them with you.

2. Be very careful when taking your children to public
    clinics or emergency rooms--particularly for treatment
    of burns, bruises, or other injuries which could
    possibly have been deliberately inflicted. Doctors or
    social workers at these hospitals may be quick to con-
    clude that you have neglected your children or deliber-
    ately burned or beaten them.

    When you take your child to an emergency room, be sure
    to explain just how the injury happened. If you are too
    upset or nervous to feel confident about doing this,
    take a friend with you. In fact, it's a good idea to
    take another person with you whenever you go there. If
    the hospital or clinic threatens to refuse to release
    your child, call legal services for advice *immediately*.
    And let the hospital officials know you are aware of
    your rights. Tell the doctor, nurse, or administrators
    that you will talk with your lawyer if you have any
    problem with getting your child out of the hospital.

3. When your young children play outside, always know
    where they are. They may wander into the street or
    come to the attention of someone who believes they have
    been "neglected." The danger is less in neighborhoods
    where people know each other and look out for each
    others' children.

4. If your children miss school often or their teacher
    indicates that she or he thinks they are not being
    properly cared for, you might ask for a conference or
    try to have a calm talk about what is happening. Con-
    frontation and anger may be dangerous. No matter how
    prejudiced the teacher, social worker, or other agency
    person may be, try to be rational and calm. Explain
    matter-of-factly whatever circumstances at home may be
    affecting your child's behavior. You do not need to
    feel defensive. You do have the right to make your own
    judgments about how your children live--but it does not
    pay to antagonize people who are in a position to force
    you to defend that right in court.

5. If any of your children become involved in juvenile
    court proceedings, you may be called into court if
    the judge believes that the situation at home is lead-
    ing to your child's problems. Often you do not get
    much advance notice of this appearance and you may not
    be sufficiently informed to realize that the custody of
    your child is at stake.

    You have a right to be represented in this situation.
    Do not think you will be automatically represented by
    your child's lawyer. You probably will not be. Get a
    lawyer of your own immediately.

Occasionally caseworkers, neighbors, or relatives may be
the source of complaints suggesting you are neglecting your
children or unfit to care for them. You cannot avoid contact with these people, but you can avoid much of the
serious conflict. If you realize there is a growing dispute
about your ability or fitness to care for your children, try
to talk--again as calmly as possible--to the people who may
call your custody into question. Again, it does not pay to
antagonize your caseworker--or your neighbor. Try to resolve disputes among yourselves rather than fighting major
battles in court. Sometimes a third person respected by
all those involved in the dispute can help you settle these
problems. The local minister or some other counselor you
respect and trust will be much more helpful than a judge.

If you lose custody of your children at the trial, you
should know you have a decision against you. Legal service
lawyers will often appeal your case for free. But you
should know that custody decisions are not often overturned
by higher courts. Your best bet is to follow these three
basic rules:

1. Resolve disputes of problems concerning the way you care
    for your children by talking.

2. Avoid situations which are likely to give anyone an
    opportunity to bring your custody into question.

3. Call for legal help at the first sign of trouble.

"Illegitimacy"

Q: Why are children born to unmarried women called "ille-
    gitimate"?

A: "The way I see it, it's not the child that's illegiti-
    mate--it's the parent," one old man said to another.
    Of course, it's ridiculous to label a child "illegiti-
    mate." *There is no such thing as an illegitimate child,*
    which is why we always write "illegitimate" in this
    book. Nor do we believe women who have children with-
    out being married are illegitimate. But most states
    and government agencies do believe that children whose
    parents are not married are "illegitimate," and discrimi-
    nate against these children in a variety of ways.

Q: Are there any states in which there is no "illegitimate"
    status for children born to unmarried parents?

A: Yes. North Dakota, Arizona, Oregon, and Minnesota have
    all recently adopted laws abolishing the status or the
    discrimination generally associated with "illegitimacy."
    In all other states, the status and the discrimination
    persist.   Some states (e.g., Wisconsin) will not even
    release the birth certificate of "illegitimate" children
    to their mothers--although they will to school boards,
    the armed forces, and other official agencies.

Q: How is the problem of "illegitimacy" particularly im-
    portant for women in transition?

A: There are several ways. First, if either you or your
    husband is thinking about an annulment instead of a
    divorce (for religious or other reasons), you should
    check carefully to see what your state says about the
    children of annulled marriages. Some states declare
    these children retroactively illegitimate because an
    annulment declares that you never have been married.
    Some states have specific laws saying that the children
    of annulled marriages *are not illegitimate*, but you
    should check carefully before filing for or allowing an
    annulment to be granted to see what the law is in your
    state.

    The second way this problem affects women in transition
    is in a situation where you either don't care all that
    much about a divorce, or you don't have the money to get
    one. Any children born to you for the rest of your life
    (or at least until a divorce has been granted) will be
    presumed to be the children of your husband. This is
    to "spare" them the stigma of "illegitimacy." However,
    if their real father would ever want custody, or if you
    should ever want to sue him for their support, problems

would arise. Legally these children would be the
children of your husband, and anyone else wanting to
assert rights or whom you seek to hold responsible
would have no rights or responsibilities until you (or
he) proved otherwise.

People who don't "bother" to get a divorce, and then
enter into what they consider either a common-law marriage or an official marriage are treading on very thin
ice should the undivorced spouse from marriage #1 ever
care to assert himself. That spouse could have your
second "marriage" annulled, and the children of that
marriage could become "illegitimate."

Finally, if you're divorced and you've decided you never
want to get married again--you might want to think it
over if you're planning to have any more children.
Children born to unmarried mothers are "illegitimate"
under the law.

Q: In what ways does the law discriminate against "ille-
     gitimate" children?

A: Traditionally, there have been six major areas of dis-
     crimination against "illegitimate" children: support,
     inheritance, benefits (e.g., social security, insurance,
     welfare, workman's compensation, etc.), custody, and
     name. Mothers who apply for public housing have also
     been discriminated against on the basis of their having
     "illegitimate" children. Let's look at each of these
     areas and see what discrimination has meant in each one.

     The first, and certainly the most important, is that of
     support. Here the usual rule is reversed. The mother
     has always been obligated to support her "illegitimate"
     child, while the father, traditionally, has had no such
     duty. This rule hardly encouraged unmarried fathers to
     take the institution of marriage (or fatherhood) more
     seriously! In 1973 this rule was reversed, and *all*
     children now have a right to be supported by their
     father, regardless of whether or not he is married to
     their mother. Note: A husband is *not* legally obligated
     to support the children of another father--regardless
     of whether their mother was married to the father or
     not.

     Another important area is that of *inheritance*. Until
     at least 1967 both New York and Louisiana declared that

"illegitimate" children had no right to inherit property
from their mother!   The problem is usually whether or
not they can inherit from their father or their
father's relatives. Most states say that the word
"children" in a will means "legitimate" children, unless
it is clear from the will that the person making it
intended benefits to go to the "illegitimate" children
as well. This can be shown simply by using the full
names of the children when writing a will.

Most of the problems come when there is no will. Every
state has laws which declare how property should be
divided when the property owner dies without a will.
Several states give equal rights to "legitimate" and
"illegitimate" children, others give full rights to
"acknowledged illegitimate" children. Several states
have declared that under no circumstances can "illegitimate" children inherit from their fathers without a
will naming them specifically, and still other states
have no clear position on the question.

If you are the mother of an "illegitimate" child and
concerned about inheritance, the best thing to do is to
have the person from whom the child might inherit write
a will which names the child specifically, by full
names.

In the area of *benefits* major progress has been made
toward doing away with legal discrimination against
"illegitimate" children. It has been ruled that the
word "children" in insurance policies means both legitimate and "illegitimate" children, that "illegitimate"
children have rights to social security survivors'
benefits and other benefits under certain conditions--
usually that their father supported the children during
his lifetime. "Illegitimate" children have equal rights
to medical and dental care under the Armed Services
Dependents' Medical Care Act of 1972.

In this area the law varies a great deal from state to
state and is in the process of rapid change. *If you
feel your child is being discriminated against on the
basis of her or his status as "illegitimate" you should
consult an attorney immediately*. Many local and state
agencies and businesses are not well informed about the
state of the law, or continue to have clearly unconstitutional practices because they have not been faced with
a legal challenge. Remember: *You don't have to be rich*

to bring this kind of action.   Legal service lawyers
are there to do it for free.

In relation to *public housing*, until 1967 many housing
authorities used the fact that a mother had "illegitimate" children as a basis for excluding her from public
housing. In December of 1968 the Department of Housing
and Urban Development sent a circular to all public
housing authorities stating that having one or more
"illegitimate" children *may not be used as a basis for
keeping women and children out of public housing.* It
is, however, not illegal for housing authorities to be
concerned with the "morality" of tenants and prospective tenants. It is not hard to imagine that mothers
of "illegitimate" children may often receive unfavorable treatment for this reason.

If you suspect that you have been discriminated against
by public housing officials because you have "illegitimate" children, you should consult an attorney at once.
Chances are the discrimination was illegal.

> *Most illegitimate children . . . are the result
> of a mistake. . . . The second time around we
> think represents a lack of judgment and demon-
> strates an unstable moral attitude on the part
> of the mother . . . that is inconsistent with the
> minimum moral standards the community requires.*

These words were taken from the opinion of a Maryland
court decision (*In re Cager*) which was reversed by the
Maryland Court of Appeals. The original decision, from
which the quotation was taken, illustrates the lengths
to which overenthusiastic law men (a state attorney in
this case) may go to use the law to enforce what they
consider to be "morality" in determining the matter of
custody. In the above-mentioned case, the state attorney had a suit brought to remove an "illegitimate"
child from its mother's custody on the ground that she
had "neglected" her child by giving birth to a second
"illegitimate" child! The confidential information was
obtained from cooperative welfare officials.

The traditional rule has been that mothers had a right
to custody of their "illegitimate" children, while
fathers did not. Some states exclude such fathers from
adoption proceedings when the mother has decided to
surrender the child. It is clear that in almost every

state, the fathers of "illegitimate" children do not have
the same rights as the fathers of "legitimate" children,
although in most states today, the father of "illegitimate" children can get custody if the mother dies. In
many states these fathers have a right to custody of
their children which is secondary only to that of the
mother.

Some states have laws which provide that if the father
chooses to live with his "illegitimate" child, that
child becomes "legitimate," and the father has full
rights to custody and visitation as if he and the child's
mother were married.

In the matter of *names*, "illegitimate" children have
usually been given the surname of their mothers. This
was, in fact, one of the main ways the stigma of
"illegitimacy" was applied. Any child whose last
name belonged to her or his mother was known to the
community as "illegitimate." Recent changes in the
area of the rights of women and children's names
have changed this rule somewhat. See the section on a
woman's right to her own name in this chapter for further information.

Q: Is there any way to change the status of a child who
was registered "illegitimate" at birth?

A: Yes, there are several ways, depending on the state you
live in. In all states, the child becomes "legitimate"
when you marry the father. In some states, marrying
the father is the *only* way to make the child "legitimate."

Q: Suppose I am not married when my child is born. Is
there any way I can prevent its being registered as
"illegitimate"?

A: It depends. This is one time when you may want to
assert a common-law marriage, if you have one. The
fact that you do not use the father's last name should
not determine whether your child is "legitimate" or
"illegitimate." In some states a child becomes "legitimate" as soon as it is "acknowledged" by the father.
If he is willing to take legal responsibility for the
child, and have his name on the birth certificate, the
child is "legitimate" in those states.

In some states the status of "illegitimate" has been abolished, and in others, hospitals and state bureaus of vital statistics or other agencies are no longer allowed to classify children as "legitimate" and "illegitimate." Your local legal services attorney should be able to tell you what is true for your state. Or you can write to the Attorney General of your state asking for an opinion about the legality of branding some children as "illegitimate."

Q: Is there any way to do away with this problem once and for all?

A: Sure. Abolish the status of "illegitimate." Several countries, including New Zealand, have done this without any noticeable ill effects. This could be accomplished in America either on a national or state-by-state basis. The United States Supreme Court has resisted several opportunities to declare that all discrimination based on this status is unconstitutional and illegal, but it might still come to this conclusion. Another possibility is that this kind of discrimination will continue to be abolished on a state level, either by means of legislation or suits brought by "illegitimate" children and their parents in local courts.

▶▶▶ *JERRI*

I got married when I was 15. It was in April. Only fools get married in April. At the time, I was a mother before I was a wife. I married him for three reasons. I loved him, he was able to support me, and I had his child.

My husband was in the service when we married. When he came home, he was changed. He seemed very hostile towards me and said he was in love with someone else. We really did not know each other having been apart for so long. I left him mainly because of his brutality towards me. I stayed as long as I could.

I saved money while he was in the service and bought some furniture for the house. I was used to trying to manage money when he came home. It's different for a woman . . . by instinct you have to know how to survive. I knew I could manage somehow after I left him. I went and stayed with my sister and

*family until I could get set up in my own place.
They helped me out a lot.*

*How did the breakup affect the children? I don't
think it bothered the oldest. My husband and I
alternated in taking care of him. If anything, they
were relieved to get away from him and all the problems we had living together. It was probably hardest on the unborn child. I was pregnant when I left
my husband, and I felt bitter and hostile. I was
angry because he would not work at the marriage.
We didn't know each other well, and he did not seem
the same when he returned home from the service. I
felt as though he could have tried more to make
things work out.*

*My biggest problem now is being on D.P.A. I want to
buy a home for my kids--the meager money from welfare
does not allow me to do so. I know what I want. . . .
I'm a determined person. If I were to do it all over
again, I would have three kids and a man who wants
to take care of his family. I'm not thinking about
remarrying. If I did, I would marry for security,
but I think I would rather shack. I have always
wanted to be a housewife. I don't want to work even
though I had to. I come from a big family, and my
mother worked hard to support us all. I want someone to support me and raise the family.*

FIVE: FINANCIAL RESOURCES

THE ECONOMIC REALITIES OF SEPARATION AND DIVORCE

The bizarre myth that women get rich from divorce and live luxuriously on alimony persists despite overwhelming evidence to the contrary. In theory, a wife is entitled to up to one-third her husband's income in the form of alimony, and up to one-half for alimony and child support together. Of course, two households are more expensive than one, so that even if she does get half his income for herself and the children, a mother is living on less than half of what she had before. And her half gets split at least two ways-- between herself and how ever many children she may have. Needless to say, such high alimony and support awards are exceedingly rare, and even more rarely complied with.

As a result, divorced women do not lie in bed eating chocolates and watching soap operas all day. According to the U.S. Bureau of Labor Statistics, almost half of all separated and divorced women *with children under six* work, as compared to only one-third of the married women with children of the same age. Not that there's anything wrong with working--if you get paid decently. But child care is expensive, and women with children under six cannot work without some form of child care.

No wonder over three times as many families below the poverty line are headed by women as above (37 percent of all poor families are headed by women as compared to 11 percent of those above the poverty line). A Consumer Income study published by the Bureau of the Census in December 1973 indicates that women earn approximately *half* of what men with comparable educations earn, with the median income for men with eighth-grade educations ($6149 per year) being just short of the median income for women with college educations ($6842 per year)!

Occasionally a woman will find herself in better financial shape following a divorce, but this is usually true only when she was in fairly bad shape during the marriage. For example, if the husband is not working or earns less than his wife and/or runs up a number of debts for which the wife is held responsible, she stands to see some financial advantages after the divorce.

Women who have forgone education and/or careers for marriage and motherhood are in the worst financial position following a divorce. No matter how good the settlement, she is probably going to have to work to make ends meet, and her intelligence, skills, and long years of service at home are not going to be fully rewarded in the marketplace. Women who have continued to go to school or work during the marriage are in a much better position, as are those without preschool children.

This is all said by way of being realistic, not to frighten or discourage you. If the situation seems hopeless, have patience. It really isn't. One of the most important things you can do to minimize the economic trauma is to plan in advance. Don't allow a divorce to go through without a property, support, and custody agreement that you feel represents a fair and reasonable division of the resources accumulated during the marriage. Insist that the child-support payments allow the children to live at approximately the same level they would have had there been no divorce. Otherwise they are being punished for their parents' incompatibility.

If property settlement and child-support payments are out of the question for you, you already know that your options are even more strictly limited. The myths about women on welfare are even more cruel and ridiculous than those about women living on alimony. If you were on welfare before the separation or divorce you already know what to expect and how to survive on next to nothing. There are some things

Photo by: Eva Shaderowfsky

Feminist Resources

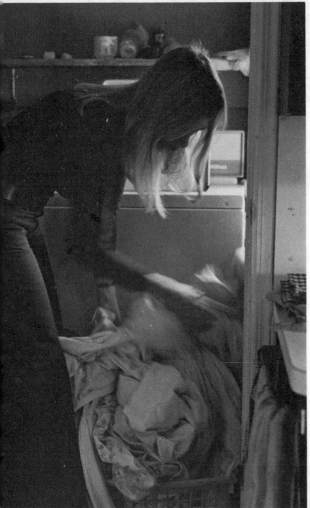

Photo by: Eva Shaderowfsky

Photo by: Diane Deitchman Tong

Photo by: Diane Deitchman Tong

you might learn about your rights from the welfare section
of this chapter that you had not realized (or ever been
told) before. Many women find themselves thinking about
welfare for the first time in their lives following a separation or divorce. This is often true if your husband just
up and left you and the children and you have no idea of
his whereabouts. If this is your situation, don't panic.
It isn't easy, but women have been surviving like this for
centuries. You will want to read the welfare section of
this chapter very carefully.

No matter how desperate your financial situation seems,
you should remember that at least now you are economically
independent and may be working your way toward a financial
security you could never have known as a wife, simply
because wives are, in most cases, totally dependent on
their husbands' economic resources and generosity.

The separation or divorce may be the kick you always needed
to continue your education, acquire skills, or pursue a
career. It will force you to become economically independent and to develop your own resources. We don't mean to
paint a rosy picture of a bleak situation, but once you
learn the ropes it may be possible to get job training or a
college education while on welfare. For those of you who
are not on welfare, your new independence will force you to
develop the job skills and other abilities you have.

Careful planning for the future and conscientious budgeting
for the present are now absolutely essential. If you are
still at the planning stage--about to negotiate a separation
agreement--the following list may help you figure what your
financial needs will be. The list includes maximum expenses
for maintaining yourself, your children, and your house.
If you have been living on a low or moderate income, you may
never have had money for all these things, and a separation
agreement or support order (or welfare) won't provide them
now. But you should seriously consider putting these types
of expenses into your separation agreement if they were part
of your pre-separation life-style.

Itemized List Of Expenses

1. Food: at home, at work, at school, for you and children.

2. Housing: rent, garage, mortgages.

3. Home Maintenance: painting and upkeep, repairs (major
    and minor appliances--washer, radio), exterior repairs

(driveway, roof, gutters), interior repairs (walls, ceilings), furniture repair.

4. Utilities: gas, electricity, telephone, water, oil.

5. Transportation: car--replacement price, registration fee, gas and oil, repairs. Other transportation expenses, including public transportation fares, parking meters, tolls.

6. Insurance: medical, car, homeowners, disability, life.

7. Medicine: (not covered by insurance) dentist, eye doctor, other specialists, drugs, vitamins, supplies.

8. Clothes: yours and children's. Clothing repair and maintenance (laundromat, dry cleaning, sewing). New clothes, shoes.

9. Household supplies and maintenance: laundry and cleaning supplies, general supplies, household replacement-- sheets, towels, etc.

10. Recreation and entertainment: movies, hobbies, sports, eating out, concerts, classes, vacations.

11. Child care and education: day care center, baby-sitter, books and supplies, school tuition, room and board.

12. Taxes: federal, state, sales, local income tax, real estate.

13. Education for wife and children: tuition, fees, books and other supplies, transportation, day care.

Once you figure out how much you need and what you are likely to get, you should set up a budget that you can live with and stick to it. We feel the importance of a budget cannot be overemphasized. You may have managed the finances in your family all along; in that case, you already know the trials of budgeting. But if you have never had a very clear idea of your family's finances, you will need to learn how to handle money, and the less you have the more strictly you will have to plan and stick to the budget.

It's hard, when you have so little money that you really can't afford anything, to think of trying to plan your spending, but we all need to, and this outline is designed to help you step by step, week by week.

A Partial Plan For Budgeting

1. First, when you get your check (pay, welfare, support,
    other) take out enough to get through the week and
    deposit the rest in the bank.

2. Pay the major bills first: rent, utilities, car pay-
    ments, insurance, credit, loans.

3. Subtract what you have paid from your total check to
    see what you have left. Compute the number of days you
    will have to live on it, and how much you will have per
    day or week.

4. This is it! There isn't any more. The money left over
    will have to pay for food, clothes, gas or car repairs,
    other transportation, and anything else you buy consis-
    tently.

5. Buy your food, the most essential items first, then
    calculate what you have left to buy the things that are
    more expensive or not absolutely necessary.

6. Try to handle expenses one week at a time. Some people
    put their money into labeled envelopes marked with what
    the money is for. Whenever possible don't buy on a
    payment plan or credit, or on the promise of next
    week's (or month's) check. You may find an emergency
    has gobbled that check before you can make the payment,
    and besides, credit is expensive. You pay a lot more
    for an item bought on credit (time) than one you pay
    cash for.

7. Try to stretch your expenses out over the month so that
    there isn't one time when all your money is needed for
    bills.

Usually, you're doing well if you can make it from check to
check. If you can save, take the amount of money you want
to put away as soon as you get it and deposit it in the
bank. You may want to open a savings account and try to
save money regularly; if it is in a savings account it will
earn interest, which it will not do in your checking
account.

Even a very small amount of savings may enable you to meet
emergencies or additional expense (like school clothes for
the children in the fall), or to take a vacation or purchase

a much-needed appliance (washer, dryer, or car). Finally,
if you are fortunate enough to get through the week, meet
all your expenses, and actually have money left over,
spend it on yourself for being so fortunate and thrifty.

You're the one who is in charge now. Maybe you always have
been and didn't know it. The money that you have, as
little as it may be, is yours and yours alone to budget,
spend, save, and you and your children are the people who
should enjoy it as well as worry over it.

JOAN

*The first strike against poor mothers is being poor,
strike two is being a mother, and there seems to be
no end to it after that.*

*You are on welfare and one day you receive a letter
from your caseworker "requesting" you come and see
her on such and such a day or your welfare will be
discontinued. You get there with time to spare,
there are ten people ahead of you, and you wait.
When you first applied for welfare, you had to give
your life history, your mother's and your father's,
and maybe any other relative they chose to pick on
that day. Next they tell you that you have to take
your husband to court for support. Not knowing any
different, you do what they tell you.*

*Up to this time, he has been an all right guy, if
you are lucky and if he has bothered to get a job.
When he receives this notice to appear in domestic
court, he blows his top. He comes to see you and
tells you that he has been helping you as much as
he can, which more times than not is true, but
that from now on you'll have to catch him first,
and out he goes. The money he was giving you goes
with him.*

*OK, back to this important visit to your caseworker.
You finally get to see her, and what do you hear?*

*"Mrs. Jones, I have heard that you are doing day
work. You should have reported this to me! I'm
afraid your grant will have to be lowered."*

*And you think, "What the hell is the sense in trying?
You are beat before you even get started."*

LIVING ON WELFARE

One of the leaders of the National Welfare Rights Organization has suggested that women who live on welfare know more
about finances than the richest man in the country. They
have to, just to survive, she insists. Fortunately, you
don't have to be a financial genius to get on to welfare.
It's a kind of training program in how to live on nothing.
Seriously, living on welfare is one of the hardest ways
to survive imaginable. But knowing your rights and insisting on them may make life on welfare a little more livable.
You don't have to take insults, prying questions, and
condescension. Welfare is not a handout but a *right*. The
information in this section should enable you to know what
to expect from welfare, what you are entitled to receive in
terms of money and other benefits, and what rights you have
if you think you are not being treated fairly.

The first step for anyone on welfare, or thinking about
applying, is to contact the local office of the National
Welfare Rights Organization. This organization is made up
of welfare recipients who have acquired a great deal of
knowledge and expertise in coping with and changing the
welfare system. Their services are open to all low-income
and poor people and to all senior citizens. To find out
how to get in touch with the chapter nearest you, look in
the local telephone book, ask telephone information, or
write:

>   National Welfare Rights Organization
>   1420 N. Street, N.W.
>   Washington, D.C. 20005

or call: 1-202-483-1531.

Now for some basic information about welfare and the rights
of welfare recipients.

Who Is Eligible?

There is one category of people entitled to state and
federally financed welfare: families with dependent children. This welfare program (called Aid to Families With
Dependent Children--AFDC) is run by the states, but half

the funds come from the federal government and the program
must meet federal requirements. People who do not fall
into this category may be eligible for general assistance
or for Supplementary Security Income (SSI; this will be
explained later). General assistance is administered solely
by the states, so it varies from state to state. Payments
in this program are usually less than in the federal program. SSI is administered by the federal government under
the Social Security Administration.

If you are a woman in transition with little income you
will probably qualify for Aid to Families with Dependent
Children (AFDC). To be eligible, you must be pregnant or
have at least one child, you must live with and take care
of the child, and your husband (or the child's father)
must be either unable or unwilling to support the child.
This means that the father of your child must be dead,
disabled, or not living with you.

In 22 states there is a program called Aid to Families with
Dependent Children and an Unemployed Father (AFDCU). There
are four requirements for this program. 1. In order to be
considered "unemployed" the father must have worked less
than 100 hours a month and earn less than enough to meet
the family needs; 2. the father must have been "unemployed"
(not working at all or working less than 100 hours a month)
for at least 30 days; 3. the father must be willing to
accept any genuine offer of work or job training; and 4. the
father must have been employed in the past.

Since all states require a father to support his children,
even if he is not married to their mother, the welfare
office will probably ask you to cooperate in getting
support from the father of your children. This may mean
several things. If they tell you you must sue him in
support court, they are wrong. You cannot be forced to
sue him as a condition of getting on welfare. You and the
children are entitled to receive welfare, and the welfare
department is entitled to sue your husband for the support
he owes for your child. You are better off letting them
sue him and getting your welfare check regularly (unless,
of course, he would pay a lot more under a support order
than you could get from welfare). You are, however,
obligated to cooperate with the welfare department in
telling them his name and address (if you know it; if you
don't you can't tell, and they can't punish you). There is
still much controversy and confusion over whether you can
be denied welfare if you refuse to give the name of the
father of your children. Several recent cases suggest that

you cannot be denied welfare or punished for refusing to
give his name, even if you know it. But most welfare
departments disagree with this ruling, and will do everything in their power to get you to give this information if
you know it. If you refuse to give this information and
are deprived of any of your welfare rights, you should contact both the local Welfare Rights Organization and a legal
services lawyer (free) *immediately*.

If you remarry, your children are still entitled to AFDC
because a husband is required by law to support his wife,
but not her children through a previous relationship.
Unless the stepfather wants to and does support the children, the welfare office must continue AFDC.

How Do You Apply?

If you want to apply for welfare, check your local telephone directory under "Welfare" and find the office nearest
where you live. Call that office and ask for an appointment. On the day of your appointment, you should bring
with you your children's birth certificates (or a statement
from a doctor saying that you are pregnant), any pay stubs
that show what your income is, and rent receipts, utilities
bills, medical bills, and any other papers that show how
much money you need. You will be given an application to
be filled out. *Everyone must be allowed to fill out an
application and be given the reasons in writing if the
application is denied. Everyone has a right to appeal if
the application is denied.* Federal regulations require
that the welfare department let you know within 45 days
after you apply whether your request has been granted. If
you have been approved, you first check will arrive with
this notification. In some states you will hear sooner.

Emergencies

If you are absolutely without money for the next day's food,
or have any other comparable emergency, call for an appointment at the welfare office in the morning and explain that
it is an emergency. In some localities, even in an emergency, it may take two days to get an appointment. Some
women have found that the most effective way to get an
emergency check is to go to the welfare office (bring your
children and your friends if you wait) and wait there until
you get your check.

How Much Can I Expect?

A good thing to remember is that you will probably not get
enough to live on adequately. The method used to figure
out how much you are entitled to is fairly complicated, and
is included at the end of the welfare section of this
chapter so that you can figure out in advance how much you
can get from welfare. This may help you in deciding
whether it is worth it to take your husband to support
court. It will also help you figure out whether you are
getting the proper amount. Welfare workers do make mistakes!

Some states use what is called a "flat grant" system which
gives the same amount of welfare to every family, regardless
of family size and expenses. The only thing that would
vary the grant is the amount of family income.

In other states, the welfare office has a set of predetermined "maximum allowances" based on the size of your family
with allowances for living expenses such as rent, utilities,
food, clothing, and incidentals. Different states also
recognize various special needs such as special diets for
pregnant women and sick people, expenses for work and education, transportation allowance for travel to regular doctors' appointments, and other regular necessary expenses.

You should ask your caseworker or a Welfare Rights Organization worker what special expenses are recognized in your
state. Your expenses will be compared to the maximum
allowances. If, for example, your rent is less than the
maximum allowance, your grant will equal your rent and so
be below the maximum allowance. But even if any of your
expenses are greater than the maximum allowance, your
grant will never exceed the maximum allowance. Your family
income minus deductions for such items as taxes and child-
care expenses (if you are working) is then deducted from
the computed grant to arrive at the sum you will receive.

You are entitled to and should demand a written statement
of how your welfare grant was determined. You should also
ask a Welfare Rights Organization worker or someone you
trust who knows the local rules whether you are getting the
right amount. Or you could use the information at the end
of this section to figure it out yourself.

Support Payments And Welfare

If you are receiving regular support payments from the

father of your children, this will be considered "income" to you and deducted from whatever amount you might receive from welfare. But if you are not actually receiving the money, despite a court order, it should not be counted as income and deducted from your grant. If you were receiving support payments when you applied for welfare but the payments have stopped since then, tell your caseworker and demand that your grant be increased.

In some places, support payments are made to the welfare department, which then issues a check to the family. If a support payment is missed, the family still gets the check from welfare. Many women have found this to be the best arrangement if it can be worked out.

You Have A Right To Appeal

Any time a decision is made against you--to reduce your grant, find you ineligible for welfare, drop you from the rolls, or increase the amount you pay for food stamps, for example--you have the right to appeal. If you want to protest such a decision, ask your caseworker for an "appeal form." This entitles you to a hearing, which is one of the most important rights you have as a welfare recipient. If you are receiving welfare, you cannot be cut off before this hearing. The hearing must be held within 60 days of the request.

Working With Your Caseworker

A basic rule to remember is that your caseworker must help you to get enough money to live on so long as your needs are not beyond what welfare is allowed to provide. *Never accept the excuse that your caseworker is too busy to help you*. If you have a very hard time reaching her, ask to speak to her supervisor.

Take care of as much business as possible over the telephone. Save your trips to the office for real emergencies (like when you don't receive a check and telephoning produced no satisfactory results). Much of your business can be done through the mail. Call your caseworker and ask her to mail the proper forms to you if you need to report an increase in rent, or want to apply for food stamps, for example. If you make a request and get no response, call again or write a letter. The trick is to find a middle ground between being so polite that nobody remembers your request and being so rude that they deliberately forget you.

If you are confused about something, ask. Caseworkers
can't read minds and are as absentminded and careless as
the rest of us. It will help your caseworker (and your own
financial situation) if you report all changes in your economic situation immediately. If you are going to need more
money because of medical expenses or moving, find out in
advance what welfare will cover. Sometimes advance notice
means the difference between welfare paying and you paying.

Any time you think your caseworker has given you some incorrect information, or you believe she or he has denied you
your rights, ask to speak to the supervisor immediately.
If you are still not satisfied, ask for an appeal form.

What Other Benefits Can I Get From Welfare?

Medical assistance: If you are getting AFDC you automatically receive Medicaid. Medicaid pays for many, but not all
medical expenses. Exactly which expenses are covered varies
from state to state. For information for your state, contact your nearest Welfare Rights Organization, or ask your
caseworker. If you believe Medicaid should pay for something welfare says is not covered, contact the nearest
legal service agency.

You may also be eligible for Medicaid if you are not eligible (or just not receiving) welfare, but your income is
low. States can give Medicaid to anyone who is "medically
needy"--all those whose income can provide for daily living
expenses, but will not cover medical expenses. As a woman
in transition with very little money, you should investigate your eligibility for Medicaid. If your income is close
to the welfare grant level, don't forget to add to the
amount welfare would actually pay you the amount you would
save in medical expenses if you were on welfare. Sometimes
this alone makes being on welfare a better choice than
receiving support payments or having another form of support.

Job training and employment: The welfare department has a
special job training program called a "work incentive"
program, "WIN." Everybody except women with children under
6 years old and mothers in families receiving AFDC is eligible for the WIN program. In addition, you must have been
receiving welfare for the past four months to qualify for
this program.

Those who are in the WIN program may have one of three job
situations: on-the-job training in the regular job market,

a special training program, or a public service job. If
you are in one of the training programs, you get to keep
the first $30 of your monthly salary and to deduct one-
third of your income from the amount used to determine your
eligibility. So you can get a maximum grant even though
you are also earning income from a regular job. This is
true regardless of whether or not you qualify for WIN. If
you work while you receive welfare, up to one-third of your
salary will not reduce your grant. If you take a "public
service" job you get no work incentive--everything you earn
may be deducted from your grant.

Everyone receiving AFDC who has a regular job is entitled
to allowance for work-related expenses such as taxes, transportation, child care, and union dues. In fact, you are
probably better off finding your own job while on welfare
than applying for the WIN program. There are not nearly
enough jobs to go around to all those who are qualified for
the program, and the training programs are, for the most
part, a joke. Welfare considers jobs for unemployed *fathers*
most important, so you're low on the totem pole, but at
least one judge has ruled this preference is really "discrimination," so if you're told you don't qualify or can't
get a job or training through WIN and you suspect it's
because you're a *mother* rather than a father, you should
see a lawyer.

What is SSI?

The Supplemental Security Income (SSI) is a federal program
administered by the Social Security Administration. It is
available to those poor people who are over 65 years of age,
or disabled, or blind. To qualify, your income must be
less than $1680 a year for a single person or $2520 a year
for a couple. Also, you must have less than $1550 worth of
"resources" if you are single, or less than $2250 for a
couple. "Resources" include things like a bank account,
stocks, or securities, but do not include the value of your
car or a home worth up to $25,000 and one acre of property.
Everyone on SSI is entitled to Medicaid.

To determine eligibility for SSI, $20 is subtracted from
your social security check, then $65 plus half the balance
is subtracted from any income you have from employment. If
this figure is less than $1680 per year for an individual,
you are eligible. The federal grant is $150 a month per
person, and some states contribute additional sums to make
the amount higher.

You can be on SSI and have children on AFDC, or you may be on AFDC and have a disabled child (blind, paralyzed, or otherwise disabled) who is receiving SSI. To apply for SSI, go to the local Social Security Administration. If you are turned down or are given less than you believe you deserve, you have a right to review. The review procedure here is similar to that used in social security.

What Is The Food Stamp Program?

Food stamps are another one of the hidden bonuses of welfare. Not that they make life easy, but if you are trying to decide whether it is worth it for you to apply for welfare, you should not forget to count in the money you would save by getting food stamps. In a close case, it might be better to take a little less cash from welfare in order to get food stamps and free medical care.

If everyone in your household is eligible for assistance, you are automatically eligible for food stamps. Food stamps are also available to people on SSI. If you are on welfare or SSI *be sure to ask for food stamps*. Your case-worker may not even mention that you have a right to them! Some people who are not eligible for welfare (because their incomes are just above the maximum grant levels) are eligible for food stamps. Check with your local welfare office to see if you are eligible for food stamps. (The maximum income allowed for food stamp recipients is $500 a month for a family of four. As in welfare, certain deductions can be made from your income before eligibility is determined.)

Food stamp grants are the same everywhere. A family of four receives $150 worth of stamps. Your income will determine how much you pay for this amount of stamps. If you are denied food stamps, or the amount you pay is increased, you may request a hearing. You should be informed of this right to a hearing at the time you apply for the stamps.

Welfare Language

Grant—the amount of money you receive each month from welfare. Your grant may be either the maximum monthly grant for your state (a set amount which depends only on the size of your family) or a grant supplement. If you have any deductible income you will receive only a supplement. That is, you will get less than the maximum monthly grant, because you are partially supporting yourself from

your own income. Your grant just brings you up to the level
of people on welfare.

Deductible income--a somewhat complicated idea. Basically,
it's the amount of money you have left over from your paycheck after you subtract many necessary expenses--what you
can count on having in your pocket to spend on groceries
and the like. See the table on "Figuring Your Welfare
Grant" for an illustration.

Gross income--the amount of money you earn before any deductions are made (e.g., social security, taxes, pension
fund).

Net income--the amount of money you take home after all the
deductions are made.

Work incentive allowance--$30 plus one-third of your income
which is not counted as income in figuring your grant. This
means you get to keep this amount "free and clear," so you
can actually have a little more each month than you would
if you received a maximum monthly grant but did not work.

FREDA

*The welfare payments here [a small town in South
Jersey] are higher than in the city--$370.00 for
myself and four children. City housing [projects,
etc.] is quite modern with sliding glass doors and
fully maintained, and only costs 25 percent of your
check including all utilities. I imagine that would
be a big help to someone unable to work with just
one or two children. The educational programs [WIN
and others] are unbelievable and go all out to make
arrangements for child care that are suitable for
you. I guess that this can be done better here than
in the city because it's a smaller community. Also,
you can usually contact your caseworker or see him
the same day.*

*The Medicaid program is also fantastic. It's avail-
able to many people, not just welfare recipients.
They pay $10-$12 for an office visit so you can imagine that the doctors just about kiss your *** and
don't mind the paperwork at all. Unlike in the city,
the specialists here all take the card. When my
daughter needed an appendectomy, I took her to the
surgeon who was chief of staff at the hospital. She*

*was in a semiprivate room and the bill was $0. I
didn't even have to pay for the I.D. bracelet.*

Figuring Your Welfare Grant

This example is meant to help you understand what welfare
does with the information you give them to determine your
eligibility and the size of your grant.

For a family of four in State X: maximum monthly grant is
$215. The family in our example consists of a mother and
three young children.

The mother works and her gross monthly income is $400.00

Her work incentive is: $246.67

            $400.00
            -30.00
            370.00
          -123.33 (1/3 of 370)
            $246.67

Her monthly deductible expenses are:

            $50.00 taxes
             90.00 rent
             30.00 day care
             10.00 transportation to and from
                    work
             50.00 utilities
          $230.00

Her gross income $400.00

minus her deductions $230.00

amount to: $170.00 which is less than $215--

the maximum monthly grant, so she is eligible. To determine how much she will receive, her caseworker will consider:

```
Her income            $246.67   (after work incentive
                                 allowance)
minus
Her total deductions  $230.00
                      _____
                       16.67    THIS IS THE AMOUNT DEDUCTED
                                FROM THE MAXIMUM MONTHLY GRANT
Maximum monthly
  allowance           $215.00
minus
deductible income     $ 16.67
                      _____
                      $198.33   THIS IS THE AMOUNT WELFARE WILL
                                PAY THIS FAMILY EACH MONTH.
```

So even though the maximum monthly grant in this state for a family of four is $215.00, this family's total gross monthly income is $598.33--$400.00 from the mother's salary and 198.33 from welfare.

```
                              _____
                              $598.33
```

This family will automatically be eligible for a set amount of food stamps for which the mother will have to pay a certain amount.

_____

DONNA

I am forty and expecting my sixth child in November. I am also a middle-class white whose husband has filed for divorce and I am supporting myself and three children by working at a Hallmark card shop for $1.70 an hour. My boss has finally allowed the two pregnant salesclerks an afternoon break of ten minutes because of our "condition."

We've never had one before. We're not supposed to sit at any time and we have thirty minutes for lunch. We walk on concrete floors all day and are tired by closing time. We want to quit but have no skills or training and doubt if anyone will hire obviously pregnant women for anything.

My husband has a good job and makes at least $1,000 per month, maybe more. He's very reticent about money--I never knew about his pay raises or bonuses or moving allowances, except from remarks made by other company wives, who thought I already knew. I really have no idea what my husband's financial

*situation is; he seems to have bank accounts in
nearly every town we've lived in--8 towns in 12
years.*

WOMEN'S WORK

Women have always worked. All during your marriage you
worked. What else would you call lifting babies and carting
piles of dirty clothes to the washer or the laundromat?
Cooking and cleaning, scrubbing and polishing, mopping and
dusting. . . . Shopping, making clothes, paying bills,
pinching pennies. . . . Nursing sick children, waiting on
your husband. What else but work? Slave labor, maybe? The
Chase Manhattan Bank has estimated that the average housewife works *99* hours a week; her labor is worth at least
$10,000, and twice that amount would be reasonable compen-
sation.

But when you sit down to write that job application or
résumé, when you are interviewed for a job, what can you
say about your previous employment? How does your employer
rate you? What was your most recent pay level? You've
acquired many skills, considerable education in a variety
of fields including nutrition, early childhood development,
child psychology, and probably some sociology and economics.
You have physical skill and stamina for which men are well
rewarded on the job market. So what are you qualified for?

You'd probably be able to do any number of jobs for which
you couldn't possibly be hired. Special training, education, or experience are often prerequisites to many jobs
you could do well if you were only given the chance. But
there's no use complaining. There is absolutely no reason
why "women's work" shouldn't be anything a woman wants and
is trained to do. The next section of this chapter should
help you think about the kind of work you want to do and
help you go through the various steps involved in getting
a job, from getting more education or training to writing
résumés and going to interviews. Before you go to apply
for that first job, you may want to consider some of the
following myths that are often given as reasons why women
should not be hired for a particular job, or why they
should be paid less than men. The following information is
some ammunition to help you combat those myths.

The Working Woman's Guide To Employment Myths

Myth #1: "Women don't need to work."

Facts: Two-thirds of the adult poor in America are women.
About 40 percent of the working women in this country must
work to support themselves and/or their families.

Myth #2: "Women don't want to work."

Facts: 43 percent of all women over 16 are in the labor
force. More women, and female heads of households, who
want to work are unemployed than men.

Myth #3: "Women are absent from work more often than men."

Facts: Men lose more time than women. This is particularly dramatic when women over 45 are compared with men of the
same age. If an employer's figures show higher absenteeism
among his women employees, it's because he only hires women
for low-level jobs with little responsibility and much boredom. To get a fair comparison, you must compare employees
at similar levels of responsibility. Boredom produces both
illness and absenteeism.

Myth #4: "There are many jobs women just can't do."

Facts: Many occupations that have been traditionally
considered "for men only" have been successfully performed
by women who have been able to get the necessary training.
This includes occupations like bricklaying, carpentry,
plumbing, and others. New technological developments are
making brute strength less and less a factor in most work,
including factory work.

Myth #5: "Women make bad bosses."

Facts: It is a blow to many a maculine ego to have to take
orders from a woman. The U.S. Civil Service Commission
study shows that men who have worked under a woman supervisor had fewer objections to women in management positions
than those who had not.

Myth #6: "Women don't qualify for the better-paying jobs."

Facts: There are proportionately more women college graduates in the work force than women with elementary school
educations. But even women with college degrees are usually
hired for clerical and secretarial work, or as salespeople.

Even in the good-paying jobs, women are promoted more slowly than men. There are far more training programs open to men with high school educations than women with the same educational level. More women are receiving higher educations today, while the concentration of women in lower-income jobs is increasing rather than decreasing.

Myth #7: "Employment laws protect women rather than discriminate against them."

Facts: "Protective" laws such as those limiting the weight a woman worker may lift are used to keep women out of high-paying jobs that require no more physical strength than lifting a five-year-old. Protective laws would be fairer if they applied equally to men and women.

Myth #8: "Raging hormones hamper job performance."

Facts: There is little scientific evidence that the physiological changes that take place in women's bodies due to menstruation and pregnancy affect job performance at all. All *workers* experience cycles of low energy which produce apathy, indifference, and a tendency to magnify minor problems. Some studies indicate that men also go through a 4-6 week hormonal cycle.

Myth #9: "Working mothers are bad for children."

Facts: This is little more than an update on the old "A woman's place is in the home" platitude. There is no demonstrated significant difference between the lives of children whose mothers stay at home and those whose mothers work. There has never been a single study made of the destructive effect of working fathers on their children!

Myth #10: "Women get equal treatment in the work force."

Facts: Untrue! Women earn, on the average, $3.00 for every $5.00 earned by men in similar positions. And the position of women in the work force is not improving, but getting worse. In 1955 women earned 63.9 percent of what men earned in America. In 1970 they made only 59.4 percent.

Looking And Applying For Jobs

Start by making a list of jobs you might qualify for. Consider all your skills and experience, and don't forget to include skills you have acquired as a wife and mother, or as a result of hobbies or other interests. Next, figure how much you will have to earn to support yourself (and your children if they are living with you). Check the want ads in the newspaper to see what kinds of jobs that you would qualify for would meet your expenses.

Before you begin your job hunt in earnest, step back and consider. Can you afford to not work long enough to investigate some new possibilities? Is your husband willing or able to give you enough money to enable you to take courses in school, enroll in college, or attend a vocational school? If you think it worthwhile to discuss this possibility with him, you might remind him that it will save him money in the long run. The sooner you are self-supporting and the better paid you are the less you will need from him.

Evaluate your skills and interests carefully. Is there any area that you are interested in, or have had some experience in, that might develop into a job possibility? Have you worked on your own car, done electrical work, carpentry, or plumbing in your own home? If you did things like these and enjoyed them, you might consider attending a vocational school or finding a training program to enable you to receive certification in these fields. Or you might be able to get a job at a local gas station, with a carpenter you know, or take courses from the local Y or women's center in the areas of your interest. Look into apprenticeship programs as well.

In other words, if you are not immediately desperate for income to meet this week's expenses, look at long-range goals and possibilities. A job which offers a chance for growth and development in the future is probably better than one which starts off at a higher pay rate but offers little hope of advancement.

Take time to ask yourself these questions:

What do I want from a job? Am I going to have to depend on my income for part or all of my family's expenses?

How much money will I need to make ends meet?

How many hours a week can I work? During what part of the day?

What qualifications do I have? Education, previous job training, experience at home or through volunteer work?

What jobs have I held?

What did I enjoy about those jobs? What did I dislike?

What kind of job do I want? Involving numbers and money,
travel, meeting people, sales? Do I prefer to work alone,
or with people? How important is flexible scheduling, independence, freedom to move around?

What am I especially good at? Think back--what areas interested you in high school, before marriage? If you can't
think of anything, you might consider taking aptitude tests,
available through career development agencies, among other
places. But beware--these tests can be quite expensive (and
sometimes a little ridiculous). Your best guide is your own
feeling and your own memory.

Are there jobs or situations which make me feel uncomfortable, incapable? Why? Should I avoid them?

After answering these questions, you should be able to have
a good idea of what kind of job you are looking for. You
should survey the job possibilities with your answers to
these questions in your mind.

Where To Look

As with housing, look first to friends and associates. Call
your friends and people you know in the area you are interested in. Often the best jobs are never advertised in the
newspapers--they are filled by word of mouth. And besides,
if you have friends who know of an opening, you are in a
better position than the applicant who comes in off the
street.

Professional organizations and unions sometimes have their
own placement offices. Even if you are not a member, they
may advise you of openings. To find out the names and
addresses of these groups, call a local school and inquire
in the department related to your field of interest. You
can also try the Chamber of Commerce, or the personnel department of a firm hiring people in your field.

College placement offices may have services for graduates
and members of the community (but don't count on it). Your
chances are much better if you keep in mind the skills and
interests you have and find organizations that are relevant
to them.

State employment agencies are not likely places to find a
job. Generally they are poorly staffed, smothered in paperwork and red tape, and have few jobs of any merit. You
should not totally ignore them, however, on the chance you
may find a lead if not a job.

The local Chamber of Commerce can give you the names and
addresses of firms which offer work in your area. You might
send a cover letter and a résumé to these firms in the hope
that they will keep your résumé on file or answer your letter with an indication of when they expect to be hiring
next. You might also try the telephone directory. Don't
expect great results by this method. Jobs are scarce, and
you usually need something more personal than a résumé to a
company selected out of the telephone directory. But *try
everything*.

A few civil service jobs are available in many different
work areas. The qualifying procedures generally take
several days, with oral and written tests given to groups
at scheduled times. Once you pass the tests, you are put
on a list of people eligible for certain jobs. Don't be
intimidated by the tests. You don't have to be a genius to
pass them. Civil service jobs generally offer better pay
than similar jobs in the private sector, and they offer
excellent fringe benefits. Getting the job often requires
a long waiting period, and the job may be tedious or dull
and require you put in strictly 9-5 hours, where a small
private employer might allow more flexibility to accommodate
your family schedule. Many civil service jobs (but not all)
require a college-level education.

Looking through the newspaper want ads is not a bad way to
find a job. Most ads are no longer separated by sex, but
if they are in your area, look under "Help Wanted, Male" as
well as "Female." Some employment agencies or career counseling facilities may help you. But be careful. Some are
just looking for more places to send their clients, and will
ask you detailed questions about other places you have
applied for jobs. You don't have to tell them.

Some employment agencies require that you sign a contract
or pay a large fee in advance. An agency that will take
your first week's paycheck as payment *after* finding you a
job is better than one that asks for money in advance with
no guarantee. If the agency indicates it guarantees a job,
be sure to write on the application next to your signature,
"For fee-paid job only." Beware of false ads by agencies

just wanting to collect résumés. They may tell you that the job is filled and then send you where no job opening exists. Some agencies will also call your current employer, tell him you're looking for another job, and ask if they can find your replacement!

Temporary agencies often require no fee and offer jobs of varying length. It has been our experience that temporary agencies may help you if you need only temporary work or just want to brush up on your skills, but it is unlikely that you will find a permanent job this way.

Writing A Résumé

A résumé is not a French dish. It is an advertisement for yourself which will convince an employer to hire you (hope-fully). You may take a résumé to an interview, send it to firms employing people in the area you wish to work in, or use it as a capsule of the information an employer might want to know about you. Most résumés contain the following kinds of information:

1. Your name (conspicuously placed, in the center of the page or to the far right or left).

2. Your address and phone number.

3. The particular job or general kind of work you are interested in.

4. Your work history, arranged in chronological order with the most recent job listed first. For each job you should list:

    name and address of the company

    dates of your employment

    name of your supervisor

    description of your duties

    skills learned, training received

    unusual accomplishments or awards earned, promotions or increased duties.

5. Your education:

    schools attended and dates

    courses taken after high school or college

    vocational schools, previous job training, in-
    service courses or institutes

6. Anything you have done related to the area you are
    looking for a job in, including:

    volunteer activities, community work, courses

    freelance work--poster design, layout, writing
    articles for community paper, teaching classes at a
    day camp, day care center, neighborhood center,
    civic activities

    sports, home maintenance, office skills.

7. Personal data, including:

    birthdate

    marital status (Either "married" or "single." "Sep-
    arated" or "divorced" flashes red lights to lots of
    employers--"unstable" is what they see.)

    dependents (If your children are young, you can
    expect to be asked who will care for them while you
    work.)

    car ownership, driver's license

    any license or certification you may have--e.g.,
    nursing, teaching, cosmetology, any trade

8. Personal references:

    name, address, and telephone number of two or more
    people who know you well and will affirm your quali-
    fications, character, etc. Bear in mind that the
    people you list as references should be people with a
    good reputation themselves. People like your minis-
    ter or priest, your child's teacher or principal,
    or your family doctor are possible references.
    Former employers, if you have any, are excellent.

Be sure to get permission from a person before using her or his name as a reference.

Using A Résumé

Usually a résumé is not the most effective way to go about getting a job. You may send out ten résumés without a single response. A résumé is often more effective for people who have some kind of professional training or education than for those who do not. By itself, a résumé is, at best, a foot in the door of a personnel office. But having a résumé that stresses your good points and plays down your limitations can be helpful in your search for a job. It can also help you focus on the information a would-be employer would want to know, and enable you to anticipate the kinds of questions he or she might ask you.

Finally, your résumé should be neat, with correct spelling, punctuation, and grammar. Have copies made on a Xerox or mimeograph machine. Carbon copies are not good. Sometimes you will want to modify your standard résumé for a particular employer.

The Job Interview

You find a likely job in the want ads and call the number listed. "Come in tomorrow at nine-thirty," says a voice at the other end. Or perhaps you have sent out your résumés and a firm has sent you a letter advising you of its interviewing schedule. What do you do next? What is expected of you?

It is always a good idea to go to a job interview, even though it may seem like a waste of time. Job interviews can range from a "chat" with the owner of a small office to a formal interview with personnel people and elaborate tests that take all day. You can't be sure which type of interview you're going to until you're there, so it's important to be prepared.

One thing to do is make a list of the questions you want to ask. Ask about salary, hours, benefits, and the like. Inquire about the range of duties, the availability of training programs and advancement, and skills needed for the job. Find out how you will be evaluated. See if there is a union (you might do better to ask employees this question). Find out what facilities and assistance will be available. How long is the job likely to last? Is there a probationary

period after which you are automatically permanently employed? What qualifications does the employer value most
in an employee?

Try to meet the people who work there. Look around, if you
can. See how they seem to work, what they are doing. Are
they relaxed, tense, or bored? Is the atmosphere friendly
and helpful, or competitive?

Find out, when possible, why the job is open. Did the
employee whose place you would fill quit? Was she fired?
Her problems may come to haunt you. Better to know in
advance.

Find out how many women are in the firm, what they do, if
it seems likely that being a woman will stand in the way of
a promotion or even keeping your job.

Interview your employer. What does she or he do? How is
her or his job different from yours? How does your employer feel about her or his job, the firm in general? Ask to
see samples of what you will be expected to do. Find out
how closely you will be working with your employer.

Be prepared to face questions about your marital status,
children, whether you plan to remarry, have more children,
what your husband does for a living, and how long you are
interested in working.

You do not have to discuss your husband's or ex-husband's
employment or lack of it. You can say that as a single or
divorced woman you are taking on the responsibility of working to support your family, and that you are sure you are
capable of doing the job.

Your interview is a chance for you to demonstrate the
qualities that your employer is looking for. Stress that
you want a stable work situation, a permanent job. When
questions are asked of you that you don't want to answer,
try to evade them, but don't antagonize your interviewer.

At all costs, *be on time*.Punctuality is highly valued.
They may keep you waiting (especially if they have many
applicants and are interviewing them individually), but
it creates a bad impression for you to be late.

Dress neatly and conservatively. An interview is not a
cocktail party, so tone down the makeup, jewelry, or

perfume. In some places it is still considered bad taste
to wear slacks to an interview (or work). Play it safe.
You should look like you could qualify for a better position than the one you are applying for.

If you expect a bad recommendation from your previous employer, warn your prospective employer. She or he is
likely to find out anyway, so you might as well tell your
side of the story. Tell it briefly, unemotionally, and
without exaggeration. Most employers identify with other
employers, so anything you say about a previous employer
may be taken as an indication of your incompetence or bad
attitude.

Check the standard salary range for the kind of work you
want to do, and, if at all possible, don't take less. You
might be able to find out what the standard range is from
professional organizations, unions, or want ads. Many
firms decide what you will be paid from your last salary.
Some employment counselors advise you list your last salary
as what it should have been instead of what it actually
was, especially if you were underpaid. We think this could
be dangerous advice.

You might consider taking less than the standard salary for a
job if it includes training in an area in which you do not already have skills, if it has good potential for raises or promo-
tions, or you are sure your options are quite limited and
this may be a choice between a job and no job. But don't
make this decision too quickly. It's easy to get discouraged, but it would be foolish to take any job that would
not give you enough money to live on.

If you think you will hate the job, the pay is impossible,
there are no benefits, or you're not going to be able to
get along with your boss or fellow workers, think hard
about whether it's worth it. Maybe you should turn down
the job if it's offered to you. If you start the job with
too many negative feelings, chances are you won't stay at
it long, and you'll be right back where you are now, with
at least one unsatisfactory employment situation on your
record (and maybe a bad recommendation). This is the
hardest decision you can make in all your job hunting,
since you probably need the money, and other factors (such
as friends you make on the job) can make even the worst
job a little better.

But when there is a possibility that you could find another

job that pays better, has more opportunity, or has other good qualities, settling for a job you know you're going to hate doesn't make much sense--unless you are absolutely desperate. Apart from your interview nervousness, is there a concrete reason why you feel this way? If so, consider: If you feel this way before you even take the job, how are you going to feel after six weeks of it?

Present yourself as a valuable person, not just another applicant. Even your prospective employer knows that there is more to you than the skills, work experience, and education listed on your résumé. That's what the interview is for--to bring out these additional assets. Stability, responsibility, enthusiasm, and persistence will endear you to the most steely employers. Even if you haven't had a paid job for a long time (or ever), you have many personal qualities that employers will value, and you have not lost the ability to learn.

If there are no jobs available in an area in which you are qualified, ask when such jobs might become available. And don't be afraid to ask for advice. Some personnel people know other companies with openings. Leave your résumé and call back from time to time to see if there are any new openings.

SEXISM AT WORK: JOB DISCRIMINATION

It is almost impossible to escape some form of discrimination on the job. There, as elsewhere, you will run into many sexist attitudes and false assumptions about the true nature and proper role of women in society. You're a freak if you're not married (or hoping to be), a bad mother if you have young children while you work, and often considered a maid-mother-playmate by your boss--all just because you are a woman. No laws are going to change these attitudes or the more subtle forms of discrimination you are likely to experience.

But *many forms of job discrimination based on race, religion, national origin, and sex are illegal.* The unfair treatment you receive may be covered by one or more federal, state, or local laws. The information in this section is intended to help you decide whether you have been discriminated against illegally and, if you have, to help you take the proper steps to put an end to the discrimination and be compensated for your losses.

Q: What makes job discrimination illegal?

A: Five federal laws and a number of state laws. The five
    federal laws include: 1. Title VII of the 1964 Civil
    Rights Act (generally referred to as "Title VII," and
    administered by the Equal Employment Opportunities
    Commission (EEOC); 2. the "Equal Pay Act"; 3. and 4.
    two Executive Orders (11246, as amended, and 11478); and
    5. the Age Discrimination Act of 1962.

In addition to these federal laws, many states have passed
fair employment practices laws forbidding discrimination
based on sex. State equal rights amendments passed in
Alaska, Colorado, Hawaii, Illinois, Maryland, Montana,
Pennsylvania, Texas, and Washington and state constitutions
in Utah and Texas also forbid sex discrimination. Some
forms of discrimination are also illegal under the Four-
teenth Amendment to the United States Constitution, which
guarantees equal protection of law to all citizens.

Q: Who is covered by these various laws?

A: Title VII is the most comprehensive of these laws, as
    it forbids discrimination practiced by any employer,
    labor union, or employment agency (or apprenticeship
    committee) which employs or has as members more than
    15 people. Employees of local and state agencies are
    covered by Title VII, including schoolteachers and
    municipal employees. Household workers and agricul-
    tural workers are not covered by Title VII. The Equal
    Pay Act covers the same categories of people, but is
    concerned with slightly different forms of discrimina-
    tion. The Executive Orders cover "federal contractors."
    This includes most universities, which depend heavily
    on federal grants. It also covers any other employer
    or agency which receives federal contracts, no matter
    how small. The Age Discrimination in Employment Act
    of 1967 protects women from 40 to 65. Different states
    also have similar acts, often protecting older women
    workers.

Did You Know These Forms Of Discrimination Are Illegal?

1. Refusing to hire or promote, or firing women who marry
    and women with young children unless the same policy
    applies to men.

2. Treating maternity (abortion, miscarriage, and related
    medical problems) differently from any other medical

"disability" in terms of employee insurance plans, benefits, or in terms of leave and pay granted.

3. Maintaining separate seniority lists for men and women, or for jobs or categories or work done primarily by men or women.

4. Using "protective" hour or weight laws to avoid paying women who wish to work at night, overtime, or lifting weights, or using these laws to keep women out of higher-paying jobs.

5. Treating unmarried fathers differently from unmarried mothers. Any company which refuses to hire or fires unwed mothers is discriminating because you can bet they don't care how many children their male employees have fathered and deserted.

6. Offering separate retirement plans or pension plans for men and women. Many employers have earlier mandatory retirement plans for women.

7. Paying men and women differently even though they are doing substantially the same job. Just giving the jobs different names or putting the employees in different departments or different parts of the plant doesn't erase the discrimination. For example, orderlies and nurse's aides, janitors and maids often do the same amount of hard physical labor; their jobs are substantially the same, but the pay levels are often quite different.

8. Using "lack of facilities" (read "bathrooms") as an excuse for not hiring women. *No "expense to the company" excuse is good enough to justify discrimination!*

9. "I didn't mean to" is no excuse for an employer, union, or employment agency who discriminates. Discrimination does not have to be willful. In this society an employer does not have to want or try to discriminate against women; he just follows along with stereotypes and prejudices.

DISCRIMINATION AT WORK--A PLUMBER FIGHTS BACK

Diane is a 26-year-old single woman who was trained as a plumber at an Opportunities Industrialization

Center school. Her first job as an industrial pipe-
fitter ended three days before the end of her sixty-
day probation period, after which she would have
been permanently employed.

Q: Why did you decide to become a plumber?

A: Well, I was a file clerk for about two years and I
    didn't like being a file clerk. I decided that I
    wanted to be something else that was more skilled,
    and I didn't have a college education. I decided
    I was comfortable fixing things, and that I would
    like to learn a skill that would involve fixing
    things, and I thought about fixing TVs and I thought
    a little about plumbing, and then I fixed a toilet
    and I decided that I wanted to be a plumber.

Q: How did you find a way to do that?

A: I looked up different ways that you could learn the
    skill, and the best thing that I could find was OIC,
    Opportunities Industrialization Center, where you
    can go for approximately a year of training, and come
    out knowing plumbing.

Q: And it doesn't cost a lot of money, right?

A: Doesn't cost anything, if you're fairly uneducated
    and fairly poor. . . . After I finished the program
    at OIC they found me a job as a pipefitter; I got
    paid about five-fifty an hour.

Q: You had a sixty-day probationary period and
    they let you go after your fifty-seventh day.
    . . . Did you think right away that something
    was going on when they let you go?

A: It was strange, because they called me up on my
    thirtieth day and they told me that I was doing
    well and they were pleased with my progress,
    and asked me if I wanted to go to the plant
    school to take after-work classes. . . . Then,
    on my fifty-seventh day, they called me up and
    told me that I wasn't working up to their ex-
    pectations of me, and that I wasn't doing the
    kind of work that the men did.

Q: What did the union do when you were released?
    Did they help you in any way?

A: *Yes, the union filed a grievance in my favor, even though I wasn't officially a union member, because they don't like to see people be kept beyond thirty days and then fired.*

Q: *What did you do after that?*

A: *I filed a complaint with the City Human Relations Commission and also with the Equal Employment Opportunity Commission.*

Q: *How does that work?*

A: *They investigate the complaint, and then if they find that the company is guilty and the employee is right, they bring the company before a board. The board tells the company that they were wrong, and the company has the right then to settle the case, in terms of back pay or whatever. If the company refuses, then the board decides what the company should do, and if the company refuses, then they'll take it to court.*

Q: *What do you do now?*

A: *Now I work for a factory that prints designs on vinyl, and I'm an assistant printer.*

Q: *How do you feel about doing industrial kinds of work instead of more traditional women's jobs like office work?*

A: *Well, factory work tends to pay better than office work if you work for a factory that has a good union.*

Q: *In another two years you'll be a master plumber, is that right? Do you intend to continue with it?*

A: *I'd like to try to. I'd like to get to the point where I could open my own business and employ other people, and that way make some money at what I learned to do.*

A Few Questions And Answers About Discrimination

Q: How do I file a discrimination complaint under Title
    VII?

A: Filing a complaint and going through all the proper
    procedures under Title VII may take a total of 2-3
    years before the problem is resolved. There are very
    strict time limits for filing your complaint, and you
    should act as promptly as possible and keep in touch
    with your EEOC counselor or attorney every step of the
    way. The basic procedures include:

    1. Filing a charge of discrimination with the regional
        EEOC office and/or your state or local Human Rela-
        tions Commission and waiting 60 days for it to act.
        If there are no satisfactory results from the local
        Commission, you go to step 2.

    2. After 60 days EEOC sends a notice of your charge to
        the employer, union, or employment agency.

    3. Next, the EEOC conducts an investigation and makes
        an effort to settle the dispute with the employer.
        If this effort fails, you go to step 4.

    4. EEOC writes a brief Opinion stating that there is
        "reasonable cause" to believe that discrimination
        exists. Once this happens, there are more concili-
        ation efforts. If these fail, you go to step 5.

    5. You receive a "notice of a right to sue."

    6. You contact attorneys and try to find one who will
        sue the employer, union or agency for you. You
        should remind the attorney that Title VII provides
        for attorneys' fees to be paid at no expense to the
        party bringing the suit.

Q: Why does this take so much time?

A: When Title VII was first drafted and the EEOC estab-
    lished, it was assumed that discrimination consisted of
    a few incidents which could be resolved by a few confer-
    ences and a little common sense. We have learned since
    then that discrimination is a very widespread practice
    in which industry and business have invested a great
    deal of money. They will often fight to the bitter end
    for the right to continue discriminating.

Q: Is there any way to speed up this process?

A: Yes. You have the right to start a lawsuit 180 days after the EEOC gets power to act on your charge. If you live in a state with Fair Employment Practices laws this means 180 days after the sixty-day period the EEOC must wait for the state Human Relations Commission to achieve some results. If your state has no Fair Employment laws, you may start your lawsuit 180 days after you file your charge with EEOC.

Q: What are the crucial deadlines for filing a complaint with EEOC or the state agency?

A: You must sue within 180 days of the date of the discriminatory act if your state has a Fair Employment Practices Act, and within 300 days if your state has no such Act. You should be aware that *most discriminatory practices discriminate against all women in your position*, not just you, so that the discrimination is not something that occurs just one day, but is a continuing practice. You should indicate "continuing" on the EEOC Discrimination Charge form in answer to the question "Most recent date discrimination occurred."

Q: What if EEOC refuses to act on my charge?

A: This sometimes happens. Write to William Brown, Chairman, EEOC, 1800 G Street, N.W., Washington, D.C. 20506. You should also know that EEOC keeps a list of private attorneys if you want to start your lawsuit as soon as possible without waiting for EEOC to go through all the steps.

Q: What's the difference between Title VII and the Equal Pay Act?

A: They overlap often, and you should sue the employer who discriminates by paying men and women different wages for what is essentially the same job under both Title VII and the Equal Pay Act. The Equal Pay Act says that jobs are substantially the same if they require the same skill, responsibility, and conditions of work. Differences between what men and women do which are "trivial" don't make the jobs substantially different. You should know that this law also forbids lowering the men's salaries to equalize the pay for men and women. Women must be brought up to the level of the men employees.

Q: What's the advantage to suing under the Equal Pay Act?

A: The Equal Pay Act provides for a full-scale investiga-
     tion on the basis of an anonymous complaint; they can
     investigate the pay practices of an employer, not just
     your specific complaint. The biggest advantage is that
     you can get *double* back pay under the Equal Pay Act,
     instead of just lost pay under Title VII.   Remember:
     The Equal Pay Act does not cover as many instances of
     discrimination as Title VII because it is only concerned
     with different pay levels.   But every time you have a
     complaint that fits under the Equal Pay Act you should
     also file a complaint with the EEOC.   The Equal Pay Act
     is administered by the Wage and Hour Division of the
     Labor Department, which has field offices in most major
     cities. This agency has the power to order that discrim-
     inatory practices be corrected as well as to help you
     with your individual problem.

Q: What do the Executive Orders cover?

A: Only employees of those who have government contracts
     are covered, but the Executive Orders require that in
     addition to compensating victims of discrimination, the
     employer must develop "affirmative action plans" to
     correct all employment discrimination. The Executive
     Orders are administered by the Office of Federal Con-
     tract Compliance, an agency of the Department of Health,
     Education, and Welfare.

Q: Are there any other remedies I might have?

A: Yes.   Check your state laws for other remedies.   You
     might try contacting a local feminist law firm, the
     local National Organization for Women chapter, or groups
     working on ratification of the national Equal Rights
     Amendment for further information.

Filling Out A Charge Of Discrimination

If you believe you have been discriminated against in any of
the ways discussed above for reasons of race, color, national
origin, or sex, you should contact the nearest office (regional
office) of the Equal Employment Opportunity Commission.   In
some states, you should also contact the state or local Human
Relations Commission at the same time. It is important that
your "Charge of Discrimination" be filed as soon as possible
after the discrimination takes place, so *do not delay* in
contacting the Human Relations Commission or the EEOC. The
form you will be asked to fill out will look something like
the illustration on the following page.

CHARGE OF DISCRIMINATION

Case File No. _____

(Please Print or Type)

1. Your Name _____

    Phone Number _____

    Street Address _____

    City _____ State _____ Zip Code _____

2. Was the discrimination because of: (Please check one)

    Race or Color _____ Religious Creed _____ National Origin _____ Sex _____

3. Who discriminated against you? Give the name and address of the employer, labor organiza-
    tion, employment agency and/or apprenticeship committee. If more than one, list all.

    Name _____

    Street Address _____

    City _____ State _____ Zip Code _____

    (Please turn over)

4. Have you filed this charge with a state or local government agency?

   Yes (When: _____)   No
               Month Day Year

5. If you charge is against a company or a union, how many employees or members?

   Under 15   Over 15

6. Most recent date on which discrimination took place: _____
                                                         Month Day Year
   (Note: You can write "continuing.")

7. Explain the unfair thing that was done to you. How were other persons treated differently?
   (Use extra sheet if necessary.)

8. I swear or affirm that I have read the above charge and that it is true to the best of my
   knowledge, information, and belief.

   Date _____   _____ (Sign here)

   Subscriber and sworn to be me this _____ day of _____ 197___ .

   _____   _____
     (Name)   (Title)

*If it is difficult to get a Notary Public to sign this, sign your own name and mail it to the
Regional Office. The Commission will help you to get the form sworn to.

REMEMBER

       good quality today means more jobs tomorrow
remember
       cars move america
remember
       they used to go deaf here
       and die
some did they did die
some even died deaf in the old days before safety
in the days when quality counted for more and you got
    what
you paid for
though some may have paid with an arm an eye their
    hearing
their head
do you know the story of the overhead crane
the one that runs above the presses the three story high
presses the presses that make america's car doors roofs
trunks there was a man on top of the press
they say they are thirty forty fifty feet high who
    measures?
he was repairing it maintenance maintaining quality
quantity industry and america
the crane driver missed him seeing him that is missed
seeing him when he did or didn't look missed seeing him
there on the top up there on the presses you have to
    lie
down when you see the crane coming
on the presses on top of them they are covered with
    grease
three inches deep slippery and no head room when the
    crane
comes you've got to lie down i know it is slippery
the maintenance man did not see the crane he didn't see
    it
they didn't see each other at all
they did gamble together
they say the crane driver lost lost a few hundred or so
they say he didn't like it but he wasn't a violent man
it was an accident he liked the guy he just didn't see
him up there on top of the press there and when he did
it was well you know too late just too late
the guy who told me said the head landed at his feet
right at his feet there where he was working
there was a big commotion everyone was excited no one
was surprised they all know it could happen they heard
it had happened before they even now expect it to
    happen
again   *an accident*

when they send me on top of the presses they tell me
these stories as i am climbing the ladder on the side of
*   the*
monstrous press   as i am standing on the top i look
*   around*
for the crane   there are three of them there
they can come from any direction   i remember to watch
out   i try not to look paranoid
they all shrug it off   these men   they live with death
they don't believe a woman can   they are proud
i wonder   when the next accident   how and when   and who
who will plan it   i try to remember
to make no debts or enemies   i want to be careful
i want to keep my head about me.

--diane devennie

EDUCATIONAL RESOURCES

Starting From The Bottom

As a woman in transition with plenty of problems and details to worry about, you may look forward to further education or training about as much as you would look forward
to wrestling an alligator. Many women in transition have
been deprived of educational opportunities, and do not
relish the thought of returning to something they may not
have enjoyed the first time around. But remember: Fear
of failure and lack of self-confidence may be keeping you
from a new job and a richer life. Education is important,
not because it shows how smart you are, but because it can
open doors for you. If you have not especially enjoyed
your experiences in school before, you should consider
continuing education anyway. Think of it as an investment
to help you achieve economic security. And you may discover that once you go to school with a definite purpose,
you enjoy learning.

Additional education may open up new job opportunities for
you. You don't have to be a nurse or a secretary if you
don't want to. The difference between traditionally
"female" jobs and those professional jobs which are more
rewarding is often "education" or training.

Of course, getting a college degree won't necessarily
enable you to find a job that you like, unless you are able
to continue your education beyond a bachelor's degree. And

that, of course, takes more time and money. Academic credentials aren't the only way to find a good job, however.
Vocational training in specific skills may be even more
valuable on the job market, depending, of course, on what
kind of job you want to do.

When considering further education of any kind, ask yourself the same kinds of questions you did when you were
thinking about finding a job. Before you left school, got
married, stopped working, what were you interested in or
good at doing? When was the last time you did anything
connected with that area of interest? What caused you to
stop? Are you still interested in it, or have you found
other things which excite you more? What are the first
steps to take in order to get back in this field?

A few more questions to consider: Can you arrange for
child care while you are in school? How much will this
cost? How much time can you afford to spend getting your
education? Are you going to have to work during the day
and go to school at night? Or are you taking a course that
will last only eight or ten months? What schools are close
enough to be convenient? What kind of transportation will
you need to reach them? Are you qualified for entrance
into the program of your choice? You can get a high school
diploma by taking an examination called the "General Equivalency Diploma" examination. This is given periodically in
your area. Call a local high school for information. In
some areas there are preparatory classes for this test.
Correspondence schools are another way of getting a high
school diploma, and sometimes you can receive credit for
high school graduation by taking courses at a local community college.

Are there scholarships, sliding scale payment plans, defer-
red payment plans, or other financial opportunities you
could take advantage of? (See the finances section of this
chapter.)

Ask yourself these questions, and give yourself credit for
being a person who is capable of doing anything you are
seriously determined to do. And since you are probably
going to work anyway, it might as well be at something you
enjoy doing and are rewarded for.

Job Training

Job training programs can be a great beginning for a woman
who has few marketable skills, or who is interested in getting into a field she has had no previous experience in.

Learning a trade which is considered "masculine"--such as electricity, plumbing, or carpentry--has both advantages and disadvantages. The pay is usually much higher in these fields than in traditionally "feminine" ones. On the other hand, you may find it very difficult to get jobs in these areas, even with sufficient skill and training. But the skilled trades do not have to be considered an end in themselves. After going to school and becoming licensed (usually this means taking a city or state qualifying test), you might want to open your own business or go on to take college courses to become an engineer or contractor.

There are three different types of job training programs: nonprofit or government-funded, private vocational or trade schools, and on-the-job training.

Nonprofit Training Programs

Under the Manpower Development and Training Act, federal funds are allotted to train underemployed and unemployed people. Government programs may be helpful to you, especially if you have little or no money. Bear in mind, however, that some government programs do not encourage women to go into traditionally masculine fields. In order to find out about programs in your area, you might contact any local "War on Poverty" agency. These are sometimes called "Community Action Programs" or the "Office of Economic Opportunity."

You should be aware that while you are enrolled in a federally funded training program you are usually eligible for public assistance and an allowance which is designed to help cover your lunches and transportation costs. In the Work Incentive Program, participants are permitted to receive both their grants from welfare and trainee allowances. Day care centers (not always the best) are available to mothers working in the WIN program.

Your state employment bureau should know of all the nonprofit training programs for which you would be eligible. It also has an apprenticeship office with detailed information about apprenticeship programs. In cities and states where the National Urban League has branch offices, you may find information about vocational and trade schools in your area from the local office.

Some programs funded under the *Man*(!)power Act include:

1. The WIN program, described in the welfare section of

this chapter. This program has had some bad publicity concerning its use as a tool to separate women on welfare from their families. Investigate the program in your area. Use it if you can use it and there are no objectionable conditions attached.

2. Operation Mainstream is available to low-income people who are having difficulty finding a job because of age, lack of training, or other reasons. It is available to those who are unable to qualify for other training programs.

3. The Concentrated Employment Program provides services and training for low-income people in cities and in rural areas.

4. Opportunities Industrialization Centers exist in nine states. Although they are not federal or state programs, they receive government funding. OIC is available to all low-income people at no cost, and offers training in trades and business skills, and grants high school equivalency diplomas as well. People under eighteen are sometimes referred to other programs.

5. Better Jobs For Women is sponsored jointly by the YMCA of metropolitan Denver and the U.S. Department of Labor. This program is using a $60,000 grant to help women who want to apply for apprenticeship or apprenticeship-like programs offering training in skilled trades. It may be able to direct you to one of these. Call or write Better Jobs For Women, 1545 Tremount Place, Denver, Colorado 80202.

Private Training Schools

These can be expensive, time-consuming, and fraudulent. Before you sign any contract with a private training school get an evaluation of it from your local Better Business Bureau and conduct your own investigation.

1. Determine that the field of study you are interested in is one that will leave you with marketable skills.

2. Write or call schools which offer the courses you need. Compare brochures to determine costs, subjects offered, length of the program, and the availability of financial aid.

3. After studying the material and deciding which courses
    and costs meet your needs, make an appointment with
    a counselor at the school. Check the classroom equip-
    ment available to you. Talk to other students. Ask
    for names and addresses of employers who have hired
    graduates from the program. Ask about the possibility
    of a tuition refund if you decide to drop the course.

4. Do not, at this time, give a registration fee or
    deposit. If possible, take home a blank copy of the
    contract and reread it. Find out if the school is
    affiliated with a national association. Make sure
    the school has a placement service to insure they
    will get you a job.

Some schools listed in the yellow pages, such as IBM computer schools, can be a good source of job training. But
be sure to find out whether the training offered by the
program is sufficient to get a job, or whether there are
additional requirements as well. Most computer programming
jobs, for instance, require a college degree in addition
to the training.

To get a list of all the trade schools in the United States,
write to the American Trade Schools Directory, Croner
Publications, Inc., Queens Village, New York, New York
11428. This booklet costs about $5.00, and is updated
every month. It does not evaluate the schools listed.
The Urban League maintains a "Skills Bank" in some cities
which does evaluate training programs and has information
about financial assistance for the programs.

Other Programs

Special Impact is a federal program related to other
federal, state, and local programs aimed at providing
work experience in fields such as home renovation, health
care, recreational development, and expansion of community social and economic programs. In order to qualify,
you must be at least 16 and "chronically unemployed."

JOBS, or Job Opportunities in the Business Sector, tries
to interest private businesses in training low-income
people. It should be available in 50 cities, and is
sponsored by the National Alliance of Businessmen.

The Public Service Careers Program provides on-the-job
training in public service agencies.

In addition to these government-funded, on-the-job training programs, you might check with community social service agencies, the Office of Economic Opportunity, and your city's Model Cities Program. Many of these agencies employ nonprofessional members of the community. The available jobs are usually related to social work. You might also contact local public schools and ask them if they know of programs or businesses offering on-the-job training.

In professions such as law and health, on-the-job training is a relatively new idea. Nonprofessional workers in these fields are sometimes called "paralegal" and "paramedical" workers.

There are also private on-the-job training programs in industry. Companies like General Electric and Bell Telephone have been training their employees in their own schools for years. Many department stores train their own employees for managerial positions. Usually these programs are only open to those who are already employed by the firm that offers the training program. Think about the skills you already have that may lead to a job with additional training available. The Xerox Corporation, for example, trains people with some background in electronics or mechanics to repair their equipment.

In some areas, on-the-job training is a new idea. Primarily to pacify angry urban poor people, the federal government has invested in programs that combine on-the-job training with career direction related to fields in which workers are needed. These programs include something called "New Careers," which is a federal program whose trainees are mostly women. It is open to adults over 22 years of age who live in families making less than $4,000 a year for a family of four. Community-based branches provide on-the-job training in health, education, and public welfare services.

As with most social service agencies, jobs tend to be in the community served, and are usually open to residents of the neighborhood. These jobs are most worthwhile for women with little or no experience in the field. If you have done work in the area of tenants' rights, welfare rights, or volunteer work in a community health clinic, you have a better chance of getting a paying job in these areas. Contact your city and state departments of health or community legal service agencies if you are interested in job training in these areas.

Although we have mentioned apprenticeship training previously, it is important to stress that this is a highly
underdeveloped area of job training for women. Better
Jobs For Women tries to help women who are interested in
such programs; however, the waiting list for openings is
usually very long and the number of apprenticeship positions small. Some unions do not wish to make their apprenticeship programs available to black people, women,
or members of other minority groups. And remember: Exclu-
sion from apprenticeship programs is discrimination, and
illegal.

Finally, the Labor Department maintains a Bureau of Apprenticeship Training which may be able to give you information
about whether apprenticeship programs are available in the
field you are interested in.

Going (Back) To College

Before you rush to enroll in a four-year academic program
from which you will emerge with a bachelor's degree and
swell the ranks of unemployed college graduates, ask yourself: "What do I ecpect this degree to accomplish?" It is
unfortunately no longer true that a college degree is a
guarantee of a decent-paying, maybe even interesting job.
In many areas you are better off with a particular skill
than a general "liberal arts" education. So if you were
interested in the college degree mostly becuse you assumed
it would help you land a good job, think about it some more.

On the other hand, if you want to enter one of the professional fields--teaching, medicine, law--you must get that
college degree. It is a prerequisite to other aspects of
your professional training. Of course, if you have the
time and money and want to go to college but don't have a
specific occupational goal in mind, that's O.K. too. If
your husband is willing to pay, by all means take advantage
of the opportunity. But remember there are costs beyond
tuition--fees, books, child care, transportation.

Once you've decided a college degree is definitely what
you want, you should begin to think about what kind of
education you are looking for. This will become clearer
if you ask yourself these questions:

1. Is your primary motive to use your degree as a stepping-
    stone to further education or to increase your earning
    potential?

2. Are you able to go to school full-time or part-time?
    During the day or at night? Is child care available to
    you in your community or where you want to go to school?

3. Would a program which included work experience (for cred-
    it) as well as academic subjects be more valuable to you?

4. Do you need a highly structured program with assignments
    and lots of direction from professors, or would you
    prefer a program which allowed for a great deal of in-
    dependent study, research, and writing?

5. Would taking a few courses over an extended period of
    time meet your needs as well as going immediately into
    a full-time schedule?

6. What areas do you most want to learn about? What sub-
    jects are most difficult for you? Should you take a
    refresher course in these areas?

7. What kind of student population would you feel most
    comfortable in? An all-woman college, a coeducational
    college, a community college with day students, or a
    residential one? Is it important to you to be around
    older, more experienced students?

Many women in transition are not eager to compete (and let's
face it, most of American education demands competition) with
younger students. You may feel your learning skills and
study habits have rusted. Younger students are probably more
adept at test-taking, writing papers, and memorizing. But
this is only because they have used these skills more recently than you have. These are not inborn gifts, but learned
habits. They demand little more than use and discipline.
You should remember that although you may not have been in
school for many years, you have not stopped learning. Your
life experiences have given you insight and discipline that
most younger students lack.

Many colleges and universities are developing special programs tailored to the needs of women entering college after
careers as wives and mothers, or returning to an interrupted
education. These are generally called "Continuing Education
Programs for Women." To see if there are any such programs
at universities and colleges in your area, you might call
the local institutions, or ask the local branch of the
American Association of University Women.

Some colleges and universities (including those with "Continuing Education for Women" programs) accept results from

the College Level Examination Program (CLEP) scores in lieu
of college credit. Depending on your score on these examinations, which are given in many different academic areas,
you can receive college credit for knowledge you have gained
outside a formal academic setting. Inquire about whether
the college or university you want to apply to accepts CLEP
scores for academic credit.

A few colleges will also give credit for certain learning
experiences you have had outside of an academic setting.
The procedure is usually to write a description of what
and how you learned and petition the faculty for a certain
number of credits. Past work such as writing, art, music,
or other accomplishments may be submitted as evidence of
your learning. These institutions are often called "Universities Without Walls" and belong to the Union for Experimenting Colleges and Universities. You may find out more
about these programs by writing to: Mr. Sam Baskin, Union
for Experimenting Colleges and Universities, c/o Antioch
College, Yellow Springs, Ohio 45387.

A few schools will waive the Scholastic Aptitude test
requirements and most will transfer credit earned at other
universities. When you have picked out one or more schools
to apply to, inquire whether any of these special provisions
for women returning to college or entering after a long
absence from any formal education have been adopted by this
school. You might also inquire whether there are any
special orientation programs for older students.

A Few Words About Survival On The College Campus

The number of contemporaries you will find in your classes
depends on several factors--whether the school has a program of continuing education for women, whether it is a
commuter or community college, and, to some extent, the
field you are studying. Ivy league, residential, and
liberal arts colleges are most likely to have only small
numbers of women who have not been in school continuously.

A woman who is isolated from campus life by family and/or
job responsibilities may be able to find a group of other
people who are attending school under similar conditions.
Many schools are beginning to have women's groups that
may be helpful. Often these groups have sponsored day
care programs for the children of students, faculty, and
community residents. If the school you attend seems obliv-
ious to the need for child care, perhaps the first step
is to seek out other women with the same problem and work
out sharing day care arrangements. You might also try to
find sympathetic women at the school and organize student
support for a university-supported day care center on

campus. Such centers are now thriving at Tufts University, De Anzo College in California, the State University of New York at Old Westbury, some state and community colleges in New Jersey, and the University of Pennsylvania. The New York Women's School in Brooklyn and most feminist-oriented colleges also provide day care.

Feminist Studies

If you are interested in studying Womankind you might be able to take a course in women's history, the psychology of women, women in literature, or any one of a number of other "Women's Studies" offered at over 1,000 American universities, or earn a degree in this area at one of the 80 colleges and universities with "Women's Studies" majors. Or you might consider Sagaris Institute, to open in Burlington, Vermont, by summer of 1975. Founders Blanche Boyd (author of *Nerves*), Dr. Joan Peters, and Ti-Grace Atkinson hope to offer a "feminist humanist" alternative to traditionally male-dominated institutions of higher education. Tuition will be on a sliding scale, based on ability to pay. Child care will be provided.

Financing Your Education

Up until now, few institutions have recognized the financial needs of older students applying to college. You can count yourself fortunate if you have a nest egg saved to cover your education, or if your ex-husband is willing to finance part or all of it. If this is not the case for you, you may find yourself caught in the same situation that has closed out many willing students from low-income families. By and large, there are few programs designed specifically for adult women students.

Some of your options include: government grants and scholarships, subsidy by businesses for their employees, individual college scholarships and work-study programs, and foundations grants such as the Upper Division Scholarship Competition. To determine if any of these sources are available to you, you should inquire at the school to which you are applying or are enrolled.

Government grants and scholarships include a program of guaranteed loans. Students accepted for enrollment in approved colleges, vocational sc ools, business schools, or universities may apply to banks, credit unions, savings and loan associations, insurance companies, or colleges. Students may borrow as much as $1,500 a year up to $7,500 from these institutions with a state agency, private non-profit agency, or sometimes the federal government guaranteeing the loan. The interest on the loan will be paid by the government for students with an adjusted family income of less than $15,000 a year. Repayment does not begin until 9 to 12 months after graduation and may be further deferred if the student serves in the Peace Corps, VISTA, or the Armed Forces.

Financial aid for students in areas of special study such as teaching, counseling, library work, health fields, social work, guidance, and vocational rehabilitation is available from the U.S. Department of Health, Education, and Welfare. Write them for further information.

Other programs include educational opportunity grants in which half your grant is supplied by the institution you attend and half is matched by the federal government (from $200 to $1,000 a year). Recipients of these grants are named by the institution they attend. National defense student loans offer long-term, low-interest loans. Undergraduate students may borrow up to $1,000 each year to a total of $4,000. Interest is 3 percent and repayment begins 10 months after graduation.

Michigan and Iowa give grants to adult students who wish to attend their state universities. Some other states also follow this policy. There are some states, however, in which continuing education programs must by law be self-supporting (e.g., Massachusetts), which means you must contribute to your tuition costs.

Some businesses encourage their employees to return to school and agree to undertake payment of their fees. General Electric is one such employer. Some businesses are reasonable about giving their employees time off from their jobs to attend school. You should investigate this policy and whether your employer subscribes to it. Frequently this may involve taking night courses or courses specifically related to your job.

Many colleges and universities offer scholarships or work-study programs or a combination of the two for their low-income students. This solution can work well if you have the time to take advantage of it. At colleges where work experience is given credit (such as Goddard in Vermont, Antioch in Yellow Springs, Ohio, Bard College in New York, and others) you may be able to make some money during your work period to help subsidize your education expenses.

This is not, however, the purpose of these programs, which are designed primarily to give "real life" experience to younger, inexperienced students. You may find this a costly and time-consuming way to get an education. Some government programs provide work-study for low-income students. These programs usually involve working for public or non-profit organizations or for the schools themselves. The amount of time students are allowed to work in these programs is strictly limited by law, and the hourly wage is fairly low.

The Upper Division Scholarship Competition awards sizable grants to students nominated by their college. It requires its recipients to be graduates of a community or junior college.

When deciding if any or all of these programs could be available to you, consult with a counselor at the school you are interested in attending. Inquire about the specific scholarships that they offer, how much, to whom, and under what conditions.

FINANCIAL RESOURCES

Getting Your Money's Worth

People who have money can take advantage of tax loopholes, high interest rates, or dabble in the stock market. They can consult with tax experts, buy with cash, and borrow at the most favorable rates. It's true that "money begets money," and no money only begets more of the same. Banks and other lending institutions love to lend money to people who already have it and hate to lend to those who don't.

Maybe you have always had to squeeze the last penny from your paycheck; or maybe you let your husband run the family finances, borrow the money, balance the checkbook. If this was the pattern in your marriage, you may find yourself desperately wishing for a financial genie to do your bookkeeping and produce money on demand. Sometimes the genie appears to beckon from catchy little jingles from the local savings and loan association or finance company. "Pay all your bills at once," "Easy credit, easy terms," "Our payment plan saves you money." Before you seek out these problem-solvers, think twice. No loan, savings plan, or credit company can give you money you don't have. They're only going to lend you some money and get you to pay a good price for the privilege of using their money and

their services. Credit is a business; if loans weren't a
good way for credit and finance companies (and banks and
savings and loan associations) to make money, they wouldn't
be doing it.

Before you beg, borrow, or steal, read the information in
this section. Having some understanding of how the money-
maker's system works may help you avoid being exploited
and help you to use your resources (limited as they are)
as wisely as possible.

Before Buying

Remember: Cash is the cheapest way to buy. Buy on credit
if you must, but know how much you are paying for the "convenience" of time payments. When buying appliances and
other large items, shop around. Try discount houses,
sales, secondhand stores (if you know they are reputable
and/or can see for yourself what shape the appliance is
in), or local garage sales where people often sell good
appliances at very low prices to avoid the expense of
moving them. If you are buying from a retail dealer,
try to find the catalogue price of an item, as they are
often marked up before they are marked "down" for sale. Take
the initiative and ask for a cash discount. Sometimes you
can get as much as 7 percent off because it costs stores
that much to use charge plans such as BankAmericard, Master
Charge, etc.

If you can, research before buying. Check *Consumer Reports*
and *Moneysworth* in the periodicals section of your local
library. These magazines usually have reliable reports on
products they have tested, but these are often only the
kinds of products people with substantial incomes can afford.

When having your house repaired, use only local, well-
recommended contractors. Compare prices and workmanship.
Estimates can vary immensely. Don't allow strangers who
come to your door to fix anything in your house. Don't sign
a job-completion certificate until all the work has been
done to your satisfaction. Beware of contractors lying
about the amount of work needed, or adding on extra
materials which are not used. Also, watch for the practice
of charging for superior materials and using inferior ones.

When salespeople come to your door, always ask for proper
identification. Check the telephone directory for the
company's listing. If you are in doubt, ask the salesperson to present an offer in writing.

Don't allow yourself to be fooled by "bait and switch" advertising, where a product is offered at a ridiculously low price to get you to come into the store. Once you are there, you may be informed that the advertised product is all sold out, and a salesperson may try to convince you to buy a much more expensive item. Sometimes you may be told that the advertised product, although still available, is markedly inferior.

Whatever you buy, get a receipt and detailed guarantee terms. *Read the receipt and guarantee terms.* Your signing or accepting the receipt means you have read and agreed to the terms, and you are legally bound by them.

Consumer Protection?

In many localities there are state or municipal agencies to protect the consumer. Unfortunately, because the real power in this country is still in the hands of the businesses, much of the bite has been taken out of consumer legislation and legislative cures for consumer abuse become meaningless. Agencies designed to help the consumer are often limited by a lack of funds and proper staffing, as well as lack of subpoena power (power to force a prospective witness to appear in court). Penalties can be levied against merchants or lenders, but there are no provisions for paying back the consumer. In short, your legal remedies for consumer abuse are few and far between, and not terribly significant. The situation varies from state to state, however, with some states--New Jersey and California, for example--having good consumer protection legislation and fairly meaningful remedies. If you believe you are the victim of unfair practices, you should consult the local consumer protection agency and/or a legal services agency. Many state attorney generals' offices have special consumer protection departments.

Because of the relative inefficiency of official consumer protection agencies, many grass roots groups have sprung up to help the low-income consumer. These groups concentrate on publicizing the unfair practices of merchants and lenders through demonstrations, picket lines, and other consciousness-raising, publicity-attracting devices.

Savings

Most of us consider ourselves doing well if we can just meet our expenses instead of going into debt. Saving seems to be out of the question. But many women in transition have found it extremely important to try to save *something* as part of their effort to build a new life for themselves. Here are some suggestions for what to do with your savings if you are fortunate enough to have any.

If you have a small amount of money, the best alternative is to put it in a savings account with a savings and loan or a federal bank. The interest rates of these banks is higher than other ("commercial") banks. If you will not need to withdraw the money on short notice, you can buy savings certificates and get higher interest. You must give the bank 3-6 months notice before cashing savings certificates. If you have to be able to get your money out quickly, you lose the interest. Christmas Clubs or other special savings accounts (vacation plans, special accounts for car purchases) are not good investments as you pay for the convenience of having a scheduled savings plan. The interest on these accounts is low. If you come into $5,000 or more, get some professional advice on what to do with it. Banks provide such services.

Don't let the level of your checking account get too low if you have the kind of account which is free so long as you maintain a certain balance. On the other hand, it doesn't make much sense to keep a lot of money in your checking account because it will earn no interest there. Checking account service charges often depend on the balance in the account and the number of checks you write per month. If you have trouble balancing your account, follow the forms on the back of your monthly statement. And *do* take the trouble to balance the account--even computers make mistakes!

Lending Institutions

You might want a lending institution for one of several purposes: a savings or checking account, a mortgage, or any other kind of loan. Before you try to borrow money, think about why you want to borrow it, where you can get the lowest interest rates and the most convenient terms, and how you will be able to pay it off. It is always best to buy with cash, and to borrow only for long-term investments (such as a house or a car), but this is not always possible, especially for women in transition who have children.

The most common lending institutions include:

Credit Unions: These are membership groups, often made

up of members of a particular church, union, or place of
employment. They collect and make personal loans and collateral loans which may be paid back on an installment
plan, often by payroll deductions. Generally these are
run by members who volunteer their services or union personnel. They are generally not set up for profit, but for
the members' convenience. For this reason, they are a good
source of loans and can offer lower interest rates than
commercial banks. The rate at credit unions is almost always 10 percent or less. Credit unions do not usually
make mortgage loans.

Commercial banks may be a decent source of credit, especially if you already have a checking or savings account with
that bank. The amount a bank will lend you depends on
what the bank thinks of you as a credit risk. The criteria are spelled out in "A Word About Credit," later in
this chapter. If you have credit and well-established contacts with your bank, you may be able to get a small loan
on a personal note (I.O.U.) payable monthly, or through a
demand loan, payable at the end of a certain period. Interest for this kind of loan runs from 7 1/2 percent and
higher. If the bank will not give you a loan on this
basis, you might be able to get a "collateral" loan" for
which you put up collateral of fairly stable value--a
savings account, a paid-off car--to which the bank holds
the title until the loan is paid off. In order to cut
down the amount of interest you have to pay, you should
try to convince the lending institution to compute it on
an annual basis, or in monthly payments on which interest
is figured only on the balance you owe on the loan as of
that month. *Remember:* The longer your loan is outstanding
the more you pay in interest.

Savings banks: If you have a savings account, you might
consider borrowing against it. This is called a "passbook
loan." You have to pay interest to the bank (6-7 percent),
but your savings still draw interest. Such loans can be
made quickly and without a lot of trouble, but while you
owe money on the loan you cannot withdraw your savings.

Savings and loan associations: These are a major source
of mortgage and home-improvement loans. Often they will
offer more favorable interest rates and more liberal terms
than commercial banks for mortgages. They do not make
personal loans, except passbook loans. Savings and loan
associations often pay more interest on savings accounts
than commercial banks.

Finance companies: These are willing to lend money with or without collateral, but they generally will lend only small amounts at fairly high interest rates--much higher than banks. They are generally paid off on an installment basis and often charge "late fees" as well. Unfortunately, people with credit problems, who are the people who can least afford high interest rates, are frequently forced to borrow from finance companies. If you are getting threatening letters, harassing phone calls, or have any other serious problems with finance companies, contact a legal services office immediately. Many of the practices of these institutions are illegal--including illegally high interest rates disguised as "service charges" and harassing phone calls.

Types of Loans

There are many different kinds of loans, but all fall within one of the following categories (usually).

1. *Demand Loans* are usually offered by commercial banks on a short-term basis (30-180 days). No collateral is required, but a good credit rating is, and sometimes you will need another person to act as co-signer (and take the risk of payment if you don't pay when due).

2. *Collateral Loans* are backed by valuable property you own. If you don't repay when due, the bank has the right to possess the property (home, securities, car, etc.). These are often long-term loans, which can remain outstanding as long as the collateral you have put up retains (or increases) its value.

3. *Personal Notes* are paid off on a monthly basis. The interest is figured on a declining basis (the more you've paid off the less you have to pay interest on). Payments and interest are often deducted automatically from borrower's checking account. You will probably need a good credit rating *and* a co-signer.

4. *Installment Loans* may be obtained without collateral, like a personal note, but the installment loan is paid off monthly. Interest may be on a "discount" or "add-on" basis (see the next section for what these types of interest mean), which is less favorable.

5. *Mortgage Loans* generally cover long-term purchases. They may extend over periods as long as thirty years.

Payments covering interest, principal, insurance, and taxes are usually required on a monthly basis. Generally a bank will lend up to 75 percent of the market value of a house.

Interest Rates fluctuate with the economy and with the type of loan.

Ask for a loan on a *Declining Interest Basis,* stressing your ability to pay and your "good" credit rating.

Types Of Interest

1. *Interest On A Declining Balance:* This is usually the best way to borrow money. You repay in monthly installments, paying interest only on what's left outstanding. Thus, the amount of interest you pay each month is less. Unfortunately, you have to be considered a very good credit risk to get this kind of loan--which eliminates many women in transition, who are forced to borrow on much less favorable terms.

2. *Discount Method:* This is similar to the "add-on" interest (below), except that interest is discounted in advance. (You sign a loan for $3,000 but only receive $2,600, the interest having already been deducted.) Again, since you are making monthly payments, the effective or real interest is higher than the one quoted. For this reason, new consumer laws require lenders to tell you both the quoted rate of interest and the rate you are actually paying. This is supposed to embarrass them?

3. *Add-Ons:* Under this method, the interest owed is added on to the amount that you borrow. If you get a $3,000 loan with $400 interest, you owe the bank $3,400, and are expected to pay the whole sum back in monthly installments over a period of time. In effect two things happen: First, you do not have full use of your loan because you are paying back monthly and, second, you are paying a much higher rate of interest than it appears.

Credit Bureaus

A credit bureau is a business which collects and/or keeps on file information about your credit transactions over a period of years. Many of these bureaus have in the past conducted their business rather unscrupulously. For instance, some of them collect information about people which is not relevant to their credit record, even employing private detectives to visit relatives and neighbors of the person who borrows money.

If you apply for a personal loan, home improvement loan, or auto loan; if you apply for credit on an appliance, open a charge account, or buy life insurance, it is quite possible that one or more credit bureaus will be contacted.

All of these credit bureaus are listed alphabetically in the telephone directory under "Credit Reporting Agencies." You can go to any of these agencies and, for a small fee, see what is in your file. If there are items which are incorrect, the bureau must reinvestigate the information. It must take out any inaccurate or unverifiable information. It must send notice of the information removed to any or all of those people who received your file in the last six months. In the event of a dispute with a merchant, you have the right to put into the file your own statement of 100 words or less, giving your side of the argument.

Ordinarily, you must go to the credit bureau in person for the information you want. They must give you the names of any firms which have received your credit record during the previous six months. You also have the right to be told promptly if a report about your character has been requested. You have the right to demand a complete disclosure of the nature and scope of their investigation. Credit bureaus are not allowed to investigate your private life, and may also give out information which is directly related to your employment if a prospective employer requests information about you. Unfavorable information which is more than seven years old may not be given out to anyone.

A Word About Credit

Discrimination against women in financial institutions has, in the past, taken many forms. The first aspect of discrimination is that a married woman has no credit in her own name unless she is the sole or major source of support for the family. Even then she has to petition to get her own credit recognized. Credit bureaus list credit references by last names and addresses, so often a married woman's credit rating is the same as her husband's.

As a woman in transition, you may have a hard time establishing credit. If you are separated but not divorced, you are still legally "married" and may continue to charge

or purchase or borrow as your husband's "agent." Your
credit rating is still tied to his--unless, of course, he
has posted notices to the effect that he will not be responsible for bills not in his own name.

Even if you have a full-time job, many credit institutions
will not give full credit based on your earnings alone.
One survey indicates that only two-thirds of all mortgage
lenders would consider a woman's full income if she were a
professional, and only one-third would consider her entire
income if she works as a nonprofessional. To make matters
worse, a few banks discount a woman's income if she is "of
child-bearing age" and married, because they insist it is
likely she will get pregnant and leave her job. Such
practices are probably illegal under state equal rights
amendments, and would probably be considered so under a
national equal rights amendment.

As a divorced woman, your credit rating--whatever it was--
is wiped out. Even though any loans, mortgages, or property deeds have been signed by both you and your husband,
and you may have worked to pay off these debts, the credit
was probably listed in your husband's name with *his* work
history, income, and record of loan repayments. This may
be one reason for keeping one's name after marriage, and
a good reason to try hard to establish credit in your own
name while married.

When making a loan, banks say that they use the following
criteria: length of residence in home, home ownership,
credit references (repaid loans, mortgages, car payments,
charge accounts).

Here's another way that credit is like money--you can only
get it if you already have some. It is extremely difficult to get credit if you've never borrowed or paid on
credit in your own name before. In addition, lending
institutions are afraid of people "in transition." They
don't like to lend to people who move from place to place,
and understand "marital difficulties" to mean that divorced
and separated people are unstable and poor risks. Although
the National Bureau of Economic Research has determined
that marital status, level of income, sex, age, and family
are *not* key factors in default risk, most credit institutions still firmly believe these are important factors.
It is possible for you to be entirely shut out of the
credit market because no one has a "right" to credit.
This is less likely to happen if you have been working
for some time and have a regular income, however small.

Personal references and people willing to co-sign loans will help you get credit in some cases. You can also request that your savings account be considered part of your assets. If you have a life insurance policy in your husband's name (especially if he pays you and you pay the premiums), you might use this as an asset. You can dig up all the bills *you* paid (and signed or got receipts addressed to you) to show your trustworthiness. You may also be able to point to participation in a credit union where you live or work, or to your consistent employment.

Finally, you can argue. You might try to convince the credit institution to consider support payments from your husband as income. This they steadfastly refuse to do, in most cases. You might argue that support payments which are made part of a divorce decree or court order are even more secure than employment, because if your husband defaults he will be held in contempt of court, which is pretty strong motivation (for most men) to make these payments regularly. Unfortunately, most credit agencies probably know the sad reality of that story almost as well as you do. You might also be able to point to an excellent work history, or, if worse comes to worst, you might pledge part of your savings as security.

If you are still denied credit, and you believe you would have received it if you were single and/or male with the same assets, consult a legal services agency and try to get a lawyer to persuade the institution to grant you credit. This may or may not work, depending on many factors. A slightly happy note to end our sad tale: Some banks have been pressured, embarrassed, and bad-mouthed into developing better financial opportunities for women. You might remind the particular bank you are dealing with of this fact and suggest they don't want to be behind the times. If your particular banker seems particularly hard-hearted, threaten to write local newspapers and women's organizations (also Chamber of Commerce and Better Business Bureaus) about the discriminatory policies of this bank. Good luck!

INSURANCE

Life Insurance

As a woman in transition, especially if you have dependent children, you may be wondering what to do about insurance coverage. Before you jump into the purchase of expensive

and possibly unnecessary insurance policies, determine how
these needs have been met in the past. Did both you and
your husband have insurance policies naming you, both of
you, or your children, beneficiaries? Where were these
policies acquired? (For instance, at your husband's place
of employment? At your place of employment? Through both?
Through a private agency?) What types of policies were
they? (Term, whole life, endowment?)

Life insurance, like taxes, may be an area where you have
had little interest and less information in the past.
Don't feel alone. Most of us have left life insurance
concerns in the hands of our agent, husband, and perhaps
during transition, lawyer. To know what you need to about
life insurance, read this section, and if you are interested
in further information, consult our bibliography. Knowing
this information can mean the difference between being at
least partially supported at the time of your husband's
death, and having to shoulder the financial burden alone.

Let us first find out what we mean when we speak about
insurance in general and life insurance in particular.
The basic purpose of life insurance is to provide an
instant sum of money to cover a financial loss. In the
lives of most people, this loss is the earnings which they
would have received if they had lived to earn it. Since
the older a person is, the more likely it is that he will
die, the cost of insurance protection must go up each year.
For example, out of a thousand people aged 25, you would
not expect many to die; out of a thousand people aged 95,
you would expect many people to die in a given year. The
cost of the insurance goes up per $1,000 in *every type* of
insurance policy as age increases. Don't be fooled just
because the premium remains the same. In most policies
sold, the premium remains the same, but the actual cost
of insurance protection--the insurance company's amount
at risk--goes down each year.

The actual cost for insurance protection in its purest
form tends to be very low compared to the type of policy
which is generally sold.

For example, the premium rate for the type of policy which
provides the most insurance protection at the least cost,
compared to the more expensive type which the insurance
industry tries to sell you, is this:

Most Protection At Least Cost: $2.28 per thousand

Compared To

Insurance Industry's Choice: $16.00 per thousand

These rates are for a man aged 30, paying on a monthly basis. Generally, the insurance agent will try to get you to buy the more expensive kind. There are policies which are even more expensive.

Insurance And The Divorce

For the woman in transition who is in the process of divorce or who is divorced, life insurance can be very important, particularly if children are involved. First, be aware of any insurance policies which your husband may have. For purposes of a property settlement, this is an asset which your attorney should consider. He may not, unless you make him aware of its existence.

If child support is going to play a part in your divorce, then life insurance on your husband is very important. Without it, if he should die, then child support would stop. Where would this leave a mother with children? Just because he may now have a policy, do not count on it for yourself. He can also change beneficiaries. The method that gives you the best control is to have him take out a low-cost policy on his life, with you as the *owner* and the *beneficiary*. Your attorney can structure this to have him send you sufficient extra money to take care of the premiums. It would be prudent to insure that he carries sufficient coverage. With a low-cost policy, he probably will; with a high-cost whole life policy, he probably will not.

Note: It is not a good idea to have your husband's present policy transferred into your name. By doing this, you make the cash value of the policy (the amount that you or your children are to receive upon his death) subject to *federal income tax*. Except for the amount already paid into the policy at the time of transfer, and your payment of premiums after the transfer, the value of the policy is taxable. This can mean loss of up to 70 percent of your total.

If, for some reason, you cannot make arrangements with your husband that are satisfactory to you, or if, as the family "breadwinner," you wish to assure your children of additional protection, stop and consider the following.

The primary purpose of life insurance is to provide the beneficiaries of the policy with economic security in the event of death or disability. If you have no children or dependents, there is little or no reason to have a policy. (If you had no car, you wouldn't buy insurance for it.) Similarly, a life insurance policy on the lives of children is usually a poor investment. Ask yourself:

Do I Need Life Insurance?

Probably the best way to answer this question is to ask yourself this: "If I were to die, is there anyone dependent on me who would suffer a financial loss?" If the answer to that question is "No," then you probably do not need insurance. You don't need it as an investment if you can put the same amount of money in a bank, or a better investment.

If the answer is "Yes," then you probably do need insurance. For example, if you are working and have children or parents who are dependent on you for financial support, then you would need insurance.

How Much Insurance Do I Need?

This depends on a number of factors, depending on your own circumstances. For example, let us say that you have two dependent children, ages seven and ten. You could determine how many more years each would need to have some kind of support and how much they would need each year. If you are covered by social security, this will probably pay something. Find out how much this would be, then you could subtract this from the total amount which you added up before. This is a simple way of doing it, but would be close enough for most situations. Obviously, the amount you will need goes down each year.

If you are planning on having your children go to college, then an additional amount may be required. Current figures from the government show college costs as follows:

	1960	1970	1980
Public college	$ 7,500	$11,000	$15,000
Private college	$ 9,500	$15,000	$20,000

This is for four years of a college education.

What Kind Of Insurance Should I Buy?

This is entirely up to you. Make sure that you are buying
it and that the insurance agent isn't selling you something
too expensive which you do not need. Below, we will go
into the different types of policies, beginning with the
lowest cost policies.

Annual Renewable Term is the lowest cost insurance that a
person may buy as an individual. This is the purest form
of life insurance protection. It gives you the most protection for the least amount of money. Each year, your
premium is based on your age, and it will go up every year
by a very little bit per thousand dollars of protection per
year. However, the amount of insurance protection you need
every year is probably going down, so the amount you pay
each year will tend to remain close to the same. If you
buy such a policy, here are things to look for:

1. Can you buy any amount, or do you have to buy a large
    policy? Choose the one which lets you buy any amount.

2. Is it renewable, and if so, for how long? The longer
    that it is renewable, the better off you are. This
    type of policy is renewable up to age 70 with better
    companies.

3. Is it convertible, that is, can I change it for a whole
    life policy later on without having to take a medical
    examination? It should be. Better companies have this
    type of policy renewable to age 65.

4. Is the premium low? Your cost should be low. One
    good company whose policy contains the above provisions
    has the following rates, which are very low. The
    premiums are per thousand of protection per year,
    payble on a monthly basis:

    age 20 $2.09   age 40 $3.43
    age 25 $2.17   age 45 $5.20
    age 30 $2.28   age 50 $8.08
    age 35 $2.56   age 55 $12.63

Generally, by age 55 your needs for life insurance may be
little if any. It is interesting to note that a "whole
life" or "permanent" policy will start out being more
expensive than this type of policy gets to be even at age
55!

Decreasing Term is slightly more expensive than an annual
renewable term policy in many cases, but it does have the
convenience of a level premium, even though the insurance
is decreasing each year. These policies can be had decreasing for ten, fifteen, twenty years or more, up to age
65. A variation of this is the *five-year-term*. The
premium for this remains level for the term of five years,
but you will pay slightly more during the first years of
this policy than the last years since the actual cost of
the protection is averaged out over the five-year period.
Generally, these policies may be renewed for another five-
year period without an insurance physical examination.

Whole Life has many other names such as "Cash Value" or
"Permanent" insurance. This is the type of policy that
insurance agents try to sell most frequently. The commissions are very much higher than for term insurance.
This type of insurance tends to give you the least amount
of current protection for the most premium outlay, at a
time when you need just the exact opposite. Built into
the premiums for this type of policy are insurance rates
for age 99! You may not even live until that age, or if
you did, what would you need insurance to protect against?
This type of insurance does build up Cash Surrender Values.
This is your own money which the insurance company holds
for you and generally pays about 2 1/2 percent interest.
You can do much better at a bank. Don't be taken in by
the concept of "it is guaranteed." To guarantee a rate
that low is probably about as risky for the insurance
company as to guarantee that the temperature in Honolulu
will not go below 50 degrees.

Endowment Policies are a very, very expensive form of
insurance. Generally, they are sold as a savings plan
for a certain number of years, normally a twenty-year
period. This type of policy is more of an enforced
savings plan than an insurance protection plan. If you
die, the company will pay the face value of the policy.
If you live, at the end of the period you can receive
the face amount in cash. That same money, placed in a
bank, would have produced a larger amount than the policy
would at the end of the period.

Dividends are not a policy, but bear mentioning. Many
companies pay "dividends." This is not a dividend in the
normal sense of the word, such as a stock dividend. Basically, it is a partial return of a calculated overpayment.
Even at that, it is not guaranteed that you will receive
it. For example, if you could buy two identical washing

machines at store "A" and at store "B," and store A charges
$175 but no dividend; store B charges $225 but tells you
that they *might* give you a $25 "dividend" at the end of
the year, would you call that a dividend? Insurance company dividends are not taxed as are other types of dividends.
Why not? Because they are returning your own money to you!

You now have a few of the basics of life insurance. A few
moments to read one or more of the books suggested could
save you hundreds, if not thousands, of dollars. One woman
who did was told by a surprised insurance agent, "You're
just a housewife; your're not supposed to know all of that!"
You could be that woman.

Health Insurance

Health insurance differs from other kinds of insurance in
that its function is as much to prevent disasters from
occurring as it is to help you recoup your financial losses
from ill health. Preventive medical insurance is now becoming popular, and it is estimated that a national health
insurance plan will be passed in Congress within the next
several years. It is doubtful that this plan, even when
passed, will prove sufficient for all citizens' health
needs. For a discussion of health insurance, see the health
chapter, "Taking Care of Ourselves."

Homeowners' Insurance

Insurance against fire, natural disasters, smoke, aircraft
damage, and explosions is usually available in some sort of
"package" form. Many homeowners buy package or homeowners'
policy insurance which includes personal liability insurance
as well as coverage for property and furnishings. Tenants
are also able to buy these types of insurance policies.
It is usually best to investigate several types of insurance "package" policies, as some may give you more than
you really need for protection. In general, the "package"
form of insurance is less expensive than if you bought
individual insurance policies covering just one area (such
as fire, windstorms, whatever).

It is usually best to buy an insurance policy which includes
liability insurance. Under a liability policy, injuries or
damages you are charged with in court are paid by your
insurance company. Injuries or damages which result from
actions of someone in your family are also covered. In
certain policies, regardless of your liability, medical
payments up to $250 will be paid.

Car Insurance

If you didn't know, car insurance is one of the most essential forms of insurance. Accidents in cars are too frequent
to take a chance on. Liability insurance, insurance that
covers financial loss you might incur from damage or property
injury suits, is generally considered the most important type
of car insurance. Larger liability policies generally do not
cost much more than smaller policies, and are well worth the
small increase in price.

Insurance which covers medical expenses of passengers in your
car is relatively inexpensive and is probably worth the money.
The maximum coverage is generally $2,000 per person.

Collision insurance, which protects the car owner from the
expenses of damages to her own car, is relatively expensive.
Deductible insurance in this category (where you agree to pay
the first $50 or $100 toward your car's repair) is generally
less expensive.

Comprehensive insurance covers your car against damage through
theft, fire, flood, and breakage of glass. Comprehensive and
collision insurance are almost always required if you buy a
car on credit. If you cannot afford several types of car insurance, the most important type to have is liability insurance, which will cover you in the event of the injury or death
of your passengers or the driver of another car. It is wise
to comparison-shop for car insurance as well as other forms
of insurance, as prices vary widely. Some states have state
insurance commissioners whose offices have useful information
comparing differing policies.

Crime Insurance

If you are relatively certain that you need crime insurance,
it will probably be expensive and/or difficult to obtain.
People who live in urban areas, especially in poorer urban
areas, face much higher costs for crime insurance than suburban and sometimes rural people do.

There is, however, a federal crime insurance program that you
may be eligible for if you live in a so-called "high crime"
area and cannot afford or get another form of insurance.
Despite the cancellation or nonrenewal of private insurance
policies, you may be eligible for this kind of insurance.
To find out more about federal crime insurance, contact
your city's Model Cities program or Federal Information
Center. In order to get this kind of insurance you must

have certain kinds of approved locks on your house's doors.

Divorce Insurance

Some states (New York is one) are seriously considering investigating the possibility of an insurance policy to be taken out by couples at the time they marry which matures at the time of a divorce and provides a minimal level of support for the children of a broken marriage. If there are no children, the wife would be able to use the proceeds to continue her education or receive job training. Happily married couples could convert the policy to education, retirement, or other benefits, or cash it in after a certain period of time. To be completely effective such a policy would have to be mandatory, its sponsors admit; most people refuse to think about divorce at the time they marry, despite the fact that 455 out of every 1,000 marriages end in divorce. As a result of many of these divorces, children and wives are left without adequate support. The purpose of divorce insurance would be primarily to put an end to the national scandal that child support and alimony payments are becoming, and stop penalizing children financially for their parents' mistakes.

►►► *CHARLOTTE*

I went to a prestigious Eastern women's college, and I always felt like a fraud. I thought they had admitted me by mistake, and that sooner or later the truth would come out. I thought I was there due to some error because I worked very hard at my courses and only made mediocre grades. Also, I was never very good at the intellectual chitchat that went on in the dormitory rooms, although I would hum a few bars and fake it. Somehow I had fallen in with a very academic crowd, and I remember being mortified on the day the Graduate Record exams were given that I was the only one on my floor was wasn't taking them--the only one on my floor who had no plans to go to graduate school. Mostly my plans revolved around getting married, and I played that for all it was worth.

This was in 1965, and every woman I knew planned to get married at some time or other. Most of my school friends planned to have careers as well. I had found a suitable candidate for marriage when I was a junior in college, and I worked on him all during

*my senior year.   By April we were engaged, and I was
thrilled.   I bought every issue of* Bride Magazine
*and collected brochures about silver patterns.   I
read an etiquette book from cover to cover so I would
know all the important things about getting married,
like how to word the engagement announcement, who
were suitable bridesmaids, and how to write proper
thank-you notes for the wedding gifts.*

*I had several wealthy friends at school who were also
getting married the summer after we graduated, and I
took my cues from them about the right way to get
married.   It would be unthinkable for them, for example,
to start a marriage without a complete place setting
for 12 of china, crystal, and silver, not to mention
having an additional set (for 8) of "everyday" china,
crystal, and silver.   So Bob and I picked out "our"
patterns and registered with every department store
bridal registry from Chicago to Boston, hoping that
friends and relatives would have the sense to check
them out before buying something ghastly.   We also
hoped our friends and relatives would come across
with the avalanche of trivets, salad bowls, demitasse
cups, relish trays, jam jars, cheese boards, candle-
sticks, silver serving dishes, bathroom towels, mono-
grammed bed linen, and hot trays that we so badly
needed to start our marriage.*

*Then there was the wedding.   My wealthy friends were
planning really big shindigs--500 guests, reception
at the country club, the works.   I yearned for that
kind of wedding, too, but my parents couldn't afford
it.   So I said that I wanted something* intimate *and*
tasteful.   *Just a few close friends and relatives.   A
champagne wedding on a beer budget, as they say.
Which we did.   I think the wedding was nice, although
I really don't remember too much about it.   I was
mostly anxious to get away on our honeymoon and then
get back to our cozy apartment so we could start
keeping house.   We had hauled in a lot of nice gifts,
and with such a good beginning, our marriage was
bound to succeed, right?*

*Wrong!   Things were O.K. at first, although I should
have been warned when Bob and I had a* huge *fight as
soon as we got back from the honeymoon about how to
arrange the loot on the closet shelves.   I thought
because I was the* wife *I got to do it, but Bob felt*

*he had just as much say in it. Anyhow, we got that
one worked out and proceeded to play out our roles
as* struggling graduate student *and* supportive wife/
secretary.

*There were a lot of things I enjoyed about our life.
We lived in an academic community and had lots of
"stimulating" people over for intimate dinners (and
they were really intimate, because our apartment,
grossly overpriced, was* tiny). *We went to concerts
and movies and read a lot and listened to classical
music. I felt very trendy. My secretarial job was
relatively interesting, and I felt I was doing an
important thing by supporting my husband while he
was in graduate school. Besides, it had a lot of
status among the other secretaries, most of whom
weren't married.*

*There were some minor (or so I thought at the time)
problems. Money, for example. Bob had a fellowship
and I was earning a magnificent $4224 a year, and
while things were pinched, we could usually afford
to do what we wanted. But Bob always made me feel
guilty about spending any money. He did all the
grocery shopping because he didn't trust me with
the money. Nowadays I would love for someone else
to do my grocery shopping, but at the time I felt he
was undercutting my wifely role. The other big
warning sign was that about six months after we were married I had a severe depression or breakdown or something. I couldn't sleep, and I was convinced that
every twinge in my body was a heart attack, a blood
clot, a tumor, or whatever. I cried a lot and didn't
want to see anyone and finally had to take a leave
of absence from my job. I stayed in bed about a
month before I could go back to work part time. Three
months and 10 refills of Librium later, I was more
or less myself again, convinced that I had just gone
through a "marital adjustment problem."*

*After that I really adjusted good. I threw myself
into every housewifely chore imaginable (except
cleaning, which has never been my thing). I started
cooking with a frenzy (by this time I was doing the
shopping and spending much more than Bob ever had
and feeling* very *guilty) and read cookbooks on my
lunch hour at work. I subscribed to* Gourmet Magazine
*and experimented with their recipes. I baked my own
bread and pastries. I never used frozen vegetables.*

I made most of my own clothes. I knitted. I crocheted.
I embroidered. I did needlepoint. I read women's
magazines frantically. There were hardly enough hours
in the day for me.

My husband managed to finish graduate school in between
eating all the home-cooked meals I prepared for him, and
he took a teaching job in another city. We rented a
house in the suburbs and prepared to live like real
adults (i.e., not like students). We wanted to have
children, but we decided to wait a few years so we
could earn some money and do it up right. I started
job hunting, and what I had in mind was a semi-glamorous
secretarial job which would enable me to dress up and
commute downtown on the train. Nothing too demanding,
but something to bring in some money and fill the time
until I became a mother.

The job I got wasn't anything like that, and it totally
turned my head around. By some sort of fluke (and I'm
still not sure how it happened) I took a job as the
administrative assistant in a community organizing
project in the black community. Those were the post-
civil rights days when blacks were setting up separatist
organizations and whites were either bailing out of the
struggle with hurt feelings or setting up groups to
combat racism in white communities. The whites in the
program I worked for were doing the latter.

Anyhow, instead of breezing into a sophisticated downtown office, I was stepping over piles of garbage outside
our office in the ghetto. I, who had never been political
and who thought civil rights activists I had met were
embarrassingly emotional, was suddenly caught up in a
whirl of meetings, demonstrations, pickets, conferences,
etc. I didn't understand all the issues (at least not
at first), but I felt like I was doing the right thing,
and I liked and respected all the people I was working
with.

Unfortunately, all this left Bob in the dust. At first
he thought that it was cute that I got so excited about
everything, but he began to balk when I spent a lot of
evenings out at meetings, preferred my new friends to
our old friends, and pressured him to move into the
city. I tried to involve him in the groups I was working with, but he felt threatened by my friends and
hostile to what we were doing.

*I could probably have continued that way and managed
to keep our marriage together ("My husband's a Repub-
lican and I'm a Democrat, so we don't talk about
politics at home, hah, hah") if it hadn't been for
our life-style conflicts. For example, I couldn't
stand his friends--they were stodgy, academic, un-
committed. My friends, on the other hand, were exciting and real--they were politically involved and wore
funky clothes and smoked dope at parties.*

*Suddenly the contradictions of struggling to end
racism by day and coming home at night to my suburban
home (cleaned by my black cleaning woman and filled
with all my china, crystal, silver, and tasteful
furniture) got to be too much. Plus I was finding
some of the men I knew very attractive, and, product
of The Fifties that I was, couldn't imagine sleeping
with someone other than my husband while I was married.
So I moved out.*

*I turned my back on my eight-room house filled with
possessions and took a furnished one-room apartment.
It was unbelievably dreary, but I felt very "pure."
At first it was just so I could be on my own for a
while and sort out what I wanted. I had to decide
if my marriage was worth struggling for (and it
would certainly be a struggle if we stayed together)
or whether I had the courage to be on my own. After
I had been alone for a month or so I knew that I
couldn't go back to living with Bob, no matter how
scared I got. I felt such freedom to do what I
wanted and not have to account for it to Bob. It
was fantastic!*

*I then embarked on what I now call my Sexual Libera-
tion period. I guess I was afraid that no man would
ever find me attractive, so I had to prove to myself
that I could seduce almost anyone. I was also
extremely curious, since I had only ever slept with
Bob. For a time I really enjoyed sleeping around,
and I felt like I was an entirely new person. But
eventually I got tired of waking up in the morning
next to a strange face and wondering what the hell I
was going to talk about.*

*Then came some bad times. I suddenly realized that
despite all the partying, I was basically alone, and I
didn't know how to live with myself. I would come
home from work, and if I didn't have a meeting to*

go to or a friend to visit I would drink a lot so I wouldn't get scared. I was very thankful that Bob and I hadn't had children, because I knew it would be a much harder struggle for me and I could never be as separate from him. But I also still wanted to be a mother, and I was worried that I would never again find anyone to settle down with and have children with. I was only 25, but I felt incredibly old and like I had wasted the best years of my life.

During this time I made some close women friends. The Women's Liberation Movement was just beginning then, and the women I knew were very helpful to me while I tried to get myself together. I began to share with other women things about myself (things I had always thought were bad and ugly) which I had never even considered sharing with Bob. It blew my mind that I could feel so close to other people when all my relationships in the past had been so social and superficial. That was a few years ago and I am still learning to live with myself.

I still want to be a mother and I am afraid that I am getting too old. I still want to be intimate with another person (or maybe other people?) but I don't want to be smothered in a relationship again. I don't want to grow old by myself, but I don't know anybody I want to grow old with. Basically I don't know what I want, but I think I'm getting stronger about figuring out what it is.

SIX: LIFE SPACE

INTRODUCTION

Among the many problems you have to struggle with during
the time of a separation, deciding where you will live can
be one of the most difficult. Finding a new place to live,
getting your husband to leave if you want to stay where
you are, moving in with relatives if you have no other
choices--making any of these arrangements can seem overwhelming. In this chapter we want to outline some of the
options you have and give suggestions about how to act on
them. It is important not to make hasty decisions about
anything in your life at this time, and this is especially
true about housing. Try not to decide about moving during
or just after an emotionally charged scene with your husband or family. ("That's it! I've had it! I'm leaving!")
If you can, think through your long-range plans (even though
you may be having trouble thinking ahead to tomorrow) and
make decisions about where you will live in terms of your
future. This can help you to prevent future problems
arising from making an unwise decision.

Note: If you and your husband own a house, you are generally
in a better position than if you are renting because it can
be an important part of the bargaining process. Keep this
in mind when deciding whether or not to leave, or when
thinking about how to get your husband to leave if he won't.
See the legal chapter for more help with this.

YOUR OPTIONS

Remaining In Your Home

Remaining in your home has many advantages. Probably the most important reason to stay is that the financial bur- dens on you will be particularly heavy if you are the one to move out. In addition to paying the rent and buying furniture, you'll be amazed at the number of extension cords, curtain rods, and kitchen odds and ends you'll end up buying. Hunting for a new home is generally time-con- suming and tedious, and is often depressing. Finding a place which meets your needs, especially for a woman with children, is difficult, as large apartments are expensive and rare. Often a separated women with children is con- sidered an undesirable tenant because of her lack of finan- cial security. Also, you and your children may feel attached to your present neighborhood through friends, jobs, and school.

If staying put makes sense for you, you might try to work out an agreement with your husband whereby he would move and allow you to remain in the house or apartment. In discussing this question with your husband, you might point out that your staying in your present home may save him money in the long run, and you may be able to bargain away something he wants in exchange for keeping the house. This is especially true if you and your husband owned your own home. If he agrees to move out, you should both be clear about who will pay what toward the rent, mortgage payments, utilities, etc.

Sometimes, especially when the separation is not a mutual decision, it may be difficult to get your husband to leave. If he says he absolutely won't go, this does not mean that you are stuck, although it won't be easy to get him out. The beatings section explains what some of your options are in this situation. If you are concerned about physical harm to yourself or your children, you can try removing your husband's possessions, changing the locks on the doors, and changing your phone to an unlisted number. If the house or apartment is in both of your names, he has a right to be there, but these tactics might discourage him. If the house or apartment is in your name only, he will be trespassing if he comes in without your permission, and you can call the police. You might try convincing your land- lord to have your husband's name taken off the lease. The section on beatings in Chapter Seven has more information on this.

Photo by: Emi Tonooka

Photo by: Joanne Kander

Photo by: Eva Shaderowfsky

Photo by: Eva Shaderowfsky

Photo by: Eva Shaderowfsky

Photo by: Eva Shaderowfsky

Photo by: Eva Shaderowfsky

Who keeps the home, who moves out, and how any money invested in a home is divided are sometimes determined by a
voluntary separation agreement. See the legal chapter for
details of how to arrange one. That section also discusses
how your moving out, or his, will affect your ability to
get a divorce, to qualify for a support order or welfare,
and to receive custody of your children.

DONNA

*I have no idea what my legal rights are and am beginning
to think that I have none. . . . I'm paying $150 a month
rent out of my $200 a month salary and hoping no emer-
gency comes up. My husband sends $60 weekly so "the
children won't starve," he says, and this is a lifesaver,
but I don't know how long, or if, I can depend on this
money.*

*Also, we were buying a four-bedroom house in Louisiana
when we were transferred here. We listed the house
for sale and came to Texas. That was last November and
the house still hasn't sold. I was there in March and
it has sunk five inches since we left and there are
large cracks in the ceilings and walls. I was told by
lawyers there that they couldn't help me in any legal
action against the realtors who sold the house because
they already represented the realtor or building in
other matters, and because I was married, my husband
would have to sign papers to bring suit and he refuses
to do this.*

*He says the house is my problem now--he quit making
monthly payments, which are larger than my monthly
check, so I can't pay them. He says if I can sell the
house, I can have anything I can get out of it. I
could certainly use the money but my hands seem to be
tied legally, and no one wants to buy a sinking house.
It can be patched up but will probably continue to
sink as it was built on a large drainage ditch, I
found out in March.*

Moving

You may decide to move for any number of reasons: Your
husband won't leave and it would be too much trouble to
get him out; he has already or may in the future hurt you
or your children; you can't afford to pay rent anywhere

and have to move in with relatives; or you want to start
your new life in a different neighborhood. We probably
don't have to tell you that the decision about where you
live will determine to a large extent your way of life
and the financial obligations you will have. It's important to think carefully how to go about it.

If your husband is adamant about your being the one to
leave, or if in general he is cooperative about the separation, you might bargain for a specific amount you will
need to find and move into a new place. Included in this
figure should be deposit and security costs on an apartment, installation and security costs for utilities, moving costs, fees for realtors or agents, essential household
furnishings, and perhaps one month's rent. If you have
this sum in your hands before you leave, the process of
finding a home in which to begin your new life will be
much easier.

In some circumstances, the children are mature and comfortable enough to want to have a say in where they live and
with whom. In other situations they may feel pressured at
having to make a decision. In the first case, they should
certainly be allowed to have a part in the decision-making.
On a more basic level, you run the risk of being deprived
of custody should you move out of the family home without
them. The longer your absence, the more difficult it may
be for you to regain custody of them, especially if your
husband objects strongly to it.

On the other hand, your situation may be so emotionally
charged that you feel you have little time or opportunity
for deliberation. If this is the case and you feel that
you will probably want custody of your children, take them
with you when you move or as soon as possible thereafter.
Arrange for your husband to visit with the children with
times and places specified in advance.

There are two situations in which you should not delay
moving out. First, if your husband is violent or abusive
toward you and/or the children. You may have to arrange
to stay with relatives or friends while you find a permanent home, so don't wait until the situation is intolerable and then march out with no place to go. Should an
emergency arise and you find yourself out with no place
to go, contact local women's centers, WMCAs, churches,
or health and welfare councils about emergency accommodations.

A second situation which calls for decisive action is when your husband is not supporting you and/or your children. In this case, most states require you to leave the house before you are even eligible for an emergency welfare check or a hearing in support court. In a few states, wives who are "separated" but living under the same roof as their husbands may be eligible for support orders. This area of the law is currently changing, with more states recognizing the fact that the price of housing often prohibits "separated" people from having two addresses.

Because of these issues and others discussed more fully in the legal chapter section on separation and the chapter on children, we strongly urge you to seek legal advice *before* you make any move. You don't need to have decided upon a divorce before you talk with a legal counselor.

Once you have determined some of your needs (size, location, what you can afford, house or apartment), you should try to check out any leads on the kind of home you are looking for. The first place to look is in the newspaper, but you should not forget to ask friends, relatives, colleagues, as word of mouth is often the best lead that there is. You might try community or school bulletin boards, reputable realtors, or find out if there is a women's center near you which has information about housing. (See p. 487 for a listing of women's centers.)

Going Home To Mother

Because of problems with finances, health, child care, or whatever, you may have no choice but to move in with relatives--your parents, sisters, brothers, aunts, uncles, cousins, or with friends or neighbors. In our experience this has turned out to be unsatisfactory for most women in transition. Some women, of course, have found their families to be a real refuge during a separation. They have received money, baby-sitting help, and encouragement during rough times. But many women find it difficult to be dependent on their families. For most of us, even when things are going well, our families feel they have the right to tell us how to live our lives. When you are separated and dependent on them for shelter and food, the situation can be intolerable. You (and your children) may be made to feel guilty about taking up space and adding to the family's expenses. And if you aren't criticized about how you are living your life, you are criticized for how you are raising your children.

The best advice we can give you if you have no choice but
to live with your family is to become as independent as
you can as quickly as possible. For the long run try to
arrange some financial resources for yourself, either
getting job training, or going on welfare, or tracking
down your husband for support. When you move in, make
sure the financial arrangements and household responsibilities are agreed upon by everybody. If you can pay
anything toward maintaining the household, do so. It
will make you feel less like you're a burden and may minimize the meddling in your life.

All of this is especially true if you have been living
with your husband's relatives. With him gone, you are
outnumbered. Again, plan how you can get on your own and
try to stay out of family feuds as much as possible. If
you have a plan to move out in the future, even if it's
a long way away, it may make the present more bearable.

Living Alone

Living alone is a very positive experience for some women
when they separate. If you decide to live alone, it may
be the first time that you are completely on your own.
You might find living alone gives you the opportunity to
develop confidence in your ability to take care of your
own needs. If you are having a difficult time going
through the separation, living alone will free you from
having to relate to other people. Because you are in
transition, you may not be ready to make commitments to
living with others. You just might need the time to re-
adjust to your own self, to experiment, to find ways of
appreciating yourself. You can be more flexible and mobile
if you live alone and have only yourself to account for.

If you have children, you will have to weigh the responsibility of living alone and being their sole support against
the benefits of having your privacy, time to overcome your
emotional crises, and a family unit more similar to what
you have been used to.

Living alone has its disadvantages as well. You may feel
the need for more people around to help you with the transition. You may feel isolated and lonely. You may worry
about your safety. Also, maintaining a place of your own
is more difficult financially. The point is to make your
decision with some forethought. You may be lonely whether
or not you live alone. You will probably find it difficult
to have your needs met by other people because they simply

cannot replace your relationship with your husband. You
should try not to have unrealistic expectations for whatever living situation you finally choose. Your goal should
be to choose the one that is the least stressful for you.

Group Living

Group living is not new to the 1970s; extended families of
aunts, uncles, cousins, etc., have existed for centuries as
mutual support systems for everyone belonging to them and
continue to do so now within many ethnic and racial groups.
Some of us, however, grew up in nuclear families consisting
of a father, mother, and children. There were occasional
variations on this idea--a single-parent home, or an aging
grandmother who lived with us. But by and large we were
used to seeing families living as self-contained units,
alone in their "own" homes.

Your first instinct as a separating or divorcing woman may
be to live alone or alone with your children. You may
find, however, that living with the right people may give
you more freedom in dealing with the financial and emotional problems of being a woman in transition. Sharing the
rent of a house or apartment can get you more space for
the money. Managing the expense of appliances, food, utilities, and even automobiles is less difficult for several
people than for one "head of the household." In a group-
living situation, you usually assume responsibility for
one *part* (instead of all) of the housekeeping chores.
Sharing the cooking, laundry, and child care can create
more freedom for a woman who is used to doing most of
these things by herself.

Shared child-rearing is a more complex matter, but many
parents are finding it worth trying. Living in a group
means that there are more adults around to share the responsibilities of children. The children have an opportunity to know adults other than their biological parents
and children other than their brothers and sisters. Many
of us have out of necessity shared child-rearing with our
parents, brothers, or sisters, but living with responsible
peers who are willing to make a commitment to our children
is different. Hopefully these arrangements can be helpful
in breaking down destructive patterns we have developed in
our family relationships.

There are definite disadvantages to group living. Women
who have lived only with their husbands and children have
been in a very different world. Living in a group can

mean more diverse emotional responsibilities, and the group
may not be able to furnish the same intimacy or privacy as
in a close nuclear family. Living with other people requires the ability to compromise and develop shared standards of responsibility, cleanliness, etc. Inevitably, old
group members leave and new ones arrive, which can be dis-
ruptive for everyone, especially the children. And it is
sometimes difficult for a woman in transition to give up
her way of functioning. Sometimes the group itself can be
unaware of its members' needs.

An important consideration is whether to live only with
women or in a mixed group. One possible way of creating a
support situation for yourself is to move in with another
woman (or women) in transition. If you have a large home
with extra space, you can ask another woman to join you.
The companionship and help of a woman who is going through
the same kinds of problems can be a great source of comfort.
One situation you should avoid, however, is living with
another woman in transition when the two of you can only
focus on your own pain. This is a time when you need to
receive comfort and give it, but if neither of you has
much energy or love to give the other, it is best that you
find other women, perhaps not in transition, to live with.

Living with men creates its own complexities. Not the
least of the considerations are your feelings about the
marriage you have just ended. If you are extremely bitter
toward your ex-husband, you may find yourself unable to
tolerate living with men. If your marriage has left you
shaky and insecure, and you wonder if any other man will
ever find you attractive, you may find yourself getting
sexually involved with men in the house, which can be dis-
ruptive to both you and the group. It seems sensible to
stay out of any especially demanding relationships with
men for a while in order to clear your mind about what
kinds of relationships with others, men and women, you
want for yourself in the future.

Groups which succeed do so because they have kept their
lines of communication open. It is destructive and unproductive to allow resentments and grievances to pass by
unacknowledged. This doesn't mean that you should be
tearing yourselves apart, but rather that honesty and willingness to deal with conflict helps to prevent it from
escalating. Many groups have weekly house meetings to
discuss what the members are feeling and to keep communication flowing. Most people who live in groups say that
it isn't the answer to all of their problems, but that it

has allowed them to develop more fully as individuals. As
a woman in transition attempting to build a new life for
yourself, you should consider whether living in a group can
help you to do this.

Many women's centers have listings of women looking for
other women to live with. Mixed groups usually advertise
for new members through word-of-mouth, food co-ops, community bulletin boards, underground papers, and college bulletin boards. If the group is already formed, interview
them when they interview you. If the group is just forming,
discuss everyone's expectations, needs, and life-styles.
Although you will never really know what it will be like
to live with a particular group until you do it, you can
at least try to make sure all of you have the same assumptions about what you want from a house.

ELINOR

*I have a son named Matthew who is 4 years old. For
the last year he and I have been living with a group
of people, and for the most part it has been good.
I moved in with the group because I am working on a
graduate degree in psychology and I just didn't think
I could make it studying and taking care of Matt, too.
Matthew's father sees him one weekend a month, and
the rest of the time I'm responsible for him.*

*Our house has 6 adults and 3 children. The other
children besides Matt, a brother and sister, are
2½ and 5, and their parents both live in the house.
In addition to that family, there are 2 other men
and another woman. At first I was very apprehensive
about living in a commune. I was worried about giving
up my privacy and afraid I would disagree with people
over everything from what kind of breakfast cereal to
buy to how to handle the children.*

*Some of my fears were unrealistic and others weren't.
Matt and I each have our own room, so I feel like I
can retreat whenever I need to. We have all worked
it out pretty well about what food to buy, how neat
the downstairs area should be kept, etc. Sometimes,
of course, I get annoyed when the smokers don't empty
their ashtrays or someone doesn't wash the dishes as
clean as I would like them to be, but those annoyances
are minor and we can usually work them out.*

The harder struggles have come because of the children. In the beginning there was a lot of jealousy among the children, usually when an adult would be playing with one child and the others would want to be included. But this has cooled off somewhat. The most problems have been among the adults. The parents in the house are trying not to be possessive of their children and to listen honestly to feedback they get from other people. But I do have more of an investment in Matt than in the other children, and if I see some inter-action I don't like between him and someone else, I can't help but want to control the situation. Other people get on me about this and say I should be looser, but it's hard to give that up when you've been a single parent for so long and when you know in the end you will be the one with responsibility for your child. Sometimes, too, I just get tired of having to deal with other people's children as well as my own and think it would be simpler if Matt and I lived in an apartment somewhere.

I really think, though, that the good parts outweigh the bad. For one thing, the kids all love each other. They fight, of course, but they really get a kick out of being together, and it's great for Matt because he doesn't have any brothers or sisters. And then there's the relief. *Relief from having to get up with him every single morning and put him to bed every single night and take him to his day care center and pick him up and feed him and bathe him, etc. Sometimes having to deal with 3 children instead of 1 is a drag, but when it's my time "off" I can really enjoy it.*

The best part, I think, is that Matt has other adults he can be with and get guidance from. Sometimes I get too wrapped up in my schoolwork to really give him the attention he needs or sometimes I just get angry with him and we slip into some old bad patterns we have, with him acting wild and me acting bitchy. Those times it's really helpful to have someone else step in. This is especially true when we have had an argument and he's upset and needs comforting but I'm too angry still to shift and be loving toward him.

I also like living in the house for me. *I enjoy the other people, especially the other women, and I don't feel as lonely as I used to when Matt and I lived alone. I'm not sure if I would want to live this way forever. It's hard being a single parent when there*

*is a family in the house--it reminds me of how things
didn't work out for me. But for right now it's really
keeping me sane. It's important for me to finish
school, and I really don't think I could be pulling it
off if it weren't for a little help from my friends.*

THE POLITICS OF PROPERTY

As a woman in transition, you should know by now that anything involving money is likely to benefit those who are
paid rather than those who pay. The system of property
ownership in this country was originally designed to enable
almost everyone (except slaves and women) to buy and own
their own little plot of land. The legal aspects of property ownership date back to the Middle Ages, as do many of
the attitudes of present-day landlords. The bulk of the
law is concerned with property ownership and contracts concerning ownership, so this is one area you should not be
involved in without legal counsel.

It has been estimated (by Emily Jane Goodman in *The Tenant
Survival Book*) that one-third of all Americans, or 70 million people, are tenants or occupy rented housing. In
landlord-tenant relationships, tenants usually get the
short end of the stick, although with the growth of tenant
organizations, this may change somewhat. There is no question that it is often more profitable and desirable to own
your own home, but if you haven't the money or aren't able
to get the property rights to your house from your husband,
this may not be an option for you.

The bottom of the barrel, as far as housing is concerned,
is so-called public housing or low-income subsidized housing. If you live in a housing project you can expect to
have to deal with burglaries, drug addiction, gang fights,
unsafe and unsanitary structural conditions. Despite the
fact that middle-class property owners receive substantial
subsidies in the form of deductions from income tax for
interest on mortgage and property taxes, it is low-income
people who are made to suffer for their subsidized housing.
While homeowners receive mortgages and tax benefits, the
tenants of housing projects have until recently had *no* control about the use of federal funding. All the decisions
had been made by the local housing authority. Somehow,
under our system of government, what started out as a
basically good idea--land ownership by everyone--has been
distorted into land ownership for profit, at the expense

of those who cannot afford to own their own homes or land.

> *The law, in its majestic equality, forbids the*
> *rich as well as the poor to sleep under bridges,*
> *to beg in the streets, and to steal bread.*
>
>   *Anatole France*
>   Source Catalog Number 2

He said we didn't take care of the apartment
She blamed Benje for writing on the porch
He didn't want any cats, but we had one
She said that the other said we made too much noise
He fixed all the hinges with matchsticks
She tore down Benje's Halloween decorations
I bawled her out
She was an old lady with a sense of private property
We lived there for six years
When we left, her feelings were hurt because I
didn't say goodbye
I went back to finish cleaning
Walked through the empty rooms
That we had grown into, like a snail shell
The space now so small and shabby
I wondered how it could have been home
Then remembered
                    the sofa here, with the Mexican rug
                    the plants there, in a tangled jungle
                    the baseball stickers Benje had glued
                            on his single, viewless window
It was really so small and shabby
Our home for six years
I went down the stairs and said goodbye to her.

>   *Phyllis Middlebrooks*

Rentals

Tenants are exploited by landlords, realtors, and a legal
system which does not provide justice under the law.
Housing agencies may not do their job, and the protective
laws that are available are not always enforced. By far
the greatest number of tenants are victimized because they
are not aware of their legal rights, do not have the money
to bring legal suit against their landlords, or are unaware
of legal sources they may go to for assistance. We hope
that the information we are able to offer will help you to
avoid victimization by your landlord. In some cities and
states there are tenant associations which may be further
able to help with your specific housing problem.

What To Look For

1. If the electricity has been shut off, ask if the lights
    may be turned on for your inspection. If not, insist
    on seeing the place in daylight and use a flashlight to
    look in dark corners and closets, and any other spot
    that does not have enough light.

2. Check the security in the building. Is there a strong
    lock on the front door? The dead-bolt type is the best.
    If there is a buzzer system, does it work? Is there an
    intercom to identify visitors? Each window should have
    a working lock. On the first floor, bars might be
    necessary. Who else lives in the building? Ask other
    tenants about the crime rate in the neighborhood.

3. Concerning the electrical system, are there sufficient
    well-placed electrical outlets in each room? Is the
    electrical system strong enough to handle air condition-
    ers or other heavy appliances? Do you have access to
    the fuse box? Check for loose wires. Lack of overhead
    lights will necessitate more standing lamps. You might
    ask the tenant what his average electric bill was.

4. Turn on the water taps. Is there sufficient hot water
    when more than one tap is running? Is there constant
    water pressure? Flush the toilet. Check for water
    spots on the ceiling; cracked wall plaster or peeling
    wallpaper can be signs of leaks.

5. Find out if the heat works. If you are to pay for heat,
    ask the tenant the amount you can expect to pay. Is
    there a duct or radiator in every room? If you see many
    portable electric heaters, it suggests there is insuf-
    ficient heat. Does the apartment have its own thermo-
    stat? Check windows for proper insulation.

6. If the apartment is furnished, find out exactly what is
    owned by the landlord and what belongs to the tenant.
    Inspect the condition of the furniture. Remember, you
    have no obligation to buy a former tenant's furniture.

7. In the kitchen, check for adequate shelf and counter
    space, electrical outlets, and proper ventilation. If
    there are portable freezers, etc., do they come with
    the apartment? Ask tenants about roaches, ants, and
    mice.

8. If you are expecting deliveries, is there some place

for them to be kept if you are not at home? What
facilities does the neighborhood have? How far is the
laundromat? Is there a grocery store open after 5 P.M.?
Transportation? Parking space? Schools? Are there
other children for your children to play with? Is the
neighborhood safe for them?

9. Does the place mesh with the life-style you have?
    What financial responsibilities does it place on you?

10. Try to speak with the tenants about any problems they
    have had. Ask them about the landlord's policy about
    things like pets, repairs, and security deposits. How
    long does it usually take for repairs to be made?

When you inspect the property, it may be a good idea to
bring a friend with you to help think of questions you
might forget and to offer another opinion. Also, you might
check the local housing codes, which are the laws designed
to insure the minimum of standards of health and safety in
living quarters. Call your city's health department or
housing inspection department to make sure there are no
outstanding violations.

Make up a written list of all damages, defects, and necessary repairs and submit it to the landlord (keep a copy
for yourself) so you cannot be blamed or charged for any
damages which existed prior to your moving in. Also, if
your landlord agrees to fix anything that is wrong with
the apartment beforc you move in, it is useful to have a
signed list of repairs he agrees to make.

Your Lease

When you rent a house or apartment, you are making a con-
tractual agreement with the landlord. A lease is a statement of the promises and duties you and the landlord agree
to uphold. Most leases are written to protect the landlord
and do not require him to supply anything except the building itself. Most of the burdens and responsibilities are
placed on the tenant. For example, as a tenant you must
cause no permanent damage to the premises, maintain the
premises in the same condition as when you moved in (allowing for normal wear and tear), use the premises for no
illegal purposes, and pay the rent on time. You may expect
to be taken to court if the lease is broken.

A lease may be either written or oral; both are legally
binding. An oral lease is usually better for you as a

tenant because you retain all the rights and protections
that the law gives you, and you don't sign any of them away.
You are most likely to get an oral lease from an individual
landlord rather than from a real estate office. If you sign
a written lease, be sure all the terms you've agreed to are
spelled out, and always get an exact copy of what you've
signed.

Leases are written to intimidate the tenant. Because of
the complicated and sometimes misleading language used, it
is a good idea to take a copy of your lease to someone with
a knowledge of the law who can check it over to make sure
that you are getting the best possible deal, or at least
aren't agreeing to anything too harmful. This person need
not be a lawyer. For less expensive and, in general, equally competent legal advice, try to find a sympathetic women's
legal center, legal secretary or law student, or tenants'
association. See p. 109 of the legal section for more on
this.

The *term of the lease* is the amount of time that you agree
to rent the house or apartment. Usually after the first
lease has expired (a year, for instance) you have an unwritten, assumed contract with your landlord that goes from
month to month. You or he must give one another thirty days'
notice if you decide to move, or if he asks you to, and he
must give you the same amount of notice if he decides to
raise the rent.

Long-term vs. short-term lease: The chief advantage of a
long-term lease (which is almost always written) is that
your rent cannot be raised during that period. Also, you
cannot be asked to leave during the term of the lease unless you break the conditions you agreed to--for instance, by
not paying the rent. The landlord *can* raise the rent when
the lease is renewed by giving you the same notice he would
be required to if he were to terminate the lease. It's to
your advantage to take a long-term lease if you are reasonably sure you will be there awhile and don't want the rent
raised, if you are planning to make expensive repairs, and
if you feel sure that you can meet the lease's requirements.
It's *not* to your advantage to have a longer lease if you
think you may decide to move before the expiration of the
term. The landlord can hold you legally responsible for
the payment of rent for the balance of the term if you
break the lease. He does not have to find another tenant
to fill out the time. Some landlords will allow you to sublet, that is, to find someone else to finish out your
lease, or they will agree to let you out of the lease if

you find them another tenant. It is usually better to arrange for a new lease for the new tenant because if you sublet, you are still legally responsible for the lease if the subleasee fails to pay it. If you do sublet, it is advisable to get the entire amount of rent from the subleasee before he moves in.

Special Provisions: At the end of the standard lease, there are blanks left for you or the landlord to add special provisions. Here are some of them which may be important to you.

1. The lease may say: "This property is to be occupied by no more than _____ persons" (this is relevant if you move in, then decide to take in extra people for company and/or to help meet rent payments) and "no children" (this varies from state to state; in Pennsylvania, for example, it is legal for the landlord to specify no children; in New Jersey, this is prohibited by statute). Both of these clauses will be important to you if you leave your husband, move into an apartment or house, then plan to bring your children to live with you. If this is a possibility, be sure there are no special provisions in your lease to prevent you from doing this.

2. Another common special provision refers to pets. The standard lease says you can't have pets without written authorization from the landlord; the clause will probably be in there even if the landlord doesn't care whether or not you keep pets. If you plan to keep a pet, clear it with your landlord and ask him to write in a special provision at the bottom of the lease permitting you to keep your pet.

3. A provision you may want to add, particularly if you are a single woman, is that your landlord can't inspect the premises or permit workmen to enter unless he gives you advance notice (except in an emergency).

4. If your apartment or house isn't ready by a certain date (if it's new, if repairs aren't completed, or if a former tenant hasn't moved out), you may want to cancel your lease and get your security deposit back (see below). You should spell this out under the special-provisions section of the lease if the date you can move in is particularly crucial for you.

5. This is the section where the list of repairs you want the landlord to make or pay for should be spelled out.

6. You might also try to include the following paragraph
    as a special provision: "The tenant's duty to pay
    rent is expressly conditioned upon the landlord's duty
    to comply with state and local laws and ordinances
    regarding the habitability of residential premises."
    If your landlord would sign an agreement with that
    clause in it, count yourself fortunate and somewhat
    protected.

7. Be careful when you ask for special provisions, since
    you run the risk of your landlord deciding you're a
    troublemaker and refusing to rent to you at all. You
    have to be the judge of what provisions are crucial
    for you and how much the traffic (i.e., your landlord)
    will bear.

Be careful not to sign your rights away: Many leases include a "confession of judgment" clause, which essentially
denies the tenant the right to defense in any legal proceedings the landlord might take. This is illegal because
it violates a tenant's right to due process of law, which
guarantees notification of legal action and the opportunity
to be heard.

"Distraint and distress" clauses are also illegal. This
means that a landlord may not take a tenant's personal
property from the premises and sell it to compensate for
rent owed.

Your Security Deposit

If you are renting, you will have to make a security deposit before you move in, which may be used by the owner
to repair damages you made, or as compensation if you
leave before your lease is up. It is usually equivalent
to one month's rent and, dependent upon state law, should
be no more than two months' rent. Be sure the amount is
specified in the lease, and that you get a receipt.

At least 30 days before the lease expires, the landlord
must notify you in writing, either that he will accept
the deposit as the last month's rent, or submit a statement
listing the damages requiring payment by you. In some
states, you may sue the landlord if he fails to give you
such notice. Also, a landlord may be required to place
your deposit in an interest-earning account, the benefits
of which you are entitled to. Contact a law student, community legal services agency, or tenants' organization for
information on this.

Rent

If your lease states when the rent is due, then it is due on that date. Most leases state that rent is due on the first day of the period for which it is paid. If your landlord wants your rent paid on the first day of the month, but you are not paid until the fifth, try to get him to change the due date and have it written into the lease. If you feel you will not be able to pay your rent from one check, try to get your landlord to write into the lease that you will pay half the rent at the beginning of the month and the other half at the end of the month.

Always get a written receipt when you pay rent. The person you pay your rent to can make an entry in your rent book and sign it, or he can give you a separate piece of paper.

The receipt should carry your name, the amount paid, the date of payment, the kind of payment (rent), and the signature of the person you paid the rent to.

Save all rent receipts. They are necessary when applying for welfare and are proof of continued payment.

If you miss a month's rent, you may receive a notice from a landlord and a tenant officer, a collection agent appointed by a court, asking for the rent and some fee. *The law no longer allows a landlord to sell or threaten to sell his tenant's property for nonpayment of rent where there has not been a court hearing.* Under the new procedure for collecting back rent, the landlord must sue you, the tenant, in court.

The landlord can have a landlord and tenant officer make a levy on your property, but this levy is meaningless. *You do not have to allow the landlord and tenant officer to enter your property,* and if he cannot see your goods, he cannot make a levy. If, however, he does enter the property and makes a levy, he can charge you a small fee for making the levy. Even if a levy is made, the landlord cannot sell your property. The landlord can only collect back rent by taking you to court.

So, if you don't respond to the notice, all the landlord can do is start an eviction proceeding. If you think you can pay, get in touch with him and tell him when you expect to have the money. Most will accept partial or delayed payment.

Eviction (I hear you knockin' but you can't come in)

Laws vary from state to state, but usually there are three *legal grounds for eviction:*

1. nonpayment of rent

2. failure to comply with the requirements of the lease

3. termination of the term (the landlord wants his property back when the term of the lease is over).

Check with an attorney or a tenants' organization about laws to protect you from illegal eviction. People have been known to come home from work or a weekend away to find the locks changed, a padlock on the door, etc. One woman in New York came home to find her apartment rented to another tenant. She was successful in a suit that reclaimed $12,000 for her. Of course you cannot expect to automatically get the same results. In some states, there are laws which prevent a landlord from evicting tenants if housing code violations exist.

Whatever the grounds for eviction, the law requires, as the first step in the eviction procedure, that the tenant be given *written* notice to vacate. This right to notice may be given up in the lease. However, the standard form lease does give the tenant a right to 5 days' notice for nonpayment of rent or breach of a condition of the lease. The notice to terminate the lease at the end of the term is left blank and filled in by the landlord when the lease is filled out.

If there is no written lease, the tenant is entitled to at least 30 days' notice, unless the eviction is for non-payment of rent or breach of a condition of the lease.

After the notice period has expired, the landlord may then file an action in municipal court for eviction. If you receive a notice to vacate, *get legal advice.* Do not panic and assume that you must leave immediately.

The next thing you can expect is a notice telling you to appear in court on a certain date. You may also receive a letter from a legal services agency offering legal representation at this hearing, if you fall within their income limits. If you are above their limits, you may want to pay a lawyer to go to court with you. But it is worthwhile to go to court even without a lawyer, to explain to the judge what happened (your husband left you, you lost your job, whatever).

If you did not receive a notice to vacate, be sure to tell this to the judge. Judgment for rent will often be waived than to be allowed to remain in the building if you have missed a number of payments, or if you have a bad relationship with your landlord.

Factors that you should consider while deciding whether or not to fight to remain include:

1. Do you want to remain on the premises? How long?

2. Do you have any defenses against the eviction itself?

3. Is it likely that they will award your landlord a money judgment which they might collect from you?

4. Are there enough delaying tactics available to force the landlord into a settlement?

You should discuss all these questions with your lawyer when you bring in your notice to vacate and notice to appear in court and together arrive at a decision which will be most beneficial to you.

Even if the court enters a judgment for the landlord, it will take at least 21 days from the date of the hearing before you can actually be put out of your home. You must also receive a notice from the sheriff at least 10 days before you will be evicted.

It is common practice for landlords to attempt to scare tenants into leaving by giving commands and notices orally but not in writing. Oral notices have no legal effect. If you are aware of this, the landlord will be caught in the mistake if an eviction suit is begun. Eviction can be delayed if the landlord does not proceed with a written notice.

Sometimes landlords try to force tenants to move by threats or by shutting off utilities. This is illegal. If this happens to you, contact a legal services agency or your own lawyer. A lawyer may be able to get the landlord to obey the law by speaking or writing to him. If this does not work, he may get a court order against the landlord.

Of course, you can also call the police if the landlord threatens to use force against you and you feel the police can offer some protection.

If the landlord threatens to remove your possessions, inform him that he will be charged with theft. That may be enough to prevent any further action on his part.

Landlords dislike having to bring legal actions to evict tenants. A suit costs time and money, $150 to $500 initially, depending on the time and legal expenses involved. More money is needed to pay for the sheriff's costs to evict someone once a judgment has been obtained if the tenant doesn't leave voluntarily. Frequently landlords are willing to negotiate when confronted with a tenant who knows his rights and is willing to put these financial burdens on the landlord. An informed tenants' organization can also make a lot of difference in the power that you really have in your tenant-landlord relationship.

Tenants' Rights And Remedies

Your landlord is required to maintain the building in compliance with the local housing codes. However, the codes are often not enforced because of large backlogs of complaints and red tape. Often, if the case is brought to court, landlords may or may not pay the fine, and still may not make the necessary repairs.

You should, however, be aware of housing violations which exist, so that you may take steps, outside of court procedure, to have repairs made.

Common housing codes require the following of landlords:

1. The property must stay in sound condition and good repair. The whole building--foundations, walls, ceilings, windows, and doors--must be kept safe, weatherproof, watertight, and free of rats, roaches, or other rodents. The roof must not leak. Wood outside must have paint or other preservatives.

2. Plumbing must be in good working condition. Each dwelling unit must have a bathroom with tub or shower and toilet, and a kitchen sink in good condition.

3. Hot and cold running water facilities and lines must be installed and properly connected.

4. Two electrical outlets or an electric light and at
    least one other outlet must be provided in each room.

5. Windows and doors must be in good condition so that
    they open and close. Some housing authorities require
    a window or ventilation shaft in every room.

6. A central heating system must be provided (except where
    the city permits separate units).

Some common housing violations are stoves that leak gas,
floors that sag, windows with no screens, sewers that
smell, and locks that don't work. If you think that housing violations exist, contact your city's health or inspection department, which will send an inspector. Be ready
to supply the inspector with a list of complaints and walk
through the apartment with him, pointing out the defective
areas. Make sure that he writes down your complaints and,
if possible, supply him with pictures. If the inspector
finds violations, he will file a complaint against your
landlord, specifying the violations and the amount of time
allowed for repairs (usually 30 days). If the landlord
fails to act, a complaint will be filed with the city
court and he will be prosecuted and fined.

Unfortunately, the landlord may not make the repairs despite all of this. If this is the case, check with your
city's health department to see if there is an emergency
repair program in effect. If so, the city will make the
repairs if your apartment or house is considered unsafe or
a health hazard and will then bill your landlord.

Plumbing Poem

i go off before the alarm
my paranoid must-not-clock
runs faster
much faster than the Westinghouse one
i wake up half an hour early
to must not--must not
you must now
not
stay in bed
over sleep
be late

in the morning
i trade pipes for pipes
nightmares of pipes

for the reality of pipes
i should wait
wait a few years and write
write my memoirs being called
"my life among the pipes"
            or
"i can't get out of the waste stack"
or better still
"out of the water closet and into the sewer"

awake or asleep always pipes
dreams of pipes
pipes that grow
and pipes that shrink
and pipes that wrap themselves around me
like 50 lb. lead snakes
binding me constricting me
but the reality
the real
the pipes not dreamt
but felt
those wonderful cold metals
those hollow tubes
from which i keep expecting my destiny to emerge
or better
wanting to construct
construct a wonderfully complicated structure
22 ideal bends
and lots of pipes
that will carry

all of my unhappiness
all of my i don't wants
all of the must nots
away around and down
down into the sewer
into the Schuylkill
i've put my faith in pipes
i trust them

i know
pipes are always
always there
are carrying
carrying waste and rot and ugliness away
are bringing
bringing fresh clean cooling consoling waters

                    --diane devennie

If your landlord will not cooperate and if there is no emergency repair program or if you do not want to wait until the city gets around to processing your complaint, you may choose to have the repairs done yourself. Start by having an inspector come and go through the procedure listed above. Then send a letter by registered mail to your landlord, letting him know that if he will not make the specified repairs, you will have the repairs done and deduct the amount from your rent. When the work is done, deduct the cost from your rent. Keep the bill as proof that you paid for the repairs. Since this will be considered as rent withholding or abatement by the courts, it is best to consult a lawyer before taking such action.

Rent withholding is in some states legal if a building is declared unfit for human habitation. In Pennsylvania, for example, tenants may pay rent into an escrow account in such cases until the landlord makes the necessary repairs. Thus, the landlord cannot evict the tenant or collect rent until the repairs are made. Although the United States Supreme Court upheld a lower court's decision in 1970 that tenants may withhold rent if housing code violations exist, rent withholding is still considered illegal in some states, so it is best to contact a legal person before making the move to stop payment. Another tactic is rent strikes. Because of the monetary power that tenants' organizations wield, they are often successful in getting their demands satisfied. For information from beginning to end about tenant organizing, rent strikes, legal resources, and almost everything you need to know about getting power in this area, you might read *The Tenant Survival Handbook* listed in the bibliography at the end of this book.

Many states now have laws which prohibit landlords from evicting tenants for exercising legal rights (such as: belonging to a tenants' organization or filing a complaint about housing code violations). Also, it is illegal in some states for a landlord to raise the rent or evict a tenant as long as rent is paid up to date when housing violations exist. Contact your city's health or inspection department or an attorney to see if such laws exist in your state.

Discrimination

The less you have, the less you'll get is generally true in the realm of housing as in other areas. You may be discriminated against by realtors and landlords for any of a number of reasons. To know what is going on is a help and to prove

it is even better. Depending on your age, race, income,
and status, you may face discrimination because you are a
woman, divorcing or divorced, poor or on welfare, black or
young or aged. The law protects you only in certain areas.

Poor women, especially non-white women or women with large
families, are stereotyped as irresponsible and incapable of
handling financial matters. Women who are in transition
may be considered even greater risks because of (sometimes
real) financial instability or supposed emotional instability. For this reason you may find it advantageous to
say that you are divorced rather than separated when talking to landlords, mortgage companies, etc. This discrimination is particularly true if you have not been receiving
pay for your work or do not have an individual credit rating,
which many of us don't have.

Laws concerning discrimination in housing vary from state
to state, and in many states discrimination on the basis
of sex is still not illegal. However, if sex discrimination is not specifically prohibited in your state by law
or by the Equal Rights Amendment, the Civil Rights Act of
1968 can be used as the basis for a case in sex discrimination.

Be alert for various types of discrimination. If you are
asked to pay higher rent or give a larger security deposit
than tenants renting at the same time as you, this is just
as much discrimination as if the landlord refused to rent
to you. The Department of Housing and Urban Development
(HUD), which enforces federal laws, cannot take offenders
to court, but may conciliate and persuade, and may have
an effect on the offender if for no other reason than that
it is a federal agency. You may call HUD, toll-free, at
800-755-7252 with a housing discrimination complaint.
Other agencies which are active in fighting discrimination and which are worth contacting are: the American
Civil Liberties Union, the National Lawyers Guild, and
the National Organization for Women.

Public Housing

If you are one of the 2.4 million people living in public
housing, you probably know better than anyone else the
lie of "decent, safe housing" supposedly provided by the
1937 United States Housing Act. There are presently
800,000 public housing units owned by the United States
government. Public housing units are notoriously poorly
constructed, ineptly managed, and dangerously unsafe for

their occupants. Women in transition living in public
housing units or forced to take public housing from lack
of money or availability of low-cost private housing are
doubly trapped by being women and by being poor.

Public housing, although under the jurisdiction of the
federal Department of Housing and Urban Development (HUD),
is administered on the local level by housing authorities
who are responsible for determining the policies of the
individual projects. The administrators of the local
housing authority (LHA) are supposed to operate within
federal guidelines in determining individual regulations
concerning rents, admissions, etc. Since they are
usually professionals who have their own homes far from
the projects they administer, their understanding of the
tenant situation is generally limited.

We do not recommend public housing to any woman who can
find an alternative. But since many women are already
trapped in public housing units, and others will be forced
to live in them, we are including a limited summary of
information and guidelines which are supposed to protect
your rights as a public housing tenant.

JOAN

*Living in public housing is both good and bad. The
rent is low, and you don't have to worry about the
utilities. The people are usually very distant. It's
hard to get to know anyone there. It seems as though
everyone is ashamed because they're not doing as well
as the next person. The people who do have a little
bit of stuff are worried about the robbers and the
junkies and the winos breaking in and stealing it.*

*I was attacked one morning, so now I'm afraid to go
in and out at certain times. It's impossible to keep
it clean, really. A few women get together and they
start cleaning; they paint and they fix it up. Within
the next few weeks or so someone else's children have
come along and completely destroyed it. The management
usually keeps the utilities well, and right now they
are putting in new windows and bathrooms. They're
fixing it up to look decent. In some sections the
people themselves are working--trying to keep it
clean. But you can imagine how hard that is. The
little kids are little devils. The teen-agers try
to run you. If you stand up to a teen-ager for*

*something, you may have your windows broken or what-
ever. If you go to the parents and say "Your child
did. . . ," the parents and the child say the child
did not.*

*The feeling in the project is mostly depression. I
am trying to get a house under the government's 235
program. I want the house because it will be something
that belongs to me. I wish that there was some way
the good women could get together and be strong enough
to fight the rest of them. They try so hard, it's just
a losing battle. The ones who are trying to keep it
clean and decent--you don't ever hear about them.*

Eligibility

Eligibility for public housing is, theoretically at least,
determined by your income and based on income limits fixed
by each LHA. For years "higher income poor" were favored,
and LHAs have been known to base their admissions on housekeeping habits, lack of furniture, marital status, and
rent payment history. LHAs have conducted investigations
of applicants to find these things out.

HUD has attempted to improve these unfair admissions policies by prohibiting local authorities from denying admission
because an applicant has an out-of-wedlock child, a poor
rent payment history, or is simply "unsuitable" in the
moral judgment of the LHA. To prevent LHA from "sitting"
on applications, HUD requires that applicants be the source
of information about themselves and that the necessary documentation not require undue expense, effort, or delay. The
Civil Rights Act of 1968, preventing discrimination on the
basis of race, religion, national origin, and sex, applies
to public housing authorities also.

It is clear that the federal government leaves a lot of
decisions up to the LHAs. LHA regulations must be posted
in a conspicuous place, be reasonable, and give consideration to factors such as the urgency of housing and the age
of the applicant, their source of income, etc. In the end,
however, it is the individual housing authority who determines whom to accept and why. HUD is supposed to be a
regulatory agency for the LHAs, but such extreme measures
as lawsuits and complaints have been necessary to force
HUD to take action against unfair and illegal LHA practices.

When you apply for public housing, there are certain pieces

of information you will most likely be asked for. Try to bring with you:

1. Birth certificates for all your children.

2. Income verification such as pay stubs and/or a letter from your employer (if you are on welfare, your case-worker should be contacted by the housing authority so that you can receive a letter from him).

3. Information regarding any medical problems you or your family have, along with a letter from your doctor.

4. Rent receipts from your former landlord or a letter from the relative you have been living with, explaining the financial arrangements you have had.

According to HUD guidelines, you should be notified of your status promptly, usually within a month of your application. Frequently there is a waiting list for apartments. You may be given a choice of three projects; ask about the length of waiting list for each. You may, however, be placed on a community-wide list (an attempt by HUD to prevent racial segregation). In that case, you will be offered an apartment in the project with the highest number of vacancies. If you reject the housing offered "without a good reason" (for instance, the apartment is too great a distance from your place of employment), your name will be put at the bottom of the list.

In two emergency cases your application may be given priority: first, if you have been forced to leave your home because the city's relocation authority has bought your property, or second, if your house has been declared un-fit for human habitation. Contact your city's relocation authority and have the caseworkers there put pressure on the LHA to admit you.

In states where separation is recognized as a legal status, you should have no trouble acquiring an apartment under your own name without your husband. As proof of your marital status, you may wish to bring the separation agreement with you.

In states where separation agreements are not recognized, the local housing authority may be skeptical about whether or not your husband will be living with you (and providing income). It would be helpful in that case to have your caseworker furnish a statement or get one from your husband's

employer verifying that he is not living with you. The
LHA cannot deny you admission solely on the basis of your
marital status.

Beware of these and other illegal practices! By requesting
receipts over prohibitively long periods of time, LHAs have
managed to delay many admissions. They have also denied an
application admission on the basis of previous nonpayment
of rent. If you are denied admission, you have the right
to know the reasons for the denial and have a right to a
hearing. If at any time during your application you feel
that you were discriminated against or treated unfairly,
you may file a grievance. This procedure is explained on
page 000.

Rent

The Brooke Amendment to the United States Housing Act
effective March 1970 prohibits rent for public housing
from exceeding 25 percent of a tenant's income. LHAs may
compute rent on the basis of your income (graded rent) or
according to the apartment (flat rate). In either case,
make sure that you are paying no more than one-quarter of
your income. In computing your income, you are allowed
an exemption of $300 for each dependent, and you are also
entitled to deduct money paid for child care if that is
necessary to your employment.

LHAs are obligated to reexamine tenants' income at least
once a year to determine if they are still eligible. The
frequency of these investigations should be specified in
your lease. Your rent is readjusted according to change
in your income; if your income decreases, so should your
rent. Always notify the management of changes in your income. If your rent is to be changed, the notice of rent
readjustment must be given to you or an adult member of
your family in writing or be sent by registered mail.

If you are found to be over the continued occupancy limits
(usually slightly higher than admission limits), you may
be forced to leave. However, LHAs are supposed to take
into account any "special circumstances" preventing you
from finding alternative housing. If you can show that
you would not be able to find decent housing in the private market, you should be allowed to stay in public housing with an increase in rent. If you must leave, you are
entitled to up to six months to move.

Your Lease

In February 1971, HUD issued a Lease and Grievance procedure that all LHAs are bound by. Unfortunately, many are still refusing to comply with the regulations. If your LHA is still violating your legal rights, you have the right to take action against them. Under HUD's lease regulations, certain types of clauses are illegal. *Do not* sign a lease that contains these provisions:

1. Confession of judgment--the tenant gives consent to any lawsuit brought against her by the landlord, and a judgment in favor of the landlord.

2. Clauses known as "distraint and distress" clauses are illegal and mean that the tenant agrees the landlord may take her property and hold it as a pledge until she does whatever the landlord determines she has failed to do (pay rent, clean, repair, etc.).

3. Exculpatory clauses--tenant agrees not to hold the landlord liable for any acts or omissions (failure to supply utilities, damage to property).

4. Waiver of legal notice by tenant prior to eviction-- tenant agrees landlord does not have to give notice before filing suit, therefore preventing tenant's defense.

5. Waiver of legal proceedings--gives landlord the right to sell or hold tenant's belongings when he feels a breach or default occurs, without notice or court determination of liability.

6. Waiver of jury trial.

7. Waiver of right to appeal judicial error or right to file suit to prevent judgment.

8. Requirements that tenant pay costs of legal proceedings taken by landlord, regardless of the outcome.

All leases must always state, among other things, the following:

1. Names of the parties.

2. Description of the premises.

3. Amount and due date of rent.

4. The fact that the management must accept rent regardless of other charges owed.

5. The utilities furnished by the management and the amounts (remember that you may or may not have to pay for heat).

6. The process by which rents and eligibility are determined, the frequency of determination, information the tenant must supply, when a tenant may request a redetermination.

7. Responsibility of management to provide tenant with a written description of the condition of the dwelling unit.

8. Circumstances under which the management can evict tenant.

Any changes in your lease must be made in writing, signed, and dated by both you and the management. If you wish to have your husband's name removed from the lease if he has left you, speak to the manager. It is usually best, in most instances, such as complaints, to speak with the manager rather than higher authorities, since he is the one with the most knowledge of your specific case and will be more likely to act. In order to make such a change it will probably be necessary for you to supply information to verify your separation from your husband.

Eviction

The LHA may not evict you other than for "violation of the terms of the lease or other good cause." "Other good cause" usually includes such things as "serious interference with the rights of others" and "malicious intent to do damage." HUD regulations strictly prevent evictions on the basis of falling into a "particular social category," such as being the mother of a child when you are not married. You may not be evicted for a change in the size of your family. You are entitled to a larger or smaller apartment.

HUD does guarantee public housing residents a means to fight arbitrary evictions by LHAs. First, you *must* be given written notice by the management not less than 30 days prior to the eviction date. You must be informed in writing of the specific reasons for the proposed eviction

and of your right to request a hearing. It is illegal for
you to be evicted without a hearing; contact an attorney
immediately if this happens.

Maintenance

The management is required to maintain "decent, safe, and
sanitary conditions" in public housing. It is a well-known
fact that these kinds of conditions are the exception rather
than the rule. In the case of any maintenance problems in
your apartment, notify the management immediately. Always
put your complaint in writing and send it to the management
by registered mail.

If the management will not make repairs, you can withhold
your rent when:

1. defects exist which are hazardous to life, health, and
    safety;

2. you requested, in writing, repairs of the defects;

3. the housing authority did not make the repairs or offer
    you an alternative apartment within 72 hours after you
    made the complaint.

The rent withholding can continue until after the defect is
repaired.

Rent abatement (withholding) is not always enough to make
the management respond. If they still do not make the
repairs, contact your city's housing code authority; LHAs
are bound by local housing codes.

When you first rent an apartment you should accompany the
manager during his inspection of it and be given a written
statement of its condition. You should also reinspect the
apartment when you vacate it to make sure that you are not
charged with nonexistent damages. (You may be charged with
damages resulting from lack of heat if you are responsible
for supplying the heat.) Deductions from your security
deposit must be itemized and in writing.

The management may inspect your apartment for the purpose
of examining its condition and making repairs. They must
give advance notice of the time and the reasons for inspection. They may enter without notice only in an emergency,
and you must be notified promptly thereafter of the time and
cause of this inspection.

Grievances

HUD requires that the tenant be given an opportunity for a hearing about any grievance or disagreement she has with management. Any complaint you have, including unfair eviction, any failure of LHA to comply with your lease, or the failure of LHA to act within HUD regulations, can be brought up at a grievance hearing.

As soon as possible after the action or inaction of the LHA, write to your manager about the complaint that you have and what action you would like to be taken. Within 5 working days, the LHA must answer you, in writing, giving the action they propose to take and notifying you of your right to a hearing. If you do not like the remedy proposed, request, in writing, and within 10 days of the LHA's letter, a hearing.

The hearing will be held by a panel of housing authority and tenant representatives. You must be given, in advance, all regulations and records of the LHA pertinent to your case. You are entitled to, and should always have, an attorney present and may bring witnesses. You must be given the chance to present your side of the story, and it is up to the LHA to justify its inaction.

Afterward, the decision must be given to you in writing, along with the reasons and evidence used. If the decision is in your favor, it is binding on the LHA and they must act accordingly. If the decision is not favorable to you, you may appeal it in court.

Buying A House

Most women in transition are not likely to have the financial resources necessary to buy a house. You may be able to make an agreement with your husband which will enable you to keep your old house, or you may be able to make a financial agreement with him where you "buy out" his share of ownership. These questions are dealt with in the legal chapter of this book. Because buying a house is a complex matter, we refer you to any of the many paperback books available on home ownership for any detailed information on the subject. Here we deal only briefly with a few of the important aspects of buying your own house.

Interest rates on mortgages are going up higher and higher. Even young married couples are finding it difficult to get loans which would enable them to buy their own house. To add to the problem, there are fewer and fewer low-cost houses available. If you are lucky enough to have a nest egg, a good job, and some carpentry or home maintenance skills, you have the best chance of getting a loan and finding a place which meets your needs. Step by step, here is how you go about buying a house.

The first thing to do is, of course, find the house you want to buy. Follow the suggestions listed in this chapter about choosing an apartment to help determine whether or not the house is right for you. Check the plumbing, wiring, etc. Find out from the tax assessor what the taxes run a year. Consider how much you will have to pay on insurance and whether or not the house, as an investment, is likely to be worth more or less five years from now.

After you have made a choice, you will be asked to sign an agreement of sale. This is not just an application, but rather *a contract between you and the seller*. Once you have signed it, you have agreed to buy the house at a future date. After you have looked at the house, the realtor will usually take you back to the office and ask you to sign the agreement. You do not have to sign the agreement then and there. You should take it to an attorney to have it looked over before signing. Be aware that after you have signed the agreement there is little that you can do to back out of the deal. Any repairs that you want to be made should be specified and put into writing in the agreement, or they probably will not be made.

The next step in home buying is obtaining a mortgage. Banks and credit companies are the most common credit institutions that lend money for mortgages. They also charge high interest rates, and have in the past discriminated on the basis of race, sex, and marital status as well as economic status. Although the Fair Housing Act of 1968 makes discrimination on the basis of race illegal, realtors and mortgage institutions use a variety of tactics to prevent integration of neighborhoods. The only recourse that citizens have are costly and time-consuming court cases, unless there are local laws with powers of enforcement which institute changes in zoning laws. Women, especially separated or divorced women, have found it particularly difficult to get mortgages. See p. 310 for more on credit.

If your income is small you may be able to get a break in the financial problems by taking advantage of little-publicized federal or private organizations which provide low-interest mortgages. Most common of all the federal programs

is the Federal Housing Administration, or the FHA. Under
the 1968 National Housing Act (section 235), the federal
government is empowered to guarantee the bank you get your
mortgage from that if you do not keep up payments, they
will. You only have to put down a small deposit, and the
interest rate is significantly smaller than that on conventional mortgages (or those offered by speculators, who
often prey on poorer people). You can apply at a bank for
a FHA loan. If the mortgage payments come to more than
20 percent of your family's income, you are eligible. Down
payments can be as low as $200.

When you apply for this kind of a loan, the application
will include questions about your income and assets. This
information will be submitted to the FHA, which will decide,
mainly on the basis of your income and mortgage payments,
whether or not you are eligible. The FHA inspects the
houses that they will subsidize, but this does not mean
that they may not need repairs.

If you live in a rural area--that is, a place with a population of under 10,000--and have been denied a conventional
mortgage, you may be able to get a mortgage through Farmer's
Home Administration with the same advantages as FHA. The
interest may be as little as 1 percent depending on your
income.

In 20 states there are Housing Finance Agencies, which are
designed to provide low- and moderate-income housing by
providing nonprofit sponsors with low-interest loans, grants,
and second mortgages. There are also local agencies such
as investment funds and nonprofit development corporations
which will provide "inexpensive" mortgages. Be careful--
not all of these are as reliable as one would expect. Contact local tenants' groups, legal services, or welfare
rights organizations for information on institutions. Also,
you can buy a house while living on welfare; speak to your
local Welfare Rights Organization for further information.

Another alternative to the traditional house-buying process
is urban homesteading. In this program the federal government sells houses which have been abandoned or have been
acquired by the government for some reason. The houses are
usually in very poor condition, so the government will
"sell" the house to you for the "price" of agreeing to stay
in the house a certain number of years and performing repairs.

HOUSEWIFE

like i tried to say yesterday
when you asked me about
"That period" of my life
& i got lost
remembering what it was like
being a housewife:
Married i was--
not to a man
but to a house, a life.

No sooner would i fall in love
with the way the sun would slant
in one square room
the house would be sold out
from under me.
I was a transient housewife
i went with the man
begged him not to leave
promised he would be free
& prayed he would leave
me alone with my house
my white walls my daffodils my
early morning bread is rising.

the House (there were many
houses but it was always
the House) was my love;
but without a man
what right had i
woman alone, to a house?

the House was my love
& onto the four walls
i projected
the corners of my soul
to hang
ornately crucified by cobwebs,
eternally disappointed.
For a housewife
there is no death & resurrection,
only another piece of her life
left somewhere
lost somewhere in transit
packed away in shoeboxes
swept into uncollected trash heaps.

For a houswife
there is no glorious reunion
of body & soul--
only a series
of small insignificant losses
until at least she feels
resigned to numbness
knowing she will never
again feel quite whole.

linda backiel

▶▶▶ CAROL

*I first got married in 1952; I was 19½. My husband
and I were both in the armed forces when we met and
married. I got married because I believed in the
old tradition, to get married, have children, and
live happily ever after. The relationship was very
confining. My husband worked most of the time, and
I was left home to take care of home and children.
I was often criticized by my husband and his mother
about the way I was raising the children.*

*I took advantage of my G.I. Bill and went to school.
Because of going to school, I had to take a part-time
job aside from my other duties. After finishing
school, I had a different look at myself. We
separated, and I felt pretty good. I was getting
out of a situation that was not too comfortable for
me. I did not feel too good about leaving the children in the custody of their father, but I saw no
other way. He and his mother had promised to take
court action for the custody of the children. I
had no money to fight this and was not equipped to
get a job paying enough money for us to live on.*

*I still see my daughter. She is 20 now, going to
college, and getting along well. The last time I
spoke to her, a few months ago, she had committed
herself to a life-style with other women. She feels
that way now but is not sure if it will always be
this way. I told her it would only upset me if it
becomes difficult for her socially or in her profession. But I don't see my son. He has rejected me
as his mother. He accepts me as his biological
mother, but the relationship ends there.*

My second husband and my 20-year-old daughter get along well together. And my two youngest daughters really love her. There is a bed upstairs they say belongs to her and her alone. She is a hard person not to like. She is a beautiful person and so very much aware of other people.

I met my second husband through some friends I had made while attending school abroad. After my divorce I was offered the opportunity to go to school in Switzerland. We married in 1964 after two very turbulent years of courting. We married because even though there was this turbulence, we still liked each other. I was about 32, he was 28.

Things were bad after the first year, but after four years they were almost impossible, so bad that I decided on therapy for myself. You know, all the shit you hear about you being too aggressive and not being patient, wanting everything now. I wanted to know if all this shit belonged to me or was it partly other people projecting some of their shit on me.

This was the first of three therapy experiences. The first two therapists did not work at all. I could not relate to them as a woman, and they were of the feeling that women's place is in the home. Women have a right to their feelings and so forth, as long as these things keep them in their place. This did not help much at home either; aside from my husband's other complaints he had added, "The therapist said. . . ." Now, really, who needs all this shit?

During my first therapy experience I was not sure of my own identity. We had decided on having another baby, and my husband was offered a scholarship to a school in Pennsylvania to get his Ph.D. My therapy was to end in June, and the baby was to be born then. This worked out as planned, and by August the children and I had moved here from New York. Misery moved with us. Two weeks after moving here I woke up one morning to find the baby had died of a crib death. What next? That my husband was in New York finishing out his job helped me to see how alone I was. When you get down and need strength, the only strength you can count on is your own.

So then I went into therapy for the second time, although I ask myself now, who did me the most good
during this period, my therapist, my husband, myself,
or the new baby I was going to have? My husband was
seeing a psychiatric social worker who was helping
him. My therapist was helping him. And of course
he was on his own side, so there I stood alone again.

The next therapist I had was different. From the
first we had an understanding that he was to help me.
I was his patient. If he had any thoughts of changing
me to suit the world, our sessions would not work,
and it was not what I wanted. He helped me to understand myself further and helped me see that either the
situation at home had to change or it would be best
if we split.

My husband finally hit me, and I decided then that
the relationship as it was then had to end. I felt
pretty good about separating at that time. Now my
biggest goal is for my husband and I to get back
together. We have discussed this. We still like
each other, and our good feelings for each other have
not been lost. He is not sure this is what he wants,
though. He went away for a while to give himself
time to think it out clearly. Until then, I can only
hope, because I would really like to try it again.
Anyway, I like a close family relationship.

SEVEN: TAKING CARE
OF OURSELVES

THE PROBLEM

Introduction

Our role as women, by tradition and by necessity, is usually taking care of other people--our children, husbands,
relatives. Often it is difficult for us to find the time,
money, and energy essential to maintaining our own physical
and mental health. We recognize the importance of talking
about health care and medical and mental health services
in this chapter for three major reasons.

First of all, even though women are the largest single
group of health care consumers, as well as the majority of
employees of the health care industry (a term which includes
pharmaceutical industries, hospitals, medical supply companies, etc.), often we seem to have little influence over
the quality and accessibility of our health care services.
Paired with our general powerlessness over the quality of
health care we receive is our own lack of information about
how to find and use the facilities that *are* available to us.

Secondly, as women, we have limited access to information
about our bodies and how they function. Rather than attempt
to deal comprehensively with this area of health care (which
is better explained in books such as *Our Bodies, Ourselves*
by The Boston Women's Health Book Collective), we are including aspects of preventive health care which may enable
you to avoid costly and prolonged illness to yourself and
children.

367

Thirdly, as a woman in transition, you will be undergoing
stress and trauma in many different areas of your life.
Women who are facing acute difficulty with finances, legal
situations, housing, and their emotional lives often become physically ill in addition to having to face the
psychological complications of their decision to separate.
Added to your own state of health (or its lack) is the burden of taking care of your children and their health care
needs, perhaps for the first time as a single person.

This chapter is designed to give women in transition the
information we need in order to keep ourselves healthy, to
use medical and mental health services when we need them,
and to evaluate the kinds of health care we are receiving.
If there is a message to this chapter, it is to learn how
to have good health so that medical treatment is less frequently necessary. We feel health care professionals
should share their knowledge with us rather than forcing
us to come to them and to pay often high fees in order to
have every ailment treated. We also want to talk about non-
medical ways of taking care of ourselves--namely what you
should know about beatings, rape, and self-defense.

In this chapter, we generally refer to doctors and health
care professionals as "he" or "him." Our reason for this
is not to discriminate against the few women doctors prac-
ticing in this country, but rather to acknowledge the reality: 93 percent of all doctors are male, and 97 percent
of all gynecologists are men. The health care system,
which once was the almost exclusive domain of women, now
employes women as 70 percent of the total labor force.
Most, however, are in low-paid areas of health care work
and do not influence policy decisions.

"The Operation Is A Success, But The Patient Just Died"

Doctors are sometimes the first to admit that the system of
health care in this country is not everything that could be
desired. It sometimes seems to us a matter of priorities.
Until recently, much of the health care available was designed as much to insure doctors and the health care industry a comfortable living as to meet the increasing health
care needs of its patients. Doctors are not exclusively
the villains. Many labor under tremendous handicaps. Even
the best physician has difficulty in giving the kind of
health care that he might respect himself for when he is
working with patients whose lives he knows little or nothing about, has little time and many patients, and is forced
to work with limited facilities.

tist: Joanna Vogelsang

Feminist Resources

Photo by: Krystyna Neuman

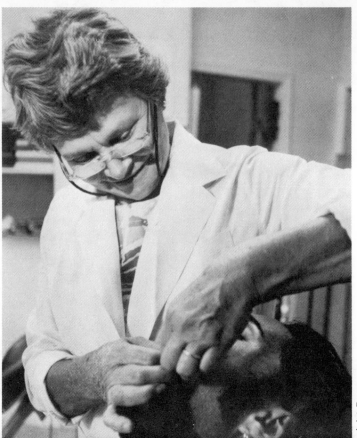

Feminist Resources

Photo by: Eva Shaderowfsky

To make the situation all the worse, there is at this time
an appalling shortage of doctors in this country. Medicine
is becoming more and more specialized, and in some areas of
medical care there is a surplus of doctors, in others a
chronic deficiency. Where you live often determines the
quality of health care available to you. Some areas (such
as rural and sometimes urban areas) have a lack of doctors
and hospitals that is devastating. For almost all of us,
medical care is expensive and hard to find. The major
cause of bankruptcy in this country is medical bills.

As women, and especially as women alone, we tend to respect
the professional status of the doctor to our own disadvan-
tage. Many of us are used to depending on his wisdom and
presumed competence even though his professional status is
no guarantee of that ability. Our lack of information
about our own bodies, combined with the fear and insecurity
all of us suffer from when we and/or our children are ill,
makes it difficult for us to ask the questions we need to
in order to find out what is really wrong and what methods
of treatment are possible. The doctor may contribute to
this by neglecting to give us information that we do not ask
for, or by treating us as if we are not capable of understanding the basis for his decisions about treatment.

We are more than a collection of misfunctioning parts, a
bundle of symptoms. We are in fact health care consumers,
and as people who are paying (and often paying a great deal)
for a service, we have a right to adequate care, explanation, and decent facilities. We believe that health care
information is too important to be left exclusively in the
hands of doctors, especially since many of us have responsibility for the care of ourselves and our children every
day of our lives, and often find ourselves alone with that
responsibility.

Is There Any Cure?

There are many people in this country working to change the
health care system. Their views range from those who think
the basic problem is one of inefficiency to those who believe that health care should not be a profit-motivated industry at all. Some groups are working to change the policies of hospitals and medical schools. Others are establishing alternative health services. The latter groups put
much emphasis on self-help, community-centered medicine,
and preventive health care. Community clinics and women's
health centers have been established where non-professional
medical workers (sometimes called paramedics) and physicians

work together to teach residents of their community about how to take care of their bodies.

In the listing at the end of this book, you will find a partial index of women's health clinics. Many are faced with the indifference or hostility of the medical establishment in their areas. Some are financially insecure and have limited facilities. For most of us there are simply not enough alternative health care services to enable us to dispense with traditional doctors and hospitals entirely. We do believe, however, that these kinds of health services are important and useful, especially since their staffs generally are sympathetic and aware of the needs of the people they serve.

A sad commentary on the health care system that serves us is the development of a whole new category of diseases called "iatrogenic" diseases. These are developed while a patient is under medical treatment when the physician is uninformed or misdiagnoses an illness. The diseases are caused by the treatment itself. Some examples include:

1. a disease caused by the side effects of a drug prescribed to us (such as methadone, which is itself addictive; barbiturates and amphetamines. Some antibiotics are known to create severe vitamin deficiencies.)

2. a disease caused by the prescribing of a drug not usually harmful by itself, but harmful in conjunction with other drugs or particular allergic reactions (such as penicillin or even aspirin)

3. a violent or fatal reaction to an anesthetic

4. methods of birth control which are not harmful to everyone, but which greatly aggravate tendencies of susceptible women (such as the IUD, pills with high levels of hormones, etc.)

5. sloppy, inefficient, or unsafe techniques used in surgery or obstetrics.*

———————

*From *Our Bodies, Ourselves*, The Boston Women's Health Book Collective.

marie curie

those little orbs were a horoscope
for marie curie, whose name has two R's
for radium, the nights she walked by them
the pockets of ore blinked violet
like newborn planets in their little cups

if she had wanted to, she could have worn
them around her neck, those seeds, or
swallowed them and smuggled them out of the country
or have used them for nightlights
if she had wanted to, she could have planted them,
buried them, given them back
she could have used them for paperweights

instead, they were given to me
in science class,
from marie curie

they will always remind me of
atoms dancing like courting ostriches,
the theory of nuclear reactors
einstein and the rosenbergs
and the image of fallout, always falling
weightless, soundless, with no visibility
and no gravity, like a slow snow
drifting through my body

not that marie curie knew
when she was wearing her body
in her lifetime in those days
dragging it along until it wearied her
and she had to give it up

I remember about x-rays and pacemakers

the problem is only, as always, in my mind
where I see her in the dark, alone in
her laboratory, looking down at the ore
as if it were the sky.

--Susan Daily

PREVENTION: LOOKING OUT FOR OURSELVES

"There's No One To Mother Mother When She's Sick"

Even in the ideal situation, women often find that they haven't the time or information that they need to take care of their health care needs. While "Mother" is taking care of everybody else's health care needs, her own may be pushed to the end of the list. In times of stress, like the period of separation and divorce, we often find ourselves with so many problems that we hardly know where to start to solve them. It is important to be aware of the connection between our bodies and our emotions. Often when we feel run-down, anxious, depressed, or harried, there is a physical as well as psychological basis for our feelings. As difficult as it may be to deal with our financial, legal, and emotional situations as women in transition, we should try to remember to include health care (for *ourselves* as well as our children) as one of our immediate needs.

Preventive medicine is not well established in this country mainly because it is more profitable (and much more simple) to treat sick people than to try to keep everyone healthy. We are concerned with prevention because the consequences of illness for a woman in transition are even greater than for women in a family situation. For one thing, being ill costs you time and money. It will almost certainly mean that you will lose money from your job. Also, if you are the sole support and counselor for your children, you will have to find a temporary replacement or leave them on their own. Being ill, especially seriously, is every woman's nightmare, and during the period of transition it can be yet another problem for a woman already overburdened with responsibilities. Knowing about our bodies and noticing medical problems before they develop into major illnesses can help all of us to be more secure in other facets of our lives.

The health care facilities available to us, of course, have everything to do with how promptly we take care of our health care problems. One of the few times that women receive the health care they need is during pregnancy. Sometimes our children receive better treatment (as far as regular checkups, vaccinations, early diagnosis of illness) than we do. Poor people in general receive health care much less frequently, and sometimes of a more inferior quality, than more wealthy patients. Some of us can afford private physicians. Many of us cannot. The vast majority of women in transition are dependent on clinics, hospitals, and

institutions that are low-cost. For all of these reasons
we feel it is most important that you read and refer to the
section of this chapter dealing with preventive health care
information.

A Partial Medical Checklist For Women In Transition

As a woman in transition, you may find your social patterns
(as well as almost everything else in your life) changing.
You may find yourself suffering from emotional and physical
reactions to your separation. We have found that most women
who go through separation and divorce have reactions not
unlike the grieving period of a mourner. You may find
yourself crying a lot, sleeping a great deal or not at all,
eating more or less, becoming sexually involved with men or
abstaining from social contacts entirely. Naturally, the
pattern varies from person to person.

Unfortunately, "women's medical problems" have much the
same status as "women's work." Even a well-intentioned
doctor cannot, in most cases, be aware of every medical
problem you might be having. If you just feel generally
miserable, you should not rule out the possibility of a
medical cause. There are many good books available which
concern each of the problems we discuss here. We do not
intend to go into any comprehensive discussion about these,
only to present them as areas of concern to you as a woman
taking care of herself.

The following questions are designed to help you check your
health:

Are you using a method of birth control?

Many women leaving a marriage find themselves discontinuing
the method of birth control they have used in the past, or
uncertain of what type of contraceptive they might want to
use. As unromantic as the topic of contraception is, this
is no time to sacrifice common sense to romance. If you believe that you may be likely to become sexually involved
with men, you should use a method of birth control.

Each type of birth control has its advantages and disadvantages. None is totally satisfactory for all women. "The
Pill" is generally considered to be the most effective
means of preventing pregnancy. It works by utilizing hormones which are associated with menstruation. Not all
women want to or are able to use "The Pill." If you decide
to use this method of birth control, your doctor should ask

you if anyone in your family or you have a tendency toward
blood clots, high blood pressure, breast cancer, diabetes,
migraines, or other factors which might make it dangerous
for you to use this type of contraceptive. You should also
return to your doctor for checkups and if you experience
any side effects.

Other methods of contraception include the IUD (internal
uterine device), a coil which is implanted in the uterus
that causes the uterus to be unreceptive to eggs; the dia-
phragm, used with spermicidal cream or jelly; vaginal
spermicides which block the passage of the sperm; and condoms (used by the man). If you are certain that you do not
ever want to have children again, you might consider the
possibility of sterilization. Usually this is done by
removing a section of fallopian tube and tying the ends
back. Many black and poor women have, in the past, been
victims of forced sterilizations, especially in the South,
but paradoxically enough, it is sometimes difficult to find
a doctor who will perform this operation if you do not fall
into that category. Planned Parenthood, Zero Population
Growth, and the Association for Voluntary Sterilization can
help you find someone who will, if this is what you want.

In most areas, branches of Planned Parenthood or their
equivalent (community clinics, women's health services) can
give you information which may enable you to make a decision about what kind of contraception you are interested in.

Is it possible that you have been exposed to venereal disease?

There is at this time literally an epidemic of venereal
disease in the United States. It is not now, and never
was, a disease exclusive to poor and non-white people, so
the prestige and status of the man you become involved with
is no guarantee he is not a carrier. There are two kinds
of VD, syphilis and gonorrhea, and both are acquired through
sexual contact with a person who has them. You can keep
yourself from acquiring VD by using contraceptive foams,
jellies, creams, or having your partner use condoms.

If you suspect that you have VD, many states have clinics
where you can be tested and treated. You should get in
touch with your state's Division of Public Health, Planned
Parenthood, or a local hospital or hotline. In Pennsylvania,
a VD hotline called Operation Venus takes toll-free calls
from 9 a.m. to 9 p.m. at 800-523-1885. They refer their
callers to the nearest medical facility. At most clinics

you will be asked the names of people you have had sexual contact with. If you decide not to give their names, you should take responsibility for calling them before they reinfect you or other people.

Because women frequently have no symptoms of gonorrhea at all, it is extremely important that you go immediately to a medical facility or clinic if you suspect you have been infected. The usual treatment for VD is penicillin or tetracycline. Natually you should not have sexual intercourse while you are infected. You should not drink alcoholic beverages while being treated. You should return to your doctor or clinic immediately if you experience what could be an allergic reaction, such as swelling of the face or throat, or a rash.

Have you noticed any important changes in your body such as a change in your menstrual cycle?

Many women find that their bodies become unbalanced by emotional stress and strains and that frequently this can affect the timing or flow of their periods. It is important to realize that nothing that happens in our bodies is completely isolated from everything else. Women who are first beginning to take oral contraceptives sometimes find that their menstrual flow is lessened or evened out, that their cramps may have become less frequent or even have stopped. Sometimes, in periods of change and crisis, the opposite occurs. Women going through menopause, of course, often find their menstruation erratic. There are many factors which can affect our bodies, physical and psychological, and inconsistency in our menstrual patterns is one indication of change somewhere in our lives. A good general rule in this case as in others is that if your body is behaving differently, it is time to have a checkup by a competent physician. Do not be alarmed if you find your menstrual cycle to have changed somewhat, but in order to be confident that everything is all right, seek medical counsel.

Some women in transition find themselves going through important physical changes at the time of their separation or divorce. Pregnancy is probably the most common, and most dramatic, of physical changes a woman can experience as a "healthy" person. Being pregnant does not insure that a woman is happily (or otherwise) married, that she lives with her husband, or that she is not experiencing the emotions of a woman in transition. It does insure that she needs greater medical care, more rest and nutrients, and is

especially vulnerable to complicated psychological reactions. A pregnant woman going through separation and divorce especially needs the support of women friends or her
family, good meals, and frequent medical checkups.

Women who have just gone through pregnancy often find themselves victims of emotional cycles. This period of time
(called postpartum) is often marked by depression, anxiety,
anger, or feelings of abandonment. Naturally, a woman does
not feel better going through this emotional cycle when she
is justifiably upset by the complications of ending a marriage. An important thing to realize is that it is not
"abnormal" or inhuman for a new mother to sometimes regret
or even hate herself and her child for its birth. Any form
of illness or surgery frequently requires a recuperative
period of time during which there are often depressions
("the blues") and fears. This is a time when a woman needs
and deserves special understanding and frequent health care.

Women who are going through menopause during their time of
divorce may find themselves having similar reactions to
those of women who have just given birth.

The physical reality of menopause is that changes in one's
body chemistry are occuring because of a lowering of hormones. For this reason, sometimes the prescription of hormones lessens the unpleasant aspects of menopause. Some
women experience hot flashes. (Often these can be alle-
viated by hormone prescription.) Other problems associated
with menopause include vertigo, palpitations, gas, nausea,
muscle aches, and exhaustion. Much of the depression and
concern women going through menopause face is as closely
associated with actual physical changes as psychological
factors. Because a woman in transition faces feelings of
lack of self-worth, frustration, and anxiety even when in
the best of health, again we feel that this is a time to
find friends or family who can be sympathetic and sensitive
to your needs, and that responsible and frequent medical
attention is advised.

Not Just A Woman's Disease: Cancer

As a woman in transition, you certainly do not want to have
to think about a terminal illness. Many of us find even
the word "cancer" a monstrous inhabitant of the dark corners
of our minds. It is, however, important to know that there
may be a connection in some instances between cancer and
certain types of oral contraceptives. You should also know
that since you are the most important person in the world

to yourself and your children, you have the right to save
yourself from this illness. There are many forms of cancer,
but most can be caught and treated successfully. The
essence of successful treatment is *time*. This is why you
should have a Pap smear taken twice a year by your doctor
or gynecologist and why you should know how to give yourself a breast self-examination.

Cancer is the leading cause of death in women, and breast
cancer makes up one-fifth of all cancer in women. It is
not difficult to examine yourself for lumps or differences
in your breasts, and knowing how and doing it can prevent
the spread of cancer. Women should examine themselves once
a month. A few days after menstruation is a good time,
since during menstruation the breasts may be tender or
swell.

1. Stand in front of a mirror and first, examine the shape
    of your breasts. Look to see if they differ. Put your
    hands at your sides, over your head, at your hips.
    Look for a flattening or bulge in one that is not in
    the other.

2. Notice if there is a puckering in one and not the other.
    Check to see if there is a discharge from the nipple,
    or a reddening or scaly crust on the nipple. If the
    nipples are shaped differently from each other, and if
    one is hard and inelastic, you should be suspicious.
    Make sure that any sores on your breasts and nipples
    are not cancerous.

3. Lie down with your arm under your head. Examine the
    breast on that side of your body. Take your hand and
    move it with your fingers flat in a circular or back-
    and-forth motion around the entire breast. Move from
    the center in a spiral motion outward, and cover the
    entire area.

4. The most common area for tumors is between the nipples
    and the armpit, so be especially thorough in that area.
    You are looking for an abnormal thickening, a hardness,
    or a lump.

5. Repeat the same process on the other side of your body.

It is a good idea to examine yourself at the same time of
the month so that you can grow used to how your breasts
usually look at that time. If there is anything unusual,

you should have it investigated as immediately as possible.
Don't panic! A lump can be an indication of a cyst. Many
times a lump may not be cancerous, and even if it is,
prompt diagnosis can determine if the cancer has spread,
and whether complete or only partial surgery is necessary.
Time is of the essence. Don't delay.

The American Cancer Society has films and literature on
breast self-examination available from their national office
at 219 E. 42nd St., New York, N.Y. 10017. Their phone number is 212-867-3700.

You should be aware that women whose families have had a
history of breast cancer, women who have not had children,
and women who have had children later in life are most often
vulnerable to breast cancer. Women who nurse their children seem to have a lower incidence of breast cancer. If
there is a history of breast cancer in your family, you
should self-examine your breasts once a month and see a
gynecologist or physician four times a year.

Cervical cancer is the second most frequently occuring cancer in women.

It is likely to occur in middle-aged women, and seems to
seldom occur in nuns and celibate women. Cervical cancer
can be checked by frequent gynecological checkups. A *Pap
smear*, which involves the extraction of a small piece of
tissue from the cervix, is the usual test for cervical
cancer.

There seems to be some evidence that cervical cancer occurs
more frequently in women who have had a greater number of
sexual relationships. According to Carol Mindey in *The Divorced Mother*, early marriage followed by divorce seems to
be a factor in cervical cancer, perhaps because multiple
sexual relationships increase the likelihood of passage of
a cancer-stimulating agent.

Stress-Related Health Problems

As we said at the beginning of this chapter, a woman in
transition has more reason than anyone else to take care of
her health, but because of all the pressures and tensions
of separation and divorce, it may be more difficult for her
to do so. During the period of transition, while you are
trying to pull together your life and keep yourself and
children somewhat stable, you may find your nerves strained,

your mind frenzied, and your body exhausted. Stop and consider:

Have you found yourself gaining or losing a great deal of
weight?

Food plays an important part in most of our lives. For
many of us it has an important psychological function as
well as a physical one. Sometimes women eat in order to
make themselves feel better when they are depressed. Sometimes, by not eating foods which give you the nutrients
that you need (because of lack of time, money, convenience)
you can literally never eat enough to be satisfied. Ask
yourself if your eating habits have changed, and if so, how
and why.

Some women find that meals, the time when the family was
once all together, can be an especially difficult time.
You may literally be unable to eat. Other women simply
cannot cope with working, legal problems, and financial
responsibilities, and eat properly as well. Our feeling
is that food should not be used as a consolation for
other things in your life that are going wrong. (Most of
all, because it *can't* console you.) Neither should you
punish yourself by not eating. A great deal of weight
gained or lost in a short amount of time is definitely a
danger signal which should alert you to the need for medical attention. Rapid gain or loss of weight could be
associated with drugs you have been taking, thyroid dis-
orders, or even tumors. If you feel a large part of your
eating habits is tied up to psychological reactions to your
separation, you should seek out other women and talk to
them about your feelings. If you cannot find anyone to
talk to, talk to anyone who is sympathetic and level-headed,
be that a therapist, a relative, or a neighbor.

Are you drinking too much?

We live in a country which has all too few resources for
women undergoing crisis and unhappiness in their lives.
If you have found yourself slipping into a pattern of ill
health like compulsive drinking, it is time to put on the
brakes and stop and think. First of all, you are not alone
in either your feelings (anger, depression, anxiety) or
in your reaction (in this case, drinking too much or too
often). There are many women, both married and single,
who find themselves using drugs of all kinds to help them
through their depression. (Just because it is legal,
you should not think that alcohol is not a drug. It is

a drug, and a drug that can create physical dependency.)

Unfortunately, alcohol doesn't really help. We all face
periods in our lives when we need more help from people we
care about in order to go on functioning. Dependency on
drugs such as alcohol and barbiturates is wrong, not
because of moral reasons, but because they add physical
and emotional problems to the ones that are already overwhelming us. If you believe that you have a health problem with drinking, it may be time to look for help.

1. Have a complete medical evaluation with a doctor
    you trust.

2. Talk to someone--your doctor, a member of your commu-
    nity, even your priest or minister--whom you believe
    knows about alcohol counseling programs in your neigh-
    borhood or city.

3. Seek out and talk with other people who have gone
    through your situation (the more that they have in
    common with you, the more likely it is that they
    will be able to help). Find out how they managed
    to deal with their problems, of which drinking is
    only one.

4. Stop for a while, or if you can't, try to cut down.

There are programs and groups available to people who have
drinking problems. You might want to see if there is an
Alcoholics Anonymous in your community. We believe that
people who have the opportunity to talk with other women
especially, can often draw strength from their shared
experience. In order to become healthy, independent
people, we have to free ourselves from both physical and
psychological dependencies.

Have your sleeping habits changed?

Sleep, like food, is often a means of escape for women
undergoing traumatic experiences. How much sleep anyone
needs is dependent on the individual. You know, however,
if you have been suffering from insomnia every night since
you and your husband have separated, that something is
going wrong. Drugs, stress, poor nutrition, and illness
all affect sleeping patterns. Most of the time when you
are unable to sleep it means that you are tense, nervous,
or depressed. Some relaxing techniques such as meditation,
yoga, dance, a warm bath, or a glass of warm milk (calcium

is a fine natural sedative) might help you if you find
that you can't relax enough to sleep. It is the root of
the problem that you want to get at, however. Don't
allow all the problems of the day to build up inside your
head at bedtime. If you have a problem that is worrying
you, take it apart, think of possible solutions to it,
the steps involved in solving it, etc. Then try to forget
it. Do something relaxing that you enjoy.

If, on the other hand, you are sleeping every spare moment,
it could be an indication of physical and emotional exhaustion. You should get a medical checkup, perhaps find
time to get an extra hour's sleep at night, or plan your
day so that you can take naps. Drugs such as amphetamines
(diet pills) make sleep impossible. Sedatives and barbiturates which are sometimes prescribed as "sleeping pills"
can lead to physical dependency and should be resorted to
only after everything else has failed.

About Drugs

There are times in every woman's life when she suffers
from feelings of loneliness, desperation, and inadequacy.
Women in transition often find themselves alone at the
very moment when they most need companionship. Sometimes
they are facing problems they have always felt overwhelmed
by, and now they are having to face these things alone.
When the burden of taking care of themselves and their
children becomes too great, they may turn to their physician or clinic to get something to help them through it.
It is unfortunate but not infrequent that doctors will
casually prescribe "mood-altering" drugs such as sedatives
and sometimes barbiturates.

Sedatives are drugs which relax your body so that you can
go to sleep. Non-prescription sedatives are virtually
harmless. Usually they contain the same medication as
antihistamines, and rely on one of the side effects of
these drugs, sleepiness. Barbiturates are dangerous and
addictive, and work on a different principle.

Barbiturates work by depressing the central nervous system
They build up in the body, creating a tolerance, so that you
have to take more and stronger drugs in order for them to
work as they did in the beginning. Barbiturates have long-
term effects such as: impaired motor coordination, deter-
ioration of mental and emotional judgment, difficulty with
vision.

Barbiturates include: Miltown, Equanil, Librium, Valium, Seconal, Nebutal, Amytal, Tuinal, and phenobarbital. Barbiturates can be fatal when taken with alcohol. The combined effect of alcohol and barbiturates is greater than either would be if taken separately. In addition, barbiturates remain in the body a longer time than alcohol, so even the next day you may feel the effects. Barbiturates can be more addictive than heroin, and withdrawal from them can be as unpleasant. In short, barbiturates are extremely dangerous to your health and should be avoided in prolonged usage. If you can't sleep, take a non-prescription sedative or a glass of milk. Do not rely on barbiturates to help you through the night.

Amphetamines work by speeding up your motor functions: breathing, circulation, body coordination. "Pep pills" and "diet pills" are usually amphetamines. Women often take amphetamines because they want to lose weight, or because they feel lifeless, tired, or depressed.

Amphetamines decrease the appetite. They do this for only three or four weeks, however. Like other addictive drugs, they destroy important vitamins and minerals in your body. They increase body temperature, metabolism rates, and often induce a feeling of nervousness, inability to sleep, and, in later stages, paranoia. Amphetamines are just as addictive as barbiturates and are a poor "cure" for tiredness or obesity.

When you have been given a prescribed drug, you should always find out:

1. How it works and what it does. (Does it relieve pain, create antibodies, cause the heart to beat more frequently, induce sleep?)

2. What side effects the drug may have (such as bloating from birth control pills, dry mouth, nausea, light-headedness, drowsiness).

3. What kinds of drugs should never be taken together (aspirin and coumadin, penicillin and tetracycline, alcohol and barbiturates).

4. Contraindications (things which would make it dangerous for you to take a certain drug, such as other medications you are taking, allergies, a tendency toward cancer, or high blood pressure in women who are taking "The Pill").

You should usually get your doctor to prescribe a drug by
its generic rather than brand name. Prescription by generic
name is cheaper and usually has the same value as prescription of "name" drugs.

Shop around for drugs. Most pharmacies are now permitted
to list the price of their drugs. They may not, however,
if they choose not to. You can be relatively certain they
will not give you that information over the telephone.
Look around and compare. One store may in fact be substantially cheaper than another.

You should know as much as you can about any drug that you
are taking. In many situations we are dependent on the
doctor's judgement about what kind of medication we need.
Doctors are human also. If you wonder about the possibility of changing your medication, talk with someone else
who shares your medical problem and find out what their
doctor prescribed. What is best for one person is not
always best for another, but this way you can at least
ask your doctor what the merits of various forms of medication are.

We are a drug-dependent society. Our feeling is that the
less you can use them, the better. Remember to keep all
your medication out of the hands of children, and watch
closely for signs of developing dependency (such as a higher tolerance level, discomfort when you do not take drugs
you usually do). Remember that doctors can make mistakes
in prescribing drugs, and if a medication is having an
unpleasant effect on you, see if he can change it. If you
go to clinics or drugstores where the directions and warnings about drugs are not typed onto the label, call your
doctor and ask him to specify that they will be in the
future.

Health Emergencies

Often, when we are ill, it seems more trouble than it is
worth to go to the doctor or clinic and wait for medical
attention. Some illnesses, such as viruses, have no
immediate "cure." You simply have to rest and wait for
them to be over. In some cases, however, the problem won't
go away or heal itself, and a doctor is needed. If you or
your children are suffering from any of these symptoms, it
is time to go to a medical professional.

• Diarrhea that doesn't stop in days.

- A headache that won't go away.

- Palpitations, chest pains, heart discomfort.

- Shortness of breath when you aren't active.

- Earaches.

- Backache or bone ache that doesn't go away.

- Lumps under the skin, growths on it.

- Fainting, dizzy spells, fits.

- Wound that gets infected, oozes pus or a discharge.

- Severe pain in chest, arms, neck, with coughing.

- Paralysis of part of your body.

- Blood coughed up, passed in urine, feces.

- Burning with urination, discharge.

- Fevers without visible cause.

- Drastic weight changes.

- Cold or flu that doesn't go away in a week.

- Toothaches (can spread to gums, mouth).

- Problems with vision (blurring, distortion, headaches).

First Aid

Women in transition are often the sole guardians of their own and their children's health. In an emergency situation (and every mother has known at least one) she is the one who has to make split-second decisions, calmly and without panic, in order to save her child's life. For this reason it is important that you have some information about first aid.

The principles of first aid are pretty much common sense, and if you decide to take a course in it you may find yourself knowing more than you thought that you did. Knowing what you are doing greatly decreases your likeliness to panic, and increases the chances of the victim's survival.

In first aid, you can learn how to check out body functions (heartbeat, respiration, pulse) and sometimes prevent them from worsening. (For instance, most wounds respond to direct pressure applied with a clean cloth or bandage, slowing down the loss of blood.) You won't, however, be able to deal with any major medical disasters, such as very deep wounds, chest wounds, internal bleeding, extreme burns, objects driven into the eyes, or spinal injuries.

Have on hand in your home, and while traveling, a first aid kit containing: a thermometer, aspirin, bandages, tweezers, antiseptic lotions, first aid cream, and lotions like calamine to relieve insect bites and skin infections (such as poison ivy).

You can probably find places where you might take a course in first aid in your community. Some community programs have been set up, and schools, churches, YWCAs, and YWHAs often have courses every few months. A useful and easy to read book on first aid is *H.E.L.P.* (Home Emergency Ladies' Pal), available for $1.00 plus postage from XYZYX Information Corporation, 21116 Vanowen Street, Canoga Park, California 91303.

It is a good idea to have on hand near your telephone the numbers of your doctor, emergency hospital nearest you, fire department, and police department. Some communities have poisoning hotlines, and if yours does, you should keep their number in sight as well. The American Red Cross has books, classes, and first aid information they can make available to you.

Dental Care

Dental problems can wipe out the life savings of poorer families, and often do. Dentists are expensive and busy professionals, and practically the only way to prevent the cost and pain of correction (especially for young children) is keeping the problem from developing to begin with. The information that we include here may seem like "kid stuff" to you, but the cost of a dentist, especially for women who have several children, should be enough motivation for you to take it seriously.

The general preventive measures we should all practice frequently are:

1. To brush our teeth after every meal, brushing up the
    bottom teeth and down on the top. Dental floss used

between the teeth will drastically reduce decay, and gentle sideways brushing under the gums will prevent gum disease. For more details, see *The Tooth Trip*, listed in our bibliography, which is available in paperback.

2. Eat proper foods--crunchy ones like fruits and raw vegetables are natural teeth cleaners. This is especially important for young children who have not yet developed the coordination to brush properly. Gummy, sticky carbohydrates like mashed potatoes, undercooked rice, and sticky candy readily cause decay and gum disease.

3. Look at your teeth. You don't need to be a dentist to see if something is grossly wrong. Holes and black spots may be decay and should be checked. Run your finger along your or your children's teeth. If you come up with a white gummy film, you're not brushing well enough in that area, and tooth decay will be on the way!

4. Visit a dentist once or twice a year (more often for children) and get all cavities filled, teeth straightened, and dental problems corrected *before they require major work*. Tooth problems do not get better by themselves. They get worse and more expensive instead. (Be true to your teeth or they will be false to you.)

5. Get fluoride, if it is not in your community's water supply, painted onto the teeth or in pill form, especially for your children.

Dentists, like doctors, should treat you with respect. You should be able to get a second opinion about any treatment your dentist suggests. You should be able to stop any procedure that you do not want or do not understand at any point. A dentist who is worth your money will try everthing he can to save your teeth rather than replace them.

The majority of dental work in this country is not what it should be. This is largely because good dental work takes more time than dentists are willing to give. Since the faster the dentist turns out work, the more profit he makes, and since there is no one to supervise the work that most dentists do, the result is generally poor care. It's therefore not only important to go to a dentist, but also to evaluate his work.

Some basic ways to evaluate your dentist are:

1. Does the dentist give you a complete cleaning and
    X-rays? This should take at least a half hour. If
    the dentist doesn't teach you proper brushing and
    flossing as well as explain the effect of a good diet,
    he is just not interested in preventing tooth decay.
    This may be more profitable to him, but is costly to
    you.

2. Does the dentist give you the complete picture of
    everything that needs to be done before he starts
    work? It is in the dentist's economic interest that
    you remain in the dark as to what is being done and
    why.

3. Does the dentist pull teeth? This is the fastest but
    most damaging treatment to give. Missing teeth cause
    the remaining teeth to shift and be more susceptible
    to gum disease and decay. With endodontics (root canal
    work) you should almost never have to lose a tooth. It
    is much more expensive and time-consuming to replace a
    missing tooth than to try to save it.

4. Does the dentist polish fillings? Polished fillings
    are longer-lasting and have a better shape. Look at
    your fillings--are they shaped like a tooth or are they
    shapeless masses? Improperly shaped fillings function
    poorly and fall out early.

5. Does the dentist take a medical history before he
    starts working? (Certain diseases such as rheumatic
    fever and diabetes will affect your dental work.)
    X-rays are dangerous to a fetus, especially in the
    first three months when it isn't visibly obvious that
    you are pregnant. Dentists should not take X-rays
    during pregnancy except in an emergency, and when they
    do, they should cover you with a lead shield.

6. Is your dentist constantly rushed? If he is working
    on four patients at once, always running, the odds are
    good your dental work will suffer.

Nutrition

As a woman who is now alone, you may have found your patterns of cooking and eating have changed. "You are what
you eat" a popular slogan says, and to some extent this is

true. Poor nutrition can result from not eating a balanced diet, not eating enough, or eating too much of the wrong things. Nutrition is always left up to women, who are supposed to dose their children with abundant, healthful meals. No one tells us, of course, what those meals are, or how to get them when we haven't the money required to buy the food we need, or how to cope with lack of time we have to cook them.

In exhaustion and desperation we turn to prepackaged foods, frozen vegetables you can cook without dirtying a pot, frequent snacks, or TV dinners. It is not reasonable that the burden of being healthy and having healthy, well-fed children should fall onto the shoulders of women simply because we are wives and/or mothers. A woman who is concerned about good nutrition does not necessarily even have access to the information she needs. This is why we have included this section in this chapter.

Poor nutrition and vitamin deficiencies resulting from it cut across all class and race lines. Generally it is true that people who have less money may eat less nutritiously, but all of us, from the middle-class housewife in the supermarket to the urban mother at the corner store, are paying a great deal of money for what may be inferior food.

A "balanced" diet means simply that you eat foods containing all of the three essential nutrients: protein, carbohydrates, and fats. We need a proper balance between these nutrients as well as vitamins and minerals in order to be healthy. In addition, when we are suffering emotional and physical disturbance, we need more vitamins than we can receive from our food alone. A woman who is in transition, pregnant, ill, or under stress needs consistent and nutritious meals, and perhaps vitamin supplements.

A meal which contains all three substances is better for you than a meal made up mostly of one nutrient. When our blood sugar level drops, we become hungry and dizzy. A meal of bacon and eggs, milk, toast, and juice, for instance, will give us needed protein, carbohydrates, and fats and will sustain us for hours. A meal of pastry, coffee, and sugar is mostly carbohydrates and will cause our blood sugar level to rush upward (a kind of high!) and plummet back down in just an hour or two. Then we feel irritable, hungry, sleepy, and faint. A more balanced meal is a better buy nutritionally because it works longer to keep us full and energetic.

Some general rules about nutrition:

1. Processed foods, such as bleached white flour, many
    cereals, frozen pre-prepared concoctions, sweets, and
    supermarket snacks are generally lacking in vitamins
    because of the processing they go through. They also
    frequently contain additives to keep them from deteri-
    orating. You don't need those additives in your body.
    They are usually chemicals which do nothing positive
    for your health, and may be harmful in prolonged and
    concentrated amounts.

2. Whole grain cereals (such as wheat and rye) and flours
    contain many more vitamins than bleached white flour.
    Fresh vegetables and fruits are usually more nutritious
    than frozen and canned versions.

3. Meat, cheese, milk, and eggs are good sources of "whole"
    or complete protein. Even if you could afford to, it
    is not necessarily a good idea to make your major source
    of protein meat. Other sources give needed vitamins
    meat does not. (Soybeans, wheat germ, liver, and
    yogurt are all high in protein and vitamins.)

Of course, the food we are able to eat depends on our time,
money, and access. Families that are not wealthy have been
finding it difficult to buy meat, and even cheese is expensive. Women in transition are likely to be short on time
and money. We know that it is difficult to find the time
to cook a meal "from scratch" and even more difficult to
convince our families to change what they are used to eating.
We do not expect you to run out to the local health food
store and bring home fifty dollars' worth of organic wheat
germ. We do suggest that you make an attempt to cut down
on carbohydrates (which most of us eat much too much of),
sugar, and "junk" foods. They are both expensive and
wasteful and if your children fill up on them they are
likely to have poor eating habits, bad teeth, and grouchy
temperaments.

Where food is concerned, the one thing we are all aware of
is that it is expensive. One solution that might be applicable to you as a woman in transition is food cooperatives.
Food co-ops are groups of people who volunteer their labor
and purchase large amounts of food wholesale at their
city's central distribution point. The savings are then
passed on to the members. You generally have to pay a
membership fee (usually very little) and volunteer a few
hours of your time each month. Food co-ops may not be

practical for a working mother who may not wish to put in
an order for her food a week ahead of time. They do, however, usually have a better quality of dry goods, produce,
and dairy products than grocery stores and supermarkets.
Their prices are usually a great deal lower than commercial food establishments.

Keeping Fit

Our bodies have been used and abused over the years to the
point where it may seem difficult to return to a state of
physical fitness. Although some aspects of our lives as
women involved exercise (after all, we do lift those
thirty- and fifty-pound children, move furniture, and cart
laundry and groceries from place to place), most often
the physical work we do does more to strain and pull our
bodies than to build them up. If we have to work at jobs
which keep us sitting or standing all day, or which have
us bending and twisting our muscles unnaturally, we probably have experienced all the discomfort of physical
activity without much of the pleasure.

The phrase "physical fitness" conjures up gruesome images.
Some of us have never been able to get involved in physical activities except stand-in-place exercises, second-
rate gym classes where neatness counted for more than
enthusiasm, and years of constant exhaustion. Nobody
wants to come home from a day full of unpleasant physical
activity and face more of the same. Exercise isn't
supposed to be torture. It used to be that group games
and dances were part of small-town and village life. Now,
access to physical recreation areas and people to play
with is mostly restricted to men and women who have the
time, money, and opportunity.

If you are not in school, you probably won't have access
to a gym or tennis court or swimming pool (unless there
is a YWCA or community recreation center that you can
use). You may have trouble finding other women to play
a team sport, or the facilities may not be, in practice,
open to women. You may be able to find a Y, community
center, health club, or public school which is open to
women if you look hard enough and have enough people
interested to help you push for use of them.

If you can get the money together, and there is something
that you are interested in learning--whether it is swimming, tennis, self-defense techniques, bicycling, jogging--

then by all means do so. If there are other women around
interested in a sport or activity that you are, maybe you
could pool your resources and try to work out baby-sitting
arrangements, transportation, or group rates. Try to build
up your muscles gradually (but don't be afraid to push
yourself to do a little better, either). Do what you enjoy
doing. Try to make the time for it, and don't let yourself
be cheated out of the time you put aside for yourself. By
getting frequent exercise you may find yourself more relaxed,
energetic, and confident. You will certainly be more
healthy.

If you are really isolated, and can't find other people to
do things with, or facilities to do them in, there are
exercises you can do alone. You might want to go to the
library and find some books, and practice the techniques
they suggest. Don't let anyone cheat you out of your physical good health. We need to be strong and healthy people
if we are going to be able to make it through the crises in
our lives.

HOW TO FIND AND CHOOSE: OUR RIGHTS AS HEALTH CARE CONSUMERS

The image of medicine that flickers across our TV screen is
greatly different from the reality that many of us face when
we need health care services. A woman in transition often
finds that the bottom has dropped out of her financial
security, and that this has consequences in the kind of
health care that is available to her as well as other areas.

The less money that we have, the more dependent we become
on institutions. Few of us can really afford a private
physician, and in any case, there are fewer general prac-
titioners or family practice doctors around. More often
the case for us is that we go to clinics or hospitals, see
doctors only when it is necessary, and find ourselves
amazed at the cost of prescriptions and medical help.

A woman in transition who finds herself moving to another
neighborhood needs to find the health care services that
will give her the most for her money. Women who live in
isolated rural areas, and some women who live in urban
areas, may find that there is no element of choice involved.
There is one hospital, one clinic, or one physician available, and that is that.

As a woman going through separation and divorce, you probably wonder how to find services in your community, how to
use the health care facilities available to you, what you
have the right to expect for your money, and how to pay for
medical services. These are the areas of health care con-
suming that we deal with in this section.

How To Find Health Care Services

The logical place to look for health care services is from
your friends, family, and neighbors. If your family or
neighbors have one consistent physician or clinic that they
use, find out from them what hours the facilities are open,
what the fees are like, what insurance or payment plans they
accept.

If you can afford a private physician, you might consult a
free or community or women's clinic and find out who they
recommend. You can call the hospital nearest to you and
find out if they have physicians affiliated with them who
take private patients. Most of the time you are better off
going to a decent clinic, unless you are in need of a
specialist of some sort (gynecologist, obstetrician, etc.).
You might look into group practice. Some physicians work
with several other doctors. They may be specialists in the
same area or in various areas. If you need to find out what
is wrong and do not know for sure, a multi-specialist group
may have a broader range of experience and information and
may actually save you money by making an accurate diagnosis
more quickly than a single physician might be able to. In
general, however, group practice does not mean reduced fees.

Some of us, of course, cannot afford health care that is
not very low cost. If you have a health insurance program,
you should find out what facilities they can refer you to.
Some health insurance plans have their own clinics, doctors
and hospitals. (They vary in expensiveness, quality, etc.).
You should make sure that any health insurance that your
husband has continues to cover you and your children. (For
more about health insurance, see p. 318.)

If you have Medicare or Medicaid, you will have to get your
health care from doctors, hospitals, and clinics which accept it. Private hospitals, and some voluntary and nonprofit
hospitals do not accept patients on Medicare or Medicaid,
or people who cannot afford to pay.

You may be able to get good information about services from
the local social agency council. They are usually called

Health and Welfare Councils or Community Councils, and the
information that you will be able to get will probably vary
greatly depending on the sex, knowledge, and honesty of the
person you speak to. Many communities have mental health
center networks and traditionally family service (counseling) agencies. There are also agencies which have a particular disease or condition in their names. Some of these
may not be helpful to you, as they were founded to raise
money for research. Many of the newer ones have a self-help
character, particularly in dealing with economic and social
aspects of their members' health problems. Agencies dealing
with epilepsy, heart disease, diabetes, etc., fall into this
category.

How To Use The Facilities Available To You

It is of the greatest importance that you have a physician
somewhere (whether at a hospital, in private practice, or
at a clinic) who has your complete medical record. If there
is a permanent staff member at a hospital who has treated
you, remember his name and make sure he has knowledge of
your medical history. If none of these things are relevant
to your situation, if you travel a great deal or seldom
see any particular doctor, you should keep your own medical
record containing information such as: *when* you saw a doctor, *why* (what were you treated for), *how* you were treated,
where you saw him, his name and/or specialty. You should
also have information about medications and drugs you have
had bad side effects from, allergies, medical problems in
your family, hospitalization, etc. A good doctor will ask
you all these things.

By having your medical history in the hands of someone you
trust, you prevent yourself from being treated with a drug
you are allergic to and aid the diagnosis of your problem a
great deal. Doctors admit patients to hospitals. In a
time of emergency, the doctor who has your records should
be contacted.

If you find a good clinic, keep going to it. Clinics vary
according to their interest and concern for the community
they operate in, who set them up, and for what purpose.
(For example, women's health clinics, community clinics,
and self-help groups differ greatly in attitude and priorities from municipal hospital clinics.) In general, most
clinics are crowded and understaffed, so you should prepare
yourself for a wait and bring someone with you. As we said
before, make sure that you have your clinic specify that
your druggist write the name of the medication and its

instructions on the label of the bottle. Also, be sure to
bring health insurance information.

If you have any particular doctor, ask for him and remember
his name and usual hours. In many clinics, especially in
teaching hospitals, there may be a rotating staff--you
may not have the same doctor longer than six months. Make
sure you know who has your files.

Emergency rooms are *expensive* and definitely should not be
used if there is an alternative. In many areas the emergency room is flooded with patients who have no alternative
clinics.

In An Emergency

You should always know the name, location, and shortest
route to the hospital nearest you. (You should also be certain that that hospital will admit you in an emergency--
some private hospitals, nonprofit, and voluntary hospitals
do not admit patients who cannot pay, have Medicare or Medicaid, or have health insurance that they do not honor).

> *In New York in 1970, 537 people died in ambulances
> transferring them to low-cost municipal hospitals
> after they had been turned away from voluntary
> hospitals they could not afford.*
>
> *Ellen Frankfort*
> Vaginal Politics

Before an emergency happens, find out from neighbors and
friends if there is one particular hospital that is better
than others in your area. In case of emergency, ask to be
taken there.

In an emergency situation, you should remember the following:

1. If you have a private, personal physician, and he is
    affiliated with a hospital, that is the hospital you
    will be admitted to. Call him and have him meet you
    at the hospital, if possible.

2. Have someone whom you trust go to the hospital with you.
    On the way, tell them what happened, what your symptoms
    are, what drugs and medications you are already taking,
    and any allergies or medications you have bad reactions
    to. This will help you to remember, and if you become
    unconscious, enable them to tell the doctor. The

doctor should ask you these things. If he doesn't,
tell him.

3.   Know what your medical insurance plan is, and bring the
      card.

4.   Find out who is treating you if you haven't a private
      physician. What level of practitioner they are (intern,
      resident, whatever) and who the supervisory doctor is.

5.   Find out what contraindications there are connected with
      any medication you are given (side effects or factors
      which might make taking the drug dangerous). Also what
      drugs the medication should *not* be taken with.

6.   Find out what treatment you are being given for what
      illness, and why that particular treatment was decided
      on.

7.   Do not allow the hospital personnel to tell you that
      nothing is wrong with you if you know otherwise. Don't
      leave until you are satisfied with the treatment you
      have received.

Some Basic Rights

None of us enjoy being helpless, and there is seldom a time
that we feel more helpless than when we are women alone and
we, or our children, are sick. No matter how well we know
the failings and weaknesses of clinics, hospitals, and
doctors, one continuing, strong emotion that we feel in
times of need is that *they are there to help us and they
will make everything better*. But while the former should
be true, it sometimes doesn't seem to work out that way;
and while the latter is sometimes an unrealistic expectation, we need to believe in its truth.

As a patient or a relative or friend of a patient, you do
have the right to certain things. We reprint these lists
from *Our Bodies, Ourselves* in order to remind you of your
legal and consumer rights, in the hope that if you should
be ill you might avail yourself of them:

WHAT TO EXPECT FROM YOUR HOSPITAL

   *1.   Clear explanations about all charges and fees, as
        much in advance as possible, item by item. Also,
        explanations of what your hospital understands*

*about the coverage offered by your particular
insurance policy (if any).*

2. *Answers to your questions about any tests and
    procedures performed in the hospital, their
    purpose and nature, costs and possible risks.*

3. *Acceptance of your refusal to sign waivers and
    permission forms, whether or not you understand
    them.*

4. *Explanation of any anesthesia services that are
    anticipated; the purpose or necessity, the type
    of anesthesia used, the relative cost of this
    and other types, and by whom the anesthesia
    will be administered (the doctor himself, or
    another colleague; a nurse-anesthetist; or an
    anesthesiologist).*

5. *Answers to your questions about the content,
    purpose, known effects, possible risks, and
    side-effects of any drugs ordered for you
    (either orally or by injection). Acceptance
    of your refusal to take any drug or medication,
    with or without explanation.*

6. *Acceptance of your refusal to accept any
    procedure, at any time.*

7. *Clear explanations of the hospital's policies
    on visitors and family participation in care
    and companionship for the patient, including
    any reasons and sources of authority for
    exclusion of family members or any other
    helping person of the patient's choice.*

8. *Acceptance of your right to leave the hospital
    at any time that you wish to do so, whether or
    not you have medical permission to do so, and
    whether or not all bills and charges have been
    paid.*

WHAT TO EXPECT FROM YOUR DOCTOR

1. *An accurate diagnosis of your condition, healthy
    or otherwise, at your request.*

2. *Results and meaning of any tests or examinations
    performed by him or by others at his directions,*

as soon as they are available.

3. *Indications for treatment, varieties and alter-
    natives, pros and cons of particular treatments
    in the opinion of experts other than him, as
    well as the doctor's own preference, and the
    reasons for it.*

4. *Answers to your questions about any examination
    or procedure he may perform, in advance of or at
    any time during the performance of it. Stopping
    any examination or procedure at any moment, at
    your request.*

5. *Complete information about purpose, content, and
    known effects of all drugs prescribed or adminis-
    tered, including possible risks, side effects, and
    contraindications, especially of any combination
    of drugs.*

6. *Willingness to accept and wait for a second medical
    opinion before performing any elective surgery
    which involves alteration or removal of any organ
    or body part.*

7. *Answers to your questions about your body or your
    general physical health and functioning, in addi-
    tion to any particular condition. Or, encouragement
    to seek these answers from another source.*

The Price Of Feeling Good: Health Care And Insurance

A hundred years later than European countries, the United
States is preparing to enact a bill providing for national
health insurance. It is not surprising that most people
in the United States cannot afford to get sick for long.
A bed in a hospital room is typically $200 a day, and can
go higher. No one should be unhealthy because of lack of
money, but unfortunately, few of us can pay the cost of
quality health care. There is at this time no really
sufficient form of health insurance available to people
with limited funds, but in order to help you to consider
what your needs are, we are presenting this description
of insurance plans which do exist at this time.

Medicaid And Medicare

Medicaid and Medicare were the first programs set up by the
government to recognize the health needs of poor and older

people. Medicare is funded by social security deductions
from our paychecks, and is for people over 65 or disabled
persons. As anyone who is living on social security can
tell you, it is a drop in the bucket. Because some doctors and hospitals inflate their charges when a person is
on Medicare, people on Medicare have been known to end
up paying more than they had to before they had Medicare.

If you are on public assistance or welfare, Medicaid will
pay most of your hospital and medical bills (as well as
dental expenses). In some states you can apply for Medicaid retroactively, so that if you are forced to be
hospitalized and you have no money or health insurance,
you might promise to apply after you are well. People on
Medicaid can receive decent health care, especially if they
have a good physician who accepts it and does not boost
his prices. Most of the "welfare" clinics and hospital
wards, however, are grim places. Even so, Medicaid is the
only health insurance program that gives complete medical
coverage at virtually no cost.

Types Of Insurance

First dollar, or basic protection health insurance, pays the
hospital for your room, pays doctors and surgeons for their
services, and usually covers accidents which might put you
into the hospital. Blue Cross and Blue Shield are basic
protection plans.

Blue Cross pays for hospital bills and Blue Shield covers
some in-hospital physicians' and surgeons' bills. But they
do not necessarily foot the whole bill if you are hospitalized for a long time. Blue Shield pays doctor's bills only
up to a certain point and may have a variety of limitations,
depending on the situation.

The big advantage to the "blues" is that they are low-cost
and may be partially or wholly paid for by your employer.
They are nonprofit, and so return more of their customers'
money than many insurance plans, but even so have a remarkably high income for a "nonprofit" organization.

Major medical coverage is designed to cover the really
serious accidents and medical problems you may be affected
by. They are not necessarily very expensive, because the
odds of having a very major illness are less than you think.
Their structure is keyed to sharing the cost with you. In
most cases, they have a "deductible," which is a fixed
amount that you pay before they pay the rest. It may be

$100, $200, or $300, or more. It can be as much as $1,000.
For poorer families, the cost of the deductible will be a
much more sizable chunk of the family income.

A major medical plan can also be a co-insurance plan,
where they agree to pay only a fixed amount for any illness, or a percentage of the costs. The greater the
percentage they will pay, the better off you are. They
may have internal limitations, which means that they
will pay only a fixed amount toward surgical or hospital
room expenses, no matter what the total cost
might be. They usually have a "maximum" that is all that
they will pay toward the cost. Often it is $10,000 to
$20,000. Depending on the policy, the maximum may apply
to each separate illness in the family. In some policies,
the maximum isn't reinstated until the patient has gone
six months or a year without a recurrence. In others,
the maximum is renewed every calendar year.

A comprehensive major medical policy is one that gives
you first dollar coverage as well as coverage for
catastrophes. It simply has a low deductible. With a
truly comprehensive major medical policy, you don't need
Blue Cross and Blue Shield.

Recently, there have been established prepaid medical
plans that pay a yearly fee to a group of health
specialists; in return, they are supposed to supply
regular checkups, preventive medicine, treatment for
illness, and sometimes even stays in a hospital. Plans
like this include the Kaiser plan on the West Coast, and
HIP in New York. The idea is a good one, but the actual
functioning of the program is too often designed to meet
the needs of businessmen who have invested into the plan
and insurance companies than the urgent needs of the
patients.

People subscribing to these plans pay their insurance
company, which then pays the health maintenance organization. No matter how many of the services are used by
subscribers, they are still paid the same amount. For
this reason, health maintenance organizations generally
cut down on unnecessary surgery and hospitalization, and
have more of an investment in making accurate diagnoses
and giving effective treatment.

The problem with the rosy picture painted by businessmen and insurance companies when discussing
health maintenance organizations is that there

is no guarantee that promised services will be forth-
coming. Many patients still have to deal with long
waits, inconvenient hours, and shortages of doctors.
Whether or not a health maintenance program would be a
useful source of medical care for you should be determined by who runs the program, what kind of facilities
they offer, and what kind of responsiveness the program
has to the criticism and suggestions offered by its subscribers.

How To Make A Decision

In buying any form of insurance, you should remember
that what you are paying for is to have someone else
take the risk of financial responsibilities that you
could not afford alone. What you will want depends very
much on what you need. The number of children you have,
whether or not you are their sole support, etc., should
figure in your decision-making process. If you cannot
afford to pay the deductible that your insurance policy
demands, it doesn't make much sense to buy that insurance.
If, on the other hand, your husband or ex-husband has a
health insurance policy which covers your children and/or
yourself, you should make continuation of that policy
(or replacement of it by a policy in your name) a priority in your separation negotiations.

According to conventional wisdom, younger people need first
dollar insurance more than they need major medical. This
is because a young person is more likely to have less money
to pay for medical bills, but is also less likely to have
a major illness. For a middle-aged person, on the other
hand, major medical is thought to be the first need. The
ideal health insurance policy would include Blue Cross
and a major medical policy with no internal limitations
and an unlimited maximum. No such policy exists at this
time.

There is a guide to comparison shopping of major medical
policies entitled *Time-Saver for Health Insurance* available from libraries or from the National Underwriting Company, 420 E. 4th Street, Cincinnati, Ohio 45202. There are
in many states state insurance commissioners, who may
have information about health insurance available in your
state. You might also be interested in the Medical Committee for Human Rights' booklet *Billions for Bandaids*,
available for $2.25 from them at Post Office Box 7677,
San Francisco, California 94119.

Second Marriage

my mind clutters
listing assumptions you make
one: that he loves you better now
one: that the children really wanted your wedding--
(is it always other people hassling your kids?)
one: that you had to have a wedding cake
big enough to block the other time out;
and now you can't get angry because
because you are a grateful wife
though sometimes it's his explosion and
pent up feelings hurt;
your house these days:
air filled with the residues of
tranquilized sleeps,
the thickness of these pains leaving a
fog:
negation . . .

and the other assumptions:
you can come, visit us any time
we'll give you fresh air
we'll give you answers
we'll give you cheer;
when i remember your need, thoughts
stick like typewriter keys,
messages pile up in
a traffic jam of good intentions--
and what can i do with your
scrambled lumpy complaints
but ask what marriage solved anyway while
you want me to suffer too
and then confide in you

Mary McGinnis

MENTAL HEALTH

As we mentioned in Chapter Two, "Emotional Supports," some
women in transition feel that for them therapy is the best
way of coping with the many painful feelings that arise as
the result of separation and/or divorce. Most of us have
felt confused, deeply depressed, or very tired during and
after separation. Our self-esteem and will to survive
seemed at an all-time low. If our children were upset by
the separation, we were feeling guilty about that, and
other people (friends, relatives, school counselors) may

have consciously or unconsciously contributed to our
feelings of guilt. We were more likely to be depressed
than angry about our situation because women are not
supposed to express anger. Also, we may have felt that
we were responsible for our marriage's failure by not
being the "right" kind of wife. Sometimes these feelings
were transmitted to our bodies and appeared as headaches,
ulcers, and/or recourse to drugs or food or sleep as an
escape.

It is important to recognize that separation is a stressful experience and that most of these feelings are
normal reactions to an abnormal situation. We feel that
women gaining support and insight from other women is a
positive and fruitful experience. For this reason, we
are happy to see women becoming involved in consciousness-raising groups, as we suggest in Chapter Two. We
also believe, however, that eomtional problems come in
all shapes and forms, and for some women a consciousness-
raising or women's group may not be the answer to their
emotional needs. A commitment to a women's group requires
responsibility toward the other members that a scarred
and shaken woman in transition may very well not be able
to give. A self-help group which is unfamiliar with your
way of life or values or problems will not be able to help
you. Similarly, a therapist can be a good alternative for
a woman in transition if she has the time and money, and
if, of course, the therapist is sympathetic and understanding. We do not discourage women who feel they need
to undergo therapy. We do suggest that you read this
chapter and consider exactly what your expectations and
needs are.

Please remember that whether you choose therapy or a
women's group or neither, there is no blanket solution
to something as particular as emotional pain. Keep in
mind that both therapists and other women are human, with
human limitations. It is not likely that anyone but you
can solve all the problems faced by a woman in transition,
although some people can help.

Deciding If You Need And Want Therapy

The goal of any sort of therapy is to enable you to cope
with problems, understand your internal conflicts, and
develop a feeling of confidence and comfortableness with
yourself. A good therapist will help you to make important discoveries about yourself, and will help you to find
ways of using these discoveries to your own advantage.

Naturally, positive effects of therapy such as an understanding of self-destructive patterns in your life, insights into your reasons for behaving as you do, and
increased ability to deal with difficulties are valuable
for anyone. They need not be obtained only through
therapy. Before you begin your search for a therapist,
ask yourself these questions:

1.   What has led me to feel the need for a therapist?
     Do I need short-term counseling to get me through a
     specific period of time, or problem, or a longer
     period of therapy to help me deal with self-destructive
     or uncomfortable patterns in my life and relationships?

2.   What do I want help for? What do I want to be differ-
     ent in my life, my way of thinking about myself? What
     is most painful or difficult for me to deal with alone?
     What do I feel is all right with my life? What do I
     want to remain the same?

3.   What do I want from, what do I fear about therapy?
     What kind of questions would I like to ask? How do
     I feel about needing help from someone? (Some women
     feel ashamed, desperate, panic-stricken. Others
     feel relieved that the burden won't be entirely on
     their shoulders alone.)

4.   What kind of people or situations help me when I feel
     I need help? What kind of people and situations make
     me feel worse?

5.   How much can I afford to pay? What resources are
     available to me? (Private therapists, community
     mental health agencies, etc.)

Women who decide that their needs are best met by therapy
should try to feel confident and secure about their
decision. Everyone needs help at one time or another, and
by asking yourself these questions (and answering them
honestly) you enable yourself to see what it is you
really need, expect, and want.

Women And Therapy

Often, when we see ourselves, or others see us, as unfulfilled, depressed, or unable to function, we feel crazy
and think that something is wrong with us. There is,
of course, something wrong. It can be our health, our
fears dominating us, the pressures of the outside world

or an unhappy marriage. Usually prolonged anxiety caused
by something outside us comes to be something inside us.
We may not be "crazy" at all, to begin with, but years
of fearing that we are can drive us to something close
to it. Many women face the same kinds of problems
trying to adjust to role patterns which are not healthy
and are not fulfilling. For so many different women
to demonstrate the same emotional problems suggests some
similarity in cause. In many cases, but not all, the
suffering of people may be caused by the warped and
destructive cultural expectations we live with rather
than by an unchangeable sickness from within.

The mental health field has come to be criticized both
from within and by the women's liberation movement for
sometimes molding women into patterns which are not necessarily compatible with the goals of therapy. There are, of
course, sensitive, socially and politically aware members
of the field of mental health, just as there are in other
professions. We do believe that women should investigate
all aspects of their lives when feeling depressed, anxious,
or frightened. Some women may be better off trying to
make changes in their lives, such as getting a job, refusing to do all the housework, finding a new home, getting
a divorce, etc., rather than attempting to adapt themselves
to an unsatisfactory (but conventionally accepted) way of
life. At its best, therapy can help a woman to understand
the changes that are most essential and basic to her
problem-solving abilities, and the understanding gained
from self-discovery can aid her in constructing a satisfying life.

What Is A Therapist?

A therapist is a person who has the training or skills to
help you sort out some of the problems in your life, and
to give you a time and place each week where you are free
to talk about anything that you want to. Many of the
skills that therapists learn are things which everyone
might learn--listening, an understanding of what motivates
people, the ability to hear what a person is saying be-
neath their words, picking up patterns in a person's
life, etc. However, therapists often serve a useful role
when our needs at a given moment are too great for our
friends and family to handle. In other words, therapists
have no magical powers, and what you will be able to get
out of therapy is basically up to you and how willing you
are to take a good look at the way that you live your life

and how ready you are to make changes when you are dissatisfied.

Ther are many different schools or approaches to therapy;
some therapists want you to focus on the past, some on
the present, and there are many other combinations. Some
names of methods are: Freudian, Gestalt, Behavioral,
Jungian, Reichian, Bioenergetic, Psychic. Some conventional approaches may be too traditional for your needs;
innovative methods, on the other hand, may be gimmicky
or faddish. You may want to ask your therapist if she/he
adheres to any particular approach, and what that may mean
for your therapy experience. Make sure she explains this
in language you can understand. Most often it is the
personal qualities of the therapist rather than the
particular approach which will determine a successful
experience.

A successful therapist, by our standards, is one who has
managed to use her training without becoming enslaved by
it (or attempting to enslave her patients with it). The
difficulty with the field of mental health is that until
comparatively recently its premises have been based on
the theories of white, academically oriented men. It is
always difficult to understand and aid a person who is
confused, distraught, or overwhelmed by their emotions.
Without an understanding of the life-experience and
cultural values of a disturbed person, it is even more
difficult. Unfortunately, the criterion for "mental
health" that has evolved in some areas of the mental
health field is only applicable to people who lead the
lives of therapists. In this way, black and minority
groups, poor people, and women seldom have an opportunity
to determine what "sanity" is for them, and it is taken
to be a symptom of one's illness to disagree with the
premises of mental health professionals.

A good therapist seeks to understand not only your problems but their context. A good therapist is flexible and
concerned with your development as a person more than she
is concerned with the tidiness of her theory about how
you became disturbed. A therapist who is sensitive and
aware can save your life, and many have.

We have found that many women therapists are just as rigid
in their attitudes toward women as men therapists, so
being in treatment with a woman does not guarantee that you
will have a nonoppressive experience. On the other hand,
many women therapists are getting tuned in to their own

experiences as women and are developing an understanding of women's problems which differs greatly from the textbook explanations. Your best chance for a successful experience with therapy will come from analyzing and understanding what is actually going on in the therapy relationship. Both you and your therapist should begin with an understanding of one another. Finally, we do not believe that credentials assure quality treatment, or that the more expensive a therapist is, the more likely you are of achieving success.

These are the general categories of therapists:

Social workers are usually trained in two-year graduate school programs and sometimes have additional training.

Psychologists usually have a master's or a doctorate from a graduate school. There are many different orientations in this training, but it usually emphasizes personality dynamics and behavior.

Psychiatrists are medical doctors who have at least three years of training beyond medical school. They are the most highly trained in terms of years and ask the highest fees.

Psychoanalysts are psychiatrists who have had additional training in analysis and who have undergone analysis themselves. There are also lay psychoanalysts who have had this training but who are not psychiatrists. People generally see psychoanalysts three to five times a week.

The terms *psychotherapist* and *counselor* are also used. Sometimes this indicates specialized graduate training and sometimes it doesn't. You may want to ask a therapist who uses one of these labels to clarify her training and experience.

Marriage counselors are persons who help couples work on marital problems. There is not nationwide licensing or certification procedure for marriage counselors, so someone using that label might have some of the training described above or none at all.

Encounter or sensitivity group leaders are a mixed bag. Some of them have credentials as social workers, psychologists, or psychiatrists and have had further training and experience in groups. Others have no formal credentials but have been trained under group leaders. Encounter or sensitivity groups often have one-shot sessions (one day, a weekend) and are not aimed at solving severe emotional problems but at dealing with what happens within the group. There are many of these group leaders around as well as those who emphasize non-talking therapies such as massage, yoga, or meditation. Some of them are doing exciting, experimental things and others are very destructive. You should be very careful about becoming involved in such groups and be certain that they can meet your needs.

Where Therapy Is Done

Private Practice

Most therapists are in private practice because they like the freedom from agency restrictions, and because the money is better. Private therapy takes place in the private office of a therapist, although some therapists who also work in agencies can use those offices to see private patients. You pay the therapist directly, although there are some insurance plans which reimburse you for part of the cost. Since you are paying, you can pick and choose among potential therapists and you have the freedom to leave and find another if you are not satisfied.

Fees vary in different locations with psychiatrists usually charging the most (it's up to $75 an hour in New York City now!) and psychologists, social workers, etc., charging less. We feel that many therapists in private practice charge fees which are unreasonable. They often say that a person has to pay a lot for therapy in order for it to be meaningful. We disagree. Try to work out a fee that is acceptable to both of you.

Clinics, Social Agencies, Community Mental Health Centers

If you don't have much money, you can consider going through a clinic, social agency, or community mental health center where you pay on a sliding scale. You won't necessarily receive poorer treatment there, as many therapists prefer being on a fixed salary rather than operating a private practice. However, you definitely have fewer options at an agency or clinic than if you could pay a therapist in private practice. There may be a long waiting list, and you can only be seen immediately if it is an emergency. Also, your fee may be based on your husband's income rather than what you may actually be receiving from him (if anything) and you may have to

pressure the clinic to convince them to lower their fee
to a realistic amount for you.

When you walk into the agency or clinic, the first thing
that will probably happen is that you will go through an
intake interview, which is usually done by a secretary
or an intake person who asks you questions about your
situation. Next there might be an evaluation lasting one
or several sessions. This is to help you and the clinic
clarify the important issues in your life. On the basis
of this the clinic decides whether you can be helped by
them, what kind of treatment would be best for you, and
who should see you. You may be able to request a specific
therapist you know of or ask for a woman therapist, but it
is likely that you will have to take the person you are
assigned to. If you feel very uncomfortable with this person, you should speak up. It is a waste of your time and
theirs if you do not like and trust your therapist.

Andi

*I was 16 when my parents had me committed. They ba-
sically felt I was "out of control" and that it was
better to send me to a mental hospital than to a
juvenile detention home, which was the other alternative they considered. At the time we were living in
rural Virginia, so you can imagine what kind of mental
hospital it was. In the beginning I was given 24
shock treatments--every day except Sunday, which was
pretty much standard procedure with about 95 percent
of the patients in the hospital. This was a private
hospital. We did have some therapy. We had group
therapy once a week. The psychiatrist I had, who was
supposed to be helping us, right?--his wife was in a
mental hospital for alcoholism, his son was a junkie,
and his daughter had been a prostitute and was also in
a mental hospital. But supposedly he was all right and
was going to cure the rest of us.*

*I also had to see a psychologist who spent most of the
sessions taunting me by calling me a whore and by telling me that I was attracted to him and that I really
wanted to sleep with him. All he talked about was sex.
It was his topic, not mine.*

*Most of the people in the hospital there were rural
Southerners, mostly women. Also a lot of teen-agers.
Everyone was mixed in together. Most of the time they*

seemed to be there because they didn't fit into the roles they were supposed to. Like there was a 13-year-old girl there who was committed because she was fighting with her parents. She wasn't running away, drinking, or doing dope--none of that stuff. She was committed by her parents and given 15 shock treatments as therapy because she was rebelling against her parents. They gave insulin shock there too. I never had that.

When they gave you electroshock you were taken down at about 7:30 in the morning and made to sit out in the hall. They would take you in one by one to this little room. You would be strapped down to the table. Electrodes were attached to your head. They would put this rubber thing in your mouth and say bite down and then hit you with the electricity. Supposedly, they're supposed to give you something like sodium pentothal to knock you out before they hit you with the electricity, but in this hospital they didn't do that. When the electricity hits you, you totally lose control of your body and go into convulsions. It's a horrible feeling to have that done to you. It's torture, not treatment.

In about the 8th or 9th month they took me in front of the board of 7 psychiatrists who decide what is going to happen to you. My parents were there, and they were told that I was incurably schizophrenic and that I should be committed to the state hospital in Virginia indefinitely. I think that that came about because I refused to buck under and do what they said I should do. Every time that I stood up to the staff they would take me back to the closed-off sections where the really "crazy, off-the-wall" patients were kept and would threaten me with more shock treatments. I think my fighting them was the reason for their saying I was incurable more than anything else. I think that when they said that my parents decided that it was going a little too far, and they took me out of the hospital. Later we moved to St. Louis, and when I moved out of the house again, they committed me to another hospital there. This time the psych that I had stood up for me and told my parents to get off my back, and they released me from the hospital.

Institutionalization

Sometimes a woman's therapist may feel that she needs to
be put in a mental institution and will put great pressure on her and her family to have her committed. Sometimes, it is her family or husband who pressure the
therapist. If you find yourself in this situation it
may be difficult for you to think clearly about it. You
may feel that you want to trust your therapist because
she is the person who can help you to feel better about
yourself, and may be ready to believe almost anything she
tells you about yourself. You may begin to feel that
everyone is right--that you are "crazy." If you have
been struggling along with little income, and many problems at home, it may seem to you that the hospital is the
only place to get help and be left alone to rest.

While we do believe that some women can benefit from
allowing themselves the time and space to "be crazy"
or to confront their fears and fantasies, most of the
things that occur in mental institutions (especially in
state and county institutions) work totally against improving your mental health. In some institutions women
are given electroshock treatments, heavily sedated,
lobotomized, or sexually abused by the staff and/or
other patients. Often, in order to get released, a
woman has to win the approval of the hospital staff by
proving that she is getting well--wearing makeup, doing
housewifely chores around the hospital, and in general
performing the traditional feminine roles. Again,
women who have paid for private hospitalization are more
likely to receive good care than women who are put into
state hospitals.

If there is pressure on you to consider committing yourself, we advise you to get support from people who do not
have an investment in seeing you put away but who can help
you to sort out all the factors involved. Ask friends,
another therapist, or a lawyer to advise you about your
situation. If you are committed, find one person whom
can trust who knows where you are going and who will check
up on you. Some hospitals will advise you of your rights,
but many won't; ask if there is a patient advocate or
someone on the staff who can tell you what your rights are
as a patient. Contact an attorney to advise and represent
you at future hearings. Having been institutionalized can
label you for life and can increase your difficulties in
finding jobs, getting custody of your children, etc. It
is important to be as informed as possible about what is

going on even though it may be hard for you to get that
information and to act on it.

Choosing And Evaluating A Therapist

Try to get recommendations for therapists from friends you
trust or from women's centers. If this is not possible,
most cities have a Community Mental Health Center, a
Health and Welfare Council, Family Service or Community
Council which can refer you to agencies or therapists in
private practice.

If possible, have a consultation with at least two therapists before you choose one. Some therapists charge for
this and others do not. Ask her some of the things you
think might be important to you in treatment. Is she
married? How does she feel about working mothers? Why
does she think that some people are rich and others are
poor? What does she believe that mental health consists
of? You should be suspicious if she won't answer most
of your questions, but instead wants to know why you asked
them. It will be difficult for you to share the pain that
you are feeling with a stranger, and you should trust your
feelings about this initial encounter when deciding whether
or not she will able to help you. Shop around!

As the therapy progresses, try not to be intimidated by
your therapist, especially if you feel she is not
respecting you. It is likely that in the course of your
treatment you and your therapist will disagree about one
thing or another. You should distrust a therapist who is
constantly telling you that your disagreement is part of
your illness. Sometimes, of course, it is difficult to
look honestly at yourself, and many of us avoid doing it,
but therapists may be wrong, too. The more open and
flexible a therapist is, the more likely it is that you
will be able to resolve disagreements between you. Trust
your feelings and be candid, and expect as much from your
therapist. Remember that you are paying to be helped.

If possible, join a women's group to validate what is happening in your therapy experience. Also talk to friends
who have been in therapy. While you may feel initially
embarrassed to discuss intimate problems with several
people, what is happening in your therapy should not be so
mysterious that you can't talk about it with anyone but
your therapist.

We strongly condemn therapists who seduce their patients. This happens more often than we like to believe, and women to whom it happens are usually dependent on their therapist's approval and find it difficult to gain perspective about it. Being in therapy is an extremely vulnerable position to face, and no therapist should take advantage of it, especially sexually.

There are some people who feel that going into group therapy is the only sure way to avoid the one-to-one dependency that often develops between therapist and client. It is our feeling that different women have different needs, and individual therapy may be helpful to some women at some times. Groups can be very supportive but they can also be destructive. Especially destructive are encounter groups where women patients "stand in" for women in general, and men are encouraged to work out their frustrated relationships with their wives, mothers, sisters, etc., on them. Women who are at all assertive in these types of groups are condemned as being too aggressive, sexually unfulfilled, or deviant.

Short-term therapy, such as problem-oriented or behavioral therapy, is becoming popular as a way of working on specific problems. Even if you feel that long-term therapy is beneficial to you, beware of therapists who accuse you of "running away" from your problems when you feel that you would rather terminate your treatment. If this is your honest feeling, you should be encouraged to apply your insights to your life, and to use as tools the ways of dealing with your situation you have acquired from therapy. It may be difficult for a therapist to let a favorite patient leave her treatment, but she should be honest about her feelings and should not foster an ongoing dependency.

MIMI

My husband and I made love in the bathtub, sometimes in the shower. We did it with soap bubbles sometimes--we really had a good time. My husband was in treatment with a reputable psychiatrist. Jeff told him that we made love in the bathtub and this guy told Jeff what we had done was absolutely sick. Any other two people would have gotten out of the bathtub and into bed, which is where lovemaking belonged. I don't think that we ever made love in the bathtub after that.

Beatings: The All-American Pastime?

Roman law held that a man's family was his property, and in
some ways things haven't changed much since then. In our
three years at Women in Transition we have discovered that
wife-beating is almost as much of a national pastime as
baseball. We have had calls from women whose husbands
locked them naked in a room all day until they came home,
accompanied, of course, by beatings. One woman whose husband had thrown her against a wall, causing spinal damage
which necessitated a back brace, called us when he threatened to put her into the street rather than pay her
medical expenses. Some women who have always believed it
was their husband's right to beat them called us believing
that divorce was the only means available to them to stop
beatings.

Habitual domestic violence often occurs when the husband
is drunk. Men who have a respectable image outside the
home often take out their frustrations and anger on their
wives and children--and it is only a small step further to
express that anger in beatings. Men *and* women frequently
believe that domestic violence is the husband's right, or
that it is part of the "for better and for worse" aspect
of marriage. Often when beatings continue over months and
years it may be part of a pattern within the relationship;
some middle-class women accept being beaten as part of a
complex system of punishments and rewards--two days after
the beating their husband may be "sorry" and "make it up,"
especially if they have a position in the community that
would be endangered if word got out. Poor and low-income
women, besides having little legal recourse, may live in
communities where beatings are taken as a matter of course,
where it is assumed by everyone that a woman accepts and
perhaps even enjoys such demonstrations of marital posses-
siveness. We have found that domestic violence cuts across
all class, racial, and ethnic lines.

Laws and procedures concerning domestic violence differ in
various states and localities, but until recently the
assumption has been that wife-beating incidents are merely
part of lovers' quarrels, and have no legal consequences.
Very often a woman who actually does resort to the police
will drop the charges when she is made to feel guilty or
intimidated. If a man repeatedly attacked his co-workers,
he would be considered dangerous or insane and would be imprisoned or referred to psychiatric help. But a man who
comes up before a male judge for assaulting his wife is
likely to get a lighter punishment (if any) than a street

mugger. There are agencies which deal with the problems
of battered children, but very little is being done to
help battered wives.

The logical extension of domestic violence, murder, occurs
once out of every four times within the family. Half of
these homicides are by spouses murdering spouses. Or so
the *FBI Uniform Crime Reports* tell us. In New York, Miami,
Louisville, and Charlotte, North Carolina, Crisis Intervention police groups have been trained to begin to deal with
domestic violence. Usually the teams are male and female,
and their primary goal is to separate the husbands and
wives and to get them to talk to someone else about their
quarrel. In most cases they attempt to refer the man and
woman to counseling services rather than arrest anyone.
Since arrests have always been infrequent anyway, it may
be an improvement.

For women whose marriages have already proved intolerable,
what can be done depends on where you live and what your
economic and social standing is. Most women who are
beaten are ashamed and frightened. Very often they are
too guilt-ridden or embarrassed to talk to anyone about
being beaten. It is desperately important--a matter of
life or death, in fact--that if you have been beaten you
speak with friends, family, or even a minister or priest
or doctor about the situation. For too long the privacy
of married life has served as a cover for abusive and
violent treatment of women. Unbelievable as it may seem,
it is highly unlikely that you are the only woman in your
community to be faced with this problem.

In general, there are limits to the legal remedies available to you, but the police and courts may be more
responsive to you than we have suggested here. Middle-
class and professional women are more likely than low-
income women to get response from the police and courts.
This is also true of women who live in small towns, although it can work the other way if your husband is an
influential member of the community. Many middle-class
men do not wish their standing in the community to be
jeopardized, and can be effectively threatened by legal
action. Divorce is not the only or best solution to the
problem of beatings. Divorce may be the answer to the
other problems within your marriage, but don't overlook
your other legal options to prevent domestic violence.

Here are some suggestions about what to do if your husband,
ex-husband, boyfriend, or ex-boyfriend is beating you.

Practical Steps

If you are not living together or if you are and you want
to keep him out, change the locks on your door. If you
know when he is likely to come, have friends, neighbors,
or relatives there. Or have a prearranged signal so that
you can call them quickly when he comes. The best solution
is to never see him alone, but if this is not possible,
try to keep self-defense tips in mind (see the self-defense
section of this chapter) for when the situation occurs.
If you have no intention of using self-defense against him,
of course, it makes no sense to attempt to learn the techniques.

If your house or apartment is in your name and he comes in
without your permission, he is trespassing. If he breaks
in, he is breaking and entering. *He* may think he has a
right to be there. Even the police may think he has a
right to be there, but legally, he does not. If the house
or apartment is in his name also you do not have a legal
right to keep him out, but you can try practical things
like changing the locks to "discourage" him. If this
doesn't work, you may have to stay with friends or relatives at the times you expect him to appear.

If he gets in and is threatening you or actually beating
you, call the police if you can. Or have a friend call.
Yell *"FIRE"* or *"THIEF"* as loud as you can. Other people may
call the police. Whoever calls the police should not
mention that the person who has broken into your place is
someone they know (or you know)--the police will be less
likely to come. In some neighborhoods, of course, they
just won't come. If you know that that is the case in
your neighborhood, or you don't want them to come, then
you must depend on friends, neighbors, prevention, and/or
self-defense.

If your beatings are part of a pattern and you can know in
advance when he is likely to come and beat you, you can go
to the precinct near you and speak with the head policeman.
Tell him, "You are supposed to be here to protect me. I
have been beaten before and I have good reason to think he
will be coming again on _____ at _____ and I would like
you to be sure he doesn't get in and beat me again." Your
success will vary depending on where and who you are, but
in general you have a better chance than if you called them
at the time the beating was occuring.

What the police will do when they come will vary also.
They will not want to arrest your husband for beating you

up. They are more likely to arrest a stranger, an ex-boyfriend, etc. They are more likely to arrest if weapons are involved or if you are badly hurt. The usual procedure is to take him for a walk. He stands a greater chance of getting arrested if he already has a record, especially if there are weapons offenses. Otherwise, he will either not be arrested, or be out in a few hours without having to put up bail. This leaves you with a very angry man on your hands, and it would be wise to get yourself out of the immediate situation if you can.

In short, calling the police is no long-term solution, but is sometimes a good idea if you are desperate, if he's anxious not to get in trouble with police, if he already has a record, or if he has a reputation within the community that he is anxious to protect. Whether the police come or not, you should not be alone. Have your closest friends or relatives come and stay with you for a while after he leaves. He will be less likely to return, and you can tell your story to them and they will help you remember what happened later if you press charges.

Pressing Charges

Procedures for pressing charges are different from place to place, and if you are being beaten frequently you should check on the procedure in your area. You have to make the decision whether it is worth the trouble to prosecute him. Again, if he is afraid of the law or has a reputation to protect, just the threat of prosecution may be effective.

Pressing charges will take a lot of your time and energy. You will have to tell your story over and over again to the police and court personnel. Your husband may not show up for hearings so you may have to go to court repeatedly. He does not have to have been arrested in order for you to file a private criminal complaint. Go to your municipal building or city court and tell them that you want to file a complaint. Usually it costs $10-$15, but it is free if you are on welfare and bring down your card. You *do not* need a lawyer to file the complaint, but it may be a good idea to speak with one as the prosecutor who is representing you may never speak with you at all.

It is important that you go down to the court right away. Don't wait more than a day to complain. You need to show evidence of his actions--bruises, broken limbs, scars, whatever. Before you go to the court get the story fixed

in your mind. Tell it to friends, and practice telling it
to them as if you were telling it to a district attorney or
judge:

What time did it happen?

Exactly where were you?

Did he say anything? Threaten you with anything?

Did you try to get away from him? How?

If not, why not?

Did you call for help? If not, why not?

Take a friend with you to any and all meetings with district attorneys, judges, and police officers. She can
give you a lot of support even if she doesn't say anything.
Better still, if you're nervous or expecting to get a hard
time, take along a social worker you trust, or another pro-
fessional--minister, doctor, lawyer, etc.

If, on the day of the court trial, he does not appear, the
court will issue a bench warrant for his arrest. This
means that he will be able to be arrested by any policeman
who comes across him. The charge is contempt of court,
which usually carries a fine and perhaps a period of imprisonment.

If He Is Found Guilty

If he is found guilty he'll probably be put on probation,
with a condition of his probation that he's not allowed
to go near you (or at least not to beat you up again) or
he'll go to jail. Sometimes he'll also have to post a
bond (sometimes called a "peace bond") of perhaps $200
which he will forfeit if he beats you up again. You
should have a certified copy of the probation order and
keep it handy. If he comes back you can show it to the
police when they come; then they will be more likely to
arrest him.

Other Legal Preventions

Other legal preventions you might take include getting a
lawyer and having him make up a peace bond which insures
your husband will forfeit money if he violates the conditions of the agreement. You might also go to court and

have them issue a "restraining order," which orders him to leave you alone or face contempt of court.

You might also get him to sign a separation agreement like the one in the legal chapter. It may be that all you need is the first few paragraphs, including the one about promising not to molest each other, and to leave each other alone. If he violates this, you will have more to back you up in court, and you may give the police more reason to arrest him by showing them the agreement.

The Way From Here

As we have said, divorce is generally not the solution to domestic violence. One of the disadvantages of any legal action you can take as a woman in transition is that your case may not come up for months, and you may have to live at home with the man you are taking to court but are probably financially dependent on. If this is your situation, try to get him to leave. Change the locks. Stay with relatives or friends as a last resort. Remember not to leave without your children--you don't want them to take the beating for you.

Many women stay in intolerable situations for years because they would have a hard time supporting themselves and their children on a low income or welfare. In London, England, a center has been set up where women can go to get away from their husbands until they can get established on their own. It is likely that similar centers will eventually be established in this country, but we don't know of any yet. Some women's centers do provide emergency housing for women in transition on a short-term basis.

If you are in transition, you may find that your husband takes the opportunity during child visitation to beat you. If this is your situation, go to the court and say that you want the visitation under court supervision. Work out arrangements where he meets the children somewhere else, or at the least, have someone with you when he comes. If he beats you after you have made this agreement in court, he can be charged with contempt of court and arrested.

The best self-defense is prevention, especially since many women do not have the time or energy to learn self-defense, and others cannot bring themselves to apply it. If you are concerned with learning martial arts or self-defense techniques, you might investigate the section on self-defense

in this chapter. Remember that in order for self-defense
to be effective, it must be disabling. You don't want to
make your husband just angry enough to hurt you worse. If
you can use any of the legal or preventive techniques in
this chapter, they may be a better solution to your problem.

Rape

Who Gets Raped And Who Does The Raping

To be a woman and to fear rape are almost synonymous in
the United States. And for good reason: Forcible rape is
the most frequently committed violent crime in this country
today. Fear of rape is one of the conditions that keep
women from developing as active, independent people. As
a woman in transition, alone perhaps for the first time,
you may have reason to think again about all the fears
and dangers you have been faced with since childhood. One
important factor is, of course, that you now have to depend
on *yourself* primarily for your safety and development as a
person. Another factor is that, as a woman alone, you may
be concerned with developing new relationships with men,
and the likelihood of your avoiding rape depends a great
deal on your common sense, ability to anticipate dangerous
situations, and understanding that rape is not something
that only happens to other people, on the street, by a
stranger.

The Federal Bureau of Investigation Uniform Crime Report
says that there were 49,430 forcible rapes in 1972. These
rapes were reported, but the majority are not. Some
sources estimate the number of unreported rapes as high as
ten times the reported total. Each year, the total of reported rapes grows higher. It has been said that there is
a universal curfew on women in this country. But it is, in
many ways, an international situation. Only in a few countries (China is one) are women relatively free from fear
of rape. Freedom from rape is *not* acquired by living in a
"safe" neighborhood, dating the right sort of men, or by
virtue of age, social status, or marital status. Any
woman, of any age, living anywhere is a potential victim
of rape.

The myths about rape are just that, myths. Most women who
are legally (forcibly, without consent) raped are attacked
by men of their own race, usually men who are *not* legally
"insane" (in fact, rapists, with the exception of child
molesters, are considered the most "normal" of prison

inmates), and most often without "provocation." You don't have to be a college coed in a miniskirt walking through a "bad section" of town. Most rapes occur, in fact, in the home of the victim, and many women who are raped are the victim of a man they have met before or know. In fact, the myths about rape are so different from the reality, it is hard to understand how they have been perpetuated. Our suspicion is that rape is so much a part of our culture that the sustaining of these myths is necessary to hide the frequency and pervasiveness of rape. In this society, any man can be a rapist, and any woman, his victim.

If sex is a commodity to be bought, stolen, or won, it is easy to see that the line between accepted sexual overtures and rape blurs considerably. Rape is very much a thing that men do to other men through their women. In most wars, the victor celebrates his conquest by the rape/ conquest of his enemy's women. In the United States the greatest violence generally occurs in group rapes ("gang bangs") where men are as anxious to prove their masculinity to other men as they are to have "free" sex. Most rapes are planned, not spontaneous, and group rapes are almost always planned. Since sex seems to be readily accessible to most men, it seems likely that the immediate availability of sex favors is less important to the rapist than the brutality and violence that often accompany rape.

CHERYL

When I was at the supermarket that afternoon this teenage kid standing next to me in the frozen food section said he sure would like to get a piece of my ass. I was wearing a short skirt and I guess that I looked pretty attractive, but when he said that it made me wish that I was wearing work overalls. I felt like hitting him with the frozen pizza, but all I did was move away. I thought, "I don't need this today." My daughter, who is 15 months old, was screaming because it was past her naptime, the store was out of half the things on my list, and I was sneezing because I was getting a cold. All I wanted was to get home and get in bed. My husband and I are separated and it seems like I get sick more often than when we were together.

I brought my daughter into the apartment and was unloading bags of groceries from the car. I guess that I didn't see the man when he slipped in the door. I brought in the last bag, locked the apartment door behind me, turned around, and there he was. I had seen him around the neighborhood before but I didn't know who he was.

I was so shocked, but I managed to say, "What are you doing here," or something like that. He said he wanted money, so I got out my wallet. My hands were shaking. As I handed him what was in it he grabbed my arm and pulled me down on the floor and pulled my skirt up and my pants down and unzipped his pants. I was paralyzed. I had tried to imagine many times what I would do in this situation, and here it was. I did nothing. My daughter was screaming the whole time and I was afraid if I resisted him he would hurt her. Besides, the only thing that I could think to do was to gouge his eyes, and I couldn't bring myself to do that.

He stuck his penis in my vagina and I can't remember how long he was in there. All I remember was him sort of grunting and then getting up. He zipped his pants, picked up the money which had dropped on the floor, and kicked me in the ribs on the way out. It was awful. I just kept saying thank God my daughter and I are still alive. I lay there for a long time. I didn't know who to call. I wanted to call my husband but I was afraid that he would be angry and blame me for what happened.

The Victim Becomes The Criminal

Only in the case of a rape trial is the jury instructed to be skeptical of the testimony of the victim. In the California Penal Code, this provision states:

A charge such as that made against the defendant in this case is one which is easily made and, once made, difficult to defend against, even if the person accused is innocent.

Therefore, the law requires that you examine the testimony of the female person named in the information with caution.

In short, in the guise of justice, it is the victim who is forced to prove the act took place (usually without other witnesses), that it took place without her consent, and that she is "moral" enough for her word to be taken concerning the occurrence. If you have led what other people might consider an immoral or promiscuous life (such as seeing other men than your husband if you are separated),

your chances of being believed by the judge or jury are
lessened.

"Once defiled, a woman can never be violated again" is an
attitude common to police, courts, juries, and society at
large. All those years of television and movies where the
woman says "no" and supposedly means "yes," melting into
her seducer's arms, seem more real in the eyes of many
men than the confused, frightened, or incoherent testimony
of a woman who has been raped by a fine, upstanding member of the community. A woman who has in any way deviated
from conventional morality, who is black or poor, or who
is divorced or separated, may find her credibility denied.

Many men identify with rapists, viewing rape as a just
punishment for the immorality or "frigid" characteristics
of a woman, but feel that their own women should be kept
on a pedestal, dependent on *them* for protection from other
men. Women who believe the myths about rape may find themselves thinking, "She must have done something to lead him
on," especially if the defendant reminds them of their
sons, neighbors, or relatives. In the case of legal action,
the district attorney's office takes on the role of husband,
exacting its punishment provided the woman is judged to be
the "right kind" of woman (virginal, married, virtuous).
The job of the defense lawyer is, of course, to discredit
the testimony of the woman and make his client appear to
be the victim. Unfortunately, this is often easily done,
the groundwork already prepared in the minds of the jury
or judge. It is a short step from the presumed immorality
of the victim to the acquittal of the rapist.

If You Are Raped

The legal definition of rape attempts to distinguish between
sexual intercourse and rape, and requests that three conditions be met before rape can be charged and prosecuted:
Penetration must have occurred; the threat of force must
have been used; and you must not have consented.

If you were unconscious, drugged, intoxicated, or insane,
incompetent, underage, or senile, you are ruled not capable
of giving your consent. If you resisted, or the threat of
force was so great that you couldn't resist, consent is
also considered not to have been given.

Many women who have been raped said that there was nothing
they needed afterward as much as comfort from a friend.

If you have a close woman friend, she should be with you
while you go through the medical and/or legal processes
and be available for comforting and consolation. You may
want to go home with her, if you live alone. You should
not have to be deserted at this time. In some cities
there are rape clinics set up and staffed by women. They
may provide medical care, someone to be with you during
this time, and have groups or counseling services. By all
means get in touch with them if you need advice or their
services. You can find a partial listing of rape clinics
in the section at the end of this book that lists women's
centers.

If you have been raped, you must decide as soon as possible
whether or not you wish to press charges. If you do not
want to press charges, you need to arrange for your own
medical treatment. You should call a friend to be with
you and to take you to a doctor you know and trust.

Many hospital clinics will not treat rape victims, and
may in fact call the police to have you transported to
another hospital. The rationale for this is that they do
not want to become involved in legal problems.

You need to have a general physical examination for injuries, an internal examination, and a preventive injec-
tion of an antibiotic such as penicillin. If you have
been impregnated, there is a chemical called "stilbestrol"*
which consists of large doses of estrogen and which will
prevent pregnancy if taken within 72 hours of intercourse.
You should have tests for both syphilis and gonorrhea.

If you decide to press charges, you must notify the police
at once. Do not change your clothes or wash away blood
or semen. As contrary to your natural instincts as this
is, you will need to have samples taken as evidence. This
is the time to have a friend with you. Write down your
experience, tell it to her, and have her stay with you
while you are questioned by the police. The police will
probably ask you to repeat your story several times, and

---

*There has been a lot of controversy over stilbestrol,
which has been given in large doses over a long period of
time to increase fertility. It has been associated with
vaginal cancer in the daughters of women who have taken
it. However, the FDA has found no serious side effects
when small doses are given for a short time and has approved
its use as a "morning after pill." *(Women Organized
Against Rape Handbook*, Philadelphia, 1973, p. 3.)

may be harsh or insulting to you. A few cities have all-
women investigative rape units, but in most cases you will
be dealing almost exclusively with men.

You will probably be upset and confused about what happened
and have a difficult time telling the story clearly. It
may seem that *you* are being accused of seducing the rapist.
Even when police are sympathetic to you, it is their job to
investigate the crime with the same skepticism the defendant's attorney will show. You do not have to suffer
abuse from them, but you are naive if you believe that they
will show you the sympathy and concern that you need at
this time.

You should try to be as clear and consistent in your story
as possible, because the police will be doubtful if you
are not. You should tell them everything that you remember, whether it seems important or not. You will be taken
to the hospital, where you will be given the tests listed
above with the addition of a fluid sample to determine if
there is sperm in your vagina; if all the tests are not
given, you should demand that they are. Make sure that
the records made at the hospital are careful and complete,
and if you have extended bruises, you should have photo-
graphs taken of them, because doctors do not record them.
If the doctor has not noted something you feel is important,
tell her/him. You need the doctor's testimony to prosecute
your case.

When you decide to prosecute in rape cases, you are the
complainant. Usually the district attorney's office acts
as your lawyer. You do not need to hire a private lawyer
to prosecute your case, although you may want to have one
to counsel you during the proceedings. The D.A.'s office
makes the decision to prosecute or not, and generally decides to do so only when there is a good chance of getting
a conviction so that they will have a high conviction rate.
Understanding this may make it more comprehensible when you
feel as if you have fallen into a looking-glass world
where you are surrounded by men who identify with your
attacker.

The best defense that the rapist has is damaging information about your reliability as a witness. *Before* you call
the police, consider the accusations that may be leveled
against you. Some of the things that can put you in a
damaging situation are: If you are not a virgin; if you
are separated or divorced; if you were hitchhiking, are
mentally "unstable," or have been in trouble with the law.

Under law, your husband (even if you are separated) can never be accused of rape.

You will be asked to sign a complaint. You will have to describe your attacker to a police artist and identify him from "mug" shots or a lineup. Some police have been known to pressure women into identifying mug shots that are not definitely the rapist. Do not allow your testimony to be used to convict the wrong man. Remember, the rapist is still loose if they convict the wrong person! Frequently, women are asked to take lie detector tests. They are not necessarily reliable, and cannot be used as evidence in court. You do not have to take one if you do not want to. Be aware, however, that if the police do not believe you they will not be likely to make much of an attempt at prosecution.

Unfortunately, you must make up your mind whether or not you want to prosecute the rapist almost immediately after your attack. You should consider seriously whether or not the mental anguish and physical effort of prosecution is worth your while. Many women feel that it is essential to prosecute in as many cases as possible in order to put rapists behind bars, and stem the increasing incidence of rapes. Most rapists plan their rapes and are often repeaters, usually managing to accomplish several rapes before they are even brought to trial.

We do not mean to discourage women from reporting rapes. Realistically, however, we point out that prosecuting a rapist is a time-consuming and often grueling experience. While you must decide within minutes whether or not to sign a complaint, it may be months or even a year before your attacker is brought to trial. Every step of the way, the legal machine will operate in his defense, protecting him from your allegations and subjecting you to intensive scrutiny from the police, the courts, and the jury. If in fact you manage to bring a repeat offender to conviction, it may be worth it to you. There is no guarantee that this will be the end result, however. Only you can decide if your legal recourse is worth the effort. Undoubtedly, whether or not you have support and counsel from friends, family, or other women should play a part in your decision.

Indira Ghandi was discussing the increase in rape with several of her cabinet ministers. In the search for solutions, one minister suggested a curfew for women beginning at a certain hour of the evening. Indira Ghandi responded, "But if it

is the men who are doing the raping, shouldn't
it be a curfew for them, instead?"

Women Organized
Against Rape Handbook

SHARON

I was raped out of stupidity. Mine. I had hitch-
hiked almost all over the country, already a pretty
stupid thing to do, coming close to being raped,
but always managing to get out of it at the last
moment. This was when I was living with this man
in California. I had stopped sleeping with him,
using contraceptives, or so I thought. I had a
fight with him and decided to hitchhike the three
hundred miles or so to my grandparents' house.
Before I even got to the expressway I had decided
that that was stupid and that I might end up dead,
so instead I went into this hotel to use the phone
and see if I could get money for a bus. The phone
in the lobby wasn't working, and this man offered
to let me use the phone in his room. Even I should
have known better, but I was too upset to think
straight. He raped me. I didn't resist.

The worst part was that he locked me in his room
and left. I imagined that he would come back with
friends, or that he would do it again and kill me.
A friend of his had come and he let me go. I ran
down the street. It was eight or ten hours since
I left. I felt ashamed of myself, dirty, and stupid.
It was night and not a very safe part of the city.
I ran all the way home. When I got there no one
was there and I didn't have any keys. I didn't
want to tell anyone. I felt it was my fault.
Going to the police would have been the last thing
that I would have done. I figured they would probably have arrested me for prostitution or something.
Finally someone came home and I told them what had
happened. I cried for the first time, but it didn't
make me feel better. After that I slept a lot and
tried to block it out. For some kind of perverse
sort of reason I started sleeping, making love with,
the man that I was living with. (Maybe to feel
secure or to win back his approval of me.) Five
months later I had to have an abortion. I never
knew if it was because of the rape or not. I thought

*it probably wasn't. Up until they rushed me into the
hospital, I never had any medical treatment connected
with the rape at all. I felt more alone than I ever
had before. I didn't talk to anyone about it. The
abortion was as bad as the rape. No one helped me
through any of it.*

Self-Defense

Women In Transition And Self-Defense

If you have always depended on the protection of a man (your
father, brothers, boyfriends, husband), the experience of
separation or divorce may cause you to become interested in
self-defense for the first time. Having complete responsibility for yourself and your children may make it essential
that you begin to concern yourself with potential dangers
to you and them.

Almost all of us, of course, have experienced fear for our
safety at one time or another, although the illusion of
being "protected" is maintained especially in the middle
and upper classes. In the final analysis, who really protects us, and from whom? Or as Mae West said, "Every man
I've ever met wanted to protect me. Couldn't figure out
what from." Most of us have seen our "protectors" become
surprisingly like whoever they are protecting us from at
one time or another. Any woman who has been beaten or
abused by her husband or father or brother may feel that
his "protection" simply means that he will have the
privilege of assaulting her instead of a stranger.

In most cases, the only person who can really insure your
safety is you. The tools to this end are developing your
own physical strength, analyzing situations before they
become dangerous to you (in your home, in the street, on
public transportation), and having in advance a good idea
of the self-defense techniques you can and will use in
defending yourself. This chapter, of course, is no replacement for more complete self-defense information available
from other sources. In the bibliography in the back of the
book you will find books and pamphlets which more specifically and in greater detail discuss self-defense for women.

Self-Defense Classes And Martial Arts Training

The best means of self-defense for you may be martial arts
training or self-defense classes. Self-defense classes are

usually short-term and emphasize effective street-fighting techniques; martial arts classes give training in various oriental fighting techniques such as karate, judo, kung fu, aikido, etc., and require an ongoing commitment to train. Self-defense classes are often given in Ys and community centers. Or, there may be a women's class given by your local women's liberation group or center.

If the thought of building up your muscles, having to go to classes, and having to commit yourself to a long period of training before you can be sure of your ability to defend yourself seems undesirable or impractical to you, perhaps you should attend self-defense classes, especially those run by and designed for women. The martial arts do not necessarily give you immediate self-defense information. You should be aware, however, that self-defense is like any other athletic activity--it requires practice. Even if you choose "street-fighting" classes over martial arts training, you must be certain that you will practice the techniques, develop your physical stamina, and commit yourself to your development in order to have much of a guarantee of effectiveness.

The advantages of becoming involved in a martial arts training program over a long period of time are numerous. You will gain the opportunity to learn about your body's strength in a consistent, disciplined manner. You will be learning techniques that you may need to defend yourself, and you will be able to practice and perfect those techniques in your classes. You will probably learn to think of pain as something to have control over, instead of having to be paralyzed by the fear of it. You will improve your muscles, your reflexes, and your general state of health. You may learn for the first time to associate physical courage and aggressiveness with yourself. Probably you will begin to be aware of the potential for self-defense in situations you used to be intimidated by. Your confidence and strength may be increased. You should begin to feel that *you* have control over what happens to you. If you have classes with men, you will have the opportunity to compare yourself to them and to see their vulnerability.

Selecting A Self-Defense Class

- Learn what types of training are available at which schools (judo, karate, etc.) and the quality of training within their field. Decide which style is most appealing to you.

- Find out the time, length of classes, and number available and decide if you will have time to train often
  enough to make it worthwhile. (Ten classes, once a week,
  will probably not be sufficient to insure your ability
  to defend yourself--although it might be enough to help
  you decide if this is really what you want to do.)

- Be wary of any school that promises more than it can
  deliver (complete competence in several months, for
  example). No one can tell you in advance how quickly
  you will be able to advance in skill. (Several years
  are generally required to reach the upper belt level
  in most styles.)

- Learn what is emphasized in the school: exercises,
  meditation, free fighting, self-defense, tournaments.
  Is this what you want?

- Find out how students progress in the school. Most
  martial arts schools are highly structured, and while
  rank is not the same thing as skill, there should be
  a reasonable correlation between the two.

- Watch several classes. Decide if you feel comfortable
  there. Many classes are extremely disciplined, which
  in most cases is good, but look elsewhere if you are
  going to be too uncomfortable within the structure.
  Notice if the students have respect for and confidence
  in their instructor(s) and talk with them about how
  they feel.

- The chief instructor should have a black belt.

- The school should not cost more than $30 a month for
  three lessons a week.

Defending Yourself--Self-Defense And Prevention

Most women do not have the time, energy, or money to train
for extended periods of time in a martial art. If this is
true for you it does not mean that you will have to stay
home unless you are with a man or a group of people. There
are a number of self-defense techniques which you can and
should learn to protect yourself.

First, it is important to remove potential dangers from your
life whenever possible--keeping doors and windows locked,
opening the door only when you know who is there, not

putting your name on the mailbox or in the phone book as
Mary Jones, but as M. Jones, etc. It is also important to
develop a nose for danger and to avoid situations which
have potential for trouble whenever possible. This means
walking down well-lit streets, entering a public building
if a man is following you, etc. If you find yourself in
a dangerous situation, you must try to remain calm and
assess the situation.

• If you can leave the situation, then by all means do.

• If you are outside, and there are people nearby or a well-
  lit area, or houses, get to them as quickly as you can.

• Do not panic, but move as quickly as possible no matter
  what you have decided to do.

• Ask for help, scream *"Fire"* or *"Police"* (not *"Help"* or
  "Rape"), surprise your attacker, spit at him or do something he does not expect, and if there is somewhere to
  run to, run.

• If you cannot run away, do not try to talk him out of
  whatever he wants to do. Conversation may not help
  you, and it may encourage him, especially if you are
  pleading, acting helpless, etc. (If you talk to him
  in order to divert his attention, that is something
  else.)

• Try to remain as calm as possible, keep your body
  functioning, keep thinking, don't allow yourself to
  become hysterical.

If your attacker has gotten hold of you and seems unlikely
to respond to anything else, or if you are certain he means
to harm you, the only way out is to attack him before he
has the chance. (Do not attack him if he has a gun unless
you are suicidal. There are self-defense techniques to use
when faced with someone carrying a gun, but they take
extreme self-control and expertise and can result in
greater danger.) If you have to hurt him, you have got to
do it quickly, with great force, and must hurt him badly
enough that he can't pursue you.

• Don't indicate in advance what you are going to do.
  Don't swing your arm or leg back so that he can anticipate your blow.

- Don't flail about with your arms, beat on his chest, wave your limbs around, get off-balance. Use your fingers, fists, knees, feet, legs.

- Aim for the eyes, the nose, the temple, Adam's apple, behind the ear, under the breastbone, neck, kidneys, or knees. In most cases it is not advised to try to kick your attacker in the groin. That's what he expects you to do. If you kick him hard enough in the knee you may throw him off-balance and get free.

- Most women have much stronger legs than arms, and most American men are unused to being attacked with legs. Make sure that your kicks are direct, quick, and aren't obvious before you make them. Don't let him grab your foot and pull you down. Pull it back as fast as you kicked out.

- If you are going to hit him with your fist, extend the knuckle of your second finger and punch quickly and directly. You punch with the space between your joints. When you punch or kick remember it has to be incapacitating. He's not going to give you a second chance.

- Don't waste time worrying about him after you have broken his hold. He wasn't worrying about you, was he? *Run.*

At home, make sure that you have locks on most points of access. Insist that the entranceway and alcoves be lit and have locks on the doors to the outside. Know where the most likely points of entrance are and block them so that anyone breaking in will have to encounter other obstacles. (You can do this with plants, especially hanging ones, books, furniture, whatever.) Don't list your full name on the mailbox or doorbell. Don't let anyone in without knowing who they are. When the bell rings, say, "I'll get it, Harry," or something like that and when you go to the door always ask, "Who is it?" Leave your lights, television, or radio on when you are out. Don't have your name or address on your keys. If your purse is stolen and your keys and identification are in it, change the locks immediately.

On the street, especially at night, when possible have someone walk with you. Wear loose-fitting, comfortable clothes and shoes. Try to wear shoes that you can run in. Don't walk through dark areas if you can help it, close to shrubs or alleys, across deserted parking lots, close to parked automobiles. If you have to run to a well-lit place do, ring the bell, break the glass if you have to. If you are attacked and have a weapon, use it fast or get rid of it so that it can't be used against *you*. Many "safety" devices are not legal. If, however, you are carrying something that can be used as a weapon that is not illegal, such as hairspray, pepper, a pick or a comb with a sharp "tail," keys, a fingernail file, have it in your hand or readily accessible and you should use it quickly and run.

You should *not* hitchhike. One of the consequences of an increase in hitchhiking in California has been an accelera- tion of women being raped, maimed, and killed. Even as we write this, however, we know that women are hitchhiking in areas where they have no other means of transportation. Don't if you don't have to. If you do have to, at the least try not to hitchhike alone, at night, or in deserted areas.

Never accept a ride from two or more men, no matter what they look like. Begin to notice license plates, car makes and years, colors. Know where you are going and don't allow anyone to take you out of your way. Before you get into the car check to see if there are liquor or beer bottles in the car, whether the man is fully clothed, whether there is a door handle on your side of the car. If possible, take rides only from women.

If you have a car, pick up women hitchhikers. If you have any doubts about riding with someone, don't. If you are attacked while riding in a car, try to get out at a red light, force him to slow down, attract the attention of other motorists. If you are attacked and have no other choice, fight back with a lit cigarette, aim for his eyes, face, nose with any weapon available to you (the car's ashtray, a book, tools).

Becoming Not A Nice Lady

As we have been writing, and as you have been reading, it has been clear that none of these things is what a "lady" is expected to do. All of us grow up being insecure about our own physical strength and many of us have a hatred of violence. In fact, probably the major contribution to the increase in deaths of women of all ages at the hands of rapists and murderers is our conditioned passivity. As women, many of us prefer to be hurt than to strike out.

This cannot continue to be true. Women are not naturally
gentle, passive, and nonviolent. Women are soldiers and have
fought in combat in many nations. No matter how "decent"
you may have cause to think you are, if you are in a situation where your life is in jeopardy, you have to be able
to care enough for yourself to hurt your attacker before he
kills you. A lot of us find it easier to become enraged
when something happens to another woman than when it happens
to us. Without the firm resolve to defend yourself by any
means necessary, no self-defense technique in the world will
be effective. Remember, when it is done to you, it is done
to a woman. Each time a man is successful at rape, beatings,
or murder, another woman is put in danger. This is no time
to be a lady! Save yourself, save all of us.

KATE

*I had never been very coordinated in grade school or
anything, so I didn't really think I would make it
in karate. But I had almost been raped once, and it
really scared me, and besides, I don't have a car
and have to walk and take public transportation a
lot and was tired of being stared at and clucked at
and goosed on my way to work. So I started in this all-
women's class which was a good thing because there
were some other women who were just as clumsy as me.*

*At first everything I did looked like shit compared
to what the other students were doing, but I kept
going because it felt so good to* punch. *When I was
little I would fight some but it was always kicking.
When I was punching I really felt* tough! *One of the
hardest things for me was to really take it seriously
when we first started sparring with each other. I was
afraid to really hurt somebody, and if we did make contact we would usually giggle or back away. I'm better
at it now, but I still have trouble with that part.*

*Anyhow, I have only been taking karate for 5 months,
but I really feel different on the street. I'm not
sure whether I could actually defend myself, but I
feel a lot more confident and I think that men sense
that and don't bother me as much. (This isn't always
true, of course.) Another thing--before I started
taking karate I used to be dieting all the time
because I wanted to be thinner. Now that I am getting
exercise regularly I need to eat more but I don't
seem to be gaining weight. I'm not* thin, *but it*

*doesn't seem to matter so much that I don't look like
a model.   I'm more interested in getting my body to
work right for me when I need it.*

▶▶▶   *DIANA*

*Jack and I had been planning to get married in March
of '62, but we eloped when I went to visit him in
Florida where he was stationed in the Navy.   Perhaps
I had my doubts about marriage (or him?) even then,
because I remember thinking as we left the justice of
the peace, "My God, you've really done it.   Now the
only way out is divorce."   That was in September of
'61, and I was not quite 19 years old.*

*What motivated my first marriage was probably a com-
bination of things.   I was a very rebellious teen-ager,
very dissatisfied with my life at home.   Marriage was
an escape, possibly a way to strike back at my parents.
And, of course, I was "in love."   Women, I assumed, got
married and had kids.   That's the way things were.
That's what you read and heard and saw around you.   I
had always said that anyone could get married, the
trick was to find the right person to marry.   (Guess I
sure missed that trick!)*

*My parents were against the marriage.   Aside from not
approving of Jack they were pressuring me to go on to
college.   Therefore, of course, I didn't.   Even college
my mother saw in terms of finding a suitable husband
with the proper class background, education, financial
resources, etc.   And at worst a degree from the right
college would give me something acceptable to fall back
on (until I found a replacement) should anything happen
to that husband or if we divorced.*

*Jack and I were married not quite three years when we
were divorced.   During that time we had two sons.   I
guess our marriage really started breaking up when he
was discharged from the Navy.   Until then we were never
together more than several weeks at a time, if that long.
Even when he was in port, there would be many nights and
some weekends that he had to stay on the ship.   So although we had been married for two years, we had not
yet really lived together on a full-time basis.   It
was not too difficult to perpetuate a very unrealistic
picture of a "doll's house" kind of marriage under
those conditions.   Aside from being able to play the*

part of "perfect wife" or "perfect husband," the absences made his homecoming a special time when we each genuinely wanted to go out of our way to do things for each other.

I guess Jack really did expect a lot of waiting on him, but since I wanted to do it, it didn't matter. I was still playing house. Maybe part if it too was that since he was away so much, I had room to be me. I could do the things I wanted to do without having to consider whether or not he would object.

After his discharge, I could not possibly maintain the image he had of "perfect wife" day in and day out even if I had wanted to. He objected to anything that took me out of the house--or even out of the role of housewife. For example, I had been doing a little bit of sculpting, painting, etc., and he refused to accept my continued interest in it now that he was home. I began to see how insecure a person he really was, and I guess anything that freed me from the house-trap was pretty threatening to him. It got to the point where I practically had to ask his permission to go to the bathroom. I found it impossible to get him to talk with me about it or say anything other than it was my fault, and my friends, parents, or whoever were poisoning my mind.

Jack, being quite a dramatist, didn't make adjusting to a life without him easy. I would often discover him standing, hidden by the bushes, trying to overhear my conversations when I was out on the porch with my parents or friends. Or he might appear, unexpectedly, as I was taking a walk or out somewhere. He often would telephone with some new issue or story he thought might upset me. The whole thing was pretty unnerving.

Then came what was probably the real adjustment stage for me. It could get pretty lonely. Christopher and Patrick were only one and two years old, and I wasn't working, so I was with them in my apartment most of the time. The other people in my building were all married couples. I found that being a divorced woman excludes you from a lot of things. I think much of this was due to our couple-oriented society where no one knows quite what to do with an extra woman at their dinner party or whatever. Then there always seems to be the wife who thinks you are after her husband (or her husband is after you!).

*The time I found tough for me was along about 5:00
p.m. when all the husbands came home and everyone
disappeared into their own private, happy (I imagined)
family. I envied them and the cozy feeling they seemed
to have, although I didn't wish I were back with Jack.
Most of the friends I saw were my friends. I lost
contact with the people Jack and I met when we were
together, the ones who saw us as a couple (or me as
Jack's wife).*

*I began dating. I started doing some painting again.
I played the kind of music I liked and read the kinds
of things I wanted. I didn't have to worry that the
children or I would do something that would send Jack
into a rage. In spite of the times I felt tied down
having two children, it was good having them there.
There were times when they were a comfort to me. I
didn't see myself as a failure because my marriage
hadn't worked out, and I assumed that I would probably
remarry eventually.*

*I met George, my second husband, about the time my
divorce became final. I started seeing him, but not
exclusively. I think my father's death that winter
was an important factor in my deciding to marry him.
My father had liked George and felt that he was a fine,
upstanding, responsible man who knew where he was going.
My relationship with George didn't sweep me off my
feet but slowly grew to mean more and more. That was
a contrast to the way Jack and I started out. Then
too, he wasn't bad in bed, either! That seemed like
a pretty good combination to me.*

*We were married in July of '65, one year after my
divorce. I thought I was being very sensible at the
time. George was insistent about wanting to adopt
the children. Jack never saw or contacted them, and
at that point he was about $1,000 in arrears with child
support and was under order to appear in court. What
it boiled down to was that he "sold" the children to
us. He would sign the papers we needed for adoption
if we would not try to collect the money he owed. That
was fine with me, too. I felt that what made a father
was not a matter of the law or biology but the way you
felt and the things you did for a child.*

*George was starting his second year of graduate school
and was very much impressed with the whole intellectual,
academic community there. I think he thought of me as*

a diamond in the rough that he could polish a bit and turn into the perfect professor's wife in spite of the fact that I lacked a college education and had married only a lowly sailor before. What really bothered me was the lack of communication between us. Most of the time was spent working in his study, and he said that he didn't have time to discuss our difficulties-- there were more important things he had to do. We had been married about two years when I started seriously planning to leave him. About three months before I actually left, I discovered I was pregnant. That really threw me for a while until I decided I wanted the baby and that didn't necessarily mean I had to have George, too. I left in December of 1967. I was really happy. When my leaving became a reality, George was quite upset and wanted a reconciliation, which later we had. Adam was born in June of 1968.

The next winter I became severely depressed. I was hospitalized twice within a period of a few months. The first time was for five days and I got very little treatment. The second time my psychiatrist saw me frequently while I was there. It was really an escape for me from all the pressures outside. I remember my doctor as a sensitive, talented therapist as well as a wonderfully warm human being. George was just great during the time I was depressed. He gave me a lot of support through the whole thing. Of course, being depressed, I wasn't very threatening to him.

Later when I started doing things I was interested in, he really couldn't handle it even though he thought that was what he wanted. He really didn't want me that independent. He needed me strong enough to take care of him but not so strong as to be a threat. As I got better, things got worse between George and me. I guess I outgrew the relationship and our needs no longer dovetailed. I became aware of things I wanted. I had gained confidence in me. I became involved at the schools the boys went to. I started teaching art classes to children, I was involved in starting a child care center, and so on.

At this point George and I discussed divorce, and what it boiled down to was that we couldn't afford to live separately. Perhaps it was selfish on my part, but there he was with a Ph.D. that I had helped him (finan- cially) to get. Even the car was about to fall apart. He refused to ride in it because he thought it was *unsafe, but the children and I had to use it. And there I was, a high school dropout with three children and no job experience to speak of.*

One evening George telephoned and said that he wouldn't be coming home. That was it. This was in May of '72. We have been separated almost 2½ years now. I am getting $350 a month, and I hear I am lucky to get that. Hopefully we will be divorced.

I don't want to screw George. I really like him. He's not a bad guy, but we just can't make it together. And it's tough when your occupation has always been "house-wife." George and I had come a long way in communicating with each other, but I could not have gone back to the "old me." The "new me" was too important to give up in order to save the marriage.

It was a relief in a lot of ways, sometimes even exhiliarating, once he left. There were times that were lonely, but I think that "new me" helped in my adjustment. It's bound to be at least a bit lonely if only due to habit (having another body around). I think knowing yourself, while not a cure-all for your problems, lets you feel in control. That doesn't mean you might not ever repeat some of your old mistakes, but I think you recognize what's happening and make your own decisions. You don't feel so helpless.

At present I am living with a man. I don't know whether it will be a forever-after thing. We have problems we need to work out, and there's always the possibility we can't work them out. Will we get married? I don't know. I don't think being legally married guarantees anything but a lot of legal hassles, and it perpetuates an institution that needs a complete overhaul. The endurance of and the commitment involved in a relationship is not something you can legislate. In theory the idea of sharing the rest of my life with one person is very appealing. In practice I wonder whether it is possible or even natural.

That doesn't mean that I might not try. While I am not thinking that a long-lasting relationship is doomed from the start, neither am I thinking of something as intangible as "forever." "Forever" is a long, long time.

EIGHT: REACHING OUT

SO YOU WANT TO START A PROGRAM FOR WOMEN IN TRANSITION

Women from many different parts of the country have written
or visited the Women in Transition project in Philadelphia
to find out how we set up our program. They are interested
in doing something similar and want to know how to go about
it. In this section we will tell you what we have learned
about starting a project and growing with it.

Women in Transition, Inc., began in the winter of 1971 when
eight women connected with the Women's Liberation Center in
Philadelphia got together to plan a program for the many
separated and divorced women and single mothers who were
calling the Center. That spring and summer we got two small
grants which enabled us to hire two staff women. Except
for one period when we were on unemployment because our
funds ran out, we have been funded continuously since then,
and have grown to a staff of six. The program has undergone
many changes since it began. We have grown by trial and
error, and have set down in this section some of our most
successful ideas in the hope that we can spare you some of
our mistakes.

There are many variations of the "women in transition"
theme--programs for urban and rural areas, programs for
older or younger women, women on welfare, professional
women, and others. We will describe our own program, which

has served urban women, predominantly between the ages of
25 and 50, from middle- and low-income ranges. We hope
you will feel free to adapt our model to the resources of
your own group and the needs of the women you want to
help.

Deciding Who You Are And What You Can Handle

Probably the most important decisions you have to make concern what you want to do and, especially important, whether you have the resources to succeed. Some of the most
exciting ideas for women's programs have foundered because
there were not enough resources--womanpower, money, and
supporting services--to keep them going. The need for all
kinds of women's services is so great that most of us are
tempted to try too much too soon.

Some of the questions you should ask yourselves in planning
a program include:

1.   Is there a need for your program, or is some other
      group already meeting the same need?

2.   Who is *really* interested in working on your program?

3.   Can the interested women be counted on to do the
      work?

4.   Realistically, how much time do the interested women
      have to give?

5.   Do you have a group of women, however small, who are
      willing to work for nothing for a while (or maybe for-
      ever) to get the project underway?

6.   Is there a basic agreement as to the goals of your
      project? Do you have clearly in mind which women you
      will serve? Try writing down the goals and the target
      group to clarify your answers to these questions.

7.   Have you agreed on how to structure the project? Will
      you work collectively? Will the staff be paid? How
      much? Equal pay for all?

8.   Do some of the women in your group have skills and
      knowledge which will be helpful to the project, and
      are they willing to share these? Are those without
      these skills willing to learn? If nobody knows any-

thing, are you willing to learn together?

9.   If there are differences in class, race, sexual orien-
      tation, and/or politics, have you recognized them and
      talked about how these differences will affect the
      group? Do you respect each other?

10. Do you have a process for working out problems which
      arise as the group goes along?

11. How will you recruit and train new members for your
      staff and supporting groups?

Shaping The Project

After your group has passed some of these preliminary hur-
dles, it's time to figure out just what you want to do.
Each group will make different decisions based on the need
in its community, the interests and skills of the group
members, and how much time your group expects to devote to
the project. We, of course, set out to do *everything* at
first, from emergency housing to job referrals, child care,
legal help, and emotional support. We quickly learned
(by means of our short tempers and our great discourage-
ment) that we were spreading ourselves too thin and not
doing anything very well.

We have since narrowed our program to problems related to
separation, divorce, and single parenthood, and focused on
two basic areas--emotional support and legal help. We
decided that other supports, as much as they were needed,
were either being done by other groups or were too demanding for us to take on at that time. Employment counseling
and emergency housing, although very much needed by women
in transition, went down the drain, and we began to concentrate on things that were most needed *and* possible for
us to do. Once we defined our two major focuses--emotional
support and legal help--the sailing has been comparatively
smooth. Define and refine!

We are still struggling with a dilemma that you will also
probably face: "service project" vs. "organizing project."
That is, you want to provide a needed service, but you also
want to develop a model for other groups--you want to have
a political as well as a humanitarian effect. You may
eventually decide, as we have, that since you can only
reach a tiny handful of all the women who need your services, you will also try to have an impact on traditional

institutions and agencies serving these women--mental health centers, welfare agencies, and the like.

DEAR WOMEN'S LIBERATION:

I am a forty-year-old woman, married eight years, and living in an intolerable situation with a horrible, frightening man, who threatens my life and says he will destroy me mentally. He makes enough money and provides material things but also worships money above human life. I have one child of his, six years old, and when I married him I had a girl, who is now sixteen. I was never married before, but I was not loose-moraled then and I am not now. He is trying to destroy this young girl's life, although she is a good girl who goes to school and has a part-time job to pay for her clothes. He refers to her, and always has, as "Your Bastard." He has done this since she was eight.

I have no one to help me, and I have no job so I can take the children and leave. And I am also very unsure of myself and afraid my bad nerves and anxiety will cause a breakdown. But staying with him, I am afraid he will drive me to suicide or a breakdown. I am writing to you in desperation for some advice on the action I could or might take. This man has also, besides mental cruelty, hit me and my daughter many times. Her life, and what is left of mine, is being destroyed by a money-worshipping anal individual who hates everyone. No one is allowed in his home, children's friends or my friends or relatives, and I believe his parents (who live up the street) encourage him in this. He also drinks very heavily. He does not give me any money so I cannot go to a lawyer. I would be grateful for any advice or help you could give me against this maniac. Please help.

Sincerely,
Leona

DOROTHY

I have been married for almost fourteen years. I have a husband who has an alcohol problem who will not or cannot stop drinking. Although I am opposed to walking out on a marriage, I may get to the point when I have no choice for my own sanity, and I want to know if I feel I must do so just where I stand.

MARIE

I'm 21, and I've been married less than a year; I've never felt so broken in my life. And I don't want to spend the rest of my life the way it is now. I figure it's better that I end my marriage now while my husband and I are still young and able to keep on trucking in our separate ways instead of waiting it out a few years, and thereby possibly damaging ourselves. But it's very hard to always know what to feel and do.

Your group has to decide for itself what to focus on. Our only concrete recommendation is to *start small*. You can always expand when you get the resources and energy. Some groups which are operating programs for women in transition are focusing on emergency housing for women who need temporary places to stay until they get their lives organized. Some groups aren't interested in providing ongoing services but have come together just to write a supplement for this book in their own area. Other groups are providing legal services, and still other groups are working on the money problems of women in transition--welfare, job training, and employment counseling. Most of these projects provide some sort of discussion groups along with whatever special services they offer, since one of the best ways to help women through a crisis period is to provide a place for them to meet and talk with other women in similar situations.

You should remember that the kinds of services you decide to offer will determine what kinds of women you will serve. If you are interested in serving a particular group of women, find out what their needs are before you decide what services to offer. For example, poor women are less likely to come to a consciousness-raising group than to a session which gives them information they can use in dealing with day-to-day problems--legal information about support court or welfare rights. If your discussion groups consist primarily of young, white, and middle-class women, the poor, black, and older women will probably feel too uncomfortable (or bored, since chances are the group is not dealing with their real problems at all) to continue meeting. In our program in Philadelphia, most of the women attending the discussion groups are white and middle-class, although in some areas of the city the groups have some middle-class black women. Older women have had varied experiences in

our groups, some saying they would prefer to be in a group
with more older women. The clinic for women who wanted to
file their own divorces without lawyers was attended primarily by black women between 18 and 60.

When it became clear to us that our centrally located discussion groups were not helping poor women, we designed
the Outreach component of our program. This component
consists of a series of workshops conducted in housing projects or community centers. The workshops are usually
designed primarily around legal rights of poor women--
separation and divorce, support court, welfare, common-
law marriage, "illegitimate" children, etc. Much to our
surprise, once the legal issues have been discussed, the
participants quickly turn to many of the same kinds of
problems as are discussed in the consciousness-raising
groups. Some of these have turned into ongoing emotional
support groups within the neighborhood or project. In
these cases we provide training in group leadership skills
for interested residents.

In other words, you're not going to save the world--or even
the women of the world. Strive to set realistic goals;
small successes are worth more than grandiose failures.
One road to small successes is to identify a particular
group of women you are most qualified to help. It's a
pretty safe guess that your task force group is going to be
primarily white, well-educated, and/or middle-class. Who
else has the time, energy, and financial security to work
on such a project? A corollary to this composition of your
group is that you are most likely to meet success in working
with women from a similar background--and most likely to
meet disaster trying to work with women from vastly different backgrounds. One solution is to seek more diversity in
your task force group. Unfortunately, we have no magic
solution for attracting and supporting talented and
articulate women from poor or minority backgrounds or
older women. One solution we are trying presently is to
hire and train women from these backgrounds as new positions
on our own staff open up. This, of course, is not much
help to those of you who cannot yet afford any paid staff.

Structure: Working Collectively

"After the revolution there will be no janitors, typists,
or maids. Everyone will do her own dirty work," is an oft-
quoted plaintive reminder of our present-day dilemma.
Women's projects usually try to avoid a division between

those women (usually with middle-class backgrounds and
education) who do the interesting work and those (with less
education or fewer middle-class advantages) who do the
"dirty work"--typing, mimeographing, taking out the trash.
We don't believe that's a healthy division--with the result
that we are *all* part-time janitors, maids, and typists. The
sad fact is that there is a phenomenal amount of routine,
boring work involved in running your own program. We have
organized ourselves collectively, which means that everyone
is paid the same, has equal say in policy decisions, and has
a similar amount of routine, boring work to do.

In the beginning there were only two staff people, and they
both did everything. As the staff grew, we began to diver-
sify so that everyone was responsible for a particular area
of the program. We now have seven full-time staff people who
meet in weekly staff meetings to exchange information, make
changes in the program operation, work out financial or
interpersonal problems, and the like. Sometimes it seems
like we spend more time in meetings talking about what we
have to do and how to organize it than we spend actually
doing it. We even had meetings to discuss how each chapter
of this book should be revised! Sometimes this method of
operation seems terribly inefficient, but none of us wants
a hierarchy in which a boss tells the workers what to do.
Efficiency may be a dangerous goal--after all, Mussolini
made the trains run on time.

In addition to the staff, collectively structured, we also
have a Planning Group for the program, made up of staff and
others connected with the program in different ways--ther-
apists and others from the Emotional Support group, legal
workers from the Legal Group, and former women in transition.
The Planning Group acts like a board of advisers and helps
with policy decisions and major problems. As our program
grows more complex, however, it becomes more and more difficult to keep the Planning Group sufficiently informed so
that it can understand the problems and make meaningful
decisions for the programs. At this point in our history
we are somewhat confused as to the role of the Planning Group.

Dealing With Power And Class Differences

In theory, all staff members and members of the various
working groups share equal power in our organization. In
reality, some women are more influential than others by
virtue of their personal style, their background, or their
experience and knowledge. It has been difficult for us to

admit to and understand those differences in power and to keep them from becoming oppressive.

We have also had to admit that what were initially passed off as "personality conflicts" are in fact often much more significant conflicts, based on class and race differences. For example, we have felt a lot of tension over apparently trivial things like "punctuality"--and more serious things like meeting deadlines. The white middle-class women in our group felt that the black and low-income women were being "irresponsible" when they arrived at meetings a half hour late or failed to complete a writing project on time. The black and low-income women were, in turn, feeling judged and condemned by white middle-class standards which did not take into account the many outside pressures and responsibilities they felt.

It is impossible to resolve such conflicts without talking about the differences in life-style, opportunities, and out-side obligations which help to determine how much and what kind of energy each woman is going to be able to put into your group. For example, deadlines and meeting times cannot be as sacred to women with children or women without cars as they are to those who have more control over their own time. Differences in speaking and writing style and different ways of meeting and working with people should be recognized and valued. Writing may be a special form of torture to women without college educations, but women with fine educations can learn a lot about being more assertive from those whose grammar is not so polished.

Working out differences like these involves a lot of struggle; it requires both patience and respect for each other, and a great deal of honest self-criticism. Unless your group is totally homogeneous, conflicts arising out of race and class differences are likely to occur. We believe it is best to be as open as possible about such differences, and to try to use them to make yours a program with enough diversity to serve women from many different backgrounds.

A Few Words To The Wise

Congratulations! You've figured out what you have to offer and who you will offer it to; you've found a staff and decided what kind of working structure you want. You've even talked about how to resolve problems that haven't occurred yet! Now for office space and a telephone--right? Wrong. This may seem backward, but a telephone is the *last* thing you need.

Why? Because telephones eat time and energy. They require
elaborate schedules so that someone is always sitting by
waiting to help the first woman in transition who calls for
help. After all, if you're set up to give her support when
she needs it, you can't afford to make her call back three
or four times.

Once you have a telephone you're obligated to see that it
is answered during the times you are officially open for
business. We finally decided to limit the hours for answering general calls and would suggest you consider doing the
same. An answering service or message-taking machine can
be used when you are not answering. Women will soon learn
when they can reach you, and you'll be freed from the phone
to do the rest of your organizational work.

The same restraint goes for office space. Of course you
need it, and you need it as soon as you've got work to do
as a group. But unless you are operating a drop-in center,
you need just enough space for a few desks, cabinets, and
a small meeting area. Consider this your working-meeting-
thinking space, not a meeting place for women from all over
the area. You can always arrange to use other facilities
for large meetings.

Remember: During the earliest stages of your program, your
time might best be spent writing proposals, getting oper
ating funds and planning your program. Will you start by
offering discussion groups and emotional support, or legal
services? Do you have the resources to do both? How should
you advertise? And on and on . . . . Program planning
takes time; you need more than a list of goals and crisis-
resolving techniques.

Money

If your group has been together for any length of time at
all, you have already discovered how important emotional
support can be. You may even have resolved several crises
in this area. Wonderful. Now for the hatpin to your rose-
colored balloon: economic support--survival--money. Where
is it going to come from? How much do you need? How long
can you last without it?

We have discovered, much to our displeasure, that not only
can we not survive long without it, but that actively seek-

ing money to support our program is a never-ending job. It's
right up there with taking out the trash and mimeographing
on our list of things that nobody wants to do but everybody
has to.

Different groups support themselves in different ways. Some
use a pledge system in which women who want to support the
project contribute a certain amount every month. Others
raise funds by maintaining a speaker's bureau or bookstore.
Some raise money sporadically at garage sales, bake sales,
or benefit concerts, plays, or movies. Most of our money
has been raised through grants from private foundations, so
this is what we feel most qualified to tell you about. If
you are interested in other methods, check the bibliography
for this chapter.

Grantswomanship

We are still not sure how we managed to get our first grant,
but it certainly got us off and rolling. It was a small
grant from a women's church group. And although it wasn't
really enough to keep us going for very long, once we had
gotten funded, other foundations seemed to have confidence
in us and gave us money. Probably we got that first grant
because, first, we had a good idea for a service which was
much needed and didn't already exist, and second, we had a
well-written proposal which listed all the credentials we
could collectively muster. Credentials are golden keys.
If the women in your original group don't have impressive
credentials, you might think about forming an honorary board
of advisors who would do no work and have no power, but who
would lend you their names for the purposes of fundraising
This idea worked for us--although we were somewhat surprised
that one of our most prestigious board members, when contacted to help with fundraising, had only the vaguest re-
collection of our project. If you are going to borrow
credentials in this manner, it seems like a good idea to
keep the credentials-holders informed of your program's
activities.

We have concentrated on private foundations because government funding involves more red tape than we care to deal
with at this point. Eventually, we need to move in that
direction because government funding means more money for
longer periods. The obvious drawback to federal money is,
of course, that you are at the mercy of the political
climate in the nation.

In general, private foundations have been reluctant to give money to women's groups because they are nervous about funding innovative programs in the first place, and because they don't take women's problems seriously or can't imagine that women could successfully operate a worthwhile program without male guidance. Recently a few foundations have ventured into the area of women's projects--usually by funding "safe" projects such as reports and studies on child care, education, or legal reform. We have always described Women in Transition, Inc., as a social service program, which in fact it is, although it is also a lot more than that. Foundations have had experience with social service programs and are more likely to understand and fund these than something that sounds suspiciously new (or worse yet--something they can't understand).

Tips For Fundraising

The brief checklist below reflects our own experience, and is very sketchy. Get the basics from the sources listed in the bibiography for this chapter.

1. Start with a good idea.

2. Find allies. These might include:

    People on boards of foundations.

    Recognized community leaders.

    Church people.

    Professionals and technicians in your field (e.g., law, mental health, community organizing, employment).

    Form an advisory group; use it for introductory interviews with foundations. Get people who have a working knowledge of the funding game.

    Talk with groups who have been funded and ask how they did it.

    Use anyone who can help you!

3. Write a proposal:

    Don't mail it at random to different foundations.

Do talk with a possible foundation first about whether it might be interested, and write a proposal tailored to their interests.

Read "What Makes a Good Proposal" (listed in the bibliography for this chapter), then write your own.

> Stud it with credentials; show how the project would be structured; give job descriptions.

> Don't be too innovative; describe what you want to do in terms which will be understood and acceptable to the conservative people who give away money.

4. Approach:

community foundations

company foundations

family foundations

individual donors--those with a few hundred dollars to donate, and those who will endow you with long-term bequests.

Cultivate--that is, get the name of your group well known, go to conferences and other gatherings where you are likely to meet people who could help you. Try to remember: You aren't selling out--you're raising money to support a project to help women.

5. How to approach your targets:

Through your allies and friends, then

In person.

Be honest about your program while trying to relate it to the interest or purpose of the foundation.

Remember: People give to people--not to projects, no matter how good they look on paper.

Concentrate on one target at a time. Use the rifle, not the scatter gun.

Dress well (i.e., conservatively).

6.   Et Cetera

Get incorporated. This is a bother and can be expensive
unless you find a friendly lawyer. But it's advisable
because foundations won't give to groups unless they are
tax-exempt, and you have to be incorporated to apply for
tax-exempt status. This is because foundations want to
know exactly what they are giving to. Until you are tax-
exempt, you may be funded through a conduit (a tax-exempt
group which receives the money and then turns it over
to you). You may find that many foundations are reluctant to fund this way, because they don't know exactly
who you are when they send their checks to a conduit.
The whole idea, of course, is for foundations to write
off their charitable contributions to tax-exempt organizations so they don't have to pay taxes on the money.

Go for tax-exempt status yourself. Use influential
lawyers and others to help you. Until then, use an
established conduit if you can.

After you get the money:

> Have a good bookkeeping system and *document all
> spending*.

> Keep your foundations up to date on your activities.
> Send them reports, renew personal contacts.

> Use the media to become well known. Hold press
> conferences, develop contacts with newspeople, go
> on radio and TV shows.

> Send newsletters to your constituency, have open
> houses.

7.   How to survive once you've been funded:

Foundations usually give "seed" money for 3 years or less.

Government funding looks bad right now, but investigate
it.

Find one or more individuals willing to give long-term
bequests.

Change to a fee-charging basis?

Let us know what you decide to do because we don't
know either.

You're off! All the hard work and planning has paid off.
You've got a modest grant, a small staff, and a modest tele-
phone-answering schedule. At this point you're free to
implement your own program to meet the needs of the women
you decide to serve. Once again, there's a tremendous need
for all kinds of services, but we feel qualified to talk only
about the two areas we decided to specialize in--emotional
support and legal help.

PROVIDING EMOTIONAL SUPPORTS

Perhaps the most important thing we can do is to provide an
opportunity for women in transition to share their experiences with other women in transition. For most women, a
means of contacting other women who are dealing with similar
problems and making similar discoveries about their own lives
is more valuable than a professional shoulder to cry on.
And if your goal is to help women become whole, independent
persons, being a point of contact with peers is more valuable than telling a woman what to do.

We believe a woman takes an important step toward becoming
a whole, independent person when she can begin to see that
her own situation is not unique, but shared by many other
women. We have experimented with several ways of helping
women in transition to reach this understanding, and have
found short-term discussion groups work best for us. This
series of discussions also helps to overcome the isolation
and guilt many women are feeling at the end of a marriage.
The discussions, each of which focuses on a specific topic
like "Why did I marry?", also make it possible for women
to understand the social and cultural forces which shape
the experiences of all women in transition.

These are basically self-help groups, where peers counsel
and give support to each other, but there are also two
group "sisters,"trained in group skills, who act as
"facilitators" for the group. For women who need more
intensive help than can be provided in a peer-group setting,
we maintain a list of women therapists. The following
are some of the things we have learned about providing
emotional supports for women in transition.

Screening

Whatever kind of project you develop, you will need to have some idea of how to handle the calls you receive. It is advisable to have some kind of screening process so you will be able to refer women you can't possibly help to other sources of support. You will probably want to have some kind of "intake form" to help you get the information you need in order to make this decision. Don't throw up your hands just because you have no formal training in the area of mental health. It is possible to learn how to decide from a casual conversation whether a woman would get more out of a discussion group or a one-to-one interview with a mental health professional.

If you are planning to provide emotional supports for women in transition, it is a good idea to have a woman with mental health skills, training and/or experience affiliated with your project. If you are lucky she will work for free as a consultant to your program. This person can be invaluable in helping you develop some guidelines for screening and counseling women, and can act as a backup if you have particular questions about how to handle a situation. She can also help you train new "group sisters" in group leadership techniques. We want to stress, however, that you should not always defer to a therapist because she is an "expert." Her training plus your sensitivity to other women and the combined experience of both should make a strong emotional support component for your program.

General Counseling Guidelines

The following information is meant simply to be used as a guideline for helping women who may call or come in to your office. There are no set rules in counseling. There are some skills that can be learned from experience and feedback from others. Common sense and your own intuition are some of the most valuable and worthwhile skills you will need. Instead of worrying about whether you are "doing it right," try to relax and relate to your client as spontaneously as possible.

The following suggestions are in no particular order. They represent what we consider some of our most important lessons in "counseling," learned by trial and error from hundreds of women in transition.

1. Listen. Listen first. Don't be in a hurry to give
    advice. Try to understand what is underneath the words,
    what the person is feeling.

2. You need to be calm. If you can't be calm, find someone
    who can be. As you listen, try to be accepting. If
    you're calm and listening, you can start responding.
    Try to help the woman clarify her situation.

3. Don't put words into people's mouths. Clarify by re-
    stating what she has said and by asking leading questions
    which allow her to clarify further.

4. If you don't understand what she is saying, tell her.
    If you feel confused, chances are she is too. Say
    things like, "I really don't think I understand what
    you are saying," or "I'm very confused by what you said."

5. Follow your hunches and your feelings. They're almost
    always right. Get in touch with what you feel, then
    think about it. If you feel sad, chances are your
    caller does too. If you feel anxious or scared, it may
    well be because she has communicated these feelings to
    you without being able to name them herself.

6. If someone is rambling, ask exactly what the problem is
    and how you can help. If someone can't be at least
    somewhat specific and direct, it may indicate more
    complicated problems.

7. Know what you don't know. Know how to get hold of the
    information that you need.

8. Don't just accept a fantastic story, or one that seems
    quite incredible to you. There are times when people
    are trying to see how much nonsense will be tolerated.
    Be honest. Tell your caller her situation is hard to
    believe and ask for more details.

9. Try to be somewhat objective. Don't oversympathize.
    If you do a lot of the talking, she can avoid dealing
    with her problems and just start agreeing with you.
    That may make you feel great, but, in the long run, it
    won't help anyone else.

10. Get more detailed information about her living situa-
    tion. Who lives with her? Does she feel close to the
    people she lives with? What sources of emotional
    support does she have in addition to the program?

11. What about her friends? Is she isolated? What are her
     friends like and what do they enjoy doing together? Do
     they understand and support her now?

12. It's O.K. to ask about any history of emotional problems
     if you suspect there are some. It is better to be direct
     than to hedge around. Ask questions like, "Have you ever
     been on medication for emotional problems, ever been
     hospitalized?", if they are on your mind.

13. If you are talking to someone in person look closely:
     Can she make eye contact with you? Is she relaxed? Does
     she sit still or is she constantly fidgeting? Note any
     other "body language" which may indicate severe depression
     or extreme anxiety.

14. Beware of bold (and bald) accusations. Ask, "What doctor/
     lawyer/judge did that to you, and when?" Generally if
     someone blames all her problems on others, there may be
     more serious problems than she wishes to admit.

15. If someone is very upset, be very rational, concrete,
     and more directive. Tell her, "I strongly advise you do
     this tonight and that tomorrow morning."

16. If someone is in your office and starts getting violent,
     deal with it. Don't try to ignore her; someone may
     get hurt. Reassure her that you won't hurt her and that
     you know what you are doing. Be firm and reasonable, not
     threatening or screaming. Call the police if absolutely
     necessary.

Training For Initial Interviews

You might try role playing some of the typical situations,
keeping the above suggestions in mind. Ask someone with
training and experience in crisis intervention and/or groups
to conduct a training session for your group dealing with some
of the more complex problems related to:

depressions

suicide threats and attempts

drug overdoses

psychoses

paranoia

bad trips (side effects of hallucinogens, speed, barbiturates, narcotics)

side effects from common medications women might be taking (including tranquilizers).

Setting Up Small Groups

The group experience we offer is divided into two stages: First, there is a four-week "orientation" group. During these four weeks, six to ten women meet with two "group sisters" (who act as "facilitators") at a regular meeting place and time. Then, after the four weeks, if the group members want to continue, the "group sisters" become more like resources and observers to two more sessions, then the group continues without the "sisters." The group now begins to meet in the houses and neighborhoods of group members. The "sisters" are available at any time as resources if the group gets stuck. If only several women from a given orientation group want to continue, they go into another group.

Although the subject matter for "orientation" groups is structured, we leave room for the immediate needs of the women in each group. The topics focus on four major areas we feel are most important to women going through separation or divorce. They include:

1. Separation: What does it feel like to become a separate person? What are your fears, your excitements, your goals? This discussion provides a chance for group members to shed some of the feelings of isolation and share some of the excitement they may, up to this time, have been feeling quite guilty about.

LEE

I finally admitted I really wanted out, that my husband was too passive to try to work things out--he did something constructive only after I said I must have a separation. I realize now that he never could have without my moving first. I face a struggle harder than some of my sisters and easier than many others, but the seeds of strength began with my therapist (male) and grew with the women in my Women in Transition group.

JENNY

*Thank you. The support and warmth helped my hurt
from my husband walking out and leaving me. This group
opened up the whole world of women to me as being worthwhile people. I have always only had a very few women
friends. Now I am seeking women out and relating to them
on a more meaningful level. I will always be grateful
to you.*

ALICE

*The group as a whole was very enlightening and helpful
to me. For the first time I had a chance to talk about
myself with women who were really interested. It was
nice to know I was not alone and also that I was not
boring anyone with my problems. The group helped me to
gain back my self-confidence. Now I know if a problem
should arise I have some friends I can discuss these
matters with. Also, they give me confidence that I can
solve the problems on my own.*

LIZ

*I think that the thing that was most helpful for me was
the sharing of experiences which made me realize that I
was not alone in my thoughts or feelings. At times it was
hard to relate to other people's life stories, but in
general the commonality of our experiences was great
enough to make me want to listen and understand. The
group sisters got the group started and, I think, speeded
up the process of becoming acquainted with one another.
I'm sure that this would have happened if we had stayed
together long enough without them, but they provided a
necessary framework to overcome the awkwardness of a
group of strangers.*

*The group is also a good place to meet people and devel-
op friendships. I know that is something that I feel I
wanted to do because my circle of friends had narrowed
quite a bit during my marriage, and being out of school
during the summer makes it difficult for me to find new
people.*

*In general I think the group has been a positive ex-
perience for me. I've always had a feeling of being
isolated in my experiences, and it is reassuring to know
I am not. I have also learned a great deal about myself
and the way I view the world and my future.*

NANCY

*My husband and I are back together. We realize it's
still all uphill, but we've made some resolutions and
are willing to take a chance.*

*I've decided to make changes in my own life whether our
marriage works or not—mainly I'm striving for self-
respect and greater independence. I'm trying to get
back to school in September and I will be talking with
the Continuing Education for Women program at the university soon.*

*I want you to know what it meant to me to know that
Women in Transition was there for me and how much
strength that knowledge gave (gives) me.*

---

2. Marriage: Why did you get married? How have your
   feelings and ideas about marriage changed? How does
   this affect the way you see your future? In group after
   group we brainstorm reasons for getting married. "Love"
   invariably follows "security," "escape," and "children"
   on this list.

3. Needs and Goals: What are your needs now? Your goals
   for your life? How have these been met or not met in
   the past? Are there new ways to try to meet these?
   What kind of life do you want to lead? What are the
   real obstacles?

4. Children in Transition: How does separation and divorce
   affect children? How does being a mother affect your
   experience of separation? This discussion gives women
   a chance to share some of their deepest anxieties and
   guilt feelings and be reassured that they are not
   monsters or freaks.

Techniques

For more detailed information about specific techniques you
might use in small groups, consult the bibliography for this
chapter. The purpose of these topics and whatever techniques
we use is to help participants to understand themselves from
new perspectives and to see their individual crises as part
of some larger picture of the way women live. The feedback
we have gotten on these groups indicates that this perspective is one of the most valuable things women take with them
when they leave the groups.

One of our secondary goals is to demystify the group process
and group skills. We believe this is important because so
much of the powerlessness women experience is the result of
our isolation. We work alone, at home, in the classroom,
on the job. If we would break out of our isolation and our
powerlessness we must learn to work in groups. All too
often the experiences we may have in groups lead us to
believe there is some mystical power called "leadership"
that descends from on high and makes "leaders" out of ordinary mortals. We make every attempt to refute that myth
in our small groups.

Some time is set aside during each group meeting to discuss
the techniques used and evaluate their effectiveness and
the overall progress of the group that particular session.
We stress the importance of honest feedback to the group
process in the hope that participants will have learned
enough about groups to bring some new skills and understanding with them into the continuing "leaderless" group.

The purpose of the "orientation" groups, with their group
sisters and predetermined structure, is to prepare women to
take part in their own independent leaderless groups. We
discovered in our first year that leaderless groups are
often confusing and unproductive experiences for women who
have little or no experience in groups. During the second
year we began to identify and train potential group sisters.
We believe this two-step introduction to discussion groups
enables the largest possible number of women to benefit
from the experience.

Training Group Sisters

We try to provide "group sisters" from many different backgrounds and life-styles with different strengths and weaknesses. Our main prerequisite is that each feel there is

something in her life that would be valuable and useful to a woman in transition. Another requirement is that each feel she will be learning about herself and her own life by participating in the group.

We provide a day-long training session for each woman interested in becoming a group sister. Most of these women have had previous contact with the program, and many have been in small groups as women in transition. During the training session we try to get to know the sisters and give them a chance to get to know the program and see how the discussion groups are set up.

During the day we are interested in their understanding of themselves as women, what experiences they have had in groups, how they feel feminism has affected their lives, and why they want to be group sisters. We do several group exercises during the day to give us answers to these questions. Many of these exercises are explained in the pamphlet "Group Skills for Women's Groups," listed in the bibliography for this chapter. We also act out role plays of common situations which come up in the groups and look at different ways of handling them. By the end of the day we usually have some feeling about the group sisters' interests and abilities to help women in transition form an ongoing group.

Next we try to pair women with different kinds of strengths as co-leaders. Those with many group leadership skills are paired with those who have fewer group experiences but a stronger sense of their own identity as women, for example. We try to make sure that sisters with children get paired with those who don't, and older sisters with younger ones so that each group will be balanced.

During the training sessions, one of our major goals is to communicate to the group sisters that they do not have to be all-powerful leaders, that they can share their own lives and experiences with group members. They are supposed to participate as much as lead. We also try to assure them that group leaders don't always have to know what's going on in the group; they can ask others in the group to help them understand what's happening. Above all, we try to impress on the sisters that in the end it is up to the group members themselves to determine what kind of group it is and whether it will succeed.

At the end of the first four weeks, the role of the group

sisters becomes one of resource and observer rather than
facilitator. Over the next two sessions the group members
begin to take on the role of the sisters while the erst-
while leaders sit back and make their observations of the
group's strengths and weaknesses. This is, in effect, self-
evaluation for the sisters who see their own successes and
failures mirrored in the way the group is functioning without them. Finally, when the sisters have completed their
participation in the group, each writes a brief summary of
its progress and a detailed description of each session.
These are then filed for the reference of future group
sisters who can get ideas about planning their own sessions
and find help in understanding the progress of their own
groups.

We are continually evaluating how well this small group
model works and will undoubtedly revise it in the future.
But for now this is the best model we have come up with to
utilize our existing resources.

Therapy Referrals

As we suggested earlier, therapists you like and trust can
be valuable sources of information and training for your
project. You will probably also want to develop a list of
therapists you can suggest to women who want more intensive
help than they could get in a discussion group. Of course,
a woman might want to be in a group and in therapy at the
same time, which is fine provided she understands what is
appropriate for each setting.

Our referral list consists of women therapists who are sympathetic to the women's movement and who have been interviewed by us. When a woman calls us wanting therapy (or
asking about groups and we think therapy would be more
appropriate), we ask her to describe her situation and what
she wants to accomplish in therapy.

We then give her the names of several therapists we think
she would do well with. She can get back to us for other
names if none of these works out. We also send her a
"Therapy Information Packet for Women" (described in the
bibliography), which contains a number of articles to help
her evaluate her therapist and the experience she is having.
We assembled this packet because we think it is important
for women to become good consumers of mental health services.
We also call the woman back in several months to find out
if she is still seeing the therapist and how the treatment

is going. This is an important way for us to get feedback
on the therapist herself.

What Is A Feminist Therapist?

We don't really have a strict definition, but we know one
when we see her. . . . Well, it's a little more definite
than that. We have developed some general guidelines out
of our experiences running groups, our acquaintances in the
helping professions, and from listening to women who have
been in therapy and/or consciousness-raising groups in the
past few years. Here are some of our guideposts.

We think one of the most important things about a feminist
therapist is that she must make no assumption that there is
a single proper role for women, and that she work hard to
dispel the myths and stereotypes (women are naturally
better at caring for children; men are naturally more logical
and businesslike than women) which are so often used to
justify the oppression of women.

A feminist therapist would help her client understand the
relationship between the client's "personal" problems and
the stereotypes, myths, and social structure which often
create these problems. For example, a feminist therapist
might point out that a divorced woman's feeling that she is
a worthless person may have a lot to do with the fact that
marriage is considered the most acceptable career of all for
women. The therapist might help her client decide for herself whether marriage is the best career for *her*, and help
the client look at this cultural value somewhat more
objectively.

While we think that therapists often serve a useful role at
a time when a person's needs are too great for friends and
family to handle, we also believe that what is often considered a woman's mental or emotional problem is largely
the result of her being isolated from other women undergoing similar experiences.

We believe that women can often find meaningful support
from other women, consciousness-raising or discussion groups,
or groups working on a special project. We don't always
need experts to take care of problems. Finally, we must
recognize the real limitations of therapy. There are many
problems--financial problems, for example--that no amount
of support and consciousness-raising is going to alleviate.
A therapist must understand the limitations of her profes-
ion as well as its possibilities.

We are most impressed with therapists who can work in an
egalitarian manner. A good therapist is not condescending,
She does not consider her clients crazy mixed-up people
who have to be brought back to the fold. Instead, she
respects her clients and understands that her job is to
help others understand their own lives better and solve
their own problems. While we are grateful for the skills
which a therapist should have as a result of her training,
we believe that the warmth and insight usually associated
with good therapy have more to do with her personality than
with professional training. A therapist should be willing
to share her skills with her clients rather than impress
with them.

We hope that our feminist therapist has an open mind and
has explored for herself the issues that are important to
women today. In her own life and in her relationships with
people, she should work toward relationships based on equality, mutual understanding, and respect. It is hard to
imagine that a woman who has not struggled to free herself
from roles which oppress women will be able to help other
women to do so.

It is also crucial that a feminist therapist understand how
she came to have professional skills when other women do
not. We have been disappointed that many self-styled
feminist therapists believe that they have acquired professional status by virtue of their brains and hard work
alone, rather than recognizing that race and class privilege
have contributed toward their being able to get the educations which qualify them as "professionals."

It is important that the therapist make her own values
clear to her clients. Otherwise she may be imposing these
personal beliefs and tastes on her clients in the guise of
therapy. A feminist therapist should also be able to be
sincere and honest with her clients. She should be able
to discuss her own life experiences and unresolved conflicts
where appropriate. A therapist who needs to hide behind
God-like certainty (or even a big desk) may have too many
problems of her own to be very helpful to anyone else.

Another money problem: The fees charged by many therapists in private practice are beyond the reach of many
women who urgently need their services. Some therapists
will argue that people have to pay a high price before they
take their therapy seriously. This sounds ridiculous to us.
However, we are sympathetic to the problems of women thera-

pists who are struggling to make a living as professionals
and are vulnerable to criticism from other (male) professionals who might suggest that women who charge lower
fees are undercutting them or are not really worth as much
as men. Perhaps a solution would be to charge more money
to those who could afford it in order to help subsidize
poorer women who could then get the same services for a
reduced fee.

At the present we are making referrals to women therapists
only. We do this for two reasons. The most important is
that we feel it is much easier to trust a woman therapist's
understanding of women's problems than a man's. The entire
profession is riddled with the assumptions of a male-dominated society about the nature of women. Women therapists
are at least in a position to question some of these assumptions on the basis of their own personal experience.
Unfortunately, not all women therapists do this, however.
A second reason for referring to women only is to help our
sisters in the profession get established and support themselves by helping other women.

We still have questions about whether women who have always
lived in a certain amount of material comfort and security
can really understand the problems and offer realistic help
to women whose lives are plagued with economic insecurity
and downright hunger. The problem is complicated by the
fact that not only is the profession only open to people
with middle-class backgrounds, but it is also steeped in
middle-class values and assumptions, so that even the few
working-class people who do make it into professional status
have been trained to think with middle-class attitudes.

Interviewing Therapists For Referral

Listed below are some of the questions we ask therapists
who indicate they would like to be on our referral list.
We don't usually ask each therapist every question, but in
each case we ask enough questions to enable us to understand
each woman's basic attitudes and style. We do not assume
there are any right or wrong answers to these questions;
what is important to us is that the therapist has thought
about these issues.

1. Describe your life-style, job, or family situation.

2. What contact have you had with the women's movement?

3. How would you react to one of the following hypothetical
    situations?

a. A woman comes to you who does not want custody of her child.

b. A woman comes to you who cannot recognize her own needs and constantly puts others' needs first, even when these conflict severely with her own.

c. A woman comes to you who reveals that her husband or boyfriend is often physically abusive of her.

d. A woman tells you her problem is that she is "frigid."

4. What is your attitude toward marriage?

5. What is your attitude toward lesbianism?

6. How much of yourself do you think you should reveal as a therapist?

7. Do you believe it is important to have complete control over each session with your client?

8. How do you think you are most effective?

9. Do you experience personal growth as a result of your contacts with clients?

10. What does the word "professionalism" mean to you?

11. Where did your ideas about therapy come from and what do you understand "therapy" to be?

12. Why are you in private practice?

13. What are your fees? Do you ever do free consultation or evaluation? Do you charge on a sliding scale?

14. Are there women you have trouble working with or women you prefer to work with?

15. What do you think are the limitations of therapy?

16. Why are some people rich and some people poor?

17. How do you feel about this interview?

PROVIDING LEGAL SUPPORT

It was obvious to us even before our project started that
women were not getting the kind of legal help they needed.
Poor women were getting little or no legal counsel and women
who could pay were being charged outrageous fees. Women in
all economic situations were making crucial decisions about
their lives with inadequate or misleading information. Many
women had been separated for years but never divorced just
because they could not afford the legal fees. The misin-
formation, sexist assumptions, and careless treatment many
women received from lawyers was disturbing. We decided that
if the women in transition who were calling us were ever
going to be able to exercise control over their own lives,
we were going to have to learn something about their legal
rights.

We ran into a few stumbling blocks. In the beginning we
knew no lawyers and those we contacted were often reluctant
to give us information. Some felt that legal information
could be dangerous in the hands of non-lawyers; others felt
that in order for women to take their legal problems seriously they should pay for the information. (Sound familiar?
You're right. Many therapists said the same things about
the price of therapy.)

So we decided to take matters into our own hands. Those of
us who were interested in working on legal problems contacted
other women we knew with the same interests and formed what
we called the "legal group." In the beginning this group
included two law students who knew little more than we did
(nothing) about the laws about marriage, separation, and
divorce, but their presence added immeasurably to our self-
confidence.

The group had an enormous task cut out--learn all there was
to know about local law and procedure concerning marriage,
separation, and divorce. We started by reading everything
we could find in public libraries and later got up the
courage to read at law libraries. This is not necessarily
the best way to start. You can learn a lot more of practical importance from helpful lawyers, legal secretaries, and
legal workers. We were just too discouraged (and too
scared) to do the most logical thing first.

We had an immediate use for all our information; we had
been asked by a local group affiliated with the National
Lawyers Guild (a politically more radical and service-
oriented alternative to the Bar Association) to teach a

course on marriage and divorce law. Once we gained a little
confidence from our reading we returned to the law offices
to find out how practice differed from the theory we had read
in books. Next, we started compiling materials for the
course. An unplanned by-product of this activity was our
growing confidence in our ability to evaluate the legal
services we were getting from lawyers. We began to think
of other ways we could use the information we had--referrals,
evaluations of legal services, helping women to become
better consumers of legal services, and helping women to do
some of their own legal work.

During the last two years we have developed several different types of projects and services to accomplish our goal
of making legal information and services available to all
women who needed them. The information in the rest of this
chapter illustrates how we went about establishing our
group and setting up various projects. We have singled
out a few areas to work on--separation and divorce--and
ignored others--juvenile courts, adoption. Your own group
may have a different focus or a different community to serve.
The structures and problems would be very different in a
rural area, for example, or if your program were working
primarily with younger, unmarried women. We hope you will
feel free to evaluate, criticize, and modify the suggestions
which follow.

In The Beginning

Almost any project dealing with women in transition will
be flooded with questions about divorce law and procedure,
separation, child custody, and emergencies of a legal nature.
These problems need more than a sympathetic ear and some
emotional support. Knowledge of local domestic relations
law and procedure is essential if your project is going to
help women deal with these problems.

In order to do this you will need *information*. Members of
the local legal community can be valuable sources of information and training for your group. Libraries and books
are important, but book learning is dangerous if it's not
complemented by a working knowledge of how the laws are
interpreted and local customs and practices. Books don't
tell you where to file papers, how much a certain procedure
costs, or any of these important practical details. A
certain amount of your information must come from *experience*.

We gained much of our experience by doing volunteer work

at a local community legal services office interviewing
women who wanted to get divorces. Later several members
of our group were hired by this agency to do interviewing
and other paralegal aspects of divorce. Some of us took
full-time jobs in law offices and we recruited others with
similar jobs. Others continued to do other kinds of work
and chide us for our growing vocabulary of "legalese."
If you are interested in offering information and some kind
of legal services to women in your area, you should make it
a point to get some practical experience in local law
offices. Check with the local NOW chapter, women attorneys
and judges, and the local National Lawyers Guild groups
for information on what offices might be open to you.

The next step is to decide what problems you want to be
able to help with. Chances are you will be getting calls
for help in employment discrimination, discrimination in
lending or credit, landlord-tenant problems, and others
as well as separation, divorce and custody. You can't learn
everything at once, and we discovered it was much better to
have to tell some women there was nothing we could do to
help them than to try to tackle all the legal problems of
women one by one as they reached our office. We think it
is important to be selective and define the goals of your
group realistically and precisely. Do you want to set up
a reference service, a counseling service, an information
service, or a comprehensive legal services program for
women? (The latter almost requires a lawyer, a lot of money,
and a great deal of staff energy.) Are your goals consistent with your resources? Do you know lawyers who will
work with you, either formally or informally? Do you want
to provide professional services and advice, or are you
more interested in expanding the areas in which people
can act as their own advocates?

Getting Organized

We have been plagued by two organizational problems: first,
our relationship to the larger Women in Transition group
(staff, small group members and leaders, emotional support
group), and second, the relationship between new and old
group members. Despite numerous attempts on both sides,
we have never quite succeeded in clarifying the relationship
between the legal group and the rest of Women in Transition.
For a long time one of the staff members had as a major part
of her job liaison with the legal group and integrating the
legal projects with other projects. Several members of the
legal group were also members of the Planning (advisory)
Group for the program. For some of you this structural

approach to the problem will work best. For others, more
autonomy between different aspects of the program may be
better.

The second organizational problem is more serious and
perhaps more endemic to the kind of group it is. A legal
group, by its very nature, consists of a group of people
who share a body of information and skills. New members
come into the group with very little of the knowledge and
information you already share. It is easy for them to feel
overwhelmed by their lack of information and excluded by
the easy familiarity with the problems and jargon demonstrated by older members of the group.

We have developed several methods of sharing our knowledge
with new members. These include the following:

1. Periodic review of the forms we have filled out record-
    ing the questions dealt with and answers and follow-up
    given to legal calls.

2. Planning seminars in areas where we feel the need for
    further training.

3. Compiling a list of questions we are frequently asked
    and brainstorming the best ways to answer them. If more
    information is needed, we ask practicing lawyers to come
    and help at these sessions.

4. Plunging into new issues about which we are relatively
    ignorant, such as lesbian custody.

The last two activities serve two functions--the first helps
new members of the group learn basic skills and information
as rapidly as possible. The second provides an opportunity
for the entire group to learn something about which we are
all equally ignorant. New members feeling baffled, overwhelmed, or just left out because of the information gap are
quickly placed on an equal footing with older members in
meetings like these.

Deciding What Services You Can Provide

Our thought was to offer a much-needed and fairly simple
service. We would compile a list of lawyers to refer women
to in much the same way we had compiled the list of therapists. Well, we quickly learned that what seemed simple
and obvious to us was complex and problematic if not illegal

for most of the lawyers in the city. It seems the Bar
Association has decided that no one else should be allowed
to operate a referral service for lawyers. This may or may
not have something to do with the fact that there is one
referral service in town which has a list of lawyers "for
people of moderate means." Then again, we did not find
too many feminist lawyers (or others who were willing to
work on divorces, separation agreements, and custody problems for reduced fees). We gave up the idea of becoming a
reference service after becoming discouraged with the rather
bleak picture we were getting of the legal services available to women in transition. If you were on welfare you
qualified for free legal services; if your income was a
dollar above welfare level, you paid at least $600 for a
divorce.

We eventually decided that given the small number of lawyers
we could work with and the Bar Association's attitude toward
referrals, we could best use our energies to help women
become better consumers of legal services. As advocates
for better legal services, we focused on 1. legal self-help,
2. legal counseling, 3. evaluation of available legal
services, and 4. sharing information about the rights of
women in transition, especially with women in low-income
neighborhoods. When a woman called to ask us (or tell us)
about a lawyer we would send her copies of "What to Look
for in a Lawyer," and a special evaluation form we developed
called "Feedback on Lawyers," on the following page.

Individual Counseling

One of our first projects was to answer some of the questions women in transition had about their legal problems
over the telephone. Each member of our legal group took
turns either staffing the office to answer and return calls
at scheduled times (e.g., Saturday mornings) or was available for a specific period (usually a week) to answer all
the legal questions that came into the office during that
time. We kept a log of each call, the kind of questions
asked, and the information given. Periodically one of the
lawyers who had joined the group would review these forms
to see that our information was accurate.

One of the most common problems we encountered was the lack
of good legal services at rates women in transition could
afford. The question was simple--Where can I get a decent
lawyer to do a divorce at a reasonable rate? The problem
was that we had no answer. There were no such lawyers in
the city. Of course, most lawyers might do as much for a

Lawyer's Name
_____

Lawyer's Work Address   Zip
_____

Lawyer's Work Phone
_____

General evaluation:

_____recommend

_____not recommend

recommend only for:

How did you hear about this lawyer:

Your Need: separation agreement___support order___welfare___
child custody___hearing___divorce: contested___uncontested___
physical violence___other:

1. How well did the lawyer respond to this legal need?
    Did you trust the lawyer; did you feel she/he was acting
    in your best interests?

2. Did the lawyer seem to know what she/he was doing? Did
    she/he seem competent technically?

3. Did the lawyer communicate well with you? Could you ask
    questions and express concerns? Did the lawyer do the
    work *for* you or *with* you (or both)?

4. How did the lawyer come on to you--sexually, parentally,
    warmly, coldly, etc.?

5. How much did the lawyer charge? Do you think this was a
    reasonable fee based on the amount of work involved and
    your financial resources? It would be helpful if you
    listed your weekly income (salary, support money, wel-
    fare, etc.) and your husband's income. Did your husband
    pay any of the legal fees?

6. Would you recommend this lawyer to other women? If only
    in certain situations, what are they?

7. Other comments?

Your Name
_____

Your Address   Zip
_____

Your Phone #
_____

Date
_____

friend, but to most lawyers divorce was a sticky issue, not
to be touched without sufficient monetary compensation. At
this point we came to two important realizations: First,
we would be able to do nothing about this problem as long
as we continued to devote most of our energy to answering
the telephone. Second, divorce procedures were so simple
that most women could do them without a lawyer.

Thus, we eventually came to the conclusion that answering
individual legal questions over the telephone was probably
not the best use of our energy given the long-range goals
we had set for ourselves. But you should not discount this
as a possible service for your organization. During the
year that we provided this service as a major part of our
legal program we learned a great deal about the real problems of women in transition and accumulated much information and many strategies for handling these problems.
Since our staff has expanded, several staff members are
presently answering most of the legal questions that are
called into our office, leaving the members of the Legal
Group (all of whom work part-time and without pay for Women
in Transition) free to work on other projects aimed at
reaching larger numbers of women. If your group is interested in answering legal questions over the telephone, the
following suggestions may be helpful.

Answering Legal Questions

1. Screening: Many of the women who telephone us to find
    a lawyer don't really need one. Like so many of us,
    they are so mystified and bewildered by the legal sys-
    tem that they are afraid to even think about a problem
    involving the law without consulting a lawyer first.
    Sometimes you can save a woman a lot of expense and
    time by just giving her the relevant information: where
    to file a discrimination complaint or what to do if she
    has been beaten up by her husband, for example. If you
    care about the kind of legal services women are getting,
    you owe it to them to try and discover when a woman
    really needs a lawyer and when she doesn't.

2. When a woman really needs a lawyer: If the woman you
    are talking to indicates that any of the following
    statements describe her situation, you should recommend
    she see a lawyer as soon as possible. Be sure to tell
    her about free legal services if she might qualify
    (have an income close to welfare level). If she would
    not qualify for free legal services, give her the names
    of several lawyers you have worked with and/or trust.

a. If the parents cannot agree about custody and visitation for their children.

b. If there is any question or allegation of child abuse or neglect, or "unfitness" on the part of the parent, or if any agency or third person might by trying to gain custody of a child.

c. If there is a jointly owned property which cannot be amicably divided or if there are mutual debts and the parties either cannot agree or do not know who should pay what. If the separation agreement involves the transfer of any real property (usually a house), the parties should see a lawyer to be sure the deed, mortgage, insurance, etc., are in proper order and reflect their agreement.

EDITH

A few days ago I received my copy of your book. Unfortunately, it was just one day after I had seen my lawyer (the second one in two years) about filing for a divorce. Before that I had looked all over for some information on divorce and separation. I found absolutely nothing. The bits and pieces that were available were outdated. The first lawyer I tried (two years ago) was a male and was so discouraging that I wound up calling everything off at the last minute. I had two, possibly three, half-hour sessions with him and it cost me a little over $200. Now I've decided to try a female attorney. My first session (one hour) with her was far from encouraging. At least, she wasn't as depressing as the first one. I lost a lot of faith in her when she disagreed with me and said she thought the divorce laws in Pennsylvania were more than fair to women. I only wish that I had received your book a day earlier. I would have known enough not to tell my lawyer all the details, because it seems that things have a way of getting twisted around in favor of the male (90 percent of the time, anyway). This time I intend to stick it out to the end (no matter how discouraging my attorney is) and just continue to hope for the best.

---

3. Getting the whole picture: Each time a new woman calls, try to understand her total situation. Most "legal"

problems are really emotional or social problems. The "legal" part is the tip of an iceberg; sometimes your caller will be aware of this and ask for legal help first because it's easiest to ask for something concrete. Other callers may believe that a lawyer can really solve all their problems. In either case, we suggest you try to get the whole picture. How upset is your caller? Can she deal with practical matters? If not, maybe she should be channeled to an emotional support program if one is available. On the other hand, if the woman you are talking to seems to know exactly what kind of legal service she wants and does not seem interested in support groups or other aspects of your program, give her the information she needs and let her go.

4. Filling in details: Before you can be sure whether your caller is type A above (in need of other help) or type B (in need of legal services purely) you will have to know something about her problem. Unless she gives you enough information to enable you to make a sensible recommendation on your own, you should ask whichever of the following questions is relevant to her question. For example, if she inquires about separation and/or divorce you might ask:

How is she being supported presently? Husband, job, welfare, or a combination of any of these three?

Do she and her husband own any property together? If she says no, is she sure whose name is on the lease or mortgage or deed? How about the car? Any stocks or securities?

Are there any children? If so, what ages?

Is she still living with her husband? If not, does she still see him or speak to him? Does he harass her or beat her up?

Are there any debts? Problems with bill collectors or credit? Whose name is on the bills? Did she ever sign for any of the accounts or loans?

Does she have a separation agreement? If not, can she reach an agreement directly with her husband, or will they need an intermediary? Would she be interested in writing her own agreement or does she need a lawyer? (If there is much property involved she should

definitely be advised to look for a lawyer, although you
should also advise her what her rights are and what to
expect from the lawyer. Encourage her to call or write
back with information about what lawyer she used and how
she felt about his or her services.)

It is important that in every situation you explain to your
caller what her rights are, what she can do to enforce her
rights, and what consequences flow from which choices she
makes. Whenever possible think of several alternatives and
let her decide which she feels most comfortable with.

Reaching Out To Larger Numbers Of Women

Perhaps it was just the women's movement version of "mani-
fest destiny," but we soon felt frustrated by giving out
legal information to individual women on a one-to-one
basis. We were anxious to find ways to expand our services
so that many more women would have this information. It
was also becoming clear to us that women learned about our
program by word of mouth, and this meant that an overwhelming majority of those who knew about us were fairly well-
educated young women, mostly white and middle-class. The
women who most desperately needed the information we had
were older women and poor women. These women often felt
(believed) they had no rights, and there was no one to tell
them any different.

Like many others who worked in various movements for social
change, we decided that we would have to take the information to the people rather than wait for them to come to us.
The first step was to develop working relationships with
various groups at work in low-income communities. These
included the Urban League, local community action groups,
and housing authorities. This was the most difficult part
about setting up our outreach project. It took many months
to develop these relationships and convince these groups
and organizations they should work with us. Many community
groups working in minority and low-income neighborhoods are
justifiably suspicious of the women's movement because of
its traditionally white middle-class orientation. Officials
from any local or state government are, of course, suspicious for opposite reasons. You can probably handle the
latter fairly well with no additional advice from us. We
would suggest that if your group plans to work in low-
income neighborhoods, you have black and low-income women
involved in the planning stages of your outreach program.

When we presented our outreach plans to community groups

and others our approach was low-key. We tried to avoid
feminist rhetoric, "movement" and counter-culture slang.
We wore dresses or pantsuits to meetings and presentations
in housing projects and neighborhood centers in order to
show our respect for the residents. We believed that the
services and information we had to offer spoke for themselves, and that the women in these neighborhoods needed
concrete information and specific kinds of help. They
understood their "triple jeopardy" (class, race, and sex)
all too well. If you are going to work on an outreach project like this, remember: You don't have to "organize"
poor women. They can organize themselves--but if your program is carefully constructed, you can offer material
assistance.

Our outreach effort started with legal workshops in housing
projects throughout the city. The women who most desperately needed the information and services we had were concentrated in large numbers in public housing, so we took
the information and services to the projects. Cooperation
from women active in tenants' councils, some concerned
social workers, and others in the projects determined the
success or failure of a particular workshop. In some projects we arrived at an empty hall to learn that our pain-
stakingly printed leaflets, invitations, and flyers about
the workshop had never been distributed. We learned the
hard way you can't just find a time and place agreeable to
the housing authority or other official and expect women to
flock to your program. You have to have someone with some
credibility in the project or neighborhood who is working
to get women out for your presentation.

At the workshop each participant receives a mimeographed
packet containing information in question-and-answer form
covering all the topics we plan to discuss in the workshop.
These are for the participants to make notes in, refer to,
take home, or pass on. The topics covered in almost every
workshop include: separation and divorce, common-law marriage, "illegitimate" children, welfare rights, women's
rights, child support, child custody, how to get legal
services, and domestic violence (wife-beating and child
abuse).

Much time is spent in each workshop discussing the institutions on which so many of these women are forced to depend--
welfare, social security, and other social service agencies.
We discuss what an individual's rights are with respect to
these institutions and what she must do to be treated
according to her rights.

Discussions of domestic violence are quite common. For many
women this represents the first time they have been able to
admit that they are the victims of physical violence at home
and to discover that they are not alone with this problem.
We offer concrete information about legal steps to take in
this situation and discuss the fact that these steps often
prove to be meaningless. We also discuss self-defense and
encourage women to explore with each other what it means to
be poor and female in this country.

Our outreach effort is now expanding as a result of good
experiences in several parts of the city. Many of the
groups which first came together to listen to legal information and ask questions about legal problems are continuing
to meet and expanding their discussions to include health
care and medical institutions, self-defense for women,
motherhood and child-raising, and other topics such as are
often covered in consciousness-raising groups. These are
in fact emotional support groups, and we are in the process
of developing training programs for women who are interested
in acquiring group leadership skills.

Legal Self-Help

Answering questions on the phone and helping women with
individual problems had greatly increased our confidence in
our ability to provide a responsible alternative to the
lack of good legal services at prices women could afford.
Our experiences in the housing projects and neighborhoods
convinced us of the real need for such an alternative.

We had heard of women's groups in other states setting up
"clinics" to help women to do their own divorces. We
weren't sure this was possible in Pennsylvania, but we
decided to go ahead and try.

> *Even though mine was one of the first attempts,
> there was some uncertainty as to whether I could
> pull it off, I felt it well worth the effort. . . .
> Denying those lawmakers the opportunity to clean
> up on this lady's mistake is a continuing one.*

Our first two guinea pigs, coached by us through the local
laws and procedures, obtained their divorces in three to
four months at a cost of $150. And instead of high legal
fees, embarrassing questions from an unsympathetic lawyer,
and insulting treatment, these women had a new self-
confidence.

Once we knew that women could do their own divorces in this
state we had to look long and hard at the risks and the
value of trying to establish a clinic for many women to
work on their own divorces together. There were risks on
both sides. Not every woman should file her own divorce;
those with unresolved conflicts about property, custody, or
visitation, or any other conflict which could have legal
implications should not even consider beginning a divorce
until these conflicts have been finally resolved. Divorce
is a final step and not a way to solve practical problems.
Thus, women who were anxious to get the divorce over with
might be tempted by a clinic to get the divorce before
taking care of practical problems. We did not want to encourage this practice.

On the other hand, there were risks for us the minute we
opened the clinic. Members of the local Bar Association
were convinced that we would be engaging in the "unauthorized practice of law" if we opened such a clinic. "Unauthorized practice" is illegal--a misdemeanor in most
states. Thus we risked civil action against us (an order
telling us to stop the clinic) and/or a criminal action
(leading to a fine or a jail term). We debated for months.

The clinic finally opened on the first of six successive
rainy-haily-sleety Thursdays. But despite the weather, at
least twenty women showed up for the first night. Most
were not eligible for the clinic; we had set strict income
guidelines to emphasize the need for such a clinic. Only
women who could not obtain divorces from lawyers (those
whose incomes left them stranded between welfare--and free
legal services and comfort--at $600 a divorce) were accepted.
Those who lived outside the county (procedures vary from
county to county in this state) were likewise ineligible.
Finally, all those with problems or potential problems
related to property, custody, and visitation, or any other
potentially complicated situation (their husbands might
want to contest the divorce) were also eliminated.

We had planned to run the clinic for four months and wave
goodbye to all our new divorcées in April. Because our
organization and advertising for the clinic left much to
be desired, some women who had started the clinic as late
as March were still straggling through in June. We had
hoped that the group of women working on their own divorces
would act as an emotional support or consciousness-raising
group as well. Our poor planning--or was it the nature of
the project?--created much repetition and little support.
The fact that all of the women had low incomes meant they

could not afford to find baby-sitters and take public
transportation unless they were ready to take the next
step in their divorces.

We are presently in the process of redefining our own
goals for the clinic and trying to find a new structure to
meet those goals. Other groups (on the West Coast) seem
to have met with more success in integrating the consciousness-raising aspect with the divorce process. We suspect
this would be easier with middle-class women, but are
firmly committed to making divorce accessible to women like
the woman who had been deserted twenty-six years ago, but
remained "married" because she could not afford a divorce.
Her most urgent desire was to obtain this divorce in order
to marry again and begin a new life which she believed
would make her happy. While we would be somewhat disappointed if remarriage were the goal of every woman who
came to the clinic, our political goal has been at least
partially met if the clinic helps a woman to have more
control over her own life and more confidence in her ability to use this power.

The major shortcoming of our first clinic was the small
number of women who actually went through the clinic.
Once again, removing the income limitations would solve
this problem, but we know there are enough women who
absolutely cannot afford divorces and who would also meet
all the other criteria to keep several clinics buzzing
year-round. More and better publicity would have attracted many more women, but here we are in a bind. The more
publicity, the more upset the Bar Association's "Unauthorized Practice" committee becomes. This is our second
political issue to be resolved.

If you are interested in setting up a clinic for women to
do their own divorces, you will probably face many of the
same problems. We feel our own experience was a qualified
success, and are very short on recipes for successful
clinics. You might want to get a copy of *Getting Out: A
Collective Experience in Self-Help Divorce*, which is about
how to set up a self-help divorce clinic and the strengths
and limitations of that type of project within the goals of
the women's movement (see the bibliography for ordering
information).

You should also study carefully the legal/political climate in your area to ascertain the likelihood of your being
prosecuted or enjoined for "unauthorized practice of law."
Courts in California, Michigan, and New York (and perhaps

elsewhere) have considered the legal position of non-
lawyers who help others do their own divorces and the ver-
dict has generally been unfavorable. This is not to say
that you are sure to be prosecuted, or that you are sure
to lose if you are prosecuted (or enjoined). There are
some large questions and constitutional issues involved
(freedom of speech and association, among others), none
of which have been fully explored.

Of course you could probably avoid many of these problems
if you worked under the "supervision" of an attorney. But
regardless of the political climate in your area, your
group should discuss the risks and decide whether they're
worth it to your program. Possible risks, in addition to
those already mentioned, include jeopardizing funding
sources, creating problems for women in your group who are
active in the clinic and plan to become lawyers, and the
risk of having the clinic ordered to stop before all your
clients have gotten their final divorces.

If you decide to take the risk and go ahead without the
supervision of an attorney (a supervising attorney may also
be taking great risks with her career for aiding in the
unauthorized practice of law), you should do some careful
research into the membership and authority of the local
Unauthorized Practice committee of the Bar Association.
There is a national Practice Committee of the Bar Association which discusses the activities and attitudes of this
committee and which may be found in most law libraries
(see the bibliography for this chapter).

JEAN

*The first process in a divorce was filing a complaint,
in which I accused my husband of "Indignities." The
complaint was a fill-in-the-blanks form, giving names,
addresses, etc. Also there were cards for the sheriff
who delivered the complaint to my husband and a self-
addressed notification for the sheriff to send me.*

*Having filled out these forms I went to City Hall . . .
I filed the complaint, paid $37.50 to the cashier (cash
only, no checks), filed the sheriff's cards in his
office, and paid the sheriff's cashier $13.50.*

*End of step one. Now I waited until the sheriff
delivered the complaint to Steve.*

The next step was to apply for a hearing. This involved
certifying, in legal jargon on red-striped paper: a
record of the filing of the complaint, both of our current residences, expectation of no contest of the
divorce, that my husband was not in the armed forces,
and lastly the actual motion asking for a hearing. The
forms took me and my housemate about two hours to type
up, carefully following samples.

Back at City Hall, the clerk stamped and recorded my
motion and I paid my $100, in cash of course. The clerk
was doubtful that I could represent myself, but he
accepted my papers and my money anyway.

After six weeks more waiting, when I'd begun to think
I'd made some mistake I'd never find out about, I
received a letter from an attorney who informed me that
my divorce hearing would be in two weeks at his office.

Divorce hearings used to be held in courtrooms before
judges, but in Philadelphia they are now held in the
offices of lawyers appointed by the court, called
"masters." The master reviews the case and recommends
action to the court, and gets the $100 I'd paid with my
motion for a hearing.

The forms for the hearing were: the affidavit of jurisdiction, in which I had to list everywhere my husband
or I had ever lived and why Philadelphia was where I
should sue him for divorce; another copy of the non-
military service and residences affidavits; a certification that I didn't owe my lawyer any money; and a
narrative affidavit.

The narrative affidavit told the story of why I deserved
a divorce. It was strictly a "he is guilty, I am innocent" tale in black and white; too bad real life isn't
so simple. Still, it was hard to put into words the
terrible anguish I'd been through in the past year.
"He yelled at me . . . in front of our friends. I was
very embarrassed" hardly describes the situation that
had made my life burdensome.

The morning of the hearing was bright and hot, but I
decided that a sober black dress would suit the occasion.
My housemate and I took the subway and arrived at the
master's office just as he shuffled in. He was very,
very old and his hands shook violently. Oh my God, I
thought, I hope he knows what he's supposed to do

because I sure don't.

We all shuffled into a private room and I introduced myself and my friend very slowly and carefully. The master turned to her and asked if she were the one getting the divorce. I reintroduced us and began to get a headache.

I handed him the papers I had prepared. He asked if I was representing myself and I said yes. He asked me to state my current address and then my husband's. Then he slowly and deliberately picked up the first form, and intoned, "I have here the certificate of residences." Pointing to my signature he solemnly asked, "Is this your signature?" I said, "Yes." Pointing to the notary's seal he asked, "Did you sign this in front of a notary?" I said, "Yes." He put the form in the folder. Then he picked up each form in turn and repeated those two questions.

He rose abruptly and thanked us for coming. What? Is this is? Is it over? I asked when I would be hearing from him and he said that I would be hearing from the court. We shook hands and I left.

After I left with my friend I felt very lightheaded, tremendously relieved, and very silly about having been so nervous. . . . About a month later I received a letter from the master saying he had recommended a divorce. My final decree came through on June 28, 1974!

WRITING YOUR OWN SUPPLEMENT TO THIS HANDBOOK

This handbook is, in many ways, our largest outreach effort to date. But for this book to be truly useful to women where you live, it should have a supplement which lists local resources and describes local laws and procedures. Basically, this involves getting to know what services (housing, employment, legal, etc.) are available for women in the community and evaluating the quality of those services. It also involves researching local laws and regulations (divorce, support, welfare) which vary from state to state and county to county. The chapters in this book might serve as a guide to the kinds of services which might be researched, but there are others not covered here which may be important to women in your area.

If you know people who work at local agencies (legal services, welfare department, mental health agencies) who can
let you know what these agencies can and cannot (or will
not) do for women, so much the better. If not, you will
need to do more legwork. Visit agencies, talk to workers
there, talk to women who have used their services. In
other words, get to know your community's resources.

You may find some professionals reluctant to give you any
information for free which they might get other people to
pay for. In that case, don't get discouraged. Keep talking. Look for other professionals or para-professionals
in the area. Use the libraries.

When you have the information you need, you will probably
want to have it mimeographed or printed to be distributed,
either with this book or separately (or both). And please
send us a copy.

▶▶▶ *BILLIE*

> *I got married after I got pregnant. I was kicked out
> of school and was married immediately thereafter. I
> was nineteen I believe. When I was coming along, un-
> wed mothers were frowned on, so I got married. Also,
> I loved the guy very much and thought he loved me.
> We planned to spend the rest of our lives . . . you
> know, the usual Hollywood bit. He was studying to be
> a doctor and later I planned to go back to school to
> study to be a teacher. But Uncle Sam took him into
> the armed forces, and he was stationed in Georgia.
> While there he met a Georgia Peach and they were
> married.*

> *I had the first kid when he was stationed in Georgia.
> He would come home on furlough often, and when the
> first kid was two years old (and I was pregnant again),
> my mother found out that he had another wife. She had
> our marriage annulled and had the names changed. He
> went back to Georgia and his Peach and I was left with
> the two-year-old kid and the one in the chute. All
> this happened twenty-seven years ago, and I still don't
> know what or how it was done. So much for my first
> marriage, which wasn't a marriage at all.*

> *My family ostracized me after that. Unwed, pregnant,
> and an emotional wreck, I did not know of any way of*

doing anything. My parents kept my oldest kid but
would not allow the baby in the house. They farmed
him out to a lady in another section of the city.
When the baby was four months old, the lady's sister
died and she brought the baby back home. I took the
baby (it was O.K. to leave the oldest with the
family) and started walking. We spent that night in
a cell at the police station. They were really good
to us. They found a baby bottle from somewhere, put
clean sheets on the bed, took up a collection, and
gave me about $8.00.

The next couple of days were spent with the police
talking to me, trying to help me because I was a
complete emotional wreck. My mother died about a
week later and I felt more alone than ever before.
No money, scared, stupid, dumb, and nowhere to go,
nothing. I spent the next two or three years like
a bum, sleeping in the park, in overnight movies,
and subways. I finally grew tired of being cold and
hungry and took to the streets. I was young, fairly
attractive, ane was able to make a few bucks here
and there. Deep inside I was bitterly opposed to
this. I was not brought up this way and I was getting
a terrible beating from my conscience. With the help
of a few close friends I was able to get a job, a
damn good one, too, with the federal government. I
got my oldest son from my family. My youngest son
was in a foster home, but I was able to get him back.

A friend I worked with introduced me to her son and
we started seeing each other regularly. He constantly
told me he was going to marry me, but since I didn't
particularly care for him, I constantly said no, he
was not. But after about a year I began to notice
more gray strands and my middle was beginning to fill
out (not due to pregnancy). The children needed a
father image in the house, this would be a way of
having sex legally, plus this guy was very, very
intelligent. He often spoke of going to school to
get his degree, and when he finished I could stay
home, have more babies, and make gingerbread cookies
I was working two jobs then and could afford to help
pay his way through school.

Well . . . Mr. Intelligence and I got married . . .
and that ended that dream. It just did not work out
the way we had planned. His mother had planned this
big shindig for a wedding, and since neither of us

cared for all that, we decided to elope one New Year's
Eve. On our return I found out that not only did he
not want to go to school, he did not want to work. He
was supposedly driving a Yellow Cab, but the damn cab
stayed out in front of the door more than it stayed in
the garage. Totally irresponsible. Soon after I
retired from my part-time job. We had two children,
a boy and a girl.

I have always been aggressive and arrogant too, I suppose. I knew what I wanted and where I wanted to go.
I also knew what it took to get there. If you want
something, you have to get up off your ass and get it.
He thought differently. He thought all you had to do
was say it, and it would fall from the sky. Things
like that happen only in the Old Testament, I suppose.

The marriage was a flop. I see now I did that a man a
grave injustice. I thought I would be able to change
him, and that does not happen either. We separated
about six times before the final split. He would leave
each time at my request, return also at my request.
Things just got worse and worse. I became very lonely
and very frustrated and of course turned to other men
for sexual fulfillment. I went to a shrink, but I
did not tell him the truth, so there was no way for
him to help me. The shrink did find out, however, that
I had a bit of a booze problem.

I took a look around me and said if I don't get rid of
thsse sons-of-bitches I will soon lose my sanity. I
had become a martyr. All these people dumping and
dumping on me, and I had no outlet. I had this sick
tale about poor me and everybody doing this to me and
no one will listen to me. No wonder the kids were
wacky.

I started housecleaning. I found my husband an apartment, paid the rent, gave him half the furniture, and
had a van move him and all of his stuff out. This
was the only way he would leave. Gave my two oldest
boys enough money to hold them for a while and told
all of them to go make their own lives.

This left me and my youngest two. Now the living would
be easy. Wrong again. After cleaning house I bought
a home, bigger, but I still had forgotten about my
biggest problem, me. I had moved all these people,
bought me a bigger home, but I was still on booze. I

*joined an organization that helps with a booze problem.
Here I have found emotional help, I have found friends,
and I also get my spiritual needs met. I thank God
that I found them, and because of this I have been
free of booze for five years.*

*Life is still difficult. I have been divorced for
three years. When we first split, it caused a lot of
problems with the two youngest. My daughter (fourteen)
was very upset. We had to take her to a shrink to help
get her head together, and she still gets very delighted
when her father calls. My son (seventeen) is still
pent-up within, and every once in a while it sort of
oozes out. They are not so bad as before. We have
learned to talk to each other, we do things together,
cook, clean, wash, argue, fight, just have a good time.
Learning how to face each day together.*

*At the ripe old age of forty-five, I am trying to take
life one day at a time. It is still difficult being
complete financial support of myself and the children.
The cost of living is so high--schools, clothing, food.
My children eat like condemned criminals. Sometimes
just to get up to face the new day is an ordeal. I
have learned to accept these things as part of life.
I look back at what I have gone through with much
less, and today doesn't seem so bad.*

*I would like to go back to school, but I don't have the
where-with-all to do it. Maybe a rich uncle will die
and leave me enough money to do this. I would like to
get into a service type profession. I do this work
now, but as a non-professional. I would like the education so that I could really get into it.*

*I know my chances of getting married again are very
slim. I used to think I had to have a man, but I know
now that I don't. Nothing earth-shattering will happen
if I don't. If I had my druthers, I would have a man,
but I don't, so I make it. I do have a boyfriend. He
is forty-eight, has never been married, and has spent
most of his life living with his sister. I don't want
to have to go into all that. It's like raising another
kid, and I don't feel like raising any more kids.*

*But it will be all right. Today I am determined to
accept whatever comes, because I have weathered many
a storm. The kids will soon be out doing their thing.
We'll see, we will just see. . . .*

(Right) THE WOMEN IN
TRANSITION, INC. STAFF

Andi McKenna, Judy Brigham,
Margaret Cox, Mimi Galper,
Jennifer Fleming, Schree
Hicks (front)
(Photo by: Emi Tonooka)

Photo by: Eva Shaderowfsky

Photo by: A. C. Warden

(Right) THE BOOK STAFF
(left to right) Susan Daily,
Linda Backiel, Deborah
Thomas, Carolyn Washburne
(Photo by: Emi Tonooka)

(Below) THE PEOPLE WHO
WORKED ON THIS BOOK
(Photo by: Emi Tonooka)

APPENDIX

WOMEN'S CENTERS, CLINICS,

RAPE CRISIS GROUPS, AND SO FORTH

When Women in Transition was first begun, we began attempting to develop a list of programs like ours throughout the country. Because we operate on a local level, our information was less than complete nationally. To develop this listing, we sent out questionnaires to every women's group we had encountered through referral, word of mouth, schools, other listings, etc. This listing is still by no means complete. Women's groups and centers seem to spring up and disappear with equal quickness. As far as we know, most of these groups are still functioning. Where we were told the group offered legal advice or special services for women in transition going through separation or divorce, we have indicated it by an asterisk (*). When we were able to find a telephone number, we listed it. You might want to call to determine exactly what services are available.

In the chapter of this book entitled "What The Law Says," you will find listings of legal services throughout the country. Also in this chapter you will find state-by-state listings of National Organization for Women chapters. Here we list the addresses of the national offices of several organizations working with women in transition as well as

as a state-by-state listing. In most cases they should be
able to refer you to the chapters in your community.

National   National Black Feminist Organization
Headquarters: 285 Madison Avenue, Room 1720
                        New York, New York 10017
                        (212) 889-5881

                        National Organization for Women
                        National Office
                        5 South Wabash, Suite 1615
                        Chicago, Illinois 60603
                        (312) 332-1954

                        Momma Organization, Inc.
                        Post Office Box 5759
                        Santa Monica, California 90405
                        *(Publishes an article entitled
                        "How To Start a MOMMA Chapter," 50¢)*

Alaska: The Women's Resource Center
                        570 Seatter Street, #3
                        Juneau 99801

Arizona: Women's Center
                        912 E. 6th Street
                        Tucson 85719
                        (602) 792-1929

                        Alternatives for Women
                        40 E. 14th Street, #5
                        Tucson 85701
                        (602) 884-9776

                        Women's Center
                        1414 S. McAllister
                        Tempe 85281
                        (602) 968-0743

California: Berkeley Women's Center
                        2134 Allston Way
                        Berkeley 94704

                        Berkeley Women's Health Collective
                        2214 Grove Street
                        Berkeley 94704
                        (415) 843-6194

Women's Opportunity Center
De Anza College
21250 Stevens Creek Boulevard
Cupertino 95014
(415) 257-5550, ext. 455

The Woman's Center
University of California, Davis
Davis 95616
(916) 752-3372

The Woman's Opportunities Center
University Exchange, 148 Adm. Bldg.
Irvine 92664

Isla Vista Women's Center
6504 Pardall Road
Isla Vista 93017

Chicana Service Center
5340 E. Olympic Boulevard
Los Angeles 90022

Feminist Women's Health Center
746 Crenshaw
Los Angeles 90005
(213) 936-7219
(213) 936-8156

The Woman's Building
943 S. Grand View
Los Angeles 90057

Women's Resource Center
90 Powell Library
UCLA
Los Angeles 90024

Oakland Feminist Women's Health Center
2930 McClure Street
Oakland 94609
(415) 444-5676

Problem Pregnancy
Information Collective
457 Kingsley Avenue
Palo Alto 94301
(415) 329-9000

Mother's Emergency Stress Service*
c/o The Sacramento Women's Center
1221 20th Street
Sacramento 95814
(916) 442-6161

Sacramento Women's Center
1221 20th Street
Sacramento 95814

Woman's Way
412 Red Hill Avenue
San Anselmo 94960

Center For Women's Studies and Services
908 F Street
San Diego 92101
(714) 233-8984

Advocates For Women
593 Market Street, Suite 500
San Francisco 94105
(415) 495-6750

Childcare Switchboard/Single Parent Center*
4282 23rd Street
San Francisco 94114
(415) 282-7858

Haight-Ashbury Women's Health Collective
1101 Masonic Avenue
San Francisco 94117
(415) 665-9687

The Women's Legal Center
558 Capp Street
San Francisco 94110
(415) 285-5066

Women's Center
California State University, San Jose
Building "V"
San Jose 95112
(408) 294-7265

WOMA: Women's Alliance, Inc.
c/o Nona Tobin
Economic and Social Opportunities, Inc.
2131 The Alameda
San Jose 95126

Feminist Women's Health Center
429 S. Sycamore Street
Santa Ana 92701
(714) 836-1941

Women's Center
111 Barson Street
Santa Cruz 95060

Womancare, Inc.
1050 Garnet
San Diego 92109
(714) 488-7591

Cooperating Local Agencies For Single Parents
c/o Rita Machi
1315 Gertrude Street
San Diego 92110

L.A. Radical Therapy Collective
245 Mill Street
Santa Monica 90291
(213) 399-1248

The Stanford Women's Center
3rd Floor, Clubhouse
Stanford 94305
(415) 497-3114

Women's Switchboard
Box 597
Venice 90291
(213) 388-3491 (12-6, Wednesday-Saturday)

Colorado: Virginia Neal Blue Women's Center
Room 225
Adams State College
Alamosa 81101
(303) 589-7771

Virginia Neal Blue Women's Resource Center
c/o First Methodist Church
420 North Nevada Avenue
Colorado Springs 80902

Virginia Neal Blue Women's Center
YWCA
1545 Tremont Place
Denver 80202
(303) 222-0879
(303) 222-0870

Women In Transition House
1895 Lafayette Street
Denver 80218
(303) 255-2435

Virginia Neal Blue Center
Mesa Junior College
Grand Junction 81501
(303) 248-1498

Virginia Neal Blue Women's Center
Arapahoe Community College
Littleton 80120
(303) 794-1550, ext. 262

Virginia Neal Blue Women's Resource Center
San Luis Valley Area Vocational School
Sherman Avenue
Monte Vista 81144
(303) 852-5977

Virginia Neal Blue Women's Center
Office of Admissions
Southern Colorado State College
Pueblo 81001
(303) 549-2461

Women's Information Service of Pueblo*
2501 W. Northern
Pueblo 81104
(303) 543-0245

Connecticut: Women's Center
11 Amity Street
Hartford 06106
(203) 523-8949

Center for the Person in Transition*
26 Turnbull Street
New Haven 06525
(203) 624-5715

Information and Counseling Service
  For Women
215 Park Street
New Haven 06520
(203) 436-8242

Women's Liberation Center
11 N. Main Street
South Norwalk 06854
(203) 846-1285

Women's Center
U-118, c/o University of Connecticut
Storrs 06268
(203) 486-4738

District of   The D.C. Women's Center
Columbia: 1736 R Street, N.W.
                       Washington 20009
                       (202) 232-5145

                       Washington Rape Crisis Center
                       Post Office Box 21005
                       Kalorama Station
                       Washington 20009
                       (202) 333-RAPE (7:30 a.m. - 12 midnight)

                       Women's Clinic
                       c/o Washington Area Free Clinic
                       1556 Wisconsin Avenue, N.W.
                       Washington 20007
                       (202) 965-5476
                       Clinic operates from 9 a.m. to noon Saturdays

                       Domestic Relations Project*
                       c/o The D.C. Women's Project
                       1736 R Street, N.W.
                       Washington 20009
                       (202) 232-5145

                       Washington Opportunities for Women (WOW)
                       1111 20th Street, N.W.
                       Washington 20036
                       (202) 872-8097

Delaware: Women's Resource Center
                       c/o D.E.A.
                       1626 N. Union Street
                       Wilmington 19806

Florida: Options, Inc.
                       1825 Hendricks Avenue
                       Jacksonville 32207

Tallahassee Women's Educational
    and Cultural Center
University Box 6826
Florida State University
Tallahassee 32306

Hawaii: Women's Center
                   Action Task Force on Rape
                   Women's Health Center*
                   University YWCA
                   1820 University Avenue
                   Honolulu 96816
                   (808) 947-3357 or (808) 946-8844

Idaho: Women's Center Alliance (YWCA)
                   720 W. Washington
                   Boise 83702

Illinois: Center For A Woman's Own Name
                   261 Kimberly
                   Barrington 60010
                   (312) 281-2113

                   Women's Liberation Center of Evanston*
                   2214 Ridge
                   Evanston 60201
                   (312) 475-4480

                   Prelude
                   Box 1303
                   Knox College
                   Galesburg 61407
                   (309) 343-9440

                   Chicago Women's Liberation Union*
                   2748 N. Lincoln
                   Chicago 60614
                   (312) 953-6808

                   Lesbian Feminist Center
                   3523 N. Halsted
                   Chicago 60657

Indiana: The Women's Center
                   The Women's Crisis Service*
                   414 N. Park
                   Bloomington 47401

Iowa: Open Line, Inc.
                      2408 Lincoln Way
                      Ames 50010

                      Women's Coalition
                      Room 65
                      Memorial Union
                      Ames 50010

                      YWCA
                      Alumni Hall
                      Iowa State University Campus
                      Ames 50010

                      Women's Health Project/Emma
                      Goldman Clinic for Women*
                      715 N. Dodge Street
                      Iowa City 52240
                      (319) 338-3289

                      Women's Resource and Action Center
                      3 East Market Street
                      Iowa City 52240

Louisiana: New Orleans Women's Center
                      1422 Felicity Street
                      New Orleans 70130
                      (504) 486-3665

Maine: Bangor Women's Center
                      Box 914
                      Bangor, Maine 04401

                      Bath-Brunswick Women's Center
                      Main Street
                      Brunswick 04011
                      (207) 725-2512

Maryland: Baltimore Women's Growth Center
                      862 Park Avenue
                      Baltimore 21201
                      (301) 539-3588

                      Baltimore Women's Center
                      101 E. 25th Street, Suite B-2
                      Baltimore 21218
                      (301) 366-6475

Baltimore Rape Crisis Center
101 E. 25th Street, Suite B-2
Baltimore 21218
(301) 366-RAPE

Women's Law Center
Post Office Box 1934
Baltimore 21203
(301) 547-1653

Massachusetts: For The People Women's Group
637 S. Main Street
Fall River 02721
(617) 672-3118

Franklin County Women's Coalition
Post Office Box 24
Greenfield 01301
(413) 863-8239

Birth Control Information Center
85 Main Street
North Adams 01247
(617) 663-8846

New Bedford Women's Clinic
  New Bedford Women's Center
347 County Street
New Bedford 02740
(617) 999-1070

Valley Women's Center
200 Main Street
Northampton 01060
(413) 586-2011

Women's Center
c/o Southeastern Massachusetts University
North Dartmouth 02747
(617) 997-9231, ext. 697

Berkshire Women's Coalition
Box 1564
Pittsfield 01201
(413) 442-0480

Lower Cape Women's Center
Post Office Box 712
Provincetown 02657

Everywoman's Center*
506 Goodell Hall
University of Massachusetts
Amherst 01002
(413) 545-0883

Boston University Women's Center
185 Bay State Road
Boston 02215

Boston Women's Collective
490 Beacon Street
4th Floor
Boston 02115
(617) 266-9392

The Women's Counseling and Resources
  Center, Inc.
1555 Massachusetts Avenue
Cambridge 02192
(617) 492-8568

Women's Educational Center*
46 Pleasant Street
Cambridge 02139
(617) 354-8807

Alternative Center
1882 Dorchester Avenue
Dorchester 02124
(617) 436-0541

Florence Luscomb Women's Center
Salem State College
Salem 01970

Springfield Women's Union
  Springfield Women's Center*
292 Worthington Street, Room 212
Springfield 01103
(413) 732-1852
24-hour rape crisis hot-line: 737-RAPE

Boston Project For Careers
83 Prospect Street
West Newton 02165
(617) 969-2339

Clark Women's Center
Box A037, Clark University
Worcester 01610

Worcester Women's Center
905 Main Street
2nd Floor
Worcester 01610
(617) 756-2722

Michigan: Women's Crisis Center
306 N. Division Street
Ann Arbor 48105
(313) 761-WISE

Feminist Women's Health Center
18700 Woadward
Detroit 48203

Women's Counseling Center, Inc.*
13040 W. Seven Mile Road
Detroit 48235
(313) 835-3770

Kalamazoo Women's Center*
211 S. Rose Street, Room 210
Kalamazoo 49006
(616) 345-3036 (rape crisis line)

Women's Health and Information Project*
110 Warriner
Central Michigan University
Mt. Pleasant 48859
(517) 774-3762

Minnesota: Elizabeth Blackwell Women's Health Center
2000 S.5th Street
Minneapolis 55404
(612) 335-7669

Minnesota Women's Center
306 Walter Library
University of Minnesota
Minneapolis 55455
(612) 373-3850

Women's Resource Center*
2104 Stevens Avenue
Minneapolis 55400

Mississippi: Jackson Women's Coalition
                    622 N. Jefferson Street
                    Jackson 39202
                    (601) 355-8030

Missouri: Columbia Women's Center
                    501 Rollins
                    Columbia 55201

                    Women's Liberation Union
                    5138 Tracy
                    Kansas City 64110
                    (816) 333-4155

                    UMSL Women's Center
                    8001 Natural Bridge Road
                    St. Louis 63121
                    (314) 453-5380

                    Women's Resource Center
                    Washington University
                    St. Louis 63130
                    (314) 863-0100, ext. 4848

Montana: Women's Place
                    c/o YWCA
                    600 Orange Street
                    Missoula 59801
                    (406) 543-7606

                    Women's Resource Center
                    University of Montana
                    Missoula 59801

New Hampshire   Concord Women's Center
                    130 Main Street
                    Concord 03301
                    (603) 224-3412

                    Keene State Women's Center
                    Keene State College
                    Keene 03430
                    (603) 622-9721

                    Manchester Women's Center
                    104 Middle Street
                    Manchester 03430
                    (603) 622-9721

New Dynamics Associates
Box 92
R.F.D. #5
Laconia 03246
(603) 524-1441

Portsmouth Women's Center
YWCA
40 Merrimac Street
Portsmouth 03801
(603) 436-0162

W.I.S.E.
Post Office Box 1132
Nashua 03060
(603) 882-8482

Upper Valley Women's Center
11 Lebanon Street
Hanover 03755
(603) 643-5981

New Jersey: Bergen County Women's Center
166 Main Street
Hackensack 07601
(201) 342-8958

YWCA Women's Center
Upsala College
East Orange 07019
(201) 266-7213

EVE (Education, Volunteering, Employment)
Kean Building
Newark State College
Newark 07083

Women's Rights Law Reporter
180 Washington Avenue
Newark 07102
(201) 648-5577

YWCA Women's Center*
395 Main Street
Orange 07050

New Mexico: Women's Center*
                     Las Lomas N.E.
                     University of New Mexico
                     Albuquerque 87106

New York: The Sisterhood of Black Single Mothers*
                     Post Office Box 155
                     Brooklyn 11203

                     Union Center for Women*
                     8101 Ridge Boulevard
                     Brooklyn 11209
                     (212) 748-7708
                     (212) 965-4271
                     (212) 372-5370

                     Women's Center*
                     Brooklyn YWCA
                     30 Third Avenue
                     Brooklyn 11217

                     Buffalo Women's Center*
                     Station H
                     Post Office Box 1411
                     Buffalo 14214
                     (716) 882-8721

                     Alternate Health Board
                     Weigel Health Center
                     SUC at Buffalo
                     1300 Elmwood Avenue
                     Buffalo 14222

                     Divorce Information Center*
                     Ethical Humanist Society Building
                     38 Old Country Road
                     Garden City, Long Island 11530
                     *(Tuesdays 10 a.m. - 1 p.m.,
                     Wednesdays 7:30 p.m. - 10:30 p.m.)*

                     Women's Liberation Center of Nassau County*
                     14 West Columbia Street
                     Hempstead 11550
                     (516) 292-8106

                     Ithaca Women's Center*
                     101 North Geneva Street
                     Ithaca 14850
                     (607) 272-6922

Barnard College Women's Center
100 Barnard Hall
New York 10027
(212) 280-2067

Lesbian Switchboard
243 W. 20th Street
New York 10011
(212) 741-2610

New York Women Against Rape
243 W. 20th Street
New York 10011
(212) 675-7720 *(6 - 10 p.m.)*

Women's Action Alliance, Inc.
370 Lexington Avenue
Room 601
New York 10017
(212) 658-0800

Healthright, Inc.
Women's Health Forum
156 Fifth Avenue
Apartment #1229
New York 10010
(212) 691-1140, 691-1141
*(This agency does not do health care
or referrals but is available for
literature concerning women's health
problems.)*

Women's Counseling Project
112 Earl Hall
Columbia University
New York 10027
(212) 280-5113

Women's Law Center *
1414 Sixth Avenue
New York 10019
(212) 838-8118

Women's Center in Islip*
855 Montauk Highway
Post Office Box 164
Oakdale 11769
(516) 277-0772

Oswego Women's Center*
286 Washington Boulevard
Oswego 13126
(315) 342-1294

Poughkeepsie Women's Center, Inc.*
Post Office Box 1226
Poughkeepsie 12601
(914) 462-1796

Women's Self-Help Collective*
Richmond College
Room 538
130 Stuyvesant Place
Staten Island 10301

Rockland County Women's Center*
Post Office Box 527
Valley Cottage 10989

North Carolina: Human Sexuality Information and
                      Counseling Service
                   Suite B
                   Carolina Union UNC-Chapel Hill
                   Chapel Hill 27514
                   (919) 933-5505

                   Charlotte Women's Center
                   1615 Lyndhurst Avenue
                   Charlotte 28203

                   Durham Women's Center-YWCA
                   515 W. Chapel Hill Street
                   Durham 27701
                   (919) 688-4396

Ohio: Women's Center
                   415 T.U.C.
                   University of Cincinnati
                   Cincinnati 45221

                   Women Helping Women
                   2699 Clifton Avenue
                   Cincinnati 45220

                   Cleveland Women's Counseling Center*
                   Post Office Box 20279
                   Cleveland 44120
                   (216) 321-8585

University Women's Center*
Case Western Reserve
Hitchcock Hall
11205 Euclid Avenue
Cleveland 45387
(216) 368-2647

The Tani Gomen Feminist Rape
  Crisis Center
Post Office Box 4442
Columbus 43212
(614) 291-9751
(crisis) (614) 221-4447

University of Dayton Women's Center
Box 612
University of Dayton
Dayton 45469

Women's Center*
1309 N. Main Street
Dayton 45405
(513) 228-1203, 223-3296

Oberlin Women's Service Center*
92 Spring Street
Oberlin 44074
(216) 774-HERS

Women's Resource Center
c/o Carol Horst
540 S. Campus #8
Oxford 45056

Oregon: Women's Clinic
c/o Jan Hollender
972 W. 4th Avenue
Eugene 97402

Women's Bookstore/A Woman's Place
700 S.E. Grand Avenue
Portland 97214
(503) 234-8703

Women's Health Clinic
4160 S.E. Division
Portland 97214
(503) 234-9774

Portland Chapter of MOMMA*
5244 N.E. Everett
Portland 97213
(503) 232-1239

Women's Studies Union
Portland State University
Post Office Box 751
Portland 97207
(503) 229-4459

Pennsylvania: Reproductive Health and Counseling Center
Crozer Chester Medical Annex
15th and Upland Avenue
Chester 19013

Women's Center*
YWCA
41 N. Third Street
Easton 18042
(215) 253-2523
(215) 258-6271

Lancaster Women's Center*
230 W. Chestnut Street
Lancaster 17603
(717) 299-5381

Germantown Women's Center*
YWCA of Germantown
5820 Germantown Avenue
Philadelphia 19144
(215) GE8-6266, ext. 30

Kensington Area YWCA*
174 W. Allegheny Avenue
Philadelphia 19133
(215) RE9-1430

Women In Transition*
4634 Chester Avenue
Philadelphia 19143
(215) SA4-9511, SA4-9512

Women's Center - South
180 Woodhaven Drive
Pittsburgh 15288
(412) 563-5043

Rhode Island: Higher Education Resource
                        Services (H.E.R.S.)
                     Box 1901
                     Brown University
                     Providence 02912
                     (401) 863-2197

                     Women's Liberation of Rhode Island
                     Post Office Box 2302
                     East Side Station
                     Providence 02906
                     (401) 861-5511

Tennessee: Nashville Women's Center
                     1929 21st Avenue South
                     Nashville 37212
                     (615) 269-5118

                     Rape Prevention & Crisis Center
                     Box 12531 Acklen Station
                     Nashville 37212
                     (615) 297-9587

Texas: Austin Women's Center
                     2316 San Gabriel
                     Austin 78705

Vermont: Vermont Women's Health Center*
                     Box 29
                     Burlington 05401
                     (802) 655-1600

                     Women's Switchboard*
                     73 Church Street
                     Burlington 05401
                     (no walk-in facilities)
                     (802) 862-5504

                     Women of Upper Valley
                     Jill Nooney
                     Thetford 05074
                     (802) 785-4559

Virginia: Rape Crisis Line
                     Roanoke
                     (703) 366-6030

Washington: Women's Resource Center
                   Post Office Box 1081
                   Richland 99352

                   Aradia Clinic
                   4224 University Way, N.E.
                   Seattle 98105

                   University YWCA*
                   4224 University Way, N.E.
                   Seattle 98105
                   *(also, Lesbian Resource Center, Third
                   World Resource Center, Women's Divorce
                   Cooperative: (206) 632-4747)*

                   Country Doctor Women's Clinic
                   402 15th Street
                   Seattle 98112
                   (206) EA2-6698

                   Feminist Coordinating Council
                   6410 Brooklyn, N.E.
                   Seattle 98115

                   Fremont Women's Clinic
                   6817 Greenwood Avenue N.
                   Seattle 98103
                   (206) 782-5788

                   Radical Women
                   3815 Fifth Avenue, N.E.
                   Seattle 98105
                   (206) ME2-7449

                   Seattle Counseling Center
                   1720 16th
                   Seattle 98112

                   The I.D. Center
                   1020 East John Street
                   Seattle 98102
                   (206) 329-0600

Wisconsin: Women's Crisis Line
                   Women's Coalition Center
                   2211 E. Kenwood
                   Milwaukee, Wisconsin 53202
                   (414) 964-7535

CANADA

Alberta: Women's Overnight Shelter
                     10348 101st Street
                     Edmonton

British Columbia: Ishtar
                     Women's Resource Center and
                         Transition House
                     Box 613
                     2961 Jackmann Road
                     Aldergrove

                     Prince George Women's Centre and
                         Community Service Centre*
                     1306 Seventh Avenue
                     Prince George

                     Transition House*
                     4830 Victoria Drive
                     Vancouver

                     Vancouver Women's Centre
                     804 Richards Street
                     Vancouver

                     Vancouver Women's Health Collective
                     4197 John Street
                     Vancouver 10

                     Victoria Women's Centre and
                         Transition House*
                     523 Trutch Street
                     Victoria

Manitoba: A Woman's Place*
                     300 Victor Street
                     Winnipeg

                     Crisis Housing Project for
                         Women in Transition*
                     62 Hargrave House
                     Winnipeg

Newfoundland   Women's Place
                     Post Office Box 5021
                     4 Prescott Street
                     St. John's

Ontario: Ottawa Women's Centre
                      581 O'Connor Street
                      Ottowa

                      MUMS* (self-help group for
                        mothers alone)
                      421 Markham Road
                      No. 1004
                      Scarboro
                        757-2155

                      The Women's Place*
                      137 George Street
                      Toronto
                        (416) 363-8021

Quebec: Women's Information and Referral Center
                      3595 St. Urbain
                      Montreal 131
                        (514) 842-4781

                      YWCA Women's Centre*
                      1355 Dorchester Street, W.
                      Montreal
                        (514) 866-9941, ext. 64, 44

Saskatchewan   Saskatoon Women's Centre
                      124-A Second Avenue, N.
                      Saskatoon

                      Women Alone (Interval House)
                      211 Fifth Avenue, N.
                      Saskatoon
                        (306) 242-7808, 244-0185

BIBLIOGRAPHY

We haven't been able to read everything that has been written about separation and divorce, but here are some books and articles we hope will be helpful. Some we have read ourselves, and we usually include any comments we have. Others have been recommended to us, so use your own judgment.

GENERAL

Books And Articles

Cisler, Lucinda. *Women: A Bibliography*. Box 241, New York, New York 10024. 50¢ per copy. A useful list of books and articles for and by women.

Grimstad, Kirsten, and Rennie, Susan. *The New Women's Survival Catalog*. New York: Coward, McCann and Geoghegan, 1973. $5.00. A comprehensive listing of women's projects throughout the country.

Poetry

The Common Woman Poems and other works of feminist poetry are available from the *women's press collective*, 5251 Broadway, Oakland, California 94618.

Resources For Older Women

Gray Panthers. A coalition for social change. 3700 Chestnut, Philadelphia, Pennsylvania 19104.

NOW Task Force on Older Women. Tish Sommers, Coordinator, 434 66th Street, Oakland, California 94609.

Prime Time. A monthly publication for older women. Marjorie Collins, 264 Piermont Avenue, Piermont, New York 10968.

TWO: EMOTIONAL SUPPORTS

Books And Articles

Allen, Pamela. *Free Space: A Perspective on the Small Group in Women's Liberation*. Times Change Press, Penwell Road, Washington, New Jersey 07882. $1.35. The story of a women's consciousness-raising group and how it grew.

Baguedor, Eve. *Separation: Journal of a Marriage*. New York: Simon and Schuster, 1972. $5.95. A woman borrowed this book from the Women in Transition Program's lending library and wrote this inside the cover: "Rip-off!! She goes back after seducing him--and has romance and candlelight for her two years of separation!"

Barbara, Judy, Kathy, Shirley, and Sue. "Consciousness-Raising." *Women: A Journal of Liberation*, Vol. 2, No. 4. $1.00 for whole issue. Write 3028 Greenmount Avenue, Baltimore, Maryland 21218. The women talk about their feelings about being in a group and how it changed their lives.

Bernard, Jessie. *The Future of Marriage*. New York: Bantam Books, 1972. $1.95. The language is somewhat academic, but it is an interesting book.

Chesler, Phyllis. "Marriage and Psychotherapy." KNOW, Inc., Post Office Box 86031, Pittsburgh, Pennsylvania 15221. 40¢. A classic and a "must" for any married woman in therapy or thinking about it.

Epstein, Joseph. *Divorced in America: Marriage in an Age of Possibility*. New York: E. P. Dutton & Co., 1974. $8.95.

Fuller, Jan. *Space, The Scrapbook of My Divorce*. New York: Arthur Fields Books, Inc., 1973. $5.95. Insightful and nice. Good photographs.

Gettleman, Susan, and Markowitz, Janet. *The Courage to Divorce*. New York: Simon and Schuster, 1974. $7.95. An excellent book which we recommend highly. The authors challenge many of the assumptions about divorce which are common among mental health professionals and in the media.

Jacoby, Susan. "What Do I Do for the Next 20 Years?" *New York Times Magazine*, June 17, 1973. An exciting article about a consciousness-raising group of middle-aged working-class women in Queens.

Krantzler, Mel. *Creative Divorce: A New Opportunity for Personal Growth*. New York: M. Evans and Company, Inc., 1973. $6.95.

LaBarre, Harriet. *A Life of Your Own*. New York: Popular Library, 1972. $1.25. We include this because it is typical of many new books aimed at the woman alone telling her that she can have a glamorous new life if she will only "think right." It is written from an upper-middle-class, almost jet-set perspective, which assumes that you have a lot of options about what kind of job to get, where to live, where to travel, etc. Keeping all that in mind, it may be a shot in the arm for women who do have some options and want help figuring out what choices to make.

Leah and Mary Jane. "Thinking about Psychiatry." *Women: A Journal of Liberation*, Vol. 2, No. 2. $1.00 for whole issue. Write 3028 Greenmount Avenue, Baltimore, Maryland 21218. This article discusses the connnections between consciousness-raising and therapy.

Mainardi, Pat. "The Politics of Housework." 5¢ plus 10¢ postage. Write New England Free Press, 60 Union Square, Somerville, Massachusetts 02143. A classic.

Ms. Magazine. "A Guide to Consciousness-Raising," July 1972. Available for 25¢ plus self-addressed business-sized envelope from Ms. Magazine, 370 Lexington Avenue, New York, New York 10017. A how-to-do-it article about setting up a consciousness-raising group.

O'Brien, Patricia. *The Woman Alone*. New York: Quadrangle
    Books, 1973. $7.95. We found this to be a very thought-
    ful and sensitive book. The author describes her own
    experiences living away from her family for two years
    and shares the experiences of a number of women she inter-
    viewed.

"Rap Groups: The Feminist Connection." *Ms. Magazine*, 370
    Lexington Avenue, New York, New York 10017. 25¢ in coin
    plus self-addressed envelope. The experiences of a New
    York consciousness-raising group and their advice to
    other groups.

Rascoe, Judith. *Yours, and Mine*. Boston: Little, Brown
    and Co., 1969. $6.95. A collection of short stories,
    some of which concern divorce.

Scott, Carol and Oken, Jean. "Divorce as Survival: The
    Buck Stops Here." *Women: A Journal of Liberation*, Vol.
    2, No. 2. $1.00 for whole issue. Write 3028 Green-
    mount Avenue, Baltimore, Maryland 21218.

Seifer, Nancy. *Absent from the Majority: Working Class
    Women in America*. 1973. The American Jewish Committee,
    Institute of Human Relations, 165 E. 56th Street, New
    York, New York 10022. $1.25. An excellent book about
    the life-style, problems, attitudes, and changes in
    working-class women in this country.

Sheresky, Norman and Mannes, Marya. *Uncoupling: The Art
    of Coming Apart*. New York: Dell Books, 1972. $1.50.
    This book has gotten a lot of publicity, but we didn't
    find it that helpful.

Syfers, Judy. "Why I Want a Wife." 10¢ plus 10¢ postage
    from KNOW, Inc., Post Office Box 86031, Pittsburgh, Penn-
    sylvania 15221. Another classic.

Organizations

Alcoholics Anonymous: If you don't know of a chapter near
    you, write or call their General Services Office, Box
    459, Grand Central Station, New York, New York 10017.
    (212) MU6-1100.

Al-Anon (for families of alcoholics) and Alateen (for
    children of alcoholics): For information about a chapter
    near you, write or call 115 E. 23rd Street, New York,
    New York 10010. (212) GR5-6110.

Fifth Wheelers and Parents Without Partners: Check phone
directory for a chapter near you.

Weight Watchers: Weight Watchers chapters are all over the
country and usually in local telephone books. If you don't
know where the nearest chapter is, write or call the
national office, 175 E. Shore Road, Great Neck, New York
11023. (516) 466-5900.

THREE: CHILDREN IN TRANSITION

<u>General</u>

Billingsley, Andrew and Giovannoni, Jeanne M. *Children of
the Storm: Black Children and American Child Welfare*. New
York: Harcourt, Brace, Jovanovich, 1972. $8.50.

Gardner, Richard. *The Boys' and Girls' Book About Divorce*.
New York: Bantam Books, 1971. For children. The best
yet written on the subject.

Gil, David G. *Violence Against Children: Physical Child
Abuse in the United States*. Harvard University Press,
1973. $6.50. Excellent.

Hanes, Mary. *Lovechild: A Self-Portrait*. New York: Lip-
pincott, 1972. $5.95.

Harrison, Barbara Grizzuti. *Unlearning the Lie: Sexism
in School*. New York: William Morrow, 1974. How some
people changed their school. Good.

Harvard Educational Review. "The Rights of Children,"
Vol. 43, No. 4, November 1973. Very abstract, but good.

Klein, Carole. *The Single Parent Experience*. New York:
Walker and Company, 1973. $7.95.

National Institute of Mental Health. *Facts About The Mental Health of Children*. DHEW Publication No. (HSM) 72-
9147. Available for 10¢ from U.S. Government Printing
Office, Washington, D.C. 20402 (Stock Number 1724-0255).
This includes brief discussions on questions such as
"What leads to child abuse?", "What are the major symptoms of mental illness in children?", and "What is the
effect of parents being away from home?" Very brief and
readable.

Non-Sexist Books For Children

A growing number of presses today specialize in "non-sexist" books for children. Of course, not all these books are of the same quality. You may want to look for the books in your local bookstore or write for catalogues at the addresses listed below.

All of Us, Inc., 175 S. Broad Street, Monmouth, Oregon 97361.

Feminist Press, Box 334, S.U.N.Y., Old Westbury, Long Island, New York 11568.

Joyful World Press, 468 Belvedere Street, San Francisco, California 94117.

Lollipop Power, Post Office Box 1171, Chapel Hill, North Carolina 27514.

New Seed Press, Post Office Box 3016, Stanford, California 94305.

Scholastic Books, 900 Sylvan Way, Englewood Cliffs, New Jersey 07632.

Sojurner Truth Press, 432 Moreland Avenue, N.E., Atlanta, Georgia 30307.

On Day Care

Boguslawski, Dorothy Beers. *Guide for Establishing and Operating Day Care Centers for Young Children*. Published by the Child Welfare League of America, 1970.

Breitbart, Vicki. *The Day Care Book*. New York: Alfred Knopf, 1974. $3.95. Maybe the most practical of all. Highly recommended.

Keyserling, Mary Dublin. *Windows on Day Care*. A report based on the findings of the National Council of Jewish Women on Day Care Needs and Services in the Communities. New York: National Council of Jewish Women, 1972.

Roby, Pamela. *Child Care--Who Cares?* New York: Basic Books, 1972. $15.00 The definitive up-to-date study. More scholarly than practical.

Shapiro, Carol. *How to Organize a Child Care Center*.
  Available from Women's Action Alliance, 370 Lexington
  Avenue, New York, New York 10017. Excellent place to
  start. Contains good suggestions and lists further
  resources for help and information.

Women's Bureau. *Federal Funds for Day Care Projects*.
  Employment Standards Administration, U.S. Department
  of Labor, 1972, pamphlet 17 (revised). When you're
  ready to do it, here's how to find money.

Help For Lesbian Mothers, Lesbian Support

Daughters of Bilitis: A national organization with offices
  in most major cities. Consult your local telephone
  directory.

Lesbian Mothers' Union, c/o Lesbian Liberation, Women's
  Center, 46 Pleasant Street, Cambridge, Massachusetts
  02139.

Lesbian Mothers' Union, 1074 Guerrero Street, San
  Francisco, California 94110.

Consult the local telephone directory for the local
chapters of the following organizations:

  American Civil Liberties Union
    (Committee on Sexual Freedom)
  Gay Activists Alliance
  Gay Liberation Front
  Gay Students' Union
  Gay Switchboard
  Lesbian Center
  Lesbian Hotline/Switchboard
  Radical Lesbians
  Sexual Freedom League

National Organizations

American Library Association Task Force on Gay Liberation, Post Office Box 2383, Philadelphia, Pennsylvania
  19103. This group publishes an updated *Gay Bibliography*
  several times per year.

Gainesville Legal Collective, 115 S. Main Street, Gainesville, Florida 32601.

Gay Legal Caucus, 59 Christopher Street, New York, New York 10014.

Gay Women's News Service, Post Office Box 8502, Stanford, California.

Lesbian Tide, 1124 1/2 N. Ogden Drive, Los Angeles, California 90046.

Momma, Post Office Box 567, Venice, California 90291.

Mother, Post Office Box 8507, Stanford, California 94305.

National Committee for Sexual Civil Liberties, 18 Ober Road, Princeton, New Jersey 08540.

National Gay Task Force (publishes "Action on the Gay Legal Front") 80 Fifth Avenue, New York, New York 10011.

National Lesbian Information Service, Post Office Box 13368, San Francisco, California 94115.

Sisters, 1005 Market Street, Room 208, San Francisco, California 94103.

Contributions, information for lesbian custody cases urgently needed:

Lesbian Mothers' National Defense Fund, 1941 Division, Enumclaw, Washington 98002.

Lynda Chaffin Defense Fund, Box 3984, Torrance, California 90510.

Vicky and Larraine's Legal Defense Fund, 570 Harvey Avenue, Apartment #2, Kent, Ohio 44240.

Womancenter, Post Office Box 455, Penngrove, California 94928.

Lesbian Motherhood

American Psychiatric Association. "American Psychiatric Association Resolutions on Homosexuality." Write APA Division of Public Affairs, 1700 18th Street, N.W., Washington, D.C. 20009.

Klein, Carole. "Homosexual Parents." In *The Single Parent Experience*. New York: Avon, 1973. $1.95.

Klemesrud, Judy. "Lesbians Who Try To Be Good Mothers" (honest!). *The New York Times*, January 31, 1973.

LeShan, Eda J. "Homosexuality." In *Natural Parenthood: Raising Your Child Without a Script.* NAL, 1970. 75¢.

Martin, Del and Lyon, Phyllis. "Lesbian Mothers." *Ms. Magazine*, October 1973. The authors of this article have also written *Lesbian Woman*, New York: Bantam Books. $1.50. They are presently working on a book to be called *Lesbian/Mother*.

Ms. Magazine, New York. "Robin and Joyce and Family." October 1973. Robin and Joyce are collecting a book of songs, photos, and drawings. Write care of *Ms. Magazine*, 370 Lexington Avenue, New York, New York 10017.

National Gay Task Force. "Action on the Gay Legal Front." Write National Gay Task Force, 80 Fifth Avenue, New York, New York 10011. $1.00 per copy.

Reid, Coletta. "Motherhood is Powerless." *Motive*, vol. 32, No. 1, 1972. "Bringing Up Children in the Gay Community," (anon.) *Motive*, vol. 32, No. 1, 1972. This issue of *Motive* contains a "List of Contacts" across the country--but the list was compiled in 1972, so use with caution.

Directories of Interest to Lesbians

Gayellow Pages, Box 292, Village Station, New York, New York 10014. Quarterly, single issue $5.00 Classified directory of gay businesses, services, organizations, etc.

International List of Gay Organizations

GAA, Box 2, Village Station, N., New York, New York 10014.

Student Gay Groups, National Gay Student Center, 2115 S. Street, N.W., Washington, D.C. 20008.

Sources of Legal Help of Interest to Lesbian Mothers

American Civil Liberties Union, 22 E. 40th Street, New York, New York 10016 (or local chapters).

Center for Constitutional Rights, 853 Broadway, New York, New York 10003.

Center for Law and Social Policy, 1600 20th Street, N.W., Washington, D.C. 20009.

Lawyers' Committee for Civil Rights Under Law, 733 15th Street, N.W., Washington, D.C. 20005. With offices in many large cities.

Women's Rights Law Reporter, c/o Rose Basile, 180 University Avenue, Newark, New Jersey 07102.

Local Legal Aid and OEO Legal Services offices (consult your local telephone directory).

FOUR: WHAT THE LAW SAYS

Support

"The Equal Rights Amendment and Alimony and Child Support Laws," Citizens' Advisory Council on the Status of Women, Department of Labor Building, Washington, D.C. 20210.

National Organization to Insure Support Enforcement, c/o Diana DuBroff, 12 W. 72nd Street, New York, New York 10023. Chapters are forming in several cities. Reprints and a booklet available from the above address.

"Recognition of Economic Contribution of Homemakers and Protection of Children in Divorce Law and Practice," Citizens' Advisory Council on the Status of Women, Room 1336, Department of Labor Building, Washington, D.C. 20211.

Gager, Nancy, ed. *Women's Rights Almanac*. Bethesda, Maryland: Elizabeth Cady Stanton Publishing Co., 1974. Source of information on legal services list.

Divorce and Separation

Allen, Charles M. *How to Get a New York Divorce for Under $100*. Allen Advertising Co., 1973. Use with caution.

Boykin, James H. *Foreign Divorce*. Pagent Press. Very technical.

Callahan, Parnell T. *The Law of Separation and Divorce*. 3rd ed., rev. Oceanea Publications, 1970. $4.00. This gives concise information on a state-by-state basis, including residency requirements, grounds and waiting periods for divorce, and remarriage. Concise explanations of "divisible" and "foreign" divorce.

DeCrow, Karen. *Sexist Justice*. New York: Random House, 1974. Of general interest. Readable. $7.95.

Hirsch, Barbara B. *Divorce: What a Woman Needs to Know*. Regnery, 1973. $8.95, $3.95 paperback. This book is readable, but definitely oriented toward middle-class women.

Lindey, Alexander. *Separation Agreements and Ante-Nuptial Contracts*. Annotated, 2 vols. Matthew Bender, Publs., updated yearly. This is the "Bible" of lawyers who write separation agreements. Forms and paragraphs for everything you could possibly want to agree to.

Wheeler, Michael. *No-Fault Divorce*. Boston: Beacon Press, 1974. $7.50. Everything you ever wanted to know about "no-fault." Both technical and readable.

Name Changes

The Center for a Woman's Own Name. *Booklet For Women Who Wish to Determine Their Own Names After Marriage*, compiled by The Center For A Woman's Own Name, 1974. Copies may be obtained for $2.00 from Center for A Woman's Own Name, 261 Kimberly, Barrington, Illinois 60010. One-year subscription to supplements of the booklet is available for $1.00 from the same address. (Add 50¢ for postage.)

Women's Rights Law Reporter. "Married Women's Common Law Right to Their Own Surnames." Vol. 1, No. 3 is available for $1.00 from the same address. (Add 25¢ for postage.)

Ross, Susan C. *The Rights of Women*. *ACLU Handbook*, R. W. Baron, 1973. $4.95.

See pp. 211-13 for more information about name changes.

Marriage Contracts

A study group at Case-Western Reserve is interested in
exchanging information with people interested in writing
their own marriage contract. Write M. B. Sussman, Hayden
Hall, Case-Western Reserve University, Cleveland, Ohio
44106.

Child Custody

Gardner, Richard. *The Boys' and Girls' Book About Divorce*.
  Bantam Books, 1971. $1.25.

Goldstein, Joseph, et al. *Beyond the Best Interests of
  the Child*. Free Press. $1.95. A book that suggests
  new tests for judge-determined child custody. Good on
  some points, but pretty heavily laden with sexist assumptions. Most helpful in situations where parents or a
  mother is being challenged for custody of children. Less
  appropriate in divorce situations.

Griffin, Susan. "Confessions of a Single Mother,"
  Ramparts, April 1973.

Klein, Carole. *The Single Parent Experience*. New York:
  Avon, 1973. $1.95. Non-legal information and support.

Mindey, Carol. *The Divorced Mother*. New York: McGraw-
  Hill, 1970. $6.95. One woman's look at being a divorced
  mother. Readable, supportive. Definitively oriented
  toward middle-class women.

Illegitimacy

Klein, Carole. *The Single Parent Experience*. New York:
  Avon Books. $1.95. About the experience of being a
  single parent rather than uniquely about "illegitimate"
  children, but supportive of all who are raising children without partners.

Krause, Harry D., ed. *Illegitimacy: Law and Social Policy*.
  Bobbs-Merrill, 1971. $14.00. The most thorough work to
  date, with extensive bibliography. Oriented toward the
  law of illegitimacy.

National Council on Illegitimacy. *The Double Jeopardy--
  The Triple Crisis--Illegitimacy Today*. Booklet. New
  York, 1969.

FIVE: FINANCIAL RESOURCES

Employment

Albrecht, Margaret. *A Complete Guide For The Working
Mother*.   Award Books, 1970. 95¢. If you can still
find this book for 95¢ it may be one of the best buys of
the day. Answers a lot of questions about working that
women who haven't worked before, or who are returning
to work, might have.

Bird, Caroline. *Everything A Woman Needs To Know To Get
Paid What She's Worth*. McKay, 1973. $8.95. This book
is somewhat keyed to women who already have job options,
and who are mostly interested in upgrading themselves.
Caroline Bird's conception of feminism isn't quite the
same as ours, but in some respects is cheering.

Callahan, Sidney Cornelia. *The Working Mother*. Warner,
1972. 95¢. This book is less than useful if you are
concerned about practical information about how to find
a job, make child care arrangements, etc. It is a collection of essays by women who are doctors, researchers,
community organizers, graduate students, and writers.
Fine if you are interested in reading about the lives
of women who already have these jobs, but not much help
to a woman wanting to know how to get them.

Kreps, Juanita. *Sex In The Marketplace: American Women At
Work*. Johns Hopkins Press, 1971. $1.95. Some of us never
learn--just because a book has sex in the title, it
doesn't mean it has to be interesting. This is a
scholarly analysis of work patterns and possible causes
of them.

Prentice, Barbara. *The Back To Work Handbook For House-
wives*. Collier Books, 1971. $1.50. This book can help
you to decide if you want to work (if you have any choice)
and perhaps what you might like to work at, also if you
have a choice, and how to find a job. The informational
content is useful and understandable, although it does
seem to slant toward the already educated or semi-profes-
sional woman.

The Womanpower Project. *The New York Women's Directory*.
Workman Publishing Company, 1974. $2.95. If you live
in New York, you might be interested in this kind of
sourcebook listing employment agencies, social service
agencies, and interspersed with essays. It has an

interesting section on managing money including information about credit cards, banks, loans, etc., complete
with bibliography. A similar book is planned by the
Boston Women's Collective, also dealing with New York.

Women's Bureau, U.S. Department of Labor. *Continuing Education Programs and Services for Women.* Pamphlet 10.
70¢. A listing of programs tailored for women returning
to or beginning school later in life. State-by-state,
college-by-college listings.

Women's Bureau, U.S. Department of Labor, *Jobfinding
Techniques for Mature Women.* Pamphlet 11. 45¢. Somebody in Washington is determined to make older women
feel like they have useful skills, the ability to succeed, and wants to tell how to go about it. Very useful.

Life Insurance

Consumers Report, Post Office Box 1000, Orangeburg, New
York 10962. Insert, "Guide to Life Insurance." March
1974 issue.

Consumers Union, 256 Washington Street, Mt. Vernon, New
York 10550. General consumer information. Book on life
insurance.

Pennsylvania Insurance Department, Harrisburg, Pennsylvania
17120. "Shopper's Guide" series on insurance, lawyers,
health insurance, etc.

Success Achievement Systems, Inc., 3081 West Chester Pike,
Newton Square, Pennsylvania 19073. (215) 353-5500.
Consumer information and assistance in insurance, jobs
and careers, real estate, etc. Source of books and
pamphlets in these areas.

Books

Consumer Reports Editors. *The Consumers Union Report on
Life Insurance: A Guide to Planning and Buying the
Protection You Need.* Rev. ed. New York: Grossman, 1972.
$5.95.

Margolius, Sydney. *The Consumer's Guide to Better Buying.*
Pocket Books. $1.25. Nationally known consumer advisor,
formerly on the President's Consumer Advisory Council.
Syndicated columnist.

Hendricks, Randall A. "A Legal Analysis of the Sale of
    Life Insurance." Houston Law Review. Written by an
    attorney. Well-documented. For those who want to know
    even more about the life insurance industry.

"Let's Understand Life Insurance." *Consumer's Digest.*
    July/August 1974. Excellent beginner's article on what
    an insurance policy is.

Reynolds, G. Scott. *The Mortality Merchants.* McKay,
    1968. $6.95. Excellent source of understanding life
    insurance. Written for a layman.

Dacey, Norman F. *What's Wrong With Life Insurance?*
    Macmillan. $1.50. Paperback, loaded with information,
    facts, statistics, and examples.

SIX: LIFE SPACE

Books And Articles

Adams, Florence. *I Took A Hammer In My Hand: The Woman's
    Build-It And Fix-It Handbook.* William Morrow and Company,
    Inc., 1973. $9.95. Well, it's an expensive book. For
    $9.95 you really have to appreciate the drawings done by
    the author. Probably as useful as any of the other books
    of the type, but it's difficult to say if the author's
    feminism warrants the price.

Callenbach, Ernest. *Living Poor With Style.* New York:
    Bantam Books, 1972. $1.95. This book contains everything
    an ex-executive for Gulf Oil needs to know about how to
    live the life of a college dropout. Some useful and con-
    cise information can be found in this book, but the tone
    and premises of the author are insulting to women and
    poor people who never had the "choice" to "live poor
    with style."

Curry, Barbara. *O.K., I'll Do It Myself.* New York: Random
    House, 1971. $3.95. A book similar to *I Took A Hammer*. . .
    but less comprehensive and smaller. Understandable and
    sometimes funny, a handywoman's primer.

Goodman, Emily Jane. *The Tenant Survival Book.* The Bobbs-
    Merrill Company, Inc., 1972. $3.95. A very fine book
    by a feminist and lawyer giving you step-by-step informa-
    tion about tenants' rights, groups, and the law. Good
    for organizing on any level, and self-protecting.

Kanter, Rosabeth Moss. *Communes: Creating and Managing the Collective Life*. New York: Harper and Row, 1973. $4.95.

Pollard, Vicki Cohn, and Munley, Jean. "The Five of Us." *Women: A Journal of Liberation*. Winter 1971. An article that deals with a group living experience.

Slater, Charlotte. *Things Your Mother Never Taught You*. Sheed and Ward, Inc., 1974. Available for $2.25 for one volume, $4.00 for two volumes. Charlotte Slater has a syndicated column dealing with how-to-do-it information. This book is a collection of forty such articles.

Source Catalog Number 2: Communities/Housing. Chicago: The Swallow Press, Inc., 1972. $2.95. The source catalog is just that: a good source book for social action groups concerned with, in this case, housing and tenants' rights. There is information about what groups have managed to accomplish, and what possible solutions to housing problems might be. Source of our statistics on public housing.

Weiss, Michael. *Living Together: A Year In The Life Of A City Commune*. New York: McGraw-Hill, 1974. $6.95. Probably not totally useful for a woman in transition, but perhaps interesting to some.

SEVEN: TAKING CARE OF OURSELVES

General

Birth Control Handbook/The V.D. Handbook. Available from the Women's Centre, 124-A Second Avenue South, Saskatoon, Saskatchewan, Canada. 25¢ postage. Collectively prepared material dealing with birth control.

Boston Women's Health Collective. *Our Bodies, Ourselves*. New York: Simon and Schuster, 1973. $2.95. *Everyone* seems to have heard of or read this book. It has a very extensive description of how women's bodies work and what to do when they're working wrong. If there is a fault with this book it is that it seems to have been written by and for young, middle-class (or at least well-educated) women. Still, it is significant and informative.

The Boston Women's Collective, Inc. *Women's Yellow Pages*.
Published annually. $1.50. This book has listings of
many clinics; health care, employment, self-defense,
nutrition, welfare information. A new version for the
New York area will be published in 1975. Available
from 490 Beacon Street, Boston, Massachusetts 02115.

Consumer Reports. "What Women Don't Know About Breast
Cancer." March 1974, p. 264. This article lists 27
breast cancer screening centers throughout the United
States.

Edmiston, Susan. "Are You Ashamed Of Your Body?" *Woman's
Day* magazine. April 1974.

Ehrenreich, Barbara and English, Deidre. *Witches, Mid-
wives, and Nurses--A History of Women Healers*.
Feminist Press, 1972. $1.25. This is a book to look
at if you have wondered what happened to create the
mish-mash of medical services (and lack of women medical
professionals) we suffer from today. Interesting and
provocative.

Frank, Arthur, M.D. and Frank, Stuart, M.D. *People's
Handbook of Medical Care*. New York: Vintage Books/
Random House, 1972. $2.95. Very complete, explicit
descriptions of illness and the medical system. Offers
good advice, seems useful and easy to understand, and
the writers seem to have a conscience.

Frankfort, Ellen. *Vaginal Politics*. New York: Bantam
Books, 1973. $1.95. If you wonder what the connection
is between women's liberation and health care, you might
want to read this book. It's one woman's feminist perspective, and includes a few views of the self-help movement in health care. Source for many of our statistics
in this chapter.

Gendel, Evelyn S., M.D. "It's Your Body . . . Not Your
Doctor's." *Redbook Magazine*. March 1974.

Good Housekeeping. "What You Should Know About The Controversy Over Breast Surgery." April 1974.

Grimstad, Kirsten, and Rennie, Susan, eds. *The New Woman's
Survival Catalog*. Coward, McCann and Geoghegan.
Berkeley Publishing Company, 1973. $5.00. A reference
book with descriptions of books, articles, women's health
clinics, rape clinics, abortion, employment, etc. By
women, for women.

O'Neill, Nena and George. "You Can Change Your Life!" *Family Circle*. April 1974.

Pogrebin, Letty Cottin. "The Working Woman: Women Doctors." *Ladies' Home Journal*. April 1974.

Susan, Dr. *What Your Doctor Should Tell You*. Published by the October 4th Organization. 1972. Available from them at Box 14745, Philadelphia, Pennsylvania 19134. 25¢.

Women's Health Center. *Infections of the Vagina*. Available from 156 Fifth Avenue, New York, New York.

XYZYX Information Corporation. *Home Emergency Ladies' Pal (H.E.L.P.)*. $1.99. We thought this pamphlet was important enough to mention in the text. It is well-planned and easy to use and prepares you for most home emergencies from plumbing to health emergencies.

Nutrition

Davis, Adelle. *Let's Eat Right To Keep Fit. Let's Get Well. Let's Have Healthy Children*. World Publishers. $1.75 each. There's a lot of controversy about the late Adelle Davis' theories about good health. Some people claim her advice has given them results where doctors haven't. She believed most Americans are deficient in needed nutrients and vitamins--the A.M.A. does not.

Lappé, Francis Moore. *Diet For A Small Planet*. Ballantine. $3.95. A skillful study of the growing malnutrition rate in the United States and the rest of the world, and what you can do to keep yourself from being one of its victims. Recipes included.

Null, Gary and Null, Steve. *The Complete Handbook of Nutrition*. New York: Dell Publishing Co., Inc., 1972. $1.50. Everything that you ever wanted to know, and maybe more, about nutrition. Well-organized into chapters and subheadings. Usually gives sources of studies on vitamins, protein, minerals, etc.

Samuels, Mike, M.D. and Bennett, Hal. *The Well Body Book*. New York: Random House/Bookworks. $5.95. Talks about your body as a three-million-year-old healer. You have all the energy, tools, material to keep yourself fit, they say.

Mental Health

Bardwick, Judith M. *Readings on the Psychology of Women.*
New York: Harper and Row, 1972. $5.95.

Chesler, Phyllis. "Marriage and Psychotherapy." 40¢
from KNOW, Inc., Post Office Box 86031, Pittsburgh,
Pennsylvania 15221.

Chesler, Phyllis. *Women and Madness.* New York: Doubleday,
1972. $9.95. This book is also out in paperback, but
the author says it has been altered a lot and requests
that women not buy it.

Gornick, Vivian and Moran, Barbara K. *Women in Sexist
Society.* New York: Signet Books, 1971. $1.95.

Krakauer, Alice. "A Good Therapist is Hard to Find."
Ms. Magazine, October 1972, p. 33.

Leah and Mary Jane. "Thinking About Psychiatry." *Women:
A Journal of Liberation.* vol. 2, no. 2, 3028 Greenmount
Avenue, Baltimore, Maryland 21218. $1.00 for whole
issue.

Miller, Jean Baker, M.D. *Psychoanalysis and Women.*
Baltimore, Maryland: Penguin Books, 1973.

Weisstein, Naomi. "Woman as Nigger." KNOW, Inc., Post
Office Box 86031, Pittsburgh, Pennsylvania 15221. 40¢.
Also in *Psychology Today,* October 1969.

Rape

Bay Area Women Against Rape has a packet of information
including safety tactics, health services, legal information, and so forth, about rape. Available from Bay Area
Women Against Rape, 2490 Channing Way, Room 209, Berkeley,
California 94704. $1.00 plus 15¢ postage.

Csida, June Bundy and Joseph. *Rape: How To Avoid It And
What To Do About It If You Can't.* Books For Better
Living, 1974. $1.50. This book seems to have been
written as much to bring the gruesome reality of rape
to the attention of the public as to provide useful
information to the victim. It does both, although perhaps more of the former. Documents programs that have been
and are working well, and discusses legislative needs.

Freedom From Rape. Ann Arbor Women's Crisis Center, 306
N. Division Street, Ann Arbor, Michigan 48108.   25¢.

Griffin, Susan. "Rape: The All American Crime," *Ramparts
Magazine*. September 1971. Reprints available from A
Woman's Place, 5251 Broadway, Oakland, California 94518.
25¢ postage. This article was a groundbreaker when it
was first printed, and still bears reading.

How To Start A Rape Crisis Center. The Rape Center Women,
Post Office Box 21005, Kalorama Street Station, Washington, D.C. 20009.

Rape--Medical and Legal Information, Women's Center, 46
Pleasant Streeet, Cambridge, Massachusetts 02139.

Women Organized Against Rape Handbook, Post Office Box
17374, Philadelphia, Pennsylvania 19105. (215) 823-7997.

Self-Defense

Conroy, Dr. Mary and Ritvo, Edward. *Personal Defense For
Women*. 1974. Available from The Trident Shop, California State College, Los Angeles, California 90032.
$3.40. This book was excerpted in *The Sportswoman*, and
seems to be very useful for both teachers and students.
Dr. Conroy says that any self-defense technique that
takes longer than 5 seconds to immobilize the attacker
is useless, so the emphasis is on immediacy and practi-
cality.

Offstein, Jerrold N. *Self-Defense For Women*. Palo Alto:
National Press Books. $1.95. Available from National
Press Books, 850 Hansom Way, Palo Alto, California 94304.

Safety On The Streets. No. 029.01, Women's Department,
National Safety Council, 425 N. Michigan Avenue, Chicago,
Illinois 60611. 25¢.

Tegner, B. and McGrath, A. *Self-Defense For Girls and
Women*. Ventura: Thor Publishing Co., 1974. $1.95.
Available from Thor Publishing, Box 1782, Ventura,
California 93001. Many other books on self-defense at
about the same price are available from this publisher.
You might want to write to them for a listing.

EIGHT: REACHING OUT

Organizational Tips

Grimstad, Kirsten and Rennie, Susan, eds. *The New Woman's Survival Catalog*. New York: Coward, McCann and Geoghegan, 1973. $5.00.

Shapiro, Carol. "How to Organize a Multi-Service Women's Center." 1973. Women's Action Alliance, 370 Lexington Avenue, New York, New York 10017. $1.65.

Women's Action Alliance. "Introduction to the Women's Movement." 1973. Women's Action Alliance, 370 Lexington Avenue, New York, New York 10017. $2.50.

Fundraising--Books And Articles

The Bread Game. Glide Publications, 330 Ellis Street, San Francisco, California 94102. $1.95.

The Foundation Directory. Fourth edition (1972-73). Foundation Center, Columbia University Press, 136 S. Broadway, Irvington, New York 10533. $15.00. List of all foundations, boards of directors, endowments, etc. Available at most public libraries.

Foundation News. Council on Foundations, 888 Seventh Avenue, New York, New York 10019. $10.00 a year.

Jacquette, F. Lee and Barbara L. "What Makes a Good Proposal?" *Foundation News*, January/February 1973, p. 18.

Kerr, Virginia. "The Dollars and Sense of Fundraising." *Ms. Magazine*, June 1973, p. 120.

Knowles, Marjorie Fine. "Foundation Grants to Women's Groups." *Women's Studies Newsletter*, No. 5, Fall 1973. Available from The Feminist Press, Box 334, Old Westbury, New York 11568. Write for price.

Russell, Avery. "The Women's Movement and Foundations." *Foundation News*, November/December 1972, p. 16.

Fundraising--Organizations

Foundation Center, 888 Seventh Avenue, New York, New York 10019. Contains numerous directories and grants indices of foundations.

Foundation Research Service. Lawson and Williams Associates., Inc. 1019 19th Street, N.W., Washington, D.C. 20036.
Offers a variety of fundraising services for groups which
can afford their rather hefty fees.

Pacific Change, 2229 Lombard, San Francisco, California 94123.
Helps projects get seed money grants ($1,000-$5,000).

Taft Information System: A Method of Keeping Current on
Foundations. Taft Products, Inc., 1000 Vermont Avenue,
N.W., Washington, D.C. 20005.

Urban Dynamics/Inner City Fund, 111 East Wacker Drive,
Chicago, Illinois 60601.

Emotional Supports

"Consciousness Up," Box 453, Smithtown, New York 11787.
$2.00 per year. Newsletter for consciousness-raising
groups, published three times a year.

Forsman, Carolyn, compiler. *Crisis Information Centers:
A Resource Guide*. The Exchange, 311 Cedar Avenue South,
Minneapolis, Minnesota 55404. $1.00.

Women in Transition, Inc. "Group Skills for Women's
Groups." Available from KNOW, Inc., Post Office Box
86031, Pittsburgh, Pennsylvania 15221. Write for
price. Compilation of various techniques which can be
used in facilitating women's groups.

Women in Transition, Inc. "Therapy Information Packet
for Women." Collection of articles designed to help
a woman choose a therapist and evaluate her therapy
experience. Also available from KNOW, Inc.; write for price.

Pfeiffer, J. William and Jones, John E. *Handbook of
Structured Experiences for Human Relations Training*.
1970. 3 volumes, $3.00 each. University Associates
Press, Post Office Box 615, Iowa City, Iowa 52240.

Legal Supports

San Francisco Women's Legal Center. "Getting Out: A Collective
Experience in Self-Help Divorce." How to set up a self-help
divorce clinic; the strengths and limitations of that type
of project within the goals of the women's movement. Available from KNOW, Inc., Post Office Box 86031, Pittsburgh,
Pennsylvania 15221. $1.75.

INDEX

90A   1830   81

SOUTHERN

JAN 23 1987

BOUND